# Managerial Macroeconomics

## A Canadian Perspective

# Managerial Macroeconomics

## A Canadian Perspective

**Donald J. Daly, M.A., Ph.D.**
York University
North York, Ontario

1988

**_IRWIN_**

Homewood, Illinois 60430

*To Madeleine*

This book was set in Melior by Beacon Graphics Corporation.
The editors were Roderick T. Banister, Dale Boroviak, Merrily D. Mazza.
The production manager was Irene H. Sotiroff.
The drawings were done by Dan Gaeta Studio.
Arcata Graphics/Kingsport was the printer and binder.

ISBN 0-256-06000-2

Library of Congress Catalog Card No. 87–80950

*Printed in the United States of America*

1 2 3 4 5 6 7 8 9 0 K 5 4 3 2 1 0 9 8

# Preface to the Instructor

MANAGERIAL MACROECONOMICS: A CANADIAN PERSPECTIVE grew out of a conviction that business school students needed a different type of text for macroeconomics than those currently available. What was desirable was a text that provided more information on how macroeconomic theory could be *used* to provide perspective on the more important developments in the economic environment within which individuals and organizations made major decisions. It was also desirable to provide examples of how macroeconomic variables would affect sales, costs and profits. We also point out the more promising routes by which companies could reduce unit costs by increasing output in relation to labour and capital inputs. Given the importance of international trade in our time we have tried to show how issues and developments in Canada compared to similar topics in the United States, Japan and some of the other countries important in Canadian trade.

This text has been designed to meet these criteria in a one-term course. The shorter length permits the assignment of additional readings, alternative viewpoints, cases, newspaper selections, etc. A previous course in microeconomics is regarded as a prerequisite for students at the masters level. For students at the undergraduate level, a course in principles of economics is expected. The text uses charts and some simple mathematical notations but other previous courses in mathematics are not essential. Frequent use of basic descriptive statistics will familiarize the students with terms, sources and how to interpret basic tables and charts.

Illustrations have been included of how a number of the topics in macroeconomics will be covered in other functional areas that are normally included in programs in business, accounting and administrative studies in Canada.

The topics from macroeconomics that have been chosen for emphasis in the text have been selected on the basis of consistency with the available evidence and their importance in decision making. Much of the basis for that selection draws on two decades of experience with the federal government and the applied research from Royal Commissions, research groups, and consulting with governments and major corporations.

The major part of the book deals with the sources of variations in demand in the economy, using contemporary Keynesian models, with emphasis on two additional topics. One topic emphasized is the sources of economic growth over time and between countries. This is an important theme for Canada in light of the extent of the slowdown in productivity growth since 1973 and the evidence on the importance of cost and productivity problems in the performance of Canadian manufacturing. This affects Canada's performance in international trade in manufactured products, the most rapidly growing area of world trade, and also domestic performance in business investment and the unemployment rate.

A second topic emphasized is the role of monetary factors in the high rates of price increase in Canada and other countries in the 1970s and early 1980s, and the related high levels of nominal interest rates. The differential rates of domestic inflation in different countries are also a source of part of the exchange rate changes that have taken place since the early 1970s.

These two area of emphasis reflect the changing nature of economic problems in recent decades and the associated shifts in the profession and the related underlying research that has been incorporated into the text. They are important topics for students of business and are thus given greater emphasis.

Important examples of the use of realistic orders of magnitude for many of the common parameters would include the following:

1. the major factors contributing to real output changes over time and between countries;
2. the effect of changes in interest rates on business investment and housing;
3. the size of the fiscal and money supply multipliers;
4. the main factors causing inflation and high interest rates;
5. the role of lags in the system in the recurrence of cycles and the scope for using discretionary monetary and fiscal policies for stabilization purposes; and
6. the effects of changes in exchange rates and free trade on companies in the commodity-producing industries.

Key sources and references are included in an annotated list at the back of the book, organized by parts. These can be helpful for term papers in this and related courses.

This emphasis on realism and relevance has been found to be useful in motivating the student to study the text and other assigned readings carefully. It also leads to better understanding and increased interest in reading the business pages of the newspapers and financial publications. This emphasis also seems to lead to increased retention of the main themes during their subsequent careers. Classroom testing at York University has elicited very satisfying results from student evaluations following the use of the draft manuscript.

An Instructor's Manual to accompany MANAGERIAL MACROECO-NOMICS: A Canadian Perspective is available through the publisher for adopting professors. This manual contains transparency masters, additional lecture topics, and assignment material for each Chapter and Part in the book. Test items are broken down by each chapter and include comprehensive essay questions.

# Preface to the Student

This text has been designed for a one semester course in macro-economics with a managerial emphasis. We have tried to make the text easily accessible; both the vocabulary and reading level will help you understand and remember the main forces contributing to changes in the Canadian economy. The text introduces all new terms and concepts in *bold* face type, and a glossary at the back defines and explains all terms and organizations. Each chapter provides a statement of objectives at the beginning and a summary at the end.

The text emphasizes the special features of Canada as a small and increasingly open economy in a highly competitive world, with frequent comparisons with Canada's major trading partners. Theories are presented that have stood the test of time and the evidence, with examples of their use in decision making in the private and public sectors.

# Acknowledgements

Many professional colleagues have contributed to this book, some of whom are identified in end notes and the key sources and references at the back of the book. The Faculty of Administrative Studies at York University has provided support for research assistants for a number of years. Gary Wilkie, Ian Secord and Terry Shanahan have provided assistance over the years the book was being developed.

Helpful comments and suggestions have been received from reviewers, including: Donald C. MacCharles, University of New Brunswick-Saint John; Douglas J. McCready-Wilfrid Laurier University and Rocky Mirza, Vancouver Community College. Additionally, a number of reviewers provided comments on early drafts of the manuscript they are not named but their contributions are appreciated. Dennis Bockus has been of major assistance as a development editor in a careful and constructive review of several drafts with tight deadlines.

A special note of thanks is appropriate for my wife Madeleine, to whom the book has been dedicated. She put the drafts into the computer, did an initial editing, filed the evolving manuscript and helped make copies until the early hours. The book could not have been completed without her help and encouragement.

# Contents

## Part One
## Introduction       1

### 1   Macroeconomics and Managerial Decision Making       3

1-1 What is Macroeconomics?       1-2 An Introduction to the
National Accounts.       1-3 The Major Sources of Canadian
Statistics.       1-4 Microeconomic Implications of
Macroeconomics.

### 2   The Measurement of National Output and Prices       10

2-1 Why Are National Income Measures Useful?       2-2 The
Circular Flow of Income.       2-3 Coverage of Gross
Domestic Product.       2-4 Price and Quantity Changes in Gross
Domestic Product.       2-5 Personal and Government Sectors.
2-6 International Transactions.       2-7 Summary of the Coverage
of GDP.

### 3   Macroeconomic Experience in North America       28

3-1 Long-Term Economic Growth.       3-2 Business Cycles and
Fluctuations in Aggregate Demand.       3-3 Price Inflation in the
1970s.       3-4 The Role of Government.       3-5 International
Influences on North America: *1. The United States in the World
Economy. 2. Intercountry Differences in Growth Rates. 3. Growth
in World Trade. 4. Changes in the Composition of World Trade.
5. Increased Exchange-Rate Instability.*

## Part Two
## Long-Run Economic Growth   47

### 4   Natural Resources and Economic Growth   49

4-1 A Review of the Methodology of Economics.   4-2 Malthus on Aggregate Supply and Demand: *The Production of Food. The Demand for Food. Population Growth and the Labour-Supply Function.*   4-3 Subsequent Experience and Current Relevance.   4-4 Natural Resources in Canada.

### 5   Labour and Capital in Economic Growth   59

5-1 An Overview of Economic Growth Accounting. 5-2 Changes in the Level of Capital per Person Employed. 5-3 The Measurement of Employment and Capital Inputs: *The Labour Force Survey. The Definitions of Labour Force Categories. Other Data on Employment and Unemployment. Capital Input.*   5-4 Accounting for the Contribution of Inputs to the Growth in Output. Making an Estimate of Total Factor Inputs.   5-5 The Assumptions in Making an Index of Inputs.   5-6 Changing Canadian Labour Inputs in an International Perspective.   5-7 The Human Factor in Organizations.   5-8 Two Effects of Unions: *Effects of Unions on Relative Wages. Union and Nonunion Differentials in Productivity.*

### 6   Output per Unit of Input and Economic Growth   79

6-1 Estimating Potential National Income and Employment. 6-2 Main Sources of Changes in Output per Unit of Input: *Economies of Scale. Improved Resource Allocation. Advances in Knowledge.*   6-3 Changes in Output per Unit of Input in the United States.   6-4 Comparisons of Economic Growth Experience in Canada and the United States.   6-5 Factors in the Economic Growth Slowdown in North America Since 1973.   6-6 The Japanese Postwar Performance.

# Part Three
# Consumption, Investment and Business Cycles     97

## 7   The Demand Side: An Overview     99

7-1 The Classical View.     7-2 Technological Change and
Unemployment.     7-3 An Overview of the Theory of Aggregate
Demand.

## 8   Consumption     112

8-1 Keynes's General Theory.     8-2 Early Empirical
Evidence.     8-3 The Permanent-Income Hypothesis.
8-4 The Life-Cycle Hypothesis.     8-5 The Role of Wealth
and Interest Rates.     8-6 Cross-Section Evidence and Income
Redistribution.

## 9   Investment and the Multiplier     126

9-1 Business Investment — An Introduction.     9-2 Interest Rates
and Business Investment Decisions.     9-3 The Rationale for the
Limited Effect of Interest Rates on Business Spending.
9-4 Interest Rates and Housing Investment.     9-5 Summary
of Investment Spending Responses to Interest Rate
Changes.     9-6 Income and Accelerator Effects on Business
Investment.     9-7 The Multiplier in a Simple Model.
9-8 Government and the Foreign Sector and the Size of the
Multiplier.     9-9 Econometric Models for the Economy.
9-10 Is the Economy Inherently Unstable?

## 10   Business Cycles and Demand Instability     145

10-1 Research on Business Cycles.     10-2 Illustrations of
Exogenous Shocks.     10-3 The Role of Lags.     10-4 Business
Cycles in the United States.     10-5 Business Cycles in
Canada.     10-6 Why Have Business-Cycle Recessions Become
Milder?     10-7 Business Cycles and Productivity Change.

## Part Four
## Money, the Price Level, and Interest Rates    163

**11    Money and Interest Rates: An Overview    165**

11-1 What is Money?    11-2 The Role of Money in the Price
System.    11-3 Money and Interest Rates.    11-4 Money
Demand — Keynes's *General Theory*.    11-5 The Money Supply
in Canada.    11-6 Measures of Inflation.    11-7 Is Inflation a
Monetary Phenomenon?    11-8 Price Inflation in Canada Since
1970.

**12    The Supply of Money    180**

12-1 An Overview of Money Supply and Demand and Interest
Rates.    12-2 The Participants in the Money Supply
Process.    12-3 The Money Multiplier.    12-4 Other Canadian
Financial Institutions.    12-5 U. S. Monetary Policy in the Great
Depression. Appendix.

**13    The Price Level, Interest Rates, and Monetary Policy    201**

13-1 Changes in the Money Supply and Economic Activity.
13-2 Money and Real Interest Rates.    13-3 Inflation and
Corporate Accounting Practices.    13-4 Speed of Adjustment
over the Business Cycle.    13-5 Demand-Pull and Cost-Push
Inflation.    13-6 Indicators of Monetary Policy.    13-7 Lags in
Monetary Policy.    13-8 Alternative Monetary Strategies.

## Part Five
## The Role of Government    215

**14    Government Expenditure and Taxes    217**

14-1 The Postwar Performance of the Canadian Economy.
14-2 The Federal System in Canada.    14-3 Structure of
Government Expenditures: *The Historical Growth of Government
Expenditures. Distribution of Federal Expenditures. Flexibility in
Expenditures.*    14-4 Structure of Federal Revenues: *Growth in
Federal Revenues in a Growing Economy. Variability in Federal
Revenues during Business Cycles.*

**15    Government Deficits, Debt, and Financing    231**

15-1 A Review and Extension of the Framework.    15-2 Factors in the Emergence of Federal Deficits.    15-3 Effects of Federal Deficits.    15-4 Options on the Deficit.    15-5 Discretionary Changes in Fiscal Policy.    15-6 Lags and the Timing of Fiscal Policy.


**Part Six**
**International Trade and Exchange Rates**

**16    International Trade and Comparative Advantage    247**

16-1 Importance of International Trade.    16-2 Trends in World Trade.    16-3 Theories of Comparative Advantage. 16-4 Evidence on Canada's Comparative Advantage. 16-5 Japanese Manufacturing Performance. Appendix.

**17    Balance of Payments and International Capital Flows    267**

17-1 Concepts and Terms: *The Balance of Payments. Exchange Rates.*    17-2 Some Key Determinants of the Balance of Payments: *Economic Growth. Cycles in Demand and Production. Differential Inflation.*    17-3 Purchasing Power Parity.    17-4 The Price Effects of an Exchange Rate Depreciation.

**18    Instability in the International Financial System    286**

18-1 Major Changes in the World Financial System: *Decentralization of Economic Power. Evolving Domestic and International Priorities. Private Holdings of Foreign Exchange.*    18-2 Alternative Exchange Rate Systems. 18-3 Inflation during the 1970s.    18-4 The Increased Importance of International Capital Flows.

**19    International Trade in Manufactured Products    294**

19-1 Exchange Rate Changes and World Trade. 19-2 International Trade and Factor Price Equalization. 19-3 The Gains for Canada from Freer Trade.    19-4 Japan in World Trade.    19-5 The Developing Countries and Trade in Manufactured Products.

# Part Seven
# Public Policies for Growth and Stability   305

20   The Sources of Instability and Guiding Principles for Public
Policy   307

20-1 Changing Severity of Business Cycles.   20-2 Inflation.
20-3 The Causes of Persisting Business Cycles.
20-4 Alternative Guiding Principles for Stabilization Policy.
20-5 Improving Short-Term Stabilization Policy.
20-6 International Policy Aspects.   20-7 Environmental
Policies: *Commercial Policy. Adjustment Assistance. Inflation
and the Corporate Profits Tax. The Diffusion of Technology.
Labour-management Relations.*

# Part Eight
# Implications for Business Decisions   329

21   Macroeconomic Developments and Business Decision
Making   331

21-1 Business Cycles and Forecasting.   21-2 The Effects of
Fiscal and Monetary Policy.   21-3 Inflation, Interest Rates, and
Reported Profits.   21-4 International Aspects.   21-5
International Competitiveness.   21-6 Identification of Growth
Areas.

Key Sources and Selected References   345

Glossary of Major Terms and Concepts   353

Index   369

# PART ONE

# Introduction

The first three chapters provide an overview of this book as a whole. The first chapter will explain the main emphasis of a macroeconomics text designed for use in business schools and by accounting students. It will introduce some basic concepts and compare and clarify the relationship between macroeconomics and microeconomics.

The second chapter will describe the concepts and measurement of the main economic variables that will be used throughout the book. It will discuss the composition of the main sources of income on the income side and expenditures on the expenditure side of the national accounts, as well as the personal and government sectors.

The third chapter will review the macroeconomic experience in North America since 1950 in a longer-term perspective. Special attention will be given to significant developments that are explained in the balance of the book. A framework of theory helps explain these historical developments. It is essential in forecasting and, as a basis of public policy, for modifying undesirable developments. Such a framework also helps corporations respond to changes in the business environment.

# 1

# Macroeconomics and Managerial Decision Making

In the first part of the 1980s, Canada broke some historic records. During the first two years of the decade, nominal interest rates reached their highest levels in the present century. The 1981–82 recession was the most severe recession in Canada since the 1930s, and it was the first time in this century that a recession was more severe in Canada than in the United States. The unemployment rate in Canada moved above 10 percent of the labour force in the middle of 1982 and stayed there until the end of 1985. Canada was not alone in experiencing high unemployment rates; more than 32 million were unemployed in the industrialized countries in 1983. The reasons for these developments and possible measures to prevent their recurrence are the central focus of macroeconomics and therefore the focus of this book.

## 1–1 WHAT IS MACROECONOMICS?

**Macroeconomics** studies the behaviour of the *national economy as a whole*, rather than individual firms or industries. *Macro* is from the Greek work meaning "large." Some of the main topics this book covers include total national income, total employment, the general price level, the level of interest rates, and the exchange rate between the Canadian dollar and other foreign currencies.

**Aggregates**, such as national income and employment, are totals for the economy as a whole (covering such industries as agriculture, manufacturing, retail trade, government, schools, and universities). Such aggregates encompass the entire national economy. They are the *sum* of the major microeconomic variables, such as wages and profits in an individual firm or industry, employment in an individual firm or indus-

3

try, and the price for a particular product produced by these economic units. Aggregates are commonly used to compare the performance of a company or industry with the national pattern. Any major development in the economy as a whole that appears in a major statistical aggregate necessarily reflects what is happening in a majority of individual firms and industries.

The primary concern of **microeconomics**, on the other hand, is the behaviour of *the individual units,* such as households and firms. *Micro* is from the Greek work meaning "small." Individual behaviour concentrates on consumer demand theory. The study of the firm concentrates on production and cost theory. These areas of price theory explain the quantities of individual products that will be produced and how prices of such products will change compared to the prices of other products.

Thus, macroeconomics emphasizes the national totals and their behaviour, while microeconomics emphasizes the individual units and how they respond. The emphasis is thus quite different.

A further important difference is that microeconomics tends to emphasize demand and supply factors equally. Microeconomics starts off by analyzing the **demand side** for an individual product but then puts a comparable emphasis on the **supply side** and the conditions of market equilibrium for that particular industry. Figure 1–1 summarizes this type of analysis.

---

**FIGURE 1–1**   Illustrative Demand and Supply Curves

---

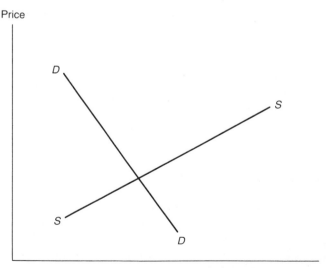

Price

Quantity per unit of time

The earlier classical economists emphasized the supply side of macroeconomics. For example, Adam Smith published *The Wealth of Nations* in 1776, more than two centuries ago. An important part of the book dealt with differences in economic performance among the major countries of that time. (Modern terminology would title such a book "The National Income of Nations.") Later classical economists continued in the same tradition, including such writers as David Ricardo and T. R. Malthus. In the present century, such authors as A. C. Pigou and Alfred Marshall continued the supply side tradition with a heavy emphasis on national income and intercountry comparisons of national income levels. And Edward F. Denison continues to work on economic growth accounting using modern concepts and data.

Lord John Maynard Keynes caused a major redirection in macroeconomics by emphasizing investment, consumption, and other concepts that stressed short-term changes in demand (see Part Three). His *General Theory* assumed no change in technology and an unchanged level in the **stock of capital.**

Macroeconomics for some decades has continued in the Keynesian tradition, with far more emphasis on the determinants of the demand side but little discussion of the supply side. Keynes and the early Keynesians did not deal with the longer-term determinants of supply, such as the effects of changes in the stock of capital. This text will discuss the determinants of demand and the extent to which the full productive potential of the Canadian economy is used.

However, macroeconomics should include some discussion of how the stock of capital and technological change affect the supply side of the economy, and this text will introduce these topics early in Part Two. There are a number of reasons for this greater emphasis on the supply side. First, since about 1973, growth on the supply side has slowed significantly in all industrialized countries. Second, important differences in economic performance between the major countries reflect differences in supply conditions. Third, supply conditions are important in corporate strategy partly because business firms emphasize productivity and costs in their planning and decision making. For example, labour income is a major component of national income, and is also important in the distribution of costs to a majority of the individual firms. The effective use of people is thus a key element in the successful performance of the individual firm.

More emphasis on the supply side is particularly appropriate in a Canadian text for business and accounting students. Some developments on the supply side are extremely important for an economy the size of Canada that is highly dependent on what is occurring in the rest of the world. In addition, many of the tools and concepts introduced on the supply side of macroeconomics can be carried over to comparable issues in corporate decision making—for example, in such areas as achieving efficiency and low cost production, factors that are important for company performance both domestically and in international markets.

## 1–2 AN INTRODUCTION TO THE NATIONAL ACCOUNTS

The concept of an aggregate was introduced in Section 1–1. The most widely used aggregate is national income. The 1986 national accounts revision by Statistics Canada emphasized **gross domestic product (GDP)**. Gross domestic product is a summary measure of the economy's current production. That is, GDP measures all the current goods and services produced within Canada's borders, both by Canadians and nonresidents, in the current period's prices.[1]

This is a shift in concept from **gross national product (GNP),** which was used in all Statistics Canada publications over the four previous decades. GNP measures only the production of Canadian nationals both within and outside Canada. The major difference between GDP and GNP involves the treatment of investment income (interest and dividends) paid to nonresidents. Such income affects the investment income component on the income side and the nonmerchandise exports and imports on the expenditure side. This shift in treatment brings the national income concepts more into line with the related aggregates of real GDP by industry and the employment data in the labour force survey. This conceptual change has had a fairly small effect on growth rates over comparable periods for the main national aggregates.

The definition of gross domestic product emphasized that this basic aggregate is measured at **"current prices"**—a reminder that an increase in the value of GDP from one year to the next consists partly of an increase in the volume of output and partly in an increase in the general level of prices for the economy as a whole.

This can be illustrated by examining the production of soft drinks. Suppose the value of production of the Can Soft Drink Company increased by 15 percent from one year to the next. If the company had increased its prices 10 percent at the start of the second period, the increase in the volume of production would be only 5 percent. One-third of the increase in the value of production was associated with an increase in production volume, but two-thirds resulted from higher prices.

A basic definition of the relations between price, volume, and value (applicable to both macro- and microeconomics) is that

$$V = P \times Q$$

where

$V$ = the value of soft drink production

$P$ = the prices of soft drinks

$Q$ = the physical count of soft drink production

Although a good management accounting system normally provides information on all three of these variables in the accounting records of the firm, you could derive the third if you knew any two of the three variables.

These same definitions are all relevant and applicable to the economy as a whole, but there are some practical problems in developing price and quantity measures for the national aggregates. A modern economy produces a tremendous number of products and brand names; new products and models are continually introduced and old ones dropped (such as buggy whips). In addition, no management accounting department produces the basic data on prices and quantities in exactly the form and coverage that would be most helpful for the national income statistician. However, the process used by the National Accounts Division of Statistics Canada (and the comparable agencies in other countries) provides a measure of price and volume that is quite useful and portrays reasonable orders of magnitude for the major economic changes in the economy. This process will be explained more fully in Chapter 2.

The main income and expenditure sides of the **national accounts** measures of GDP and the related price and volume movements are useful summaries of the past (sometimes referred to as *ex post* results). However, they are not usually sufficient to understand *why* some of the changes have occurred.

The system of national accounts also provides some sector accounts, such as the personal sector and the government sector. The **personal sector** is an important sector in terms of both the income and the expenditure accounts. Persons receive most of their income from providing services to organizations. However, they also receive income from the government, such as family allowances and old age pensions. Such income is a **transfer payment** to individuals; they provide no comparable service in return. The personal sector also pays direct taxes to the various levels of governments so not all income is available (or disposable, to use the term of the statisticians) to spend on consumer goods.

The system of national accounts also provides separate statistics for the **government sector** (broken down between the federal government on one hand and provinces and municipalities on the other). The federal government has a much greater influence on incomes and expenditures in the economy than you might think from just looking at its direct final expenditures on goods and services. For example, federal expenditures on goods and services in 1985 were about $28.3 billion, but this amount was only about one-fifth of the $113.6 billion total federal expenditures that year. Other major expenditures were $31.8 billion transfers to persons, $25.3 billion interest on the public debt, and $21.8 billion in transfers to the provinces and municipalities.[2] These other expenditures are important to the individuals, provinces, and municipalities that receive them, and the expenditures have an important indirect effect on the decisions of these groups. Sector tables can provide additional information on such important developments as interest and transfers.

## 1-3 THE MAJOR SOURCES OF CANADIAN STATISTICS

This book will use a number of tables and charts to describe past developments. Some of the examples and explanations will illustrate the types of analysis and discussion that are published regularly by the Bank of Canada, the Department of Finance, Statistics Canada, the Economic Council of Canada, the Conference Board in Canada, the C. D. Howe Research Institute, and a number of the chartered banks.

Many of these groups rely on **Statistics Canada,** Canada's centralized statistical agency, as their primary source for the statistics they use for economic and business analysis. Statistics produced by Statistics Canada include the national accounts; data on prices, industrial production, employment, and labour force data; and data on Canada's international trade.

Additional statistics are provided by such other federal agencies as the Bank of Canada, the Federal Department of Employment and Immigration, and Central Mortgage and Housing Corporation. Provincial government agencies also provide some statistics, as do administrative agencies, such as the Department of National Revenue and the Unemployment Insurance Commission.

The list of publications released by Statistics Canada is a major book itself. Statistics Canada also operates a fully computerized and regularly updated data bank called **CANSIM** (for the Canadian Socioeconomic Information Management). CANSIM provides tens of thousands of series on many aspects of Canada's economic performance. It assigns a number and gives a brief description of each series. (Various tables and charts throughout the text include CANSIM data bank numbers to identify the source of the information.)

## 1-4 MICROECONOMIC IMPLICATIONS OF MACROECONOMICS

The major national aggregates of national income summarize corresponding developments at the firm and industry level, eliminating intercompany purchases and sales. Another national aggregate is total employment. The big gain from working with such comprehensive aggregates is increased simplicity compared to working with a tremendous amount of detail.

If the economy as a whole is expanding, major increases in employment and output take place. Comparable increases in employment and output occur simultaneously within a majority of individual firms and industries. Similarly, in a period of recession, declines in output occur in the commodity-producing industries and usually in the construction industry. Thus individual firms should understand the determinants of **business cycle** expansions and contractions and be able to identify the current stage in the cycle. This text will also discuss why a minority of products and firms may be declining on a long-term basis, even if a majority of the individual units are expanding.

Later parts of the book will provide examples of the relevance of macroeconomic ideas and experience to the firm and industry. For example, labour income is a major component of national income, and it is also a major cost item to the individual firm (excluding the costs of purchased materials and services). Thus, the role of people in organizations and the effective use of their talents and abilities is an important factor in achieving excellent and successful organizations. Understanding how other countries achieve higher levels of output per hour in manufacturing is an important part of understanding recent developments in business investment and in the labour market for Canada as a whole.

Early identification of changes in the business cycle, both in direction and magnitude, has been an important topic in macroeconomic forecasting. Many of the methods developed to do so are also relevant to the individual firm and industry.

The next chapter will provide a fuller explanation of the measurement of national output and the price level.

## NOTES

1.  Department of Finance, *Quarterly Economic Review, September 1986* (Ottawa: Ministry of Supply and Services, 1986), pp. 39–45.

2.  Statistics Canada, *National Income and Expenditure Accounts, Second Quarter 1986* (Ottawa: Ministry of Supply and Services, 1986), p. 23.

# 2

# The Measurement of National Output and Prices

After reading this chapter you should understand:

1. Some basic definitions of national income and its major components on both the income and expenditure sides.
2. The coverage of the national income accounts (and some of the major sector components) and why certain transactions are included and other transactions are excluded from the major aggregates.
3. How the basic statistics are used to prepare real domestic product and the appropriate price deflators, to permit the necessary distinctions between price, quantity, and volume that have become so essential during the 1970s and 1980s.
4. The adjustments necessary to move from a production measure of national product (which is the central task of this book) to a welfare measure of national product.

## 2–1 WHY ARE NATIONAL INCOME MEASURES USEFUL?

It was pointed out in Chapter 1 that gross domestic product (GDP) is a summary measure of the value of current production of goods and services within Canada over a given period of time (usually a calendar year or a particular quarter). The major advantage of the current system of national accounts used in all the leading countries, both industrialized and developing, is the simplicity of being able to rely on a relatively small number of major aggregates to obtain a sound overview of the country's current economic situation.

An aggregate is a total of the components that constitute the broad economic categories of national income, total employment, or the general price level. An aggregate encompasses the entire national economy. It is the sum of the major microeconomic variables: wages and profits paid in a particular firm or industry, employment in an individual firm or industry, and the price for a particular product produced by that economic unit. Aggregates are commonly used to check the performance of a company or industry against the national pattern. Any major development in the economy as a whole that appears in a major aggregate necessarily reflects what is happening in a majority of the individual firms and industries within the economy.

This pattern can be illustrated by the variations in the rates of growth of **real gross domestic product** by industry in constant dollars. Real GDP by industry in constant dollars measures the *volume* of output in each individual industry; it thus eliminates the effects of any price changes. It is often built up from actual quantities of individual commodities or transactions that are produced by that industry. (The measures are designed to exclude the materials purchased from other industries.) In 1985, real GDP for the economy as a whole was 2.74 times the 1961 level—a rate of increase of 4.29 percent per year. All 36 published industry components of that aggregate increased over that 24-year period. The increases ranged from 0.75 percent per year for the metals component of the mining index (the slowest-growing industry) to 6.54 percent per year for electric power and 5.07 percent per year for the finance, insurance, and real estate industries, the two fastest-growing industries over that period.[1] The tools of economics can help explain the reasons for such differences in growth rates and changes in the aggregates. Throughout the book, some of the conclusions at the aggregate level will be related to the individual economic units within the economy.

## 2–2 THE CIRCULAR FLOW OF INCOME

A central characteristic of the current estimates of national income in Canada and other countries is that the total value of production is measured at two separate stages in the economic process. This can be seen most easily in what is usually described as the **circular flow of income.**

Consider a simplified economy that consists only of the household sector on the one hand and the business sector on the other. (We will initially ignore the existence of government and the foreign sector.) The household sector provides various personal services to business by performing work on an hourly basis (blue-collar workers), on a monthly basis (white-collar workers), or on a commission basis. Some households may also purchase bonds or stocks, thus providing funds to businesses.

Business units (companies) pay wages or salaries to the household sector (individuals) for its services. Many companies incur additional labour costs in the form of such benefits as paid holidays, contributions to pension schemes, and health benefits. Corporations also pay interest and dividends to individuals who purchase their bonds and stocks.

Companies use the services of labour and capital to produce goods and services that are then sold to individuals. These goods and services include cars, gasoline, clothing, food, barber and beauty shop services, and restaurant meals.

Individuals then pay for these goods and services with the income they earn. They do not buy such goods and services unless they expect to get a degree of satisfaction at least equal to the cost.

This flow of income and expenditures and the associated services is shown diagrammatically in Figure 2–1. The flows of financial payments are shown as broken lines and the flows of goods, services, and factor services are shown as solid lines. **Factor services** are the services provided by households to business units, such as working for a company on an hourly, monthly, or commission basis. Households also provide another service to business units: they loan funds to companies by purchasing and holding corporate bonds.

Note: the **income flows** that measure current production have to be identical to the **expenditure flows** that measure current production. The flows are defined to be equal, instantaneously, at all times and

---

**FIGURE 2–1**   Circular Flow of Income and Expenditures

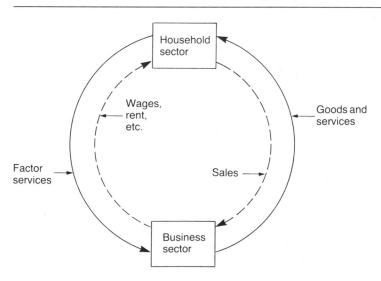

without error. If you are ever puzzled as to how some item should be treated, decide if, and how, it will show up on the income or expenditure side, and then ensure it is treated the same way on the other side of the national accounts.

We can now extend that circular-flow diagram to include more real-world applicability. Figure 2–1 assumes no government receipts or expenditures. In fact in all democratic societies, government has played an increasing role over the present century. Government receipts and expenditures are now a higher percentage of national income than they were before World War I or during the 1920s. The introduction of government is illustrated in Figure 2–2, which shows allowances for taxes collected from both firms and households (in broken lines) and increased payments to households and firms for the goods and services purchased from firms and households.

Figure 2–2 also shows another new element — purchases and sales of goods and services from one firm to another. Companies continually buy components and services from other companies (machinery; chemicals; telephone, electricity, and trucking services, and so on). Such intermediate goods and services are not sold to final consumers or

---

**FIGURE 2–2**  Circular Flow of Income and Expenditures Including Government and Intermediate Transactions

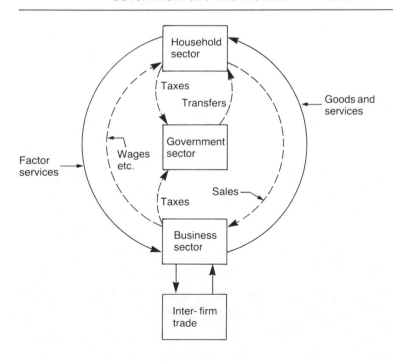

other final users and are thus not part of national income or expenditure, even though they can be quite important for the companies concerned and their employees.

## 2–3 COVERAGE OF GROSS DOMESTIC PRODUCT

By introducing income into the circular flow, we can now consider gross domestic product in a more comprehensive manner. Gross domestic product (GDP) consists of all currently produced goods and services that are purchased by final buyers through the market at market prices. There are four key points in that definition:

1. "Currently produced goods and services" means the goods and services that are produced during the particular time period (annually or quarterly) under consideration. The resale of capital items produced in a previous time period are excluded. For example, the statistics would include the production and sale of a house produced in the current year but would exclude the sale of a house built in the 1960s. Sales of new cars are included, while sales of used cars are excluded.

2. Final buyers can be consumers, businesses, or government. Final buyers are the ultimate users of the goods and services produced; they do not resell their purchased goods and services to other buyers. Consumers are the largest single category of final buyers in the North American economy. A company that buys a new piece of machinery to use in production is also a final buyer. And the government is a buyer of goods and services, such as stationery, computers, and transportation services.

3. The value of national product is based on market prices, the third major element in the definition of GDP. Market prices are the current level of prices for which goods and services sell. During a period of rising prices, GNP goes up even if the physical production of all goods and services remains unchanged. Remember, when prices of goods purchased by the consumer include indirect taxes, a similar allowance for indirect taxes paid to the government should also be included on the income side of the national accounts.

4. Prices of goods purchased by consumers include depreciation on physical assets used by the private sector (hence the term *gross* in gross domestic product). A similar amount should also be included on the income side of the national accounts.

Tables 2–1A and 2–1B, which reflect these concepts, summarize Canadian GDP data for the calendar year 1985. Note that the values

**TABLE 2–1 A** Gross Domestic Product, Income Based, Canada, 1985
(millions of dollars)

| | |
|---|---:|
| CANSIM Matrix No. 006721 | |
| Wages, salaries, and supplementary labour income | 255,569 |
| Corporation profits before taxes | 47,528 |
| Interest and miscellaneous investment income | 40,099 |
| Accrued net income of farm operators from farm production | 4,083 |
| Net income of nonfarm unincorporated business, including rent | 28,586 |
| Inventory valuation adjustment | −2,165 |
| Net domestic income at factor cost | 373,700 |
| Indirect taxes less subsidies | 47,171 |
| Capital consumption allowances | 53,725 |
| Statistical discrepancy | 1,765 |
| Gross domestic product at market prices | 476,361 |

SOURCE: Statistics Canada, *National Income and Expenditure Accounts, Second Quarter 1986* (Ottawa: Ministry of Supply and Services, October 1986), p. 2.

**TABLE 2–1 B** Gross Domestic Product Expenditure Based
(millions of dollars)

| | |
|---|---:|
| CANSIM Matrix No. 006722 | |
| Personal expenditure on consumer goods and services | 274,658 |
| Government current expenditure on goods and services | 94,971 |
| Government investment (fixed capital and inventories) | 11,717 |
| Business investment: | |
| Fixed capital | 80,856 |
| Residential construction | 25,368 |
| Nonresidential construction | 26,572 |
| Machinery and equipment | 28,916 |
| Inventories (farm and nonfarm) | 2,745 |
| Exports of goods and services | 135,961 |
| Deduct: Imports of goods and services | 122,783 |
| Statistical discrepancy | −1,764 |
| Gross domestic product at market prices | 476,361 |

SOURCE: Statistics Canada, *National Income and Expenditure Accounts, Second Quarter 1986* (Ottawa: Ministry of Supply and Services, October 1986), p. 4.

shown are identical for both the income side and the expenditure side of the accounts. Differences occur between the two sides of the accounts because the statistical data are not complete and accurate. Statistics Canada assumes that the quality of the statistics are approximately the same on both the income and expenditure side of the accounts, and it divides the statistical discrepancy equally between the two sides. This discrepancy is shown at the bottom of each of the two tables.

## 2–4 PRICE AND QUANTITY CHANGES IN GROSS DOMESTIC PRODUCT

Section 2–3 emphasized that gross domestic product is based on prices of the current period. However, it is essential to know what portion of the change in current dollars reflects a change in the general price level and what portion reflects a change in the physical quantity of goods and services produced. A basic definition is:

$$V \equiv P \times Q$$

where

$V =$  the value of production in current prices
$P =$ the price level for gross domestic product
$Q =$  the physical quantity of gross domestic product

Note that the three horizontal lines imply a definition. Also, if you know any two of these variables, you can obtain the third. For example, if you divide both sides of this definition by $P$ (the price level), you get the quantity measure of GDP.

In practice, you can obtain estimates of GDP in real terms by dividing the components of GDP for a particular year by the price indices most appropriate for that particular component of the expenditure side of the national accounts. To do so, you need some understanding of the consumer price index, probably the most widely known price index of the many available for Canada.

The **consumer price index** (CPI) measures the total change in the prices of a comprehensive, specified set of consumer goods and services that the average urban family buys on a regular basis. An index number of prices is not a simple unweighted average of price changes. Instead, each price is weighted by the proportion of total expenditures necessary to purchase the good in question.

The consumer price index, published by Statistics Canada each month, attempts to measure the movements in the total prices of goods and services consumed by a representative group of Canadian families in urban centres. Every month, Statistics Canada obtains about

130,000 prices for 490 individual items from retail outlets in 64 major Canadian centres. Products selected to construct the consumer price index are based on a 1978 survey of family expenditures.

To visualize what the CPI measures, think of a shopping basket filled with a typical range of products purchased by a representative consumer. The cost of this basket of products changes from year to year. Because the CPI uses a base year as a reference point, it is referred to as a base-weighted index. The base year of the CPI need not be the same year as the survey of expenditures. Note in Table 2–2 that the consumer had to pay more for goods and services in 1985 than in 1981 — 27.3 percent more.

In order to incorporate new products (such as minicomputers and video cassette recorders for television) and changing expenditure and price patterns, the consumer price index is rebased about once a decade. For example, in 1986 the consumer price index switched to a 1981 base (its previous base was 1971). Such rebasing does not affect the year-to-year changes of previously published series but does change the levels for overlapping years.

A base-weighted price index is called a Laspeyres index, after the French economist and statistician who first developed it. The formula for such a price index follows.

$$\frac{\sum_{i=1}^{n} p_{i}2 \times q_{i}1}{\sum_{i=1}^{n} p_{i}1 \times q_{i}1} \times 100$$

where Σ (sigma) indicates that the following quantities are all totalled:

$p_i$ refers to the price of a particular item
$q_i$ refers to the quantity of that item
$i$ refers to a specifically defined product or service
The numbers 1 and 2 refer to the base period and the current period, respectively.

The weights in the denominator above are the expenditures made by the average family in the base period. The quantities and qualities are the same in the base and the current period. This index, referred to as a fixed-basket-type price index, measures only the total price change. Items that make up a large share of the family budget have a heavier weight than items that make up a small share.

The Laspeyres index is the most widely used form of price index, primarily because of its ease in use. However, another form of price index is weighted by current weights. This type is called a Paasche index, after another French economist and statistician. Its formula follows.

$$\frac{\sum\limits_{i=1}^{n} p_{i2} \times q_{i2}}{\sum\limits_{i=1}^{n} p_{i1} \times q_{i2}} \times 100$$

The Paasche-type index is used only rarely primarily because it requires continual updating of the appropriate basket of expenditures. However, there is very little difference in the changes over time in a Paasche-type price index compared to a Laspeyres-type price index. If all prices changed by the identical amount, the two indexes would be identical. In practice, rates of price change typically differ, and the relative composition of expenditures changes. For example, with the dramatic price increases in petroleum products during the 1970s, typical consumers spent a higher share of their income on gasoline and natural gas for home heating. Such changes in expenditure composition and relative prices of different products lead to some differences between the base-weighted and current-weighted price indices. However, the extensive debates about index number formulae have tended to overexaggerate the quantitative importance of these price indices in practice.

The calculation of the price and quantity components of the changes in GDP in value terms is an important step. To illustrate the essential principles involved, Table 2–2 works through an imaginary example of the estimation of nominal GDP, real GDP, and the GDP deflator (or price index) for a simple economy in 1981 and 1985 producing only shirts and gasoline. **Nominal GDP** is based on the actual prices and quantities paid in each of the two years. **Real GDP** measures the output at 1981 prices in both years and shows an increase of 13 percent in 1985 over 1981. The **GDP deflator** (or price index) is obtained by dividing the GDP in current dollars (line 3c) by GDP in 1981 prices (line 4c). The term *implicit* (referring to the GDP implicit price deflator) is a reminder that no direct price-index measure is available. The measure derived from the current and constant dollar estimates is internally consistent with the concepts, definitions, and available data. This example shows that a major part of the increase in the value of GDP (about 50 percent) resulted from higher prices for both shirts and gasoline. Only about one fourth of the increase resulted from higher production volume.

Calculating the price and quantity components of GDP is similar in principle to this hypothetical example, but it is more difficult in practice. The difficulty occurs primarily because a much larger number of

**TABLE 2–2**    Nominal and Real GDP and Implicit Price Index,
Imaginary Economy Producing only Gasoline and Shirts,
1981 and 1985

|  | 1981 | 1985 |
|---|---|---|
| 1. Prices | | |
|    a.  Shirts (each) | $17.00 | $20.00 |
|    b.  Gasoline (cents per litre) | .30 | .40 |
| 2. Production in physical units | | |
|    a.  Shirts | 30,000 | 31,000 |
|    b.  Gasoline (litres) | 17,500 | 20,000 |
| 3. Value of production ($000s) | | |
|    a.  Shirts (1a × 2a) | 510 | 620 |
|    b.  Gasoline (1b × 2b) | 5,250 | 8,000 |
|    c.  Nominal GDP (3a + 3b) | 5,760 | 8,620 |
| 4. Volume of production in 1981 prices ($000s) | | |
|    a.  Shirts (1a for 1972 × 2a for each year) | 510 | 527 |
|    b.  Gasoline (1b for 1972 × 2b for each year) | 5,250 | 6,000 |
|    c.  Real GDP (4a + 4b) | 5,760 | 6,527 |
| 5. GDP deflator, 1981 = 100 | | |
|    (3c ÷ 4c) | 1.00 | 1.32 |

value, price, and quantity comparisons are involved in the detailed work sheets. Another difficulty is that prices and quantities are rarely available for such individual products as shirts and gasoline. Broader categories of expenditure components and price series must be used in practice. The resulting price and quantity aggregates are quite important and useful for economic analysis.

Statistics Canada incorporates new data when they become available. For example, in the 1986 revision Statistics Canada incorporated new and later price data for computers in the 1970s, leading to a significant upward revision in such series as real investment in machinery and equipment and in imports.

This introduction to the construction of the implicit GDP price index has so far ignored the significant changes in the rate of inflation that have taken place in Canada (and the rest of the world) during the 1970s. Table 2–3 illustrates important changes that have taken place over two 12-year periods, 1961 to 1973 and 1973 to 1985.

Table 2–3 shows that prices increased almost twice as fast during the second 12-year period than they did during the first. Furthermore, the rate of increase in real GDP was about 40 percent lower in the second 12-year period. The lower rate of increase in volume, however, was more than offset by the price increase. The total increase in value was higher during the second 12-year period than the first.[2] The smaller

---

**TABLE 2–3**   Value, Quantity, and Price Changes, Gross Domestic
Product, Canada, Selected Periods, 1961–85
(annual rates of change)

CANSIM Matrices No. 006722, 006723 and 006641

|  | 1961–1973 | 1973–1985 |
|---|---|---|
| GDP, current dollars | + 9.93 | + 11.62 |
| GDP, 1981 dollars | + 5.64 | + 3.28 |
| Implicit price deflator, 1981 = 100 | + 4.06 | + 8.08 |

SOURCE: Statistics Canada, CANSIM tapes.

---

increase in quantity and the more rapid increases in prices are important and puzzling developments of this period.

## 2–5 PERSONAL AND GOVERNMENT SECTORS

Thus far, we have emphasized the major aggregate of gross domestic
product, the most comprehensive summary measure of performance for
the economy as a whole. Although GDP is a useful summary of past
developments, we frequently need additional information to understand current economic developments and to develop a framework for
forecasting the short-term economic outlook. In addition to the two
tables of GDP (income-based and expenditure-based), the national
accounts include a large number of other sector accounts. We will
introduce only two of them here, namely the personal sector and the
government sector.

The personal sector includes all income sources and major expenditure areas (including savings) for the nonbusiness side of households. This sector includes income and expenditures of families *and*
receipts and expenditures of such nonprofit and voluntary organizations as churches and welfare organizations. Income sources of
the personal sector include some of the same items that are included on
the income side of the gross domestic product account—wages, salaries, supplementary labour income, etc. However, the personal sector
also receives a significant amount of transfer payments from government sources—family allowances, old age pensions, superannuation
payments, and so on. (Recipients of transfer payments perform no service for the government in return.) These payments amounted to almost
$60 billion in 1985, about one fourth of the wages and salaries compo-
nent (see Table 2–4).

The personal-income total is disbursed in essentially three
ways—expenditure on consumer goods and services, tax payments to

**TABLE 2–4**  Sources of Personal Income Canada, 1985
(millions of dollars)

| | |
|---|---|
| CANSIM Matrix No. 006726 | |
| Wages, salaries, and supplementary labour income | 255,569 |
| Net income received by farm operators from farm production | 4,070 |
| Net income of nonfarm unincorporated business, including rent | 28,586 |
| Interest, dividends, and miscellaneous investment income | 53,568 |
| Current transfers: | |
| From government | 58,816 |
| From corporations | 689 |
| From nonresidents | 685 |
| Personal income | 401,983 |

SOURCE: Statistics Canada, *National Income and Expenditure Accounts, Second Quarter 1986* (Ottawa: Ministry of Supply and Services, October 1986), pp. 10–11.

governments, and personal savings. **Personal disposable income** is the total of personal income after personal direct taxes. Individuals have the choice of either spending that income on consumer goods and services or saving it.

**Personal savings** are obtained in the personal-sector accounts as a residual, by subtracting personal expenditures on consumer goods and services from personal disposable income (total personal income less direct taxes). It is also possible to prepare direct estimates of personal savings based on changes in assets and liabilities of the personal sector. You can think of the savings of the personal sector as consisting of changes in liquid assets (chartered bank deposits and bonds), investment in physical assets (such as a home, a condominium, or a tractor for the family farm), and contractual saving. Contractual saving includes savings in a company pension scheme or a Registered Retirement Savings Plan. Paying off a home mortgage or a car loan is a form of savings also because it increases the family's net worth. Net worth is the difference between the family's total assets and total liabilities.

It is more difficult to estimate personal savings directly rather than as a residual, but this can be done. Part of the difficulty involves valuing assets (such as stocks and bonds) and separating personal holdings from corporate holdings. Direct estimates of personal savings show changes and levels broadly comparable to residual estimates of personal savings, which are the ones usually referred to.

Tables 2–4 and 2–5 show the main sources and disposition of personal income.

---

**TABLE 2–5**   Disposition of Personal Income Canada, 1985
(millions of dollars)

---

CANSIM Matrix No. 00726

| | |
|---|---|
| Personal expenditure on consumer goods and services | 274,658 |
| Current taxes and transfers to government | 78,582 |
| To corporations | 4,270 |
| To nonresidents | 529 |
| Personal saving (residual) | 43,944 |
| Personal disposable income (personal income less current taxes and transfers) | 323,401 |
| Personal savings as percentage of personal disposable income | 13.6 |

---

SOURCE: Statistics Canada, *National Income and Expenditure Accounts, Second Quarter 1986* (Ottawa: Ministry of Supply and Services, October 1986), pp. 14–15.

The other important sector is the government. We will discuss the three levels of government as a combined total to keep the presentation simple at this stage. (Part Five will return to a fuller discussion of the influence of governments on the economy, including the differing relative importance of the federal government, on the one hand, and the provinces and municipalities on the other.) Table 2–6 shows the main sources of revenue and expenditures for the three levels of government combined. When total government expenditures exceed total revenues as they did in 1985 (mainly due to the large federal deficit in the mid-1980s), the government sector is a net borrower from other sectors.

Only part of the government expenditures shown in Table 2–7 are included on the expenditure side of the national accounts. Transfer payments to individuals and families make up a significant part of government expenditures. The people who receive these payments make their own decisions as to whether to spend that income on goods and services or to save it. Government expenditures on current goods and services used directly by the government amounted to about $95 billion in 1985. Examples of such expenditures on goods and services include the salaries and wages of government employees and purchases such as stationery, telephone services, and airline tickets for Members of Parliament, Senators, and civil servants.

Some items of investment (the purchase of newly produced capital facilities) are included as government expenditures on goods and services — for example the construction of a post office or the purchase of an aircraft for defence purposes.

**TABLE 2–6**   Government-Sector Revenue, Canada, 1985, (millions of dollars)

| | |
|---|---:|
| CANSIM Matrix No. 006729 | |
| Revenue | |
| Direct taxes: | |
|    From persons | 74,864 |
|    From corporate and government business | |
|       enterprises | 15,565 |
|    From nonresidents (withholding taxes) | 1,069 |
| Indirect taxes | 58,868 |
| Other current transfers from persons | 3,718 |
| Investment income | 29,785 |
| Total revenue | 183,869 |

SOURCE: Statistics Canada, *National Income and Expenditure Accounts, Second Quarter 1986* (Ottawa: Ministry of Supply and Services, October 1986), pp. 20–21.

**TABLE 2–7**   Government-Sector Expenditure, Canada, 1985 (millions of dollars)

| | |
|---|---:|
| CANSIM Matrix No. 006729 | |
| Current expenditure on goods and services | 94,971 |
| Transfer payments: | |
|    To persons | 58,293 |
|    To business | 15,508 |
|    To nonresidents | 1,643 |
| Interest on the public debt | 40,290 |
| Total current expenditure | 210,705 |
| Saving (total revenue — total current | |
|    expenditure) | −26,836 |
| Add: Capital consumption allowances | 7,228 |
| Deduct: Investment in fixed capital | |
|    and inventories | 11,717 |
| Equals: Net lending | −31,325 |

SOURCE: Statistics Canada, *National Income and Expenditure Accounts, Second Quarter 1986* (Ottawa: Ministry of Supply and Services, October 1986), pp. 20–21.

## 2–6 INTERNATIONAL TRANSACTIONS

We are all aware of the importance of international trade in the Canadian economy. GDP for Canada (and for other countries too) includes such international transactions under the category of exports of goods and services. **Merchandise exports** include such items as sales of automobiles and trucks, newsprint and grain. The category also includes such service transactions as hotel accommodations, airline, and other transportation services to foreign com-panies and individuals, and in-surance services provided to nonresi-dents. Such exports of both goods and services provide income to the employees in companies providing such services.

However, imports make up an important part of the goods pur-chased by consumers. For example, tropical foods and spices such as tea, coffee, and many fresh fruits and vegetables are imported from abroad. Business firms also purchase many raw materials and compo-nents from foreign sources, such as automotive parts and components, books, and periodicals. These expenditures end up as income to foreign suppliers and thus must be deducted from the expenditures by Cana-dians. In effect, only the net difference between the receipts for exports of goods and services and the **imports of goods and services** need be shown on the gross national expenditure side. In practice, Canadian accounts usually show both exports and imports of goods and services separately.

## 2–7 SUMMARY OF THE COVERAGE OF GDP

Now that we have discussed the sector accounts of the personal and government sectors, it may be useful to summarize the coverage of the national accounts to recapitulate and reinforce some of the distinctions introduced. Table 2–8 summarizes some of the major expenditure cate-gories used in the national accounts and some of the sector breakdowns. The top part of the table breaks down total expenditures on final goods and services (GDP) into five basic components: consumer expenditures, private investment, government current expenditure, government in-vestment, and the international sector. These components of final ex-penditures exclude intercompany purchases and sales, which are shown separately on line C at the bottom of the table. Line B shows transfer payments to persons, which are included on the expenditure side of the government in Table 2–7 and also on the income side of the personal sector in Table 2–4. Although these expenditures and receipts show up in the personal and government accounts, they are transfers between sectors and thus are not part of final expenditures for the economy as a whole.

The national accounts also include statistics on the purchases and sales of existing assets. The most important examples of these assets are existing houses and apartments and second-hand cars, none of which involve employment in production when they are sold. However, the national accounts include commissions paid to real estate and second-hand car sales people, although commissions are only a small part of the market price of such transactions.

**TABLE 2–8**   Summary Coverage of GDP, Canada, 1985 (billions of dollars)

| Type of Expenditure | Included in GDP? | 1985 (billions of dollars) | Examples |
|---|---|---|---|
| A. Final goods and services (GDP) | Yes | 476.4 | |
| 1. Consumer expenditures | Yes | 214.7 | Autos, clothes |
| 2. Private business investment | Yes | 83.6 | |
| a. Change in business inventories | Yes | 2.7 | |
| b. Producer's durable equipment | Yes | 28.9 | Truck, motor |
| c. Nonresidential construction | Yes | 26.6 | Factory |
| d. Residential construction | Yes | 25.4 | Houses |
| 3. Government current expenditure (g. + s.)* | Yes | 95.0 | Teachers' salaries |
| 4. Government investment | Yes | 11.7 | Post office |
| 5. Net exports of g + s* | Yes | 13.2 | Cars, wheat |
| B. Government transfer payments to persons | No | 58.3 | Old age pensions |
| C. Intercompany purchases and sales | No | — | Crude oil, industrial chemicals |
| D. Private purchases of existing assets | No | — | Sales of old houses |
| E. Nonmarket activities | | | |
| 1. Housewives' services | No | — | Child raising |
| 2. Leisure time | No | — | Holidays, hobbies |
| 3. Pollution costs | No | — | Acid rain, smog |

*g + s — goods and services
SOURCE: Statistics Canada, *National Income and Expenditure Accounts, Second Quarter 1986* (Ottawa: Ministry of Supply and Services, October 1986), various pages.

We have emphasized that the national accounts measure production and are not intended to measure welfare. A number of items, although fairly important in terms of household's satisfaction, produce no cash payments through the market. We show these nonmarket activities in item E in Table 2–8. Examples include the services of housewives and the value of leisure time.

National income figures primarily measure production for the economy as a whole, but they can be adapted to provide reasonably reliable measures of welfare as well. The present measures of GDP emphasize production in the market economy based on goods and services purchased through the market. However, personal welfare can also be heavily influenced by services that do not flow through the market. The most important example of such services are the important contributions of housewives in caring for children, preparing food, doing laundry, cleaning house, and so on. To prepare a measure of welfare, you would have to impute a value to the services of housewives and add that into the value of production purchased in the market.

Some costs involved in producing goods and services in the market place may not be fully reflected in the existing measures of national income. Examples include water and air pollution and noise from factories and trucks. Estimates of such costs on third parties are only approximate.

When adjustments are made to shift from a measure of production to a measure of welfare, the percentage changes over long periods are similar to those obtained from the measures of production.[3]

Some unmeasured costs are associated with production—for instance, the costs of pollution. Unmeasured costs are included in Item E.

## SUMMARY

The major advantage in using the national income aggregates is the simplicity gained by concentrating description and analysis on a small number of key totals for the economy as a whole.

Two circular-flow diagrams were presented to show how incomes and expenditures are related to the income and spending decisions sions of the major participants.

Inclusions and exclusions from the coverage of the accounts were explained for both the income and expenditure sides of the accounts.

The connections between value, volume, and price for gross domestic product were clarified and the estimation of the GDP deflator was explained.

The accounts for the personal, government, and international sectors were introduced and recent examples provided.

The major inclusions and exclusions of the GDP totals were then summarized.

## NOTES

1. Data Resources of Canada, *Canadian Review,* September 1986, pp. 74–75.
2. It should be noted that the rate of change in volume and the rate of change in price are combined by multiplying, rather than adding the two together. For example, the change in value is equal to 1.0328 times 1.0808 (the compound rate of change in constant prices and the compound rate of change in prices, respectively), or 1.1162.

These numbers all correspond to the annual rates of change between 1973 and 1985 shown in the second column of Table 2–3.

3.  William S. Nordhaus and James Tobin, "Is Growth Obsolete?" in *The Measurement of Economic and Social Performance*, ed. Milton Moss (New York: Columbia University Press for the NBER, 1973), pp. 509–64. Comparable estimates of economic welfare for Canada have been made by Dan Usher, *The Measurement of Economic Growth* (Oxford: Basil Blackwell, 1980).

# 3

# Macroeconomic Experience in North America

This chapter will introduce you to five major topics in macroeconomics. These are:

1. Aggregate economic growth and the major determinants of growth on the supply side, both past and future.
2. Fluctuations in demand affecting the business cycle and the unemployment rate.
3. Changes in the general level of prices and interest rates.
4. The role of government on economic performance through changes in government expenditures, revenues, and public debt.
5. How developments in the rest of the world affect economic developments within Canada, as reflected in changes in international trade and exchange rates.

This discussion will summarize some highlights of economic history in North America since World War II. Some of the key problem areas will be emphasized, including some of the unique features in the economic performance of this period. In some instances, the North American experience will be compared with similar developments in the other major industrialized countries. Since world economies have become increasingly interdependent such international comparisons provide a broader perspective.

## 3–1 LONG-TERM ECONOMIC GROWTH

Since 1950, economic growth in all major industrialized countries has been exceptionally strong by historical standards. Statistical tables in this chapter show economic growth for seven major countries.

A key measure of economic growth is real GDP per employee. As shown in Table 3–1, increased worker productivity is a major reason for the economic growth that has taken place in all major industrialized countries since 1950. This table shows that the increases in real GDP per employee in every country have been more rapid from 1950 to 1973 than over the 80-year period from 1870 to 1950.

Since the days of Henry Ford and Pullman, America has prided itself on its productive industrial sector. Table 3–1, however, shows that increases in Japan and the countries in continental Western Europe were more rapid from 1950 to 1973 than increases in the United States and Canada. These increases led to significant narrowing in the differences in real income levels of GDP per employee by the 1980s. Such changes have had important effects on the size and country composition of international trade.

The selected periods are broadly representative for this group of countries. These years were selected to avoid examining the influences of economic disruption, postwar reconstruction, or temporarily high unemployment rates. The year 1870 is as early as comparable and reasonably reliable data are available for this group of countries. Some countries still experienced postwar reconstruction in the years immediately after World War II, but these adjustments were largely completed by 1950, a year of low unemployment for most of the countries shown. The year 1973 was also a year of low unemployment and the last year of high growth for most industrialized countries. The last year in the table (1986) was also a nonrecessionary period without temporarily high unemployment rates. These periods are widely accepted as important periods of analysis for economic growth. Slight differences in the years selected would not modify the main conclusions, however.

Another important measure of economic growth is total real GDP for the economy as a whole. This aggregate measure reflects the net result of changes both in the number of employees and the increases in real GDP per employee. A comparison of Tables 3–1 and 3–2 shows that increases in output per employee were usually a significant proportion of the increases in total real output for most of the individual countries, especially from 1950 to 1973. In Canada, for instance, growth in real GDP per employee for that period was 2.52 percent, substantially higher than the 1.56 percent over the previous 80 years or the much lower 1.06 percent for the 1973–86 period.

Another major development reflected in these two tables is the fact that economic growth from 1973 to 1986 was slower for each of the seven countries than the period before 1973. Both the United States and Canada experienced a slower rate after 1973 for GDP per employee and GDP than during the 80-year period from 1870 to 1950, even though that long period was interrupted by the severe depression of the 1930s.

**TABLE 3–1**   Growth Rates: Real GDP per Employee, Selected Industrial Countries (selected periods, 1870–1986)

| Country | 1870–1950 | 1950–1973 | 1973–1986 |
|---|---|---|---|
| United States | 1.78% | 2.20% | 0.38% |
| Canada | 1.56 | 2.52 | 1.06 |
| France | 1.22 | 4.73 | 2.02 |
| Germany | 1.14 | 5.12 | 2.17 |
| Italy | 0.98 | 5.75 | 1.38 |
| United Kingdom | 0.91 | 2.56 | 1.41 |
| Japan | n.a. | 7.47 | 2.84 |

Note: n.a. = not available.
SOURCES: U.S. Bureau of Economic Analysis, *Long-Term Economic Growth, 1860–1970* (Washington, D.C.: U.S. Government Printing Office, 1973) and U.S. Department of Labor, *Comparative Real Gross Domestic Product, Real GDP per Capita and Real GDP per Employed Person, 1950–1986* (Washington, D.C.: Bureau of Labor Statistics, April 1987), various pages.

**TABLE 3–2**   Growth Rates: Total Real GDP, Selected Industrial Countries, (selected periods, 1870–1986)

| Country | 1870–1950 | 1950–73 | 1973–86 |
|---|---|---|---|
| United States | 3.69% | 3.62% | 2.30% |
| Canada | 3.36 | 5.09 | 3.26 |
| France | 1.18 | 5.13 | 2.12 |
| Germany | 2.08 | 6.28 | 1.85 |
| Italy | 1.38 | 5.49 | 2.06 |
| United Kingdom | 1.72 | 3.00 | 1.39 |
| Japan | n.a. | 9.33 | 3.68 |

Note: n.a. = not available.
SOURCES: U.S. Bureau of Economic Analysis, *Long-Term Economic Growth, 1860–1970* (Washington, D.C.: U.S. Government Printing Office, 1973) and U.S. Department of Labor, *Comparative Real Gross Domestic Product, Real GDP per Capita and Real GDP per Employed Person, 1950–1986* (Washington, D.C.: Bureau of Labor Statistics, April 1987), various pages.

These differences in growth rates sometimes look small, but they can contribute to very large differences over an extended period of time. For instance, Table 3–3 compares the length of time it would take for real GDP per employee to double. With a growth rate of .9 percent per year (roughly the rate of growth in the United Kingdom from 1870 to 1950), GDP per employee would require 78 years to double. On the other hand, a growth rate of 7.6 percent per year (roughly the rate of growth in Japan from 1950 to 1973) would lead to a doubling in 10 years. Such differences over an extended period of time can modify the im-

---

**TABLE 3–3**   Years to Double, Selected Growth Rates

| Growth Rate | Years to Double |
|:---:|:---:|
| 0.9% | 78 |
| 1.4 | 50 |
| 2.6 | 27 |
| 3.0 | 24 |
| 4.5 | 16 |
| 5.2 | 14 |
| 6.0 | 12 |
| 7.6 | 10 |

SOURCE: Financial calculator, selected growth rates.

---

portance of countries as export markets and shift the balance of economic power.

The effects of compound growth rates can also be applied to corporate decision making. Suppose that you are planning for the future of a business firm, and you expect that your company's growth in needed capacity will be in line with the average increase in total GDP. Rate of growth can make a major difference on how soon you would have to double capacity. If the rate of growth were 5.2 percent per year (approximately the 1950 to 1973 Canadian rate), you would need to increase your capacity in 14 years, much sooner than necessary with the slower growth rate of 3.3 percent per year experienced since 1973. With the slower growth rate, you would need to double capacity in 22 years. This example assumed that company output increases in step with capacity. If technological advance or greater experience and higher motivation of employees also occurred, the need for greater capacity could be further postponed.

These summary statistics pose three important questions for macroeconomic theory. First, what are the reasons for the significant increases in the various indicators of aggregative economic growth in the United States and Canada from 1950 to 1973? Second, what are some of the main reasons for the more rapid economic growth in non-North American industrialized countries since 1950? Third, can economic theory throw light on the reasons for the slowdown in economic growth that has taken place since 1973 in all the major industrialized countries?

The answers to these questions are important in assessing the prospects for future economic growth. Whether economic growth for the economy as a whole will be closer to 3.3 percent per year (roughly the growth rate in Canada since 1973) or 5.0 percent per year (the growth rate in Canada from 1950 to 1973) makes a significant difference in planning future capacity levels for individual firms and industries. And the government has to predict its revenues and expenditures just like individual companies do. The government must also consider ways to encourage long-run economic growth. Both corporate managers and government planners must look at the experiences and practices in other countries to see if future performance can be improved in Canada. Are differences in economic objectives and economic policies important in explaining the different growth rates experienced by major industrialized countries, or does their apparent superior performance primarily reflect the lower initial starting points for Japan and Western Europe? These are the types of questions raised by the factual evidence summarized in Tables 3–1 to 3–3, all questions that we will be examining later in this book.

## 3–2 BUSINESS CYCLES AND FLUCTUATIONS IN AGGREGATE DEMAND

The historical experience over the last century also contains some shorter-term variations in the economy, referred to as business cycles. Business-cycle terminology distinguishes between periods of contractions, called **recessions** (when economic growth declines) and periods of **expansion** (when the growth rate accelerates). The dividing time lines between expansions and recessions are identified by **peak** and **trough** dates, as shown in Figure 3–1. Figure 3–1 illustrates the

---

**FIGURE 3–1**   Illustrative Cyclical Movement in Manufacturing Output Monthly, 1981–84

---

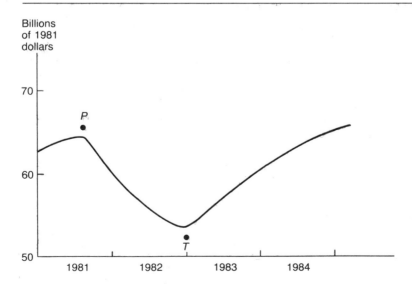

monthly levels of manufacturing production for Canada from 1981 to the end of 1984. The actual monthly data experience more month-to-month variability than is shown, but the figure is broadly illustrative of the typical changes.

The standard definition of business cycles is as follows:

Business cycles are a type of fluctuation found in the aggregate economic activity of nations that organize their work in business enterprises: a cycle consists of expansions occurring at about the same time in many economic activities, followed by similarly general recessions, contractions, and revivals which merge into the expansion phase of the next cycle; this sequence of changes is recurrent but not periodic; in duration business cycles vary from more than one year to 10 or 12 years; they are not divisible into shorter cycles of similar character with amplitudes approximately their own.[1]

The phrase *not periodic* is crucial. It clarifies that the durations of the full cycle and the individual expansions and recessions are not fixed. Examples of recent business-cycle peaks and troughs in the United States from 1919 to 1982 appear in Table 3–4. To illustrate the variation in length of expansions, the 1961 to 1969 expansion lasted 106 months, one of the longest peacetime expansions in U.S. history. On the other hand, the 1980–81 expansion lasted only 12 months, one of the shortest expansions in the historical period. Other examples can be seen in the table. The average duration of the postwar recessions (1945 to 1982) is only 11 months, while the duration of expansions is 45 months. The average duration of the full business cycle (both recession and expansion combined) is almost four years over the extended period from 1854 to 1982.

Macroeconomists speak of production, consumption, investment, and corporate profits as **economic processes,** or types of economic activity. The business cycle consists of many of these economic processes that experience varying degrees of change over the typical cycle. Some processes show a high degree of **stability,** which means they undergo small changes from quarter to quarter and over the full business cycle. Others have a very dramatic cyclical **volatility,** meaning they experience large changes from quarter to quarter and over the full business cycle. For example, personal consumption in constant dollars is very stable. On the other hand, business investment and residential construction are extremely volatile. Similar differences in volatility appear in the major income sources. Average hourly compensation is fairly stable, while corporate profits, which are the residual (difference) between corporate income and expenses, are highly volatile. These differences from one economic process to another can be seen in Table 3–5,

**TABLE 3–4**  U.S. Business Cycles: Reference Dates and Duration

| Business Cycle Reference Dates | | Contraction (trough from previous peak) | Expansion (trough to peak) | Cycle | |
|---|---|---|---|---|---|
| | | | | Trough from Previous Trough | Peak from Previous Peak |
| Trough | Peak | | | | |
| March 1919 | January 1920 | 7 | 10 | 51 | 17 |
| July 1921 | May 1923 | 18 | 22 | 28 | 40 |
| July 1924 | October 1926 | 14 | 27 | 36 | 41 |
| November 1927 | August 1929 | 13 | 21 | 40 | 34 |
| March 1933 | May 1937 | 43 | 50 | 64 | 93 |
| June 1938 | February 1945 | 13 | 80 | 63 | 93 |
| October 1945 | November 1948 | 8 | 37 | 88 | 45 |
| October 1949 | July 1953 | 11 | 45 | 48 | 56 |
| May 1954 | August 1957 | 10 | 39 | 55 | 49 |
| April 1958 | April 1960 | 8 | 24 | 47 | 32 |
| February 1961 | December 1969 | 10 | 106 | 34 | 116 |
| November 1970 | November 1973 | 11 | 36 | 117 | 47 |
| March 1975 | January 1980 | 16 | 58 | 52 | 74 |
| July 1980 | July 1981 | 6 | 12 | 64 | 18 |
| November 1982 | | 16 | — | 28 | — |
| Average, all cycles: | | | | | |
| 1854–1982 (30 cycles) | | 18 | 33 | 51 | 51* |
| 1854–1919 (16 cycles) | | 22 | 27 | 48 | 49† |
| 1919–45 (6 cycles) | | 18 | 35 | 53 | 53 |
| 1945–82 (8 cycles) | | 11 | 45 | 56 | 55 |
| Average, peacetime cycles: | | | | | |
| 1854–1982 (25 cycles) | | 19 | 27 | 46 | 46‡ |
| 1854–1919 (14 cycles) | | 22 | 24 | 46 | 47§ |
| 1919–45 (5 cycles) | | 20 | 26 | 46 | 45 |
| 1945–82 (6 cycles) | | 11 | 34 | 46 | 41 |

NOTE: Underscored figures are the wartime expansions (Civil War, World Wars I and II, Korean War, and Vietnam War), the postwar contractions, and the full cycles that include the wartime expansions.
*29 cycles.
†15 cycles.
‡24 cycles.
§13 cycles.
SOURCE: National Bureau of Economic Research, Inc.

which shows the average quarterly change over the period from 1948 to 1982.

Business cycles in Canada have essentially all the same properties as those summarized for the United States, but comparable data have not been assembled. As an example of similarities, no business-cycle

---

**TABLE 3–5**  Measures of Variability, Quarterly Series: Selected
Cyclical Indicators and Other Important Economic
Measures (average percentage changes, 1948–82)

---

| | |
|---|---|
| Personal consumption expenditures in 1972 dollars | .91 |
| GNP in 1972 dollars | 1.05 |
| Index of unit labor cost, business sector | 1.10 |
| Value of goods output in 1972 dollars | 1.32 |
| Government purchases of goods and services in 1972 dollars | 1.35 |
| Average hourly compensation, nonfarm business sector | 1.50 |
| Gross private nonresidential fixed investment in 1972 dollars, structures | 1.88 |
| Gross private nonresidential fixed investment in 1972 dollars, producers' durable equipment | 2.53 |
| Expenditures for new plant and equipment by U.S. nonfarm business | 2.68 |
| Federal government receipts | 2.75 |
| Gross private residential fixed investment in 1972 dollars | 3.98 |
| Corporate profits after tax in current dollars | 4.40 |

---

SOURCE: U.S. Bureau of Economic Analysis, *Handbook of Cyclical Indicators*
(Washington, D.C.: U.S. Government Printing Office, 1984), p. 176.

recession has occurred in Canada unless one occurred at approximately
the same time in the United Sates. About 80 percent of the peak and
trough dates in Canada from 1900 to 1985 have occurred within three
months of those in the United States. No historical evidence indicates
that economic developments in Canada have lagged behind comparable
developments in the United States, but rather they tend to move together.[2] Thus, it is not possible to use the recent past in the United
States as a guide to future business-cycle developments in Canada.

One important difference is that every recession in Canada from
1900 to 1980 was milder than the comparable recession in the United
States, as measured by the index of industrial production. It was
thought in the past that small countries would be severely affected by
even mild recessions in larger countries due to declines in exports from
small countries to large countries. (By "small" we refer to population
and national income rather than geographic area.) Small countries such
as Canada typically are more susceptible to international influences, as
measured by the ratio of merchandise exports to GDP. Canada, however,
has a much higher ratio of exports of goods and services to GDP than the
United States (25.8 percent for Canada compared to 9.2 percent for the
United States in 1985). Thus, Canada's historical experience from 1900
to 1980 refutes the view of greater instability in small open economies,
although that view continues to surface on occasion.

Business-cycle fluctuations are also reflected in developments in
the labour market and in the unemployment rate. Employment and
total hours worked tend to rise during business-cycle expansions, and

decline during business-cycle contractions. The employment changes tend to be more pronounced over the business cycle in the commodity-producing industries and in construction than in such service industries as government, hospitals, and educational institutions. The unemployment rate varies significantly over business cycles, increasing during recessions and declining during expansions. In Canada, during the 1981–82 recession, the unemployment rate increased from 7.5 percent of the labour force in early 1981 to about 12.5 percent in the latter months of 1982, the highest unemployment rate since the 1930s. In 1933, during the depths of the Depression, the unemployment rate hit an all-time high of about 20 percent.

This summary of the cyclical experience in the United States and Canada raises another new question about economic theory. What are the primary causes of these cyclical fluctuations? Economists have discussed alternative interpretations of the causes of cyclical fluctuations in modern industrial economies. One interpretation emphasizes the role of profits and investment as a central part of the cycle, but suggests that business expectations are very unstable and the resulting fluctuations in the private sector must be moderated or offset by deliberate compensating adjustments in public policy. The alternative interpretation emphasizes the effects of shocks and disturbances from *outside* the private sector as the major initiating factor in cycles. Examples of such external shocks include the impact of wars (and war finance), the OPEC price increases of the 1970s, or the effects of a weak and vulnerable banking and monetary system. Emphasis on external shocks suggests that the appropriate role for public policy would be to reduce or soften the impact of such shocks on the economy and to discourage frequent changes in public policy that could be disruptive for the appropriate longer-term decision making in the the private sector. What, if any, role does government policy have in moderating or offsetting these recurrent cycles? Why is it that business-cycle recessions in Canada have been milder than in the United States for the first decades of the present century? These are the types of questions that will be examined in later parts of this book.

## 3–3 PRICE INFLATION IN THE 1970s

Inflation has affected many countries from ancient times (the Roman Empire in the 5th century A.D.) to the present day. Some countries have experienced **hyperinflation,** when the rates of price increase exceed 45 percent — not per year but *per month!*[3] But these periods of hyperinflation tend to be regarded as special cases that occurred during periods of war or postwar reconstruction, or in countries with unstable political systems, weak financial institutions, and inappropriate monetary policies.

In North America, stability in the major aggregate-price measures was the prevailing pattern during peacetime from early in the 19th century until the start of the 1970s. The only periods of significant price inflation occurred during World Wars I and II and during the U.S. Civil War in the 1860s.

There is some interaction between the business cycle and the rate of price change over time. The most dramatic example occurred from 1929 to 1933 when the GDP price deflator fell 18.5 percent in Canada, the consumer price index fell 23 percent, the general wholesale price index fell 30 percent to its low point, and the general index of average wage rates fell 17 percent. Thus the typical declines in production and employment outlined in Section 3–2 were also reflected in declines in price and wages. The decline in corporate profits was even more marked. At their low point in 1932, corporate profits before taxes in Canada dropped to less than one-tenth of their 1929 level. Many individuals and corporations went bankrupt because of the severity of the drop in national income, employment, wages, and profits. Severe economic hardship was exacerbated in the prairies by drought and grasshoppers. In some municipalities in Saskatchewan, 85 percent of the population was on relief. The combination of relief payments and drops in tax collections created severe financial problems for a number of municipalities, and similar problems existed in other provinces.

This variation in the rate of price change has persisted historically in North America and has continued since World War II. Every economic slowdown or actual recession has been reflected in a slowdown in the rate of change in the price level. Furthermore, cyclical contractions in the rate of price change have not occurred at other times.[4]

Price developments in North America since early in the 1970s have departed significantly from the past 150-year experience of peacetime price stability. From 1974, the GDP price deflator rose more than 120 percent in Canada, a rate of increase of 7.5 percent per year. The annual rate of increase ranged from a high of 14.4 percent in 1974 to a low of 3.4 percent in 1985. For Canada, the rate of price increase from 1971 to 1985 was more than double the rate of inflation experienced during World War II and the postwar adjustment period from 1939 to 1947.

This period of price inflation in the United States and Canada since the 1970s is not unique to North America but occurred also in Japan, Europe, and some developing countries. Italy and the United Kingdom had annual rates of increase in the consumer price index in excess of 25 percent per year in the mid-1970s, and Japan had a brief period of price inflation of 20 percent per year in 1973 and 1974.

These price increases in the major industrialized countries in the 1970s exceeded those Spain and Portugal experienced in the 15th and 16th centuries due to the inflow of gold and specie from the New World.[5]

In the decade of the 1970s, the industrialized countries experienced the most widespread and rapid period of peacetime inflation of any previous decade in the last five centuries. However, in none of these countries did the rate of inflation approach that experienced during short periods of hyperinflation when the rates of price increase exceeded 45 percent per month. Furthermore, by the early 1980s, the rate of price inflation moderated in all the major industrialized countries. The rates of price increase of 10 to 15 percent per year for a number of years did not develop into galloping inflation as some had predicted.

Price increases of this magnitude in such comprehensive price series as the consumer price index and the GDP deflator were inevitably reflected in significant changes in the prices and incomes of the factors of production, such as wage rates, compensation per hour, interest rates, and corporate profits.

For the time being, let's concentrate on interest rates. By early in the 1980s, nominal interest rates in Canada and the United States (as reflected in long-term federal government-bond yields) were at their highest level in the present century. (**Nominal interest rates** are interest rates measured in current prices.) Since then, long-term interest rates have declined from the all-time highs reached in 1981 and 1982 but have not declined as much as the reduction in the rate of price increase as determined by such comprehensive measures as the consumer price index and the GDP deflator.

This summary of the fluctuations in prices and interest rates in North America since the start of the 1970s raises a number of questions for macroeconomic theory. What factors led to the widespread inflation of the 1970s? Were these same influences present in earlier periods of inflation and hyperinflation? Why didn't the widespread price increases of the 70s develop into galloping or hyperinflation? What influences led to new record highs in nominal interest rates in Canada in the early 1980s? These questions will be considered in Part Four.

## 3–4 THE ROLE OF GOVERNMENT

Government has become a more important factor in macroeconomic performance over the decades. In 1870, for example, expenditures of the three levels of government in Canada accounted for less than 5 percent of GDP. This proportion increased to 11 percent in 1929 and 22 percent by 1985. Government transfer payments also increased from 2 percent of personal income in 1929 to 10 percent in 1970 and almost 15 percent in 1985. Such increases in the relative size of government expenditures were bound to affect the economy's performance.

For most of the period after World War II, government revenues increased roughly in line with expenditures. The federal government, for example, was able to cover the growth in its expenditures, increase exemptions under the personal income tax, and reduce tax rates over the years from 1945 to 1980.

But in the early 1980s, total federal expenditures began to exceed federal revenues significantly. In the first half of 1985, current federal expenditures exceeded revenues by about 45 percent! The resulting **deficit** led to a large increase in the federal debt outstanding, and interest costs became a much larger share of total government expenditures.

The size of the deficit and the growth of the federal debt outstanding raise new questions for discussion. Were the deficits a result of the severe 1981–82 recession, or were they primarily a result of longer-term factors? Was the larger deficit an important factor in the high interest rates of the early 1980s? Should the government further increase the size of the deficit to reduce the high unemployment rate still present four years after the end of the recession?

Such issues got major coverage in daily newspapers and the financial press during the early part of the 1980s. They also triggered ongoing debates both within the House of Commons and at the major federal-provincial conferences during that period. The tools of analysis presented in Part Five will help you understand and follow such topical debates in the future.

## 3–5 INTERNATIONAL INFLUENCES ON NORTH AMERICA

Since World War II, North America has become more interdependent with the rest of the world both economically and politically. To understand what has happened in North America over the postwar period, you need to understand five major developments in the world economy.

### 1. The United States in the World Economy

At the end of World War II, the United States was a dominant factor in the world economy. It had the highest level of real GDP per employed person, a large domestic market with few limitations on trade within that market, and clear dominance in many areas of technology and managerial expertise. (Notice the very high level of GDP per employed person in the United States compared to that in the other industrialized countries in Table 3–6.) At that time, Japan's GDP per employed person was less than 20 percent of the U.S. level, partly because postwar reconstruction was still incomplete. Also, there was considerable diversity within the continental Western European countries. For the seven countries shown in Table 3–6, the unweighted average of real GDP per employed person was only about 40 percent of the U.S. level.

**TABLE 3–6**   Real GDP Per Employed Person, Selected Non-North American Countries, Selected Years, 1950–86 (United States = 100)

| Country | 1950 | 1970 | 1986 |
|---|---|---|---|
| Japan | 15.0 | 45.1 | 68.7 |
| Belgium | 46.9 | 62.1 | 82.8 |
| France | 36.0 | 61.1 | 82.0 |
| Germany | 32.1 | 61.6 | 81.5 |
| Italy | 27.7 | 59.7 | 72.9 |
| Netherlands | 56.7 | 78.1 | 88.3 |
| United Kingdom | 53.7 | 57.8 | 71.5 |
| Unweighted average, seven countries | 38.3 | 60.8 | 78.2 |

SOURCE: U.S. Department of Labor, *Comparative Real Gross Domestic Product, Real GDP Per Capita and Real GDP Per Employed Person, 1950–1984* (Washington, D.C.; Bureau of Labor Statistics, April 1987).

Since then, a number of major developments have dramatically reduced the dominant role of the United States in the world economy.

## 2. Intercountry Differences in Growth Rates

Those large differences in 1950 have narrowed drastically in the three-and-a-half decades since then. By 1986, Japan reached 70 percent of the U.S. level. The European countries also caught up to a significant degree, and even the United Kingdom began to recover after falling behind both the United States and most of the other European countries in the 1960s and early 1970s. The smaller European countries made significant gains in relation to the larger European countries (partly assisted by the emergence of free trade in industrial products under the European Economic Community). By 1986, the unweighted average of the seven countries was about 80 percent of the comparable U.S. level, compared to only about 40 percent in 1950.

The United States itself did not stand still from 1950 to 1986. Real GDP per employed person increased by more than 60 percent, a rate of 1.4 percent per year. However, increases in the other industrialized countries were even greater as illustrated in Table 3–6.

This significant narrowing in the differences in the levels of real GDP per employee has permitted dramatic increases in such an important expenditure component as consumer expenditures. Living standards, which reflect consumer spending for cars, television sets, and durables, have all increased. These countries have thus all become much more important as potential export markets for North American producers.

## 3. Growth in World Trade

International trade increased even more rapidly than real GDP. The rapid increases in exports for the major industrialized countries resulted in an increased share of GDP in all the major countries. However, the rate of increase in exports of the non-North American countries was so much more rapid that the North American share of world exports actually declined.

## 4. Changes in the Composition of World Trade

The composition of world trade has also changed significantly. Trade statistics normally distinguish between trade in manufactured products (automobiles, television sets, and machinery products) and trade in natural resource products (wheat, copper, and crude petroleum). A major development in world trade has been a dramatic increase in trade in manufactured products. In fact, world trade in manufactured products has increased even more rapidly than the production and consumption of manufactured products within the individual countries. Many producers in many countries have begun to specialize (i.e., produce fewer types of products) and purchase more components and other product varieties from foreign plants. The net result is an increase in *both* exports and imports of manufactured products.

World trade in primary products has performed differently. In fact, world trade in primary (or natural resource) products has been a falling share of total world trade since before World War I.

This declining share of natural resource products in world trade is important for Canada, since the export of natural resource products has always been an important factor in Canadian economic growth and development. The changing environment of world trade has already affected the composition of Canada's trade and industrial structure and may also affect our options and choices for the future.

There has also been an increase in the amount of receipts and payments for services, as reflected in the receipts for transportation services, international banking, and insurance and other services. However, the Canadian receipts from such services are smaller in relation to merchandise exports than in other countries, and such receipts have increased more slowly in Canada than in other countries.

## 5. Increased Exchange-Rate Instability

An **exchange rate** is the price of one currency in terms of another currency. From the mid-19th century to the start of the 1970s, the major industrialized countries tried to keep their exchange rates fixed in terms of the currencies of other major countries. Apart from periods of wars or severe depressions, these major countries managed to maintain a fair amount of exchange-rate stability. In the 1930s there were a significant number of exchange-rate changes in the major industrialized countries, but it was widely regarded at the time that those changes were primarily related to the continuing problems of reparations and war debts from World War I and the severity of the 1930s depression. Some peripheral countries in the world economy adjusted their exchange rates on occasion as well.

The International Monetary Fund (IMF), established in 1945 at the end of World War II, encouraged countries to maintain fixed exchange rates, although changes in those rates could be made under certain conditions after consultation with the IMF.

A significant change occurred in the 1970s with the more widespread adoption of floating exchange rates. **Floating exchange rates** exist when the relative international value of two currencies is allowed to fluctuate in response to international market forces. Central banks sometimes intervene to smooth out short-term fluctuations although they don't oppose longer-term and deepseated forces.

The change to floating exchange rates could be dated from 1971, when the United States announced a significant change in exchange rates and introduced a selective tax on imports. This was a major change for a country whose currency had played a key role in the world economy for decades — and for a country that actively supported IMF goals of exchange-rate stability and criticized other governments for introducing selective taxes and controls on imports.

The extent of the changes in the exchange rates of six of the major world economies can be seen in Figure 3–2 which shows the price of the individual foreign currencies per U.S. dollar since 1973. All the major currencies underwent extensive changes over this period, both up and down. The value of the Canadian dollar changed less dramatically than the other major currencies shown, but you had to pay about 40 percent more for one U.S. dollar at the end of 1986 than in the fall of 1976, a decade previously.

The extent of these changes raises two important questions. Are the factors contributing to the significant increase in exchange-rate volatility based on deepseated changes, or are they temporary, permitting the world economy to return to more stability in the foreign exchange values of the major currencies? What effects do such changes in exchange rates have on international trade, corporate profits, and the location of new production facilities?

These important developments in the world economy over the postwar period pose some questions for macroeconomic theory. Why have the real income differences between the industrialized countries narrowed to the extent that they have, and will this trend continue? What

**FIGURE 3–2**  Foreign Currency per U.S. Dollar

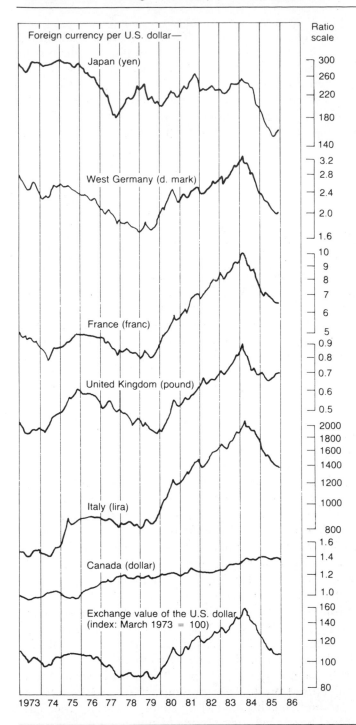

SOURCE: U.S. Department of Commerce, *Business Conditions Digest* (Washington, D.C.: Government Printing Office, October 1986), p. 106.

are the reasons for the changing composition of trade in manufactured products and natural resource products? What are the reasons for the major changes in world exchange rates that have taken place since 1971? If countries continue to experience significant differences in exchange rates, how can individual companies modify their corporate policies and strategies to accommodate such variability? These are some of the questions that will be considered in Part Six.

## SUMMARY

All major industrialized countries experienced a very high level of economic growth from 1850 to 1973 but a significant slowdown since 1973.

There have been significant differences in the rate of economic growth between the major countries, with Japan and most of the European countries experiencing more rapid economic growth than North America since the end of World War II.

Business cycles have continued to occur in recent decades, with fluctuations in such major aggregates as national income, production, employment, and unemployment. Business cycles vary in duration; some are fairly short, but others last for many years.

Some economic processes undergo only relatively small changes from quarter to quarter and over the business cycle, while other economic processes are more volatile. Corporate profits and business investment, for example, are more volatile while compensation per hour and consumer expenditures are more stable.

The inflation in the world economy in the 1970s was the most widespread by country and the most severe during peacetime in centuries. Nominal interest rates reached new peaks for the 20th century early in the 1980s. The rates of price increase tend to be faster in expansions and slower during recessions, but since the 1930s there have been no extended periods of price declines in North America.

The role of government has tended to increase in Canada over the present century, as it has in many industrialized countries. Many observers favour greater responsibility for government and its agencies to facilitate greater stability in employment and income in the country, although the appropriate steps to achieve such stability are still not fully resolved. A new element in the 1980s is the development of large federal deficits in both Canada and the United States and a rapid increase in the federal debt and related interest payments.

Important shifts have occurred in the structure of world trade. Exchange of manufactured products is growing rapidly, while trade in natural resource products has been a falling share of world trade. This shift is important for Canada because exports of staple natural resource products have been important in our economic history.

The early 1970s saw the end of more than a century of exchange-rate stability (apart from wartime periods or the severe depression of the 1930s). Changes, both up and down, in the international values of the major world currencies have taken place since the early 1970s. In Canada you would have to pay about 40 percent more for one U.S. dollar at the end of 1986 than a decade earlier, and changes for many other countries have been even greater.

The major task of the rest of this book is to develop the theory of why these major macroeconomic changes have taken place in Canada and the other major countries and to apply this framework of theory to the major economic developments that have occurred in the past. We will also discuss how governments and business firms can deal with such major changes.

The major function of macroeconomic theory is to shed light on practical problems in the economy as background for decisions by government and business. This chapter has illustrated the range of issues which we will be dealing with in the balance of the text.

## NOTES

1.  Arthur F. Burns and Wesley Clare Mitchell, *Measuring Business Cycles* (New York: National Bureau of Economic Research, 1946), p. 3.
2.  Derek A. White, *Business Cycles in Canada*, Economic Council of Canada Staff Study No. 17 (Ottawa: Information Canada, 1967); and Donald J. Daly, "Business Cycles in Canada: Their Postwar Persistence," in *Is the Business Cycle Obsolete?* ed. M. Bronfenbrenner (New York: Wiley-Interscience, 1969), pp. 45–65.
3.  Phillip Cagan, "The Monetary Dynamics of Hyperinflation," in *Studies in the Quantity Theory of Money*, ed. Milton Friedman (Chicago: University of Chicago Press, 1956).
4.  Geoffrey H. Moore, *Business Cycles, Inflation and Forecasting* (Cambridge, Mass.: Ballinger for the NBER, 1980), pp. 209–97.
5.  Anna J. Schwartz, "Secular Price Change in Historical Perspective," *Journal of Money, Credit and Banking*, February 1973, pp. 243–69.

# PART TWO

# Long-Run Economic Growth

Long-run economic growth determines the basic trends of real national income as it grows over time. These same forces affect the differences between countries in real income per capita and per person employed. Some shorter-term movements also occur around these longer-term levels and trends.

Macroeconomics must explain both these longer-term trends and the short-run fluctuations around the trends. We will follow the usual practice in economics by dealing with these theories and the related evidence in steps. Part Two will concentrate on the longer-term trends. Part Three will cover the topic of economic fluctuations.

Part Two will emphasize the theory and evidence on the supply side, which deals with the key determinants of long-run economic growth and intercountry levels of real income. Demand-side and price-level determinants will be covered in Parts Three and Four, respectively.

Chapter 4 will deal with the contribution of natural resources to economic growth. Thomas Malthus was one of the first economists to explore this topic, in the discussion of natural resources as a constraint on the growth of population. Natural resources are also important to Canadian economic performance, although their role has declined over the present century.

Chapter 5 introduces capital as a factor of production and the relevant theory on how to assess the relative contribution of labour and capital to economic growth. This chapter will also discuss the measurement of these variables. The contribution of capital to growth is important when the quantity of capital has grown more rapidly than

labour input in all the industrialized countries for centuries and especially since the end of World War II.

Chapter 6 will introduce technological change, discuss its importance in economic growth, and consider the factors affecting its creation
and dissemination. The differing speed of adoption of new technology
in different countries is a contributing factor in the differences in productivity and real income between countries.

# 4

# Natural Resources and Economic Growth

Natural resources is our first topic of discussion because of the historic importance of natural resource exports in the growth and development of the Canadian economy. In Canada, natural resource exports continue to account for a larger share of exports, investment, employment, and corporate profits than they do in most other high-income countries. In addition, the topic of natural resources and their role in economic growth was one of the early areas of discussion in macroeconomics. Thus, the topic of natural resource scarcity is of more than historical interest, for this issue reappeared in debates during the 1970s.

After reading this chapter you should understand:

1. The general methodological approach of economics.
2. The main ideas of Thomas Malthus relevant to economic growth.
3. How Malthus' predictions have performed subsequently.
4. The changing role of natural resources in Canada.

## 4–1 A REVIEW OF THE METHODOLOGY OF ECONOMICS

The first task of an economist is to develop a model that is relevant to the problem area being studied. A **model** is a framework of analysis that simplifies the characteristics crucial to an understanding of the relationships which underly that system. An example would be development of the theory of consumer demand for an individual (or a family). This theory implies that a unit (individual) would purchase more of a particular product at a low price than at a high price. In other words, the demand curve is downward-sloping with respect to price (for a given income level). This theory also implies that a high-income unit will purchase more of that product at a given price than a low-income unit. Thus, the income effect is positive, while the price effect is negative. After an understanding of these relationships has been developed for the individual unit, they are aggregated (or totalled) to develop the corresponding implications for the total market demand for that product.

Considerable estimation and testing of these relationships for consumer demands for individual products has taken place over the years. Due to the increased amount of publicly available data and the use of computers and mini-computers to make statistical estimates, the amount of estimation and testing in many areas of economics has burgeoned. This type of testing is the second step in developing economic ideas.

A third step is to evaluate the results derived from that framework of theory. The key test of a theory is to see if it works in practice. The internal logical consistency of a theory is a necessary but insufficient guide to its usefulness. If there is any apparent contradiction between theory and facts. either the theory is wrong or the facts are wrong.

An illustration of testing the theory that demand is higher at a lower price occurs regularly when store owners conduct special sales (for a limited number of items in a supermarket, a special anniversary sale at a department store, or a lower price or special financing terms on sales of new car models). The general conclusion is that if the model works in practice, keep on using it until strong evidence has accumulated from the real world to contradict the theory.

Once the theory has been disproved, economists attempt to develop a model that is both logical, internally consistent, and works better in practice.

## 4-2 MALTHUS ON AGGREGATE SUPPLY AND DEMAND

T. R. Malthus was born in 1766 and died in 1834. His justly celebrated essay, *The Principle of Population, As It Affects The Future Improvement of Society,* was first published in 1798. A revised and enlarged edition was published in 1803.[1] Malthus was critical of proposed changes to Great Britain's Poor Laws. The English Poor Law of 1601 provided grants for the needy financed by the municipality from local property taxes (similar to the current Canadian municipal welfare system). When inflation associated with the Napoleonic Wars led to an increase in social distress, it was proposed that the central government administer local grants and income supplements and extend coverage on a national scale. (These family allowances correspond to the present Family Allowance system in Canada paid by the federal government to all mothers with children under 16 years of age, irrespective of income level of the parents.) Malthus believed these proposals to be unsound and counterproductive on economic grounds, and in his essay he discussed why these proposals would be economically ineffective.

This section will restate Malthus' theory using current methods and terminology but with the essential spirit and reasoning that Malthus developed.

## The Production of Food

Malthus developed the notion of a production function, with special emphasis on the production of food. A **production function** for a particular good relates the output of that good to the various factors of production used in its creation. The **factors of production** are the resources of society used in the production of that good — labour and land in Malthus's analysis. Malthus dealt with the production of a single product (food) and two factors of production — labour (a variable factor) and land (which he treated as fixed in supply).

Central to the Malthusian model is a production function of the kind shown in Figure 4–1. The horizontal axis represents the size of population (which is closely related to the size of the labour force in his thinking). The vertical axis shows the total means of subsistence, which Malthus related to a particular country and measured in bushels or some appropriate unit of food production. The curve labelled $Y(N)$ is the production function representing the maximum amount of food production that could be produced by a number of alternative population levels with the agricultural methods then available. Malthus regarded the amount of arable land and other natural resources as fixed in supply and not subject to modification by alternative techniques of production or additional exploration.

A key part of his thinking was that if the number of people in the labour force increased, returns would diminish in relation to labour. In other words, the production function would be concave downwards, as shown in Figure 4–1. With a doubling of population (from $N_1$ to $N_2$ on the horizontal axis), there was no doubling in output. $CN_2$ is less than twice the production at $AN_1$. You will have already encountered this notion of diminishing returns and the related increasing marginal and average cost curves at the level of the individual firm in microeconomics. Doubling the labour input does *not* result in a comparable doubling of output. Thus the percentage increase in output is less than the percentage increase in labour input. Each farm labourer has only half the acreage of land to work with as initially, and food production is limited by the quality of the land, rainfall, and sunshine.

**FIGURE 4–1   Aggregate Production and Demand Functions**

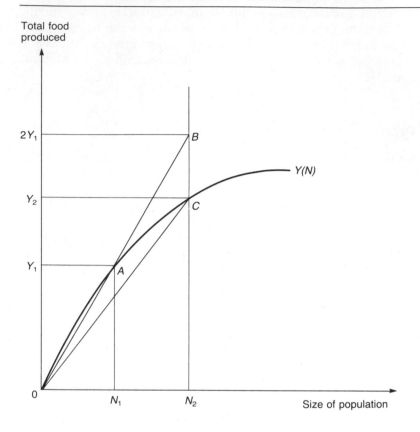

**FIGURE 4–2   Rate of Population Growth and Real GDP per Capita**

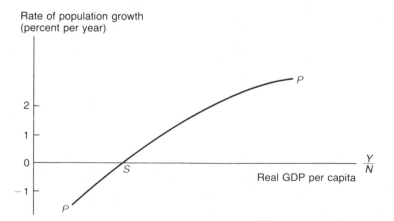

## The Demand for Food

Malthus also described a demand function for output (food). He visualized a constant demand for food on a per capita basis, so that a doubling of population involved a doubling in the demand for food. With a doubling in population, from $N_1$ to $N_2$, the demand for food increased from $AN_1$ to $BN_2$, twice as much.

These two functional relationships mean that a doubling in population over time is not associated with a comparable doubling in output and thus results in disequilibrium. Malthus visualized that one solution to this disequilibrium would be wars and starvation.

## Population Growth and the Labour-Supply Function

The third relationship introduced by Malthus was his theory of population (or a *labour supply function,* to use the modern terminology).

In the Malthusian model, the standard of living influences the size of the population, as shown in Figure 4–2. The horizontal axis measures the food consumption per capita, while the vertical axis measures the rate of population growth as a rate of change per year. Malthus's analysis depends on qualitative properties of this function and cuts the line for zero population growth from below in an upward-sloping line. This involves a drop in the rate of population growth with a lower standard of living due to a higher death rate from famine, pestilence, and other natural disasters as the population becomes undernourished, impoverished, and physically weak. An increase in the rate of population growth would occur at a higher standard of living as the death rate dropped. A higher level of food production would lower the death rate and increase the population size. That higher population would encounter the diminishing marginal-productivity problem being encountered at point $N_2$ on the horizontal axis in Figure 4–1.

The zero-population growth point is the long-run equilibrium position shown at point $S$ on the $PP$ curve. **Equilibrium** is the position that if attained would be maintained. Positions to the left of $S$ on the $PP$ curve would be to the right of $0N_1$ on Figure 4–1, while positions to the right of $S$ on the $PP$ curve would be related to positions to the left of $0N_1$ on Figure 4–1.

The rate of population growth is closely related to the supply of labour, as Malthus assumed that the working population was a stable proportion of the total population.

## 4–3 SUBSEQUENT EXPERIENCE AND CURRENT RELEVANCE

The actual developments in Britain, continental Western Europe, and the other industrialized countries since the 1800s have been inconsistent with the predictions derived from the Malthusian model. For example, in the United Kingdom population doubled between 1870 and the 1980s. Furthermore, real GDP per capita more than doubled between 1870 and 1950, and more than doubled again from 1950 to the middle of the 1980s. The increases in real GDP and in population were even greater in many of the other industrialized countries.

Malthus's economic model consisted of a production function and a demand function for food and a framework to analyze the growth of the population and the size of the labour force. Thus it had some of the characteristics of a reasonably complete economic model in the sense that it was internally consistent, but it did not predict future developments for the country in which it had been developed. It did not meet the condition of useful predictions that was set forth in Section 4–1.

Macroeconomic theory has developed considerably since Malthus because it was essential to develop a more complete framework of analysis that could better explain the facts. Economists since Malthus have recognized that in addition to labour and land, they must also include capital as a further factor of production. **Capital** represents produced goods that have a long life and are used by firms in the process of production. Examples from agriculture include the use of self-propelled combines that cut the wheat, thresh it, and separate the wheat from the chaff and the straw, all in one operation. One prairie farmer today can manage a far larger farm and raise enough grain for many more nonfarm families than was possible five decades ago.

Malthus' theory also failed to allow for technological change. **Technological change** allows more output to be produced from an unchanged quantity of labour and capital. A current practical example would be a student learning to input an essay or an assignment onto a main-frame computer or a mini-computer. Initially, the student must consult the manual for every new function on the keyboard (and the manuals are rarely "user friendly"). With additional experience and self-confidence, the student becomes faster and yet he/she and the machine are still the same factors of production. This example illustrates the importance of learning by doing and has a practical application in many work situations such as a library, an office, or a factory.

Both of these factors have been crucial in the increases in population and living standards that have taken place in Britain and the other industrialized countries since the Napoleonic Wars when Malthus was writing. These topics will be considered in the next two chapters.

Discussion in the Malthusian tradition never completely dies out, however. The notion of natural resource scarcity still occasionally reappears in popular and professional discussion, an idea logical in the Malthusian tradition with its emphasis on land and natural resources as a limiting factor in economic growth.

**TABLE 4–1**  Prices of Important Minerals Relative to Labour Costs, United States, 1900–83, Selected Years (1970 = 100)

|                | 1900  | 1920 | 1940 | 1950 | 1983 |
|----------------|-------|------|------|------|------|
| Coal           | 459   | 451  | 189  | 208  | 151  |
| Copper         | 785   | 226  | 121  | 99   | 48   |
| Iron           | 620   | 287  | 144  | 112  | 88   |
| Lead           | 788   | 388  | 204  | 228  | 50   |
| Zinc           | 794   | 400  | 272  | 256  | 97   |
| Aluminum       | 3,150 | 859  | 287  | 166  | 96   |
| Gold           | n.a.  | n.a. | 595  | 258  | 114  |
| Crude petroleum| 1,034 | 726  | 198  | 213  | 292  |

NOTE: n.a. = not available.

SOURCE: Values are the price per ton of the mineral divided by the hourly wage rate in manufacturing. Reproduced from William Nordhaus, "Resources as a Constraint on Growth," *American Economic Review, Proceedings,* June 1974, p. 24. Also, 1983 data added using the same sources as preceding study.

This idea reappeared during the 1970s at the time of the first OPEC price increase for petroleum and its products. A number of studies developed the theme that growth in population and living standards would encounter constraints from a limited supply of natural resources, especially petroleum and mineral products. At that time, the Club of Rome sponsored a study using computer simulations. A central part of those studies was a geometric increase in the demand, but slower increases in the supply of these natural resources. A compound rate of growth fairly quickly leads to such a massive increase in the demand side that supply constraints are very quickly encountered in simulations going into the 21st century. This geometric increase in demand is very much in the Malthusian tradition.[2]

You can easily test the natural resource scarcity hypothesis by examining the prices of a range of natural resource products compared to the wages per hour in U.S. manufacturing as illustrated in Table 4–1 for selected years from 1900 to 1983. (Comparable price data are not available for Canada, but developments in this country would be similar in light of the similarities of price movements when data are available.) The table shows that for every single one of the eight minerals listed, the ratio of price to labour costs was lower in 1983 than in 1900 or 1920. Crude petroleum was the only product whose relative price was higher than in 1950, and significant price declines have occurred since that date.

Natural resource price increases compared to labour costs encourage additional exploration, a greater salvage and reclamation of scrap materials, and the development of substitute materials. Plastics, synthetics, and ceramics have increased in relative importance and in some areas have actually replaced minerals. Fibre optics permit a tremendous number of telephone and television transmissions to occur simultaneously on threads that are much smaller and lighter than the copper wire they are beginning to replace.

Since 1983, actual price declines have taken place in a number of the products shown in Table 4–1. The most dramatic example is the decline of crude petroleum prices to about half the 1983 level by late 1986, but declines in other minerals and raw material prices also occurred. It is rather unusual to have that much weakness in mineral product prices while economic activity is still increasing. It is also a change from the price increases for primary products that were an important feature of the 1970s.

The price developments of the 1980s are inconsistent with the predictions of some of the studies made in the 1970s that emphasized natural resource scarcity.

## 4–4 NATURAL RESOURCES IN CANADA

The export of a variety of natural resource staples has been an important part of Canada's economic history. The fur trade was important in the initial development and settlement of Canada followed by ocean fishing (especially cod fishery off the Grand Banks in Newfoundland). In the present century, the emphasis shifted to such forest products as lumber, newsprint, wood chips, mineral products, and petroleum. A number of Canadian economists and historians have explored the staple theory of economic growth and the role of natural resources in the early stages of Canada's economic development.[3]

The historical importance of the natural resource sector continues to be reflected in the industrial composition of Canada compared to the United States. The **natural resource** sector includes agriculture, forestry, fishing and trapping, and mining (including petroleum). The natural resource industries were a relatively larger share of the national totals in Canada than in the United States as reflected in such measures as employment, wages and salaries, and the industrial composition of national income. Similarly, the natural resource share of total exports was much larger in Canada than in the United States throughout the postwar period.[4] A federal government study in 1981 emphasized the role of a number of potential large projects in the natural resource sector (including frontier development of petroleum and tar sands) as a key underpinning of Canada's economic growth in the 1980s.[5] However, the subsequent declines in crude petroleum prices and the hesitant nature of growth in real output in the commodity-producing industries in the United States in the 1980s has been reflected in a less vigorous expansion in the natural resource industries in Canada since the end of 1982.

However, the natural resource sector has been a falling share of the Canadian economy for most of the present century. This trend is appar-

**TABLE 4–2**   Share of the Work Force in the Resource Industries, Canada, Selected Years 1911–84

|                                                              | 1911  | 1941  | 1984 |
|--------------------------------------------------------------|-------|-------|------|
| Agriculture                                                  | 34.2% | 25.8% | 4.3% |
| Other primary (forestry, fishing and trapping, and mining)   | 5.0   | 5.6   | 2.7  |
| Total, natural-resource industries                           | 39.2% | 31.4% | 7.0% |

SOURCE: Statistics Canada, *Historical Statistics of Canada*, 2nd ed. (Ottawa: Ministry of Supply and Services, 1983), series D266–274 and Statistics Canada, *The Labour Force, December 1984*, (Ottawa: Ministry of Supply and Services, 1985), p. 111.

ent, for example, in the share of the work force employed in the natural resource sector in Table 4–2. This share was almost two-fifths of the work force before World War I, but it fell to only 7 percent by the 1980s, with most of the decline taking place since World War II.

The evidence in Table 4–2 suggests that, in the future, firms should be giving much more attention to labour costs and relatively less attention to the costs of natural resource products.

The decline in the relative importance of agriculture and the other natural resource industries is not unique to Canada's development but is a widespread development in the other industrialized countries as well. The declining share of agriculture and the increasing importance of service industries is a key theme in the discussion of economic growth. Agriculture and mining have experienced a falling share of employment in the major industrialized countries since before World War I.[6]

This declining importance of agriculture and the other natural resource industries raises the question of the longer-term industrial composition of the Canadian economy. If natural resource industries cannot provide sufficient employment opportunities for a growing labour force in the future to the same extent as in the past, where can that growth come from? If natural resource industries continue to experience slower growth in demand and falling relative prices, what alternatives are there for the future for a country like Canada? Where can business firms and financial institutions put their funds to obtain an adequate rate of return? We will return to these questions in Part Six when discussing international aspects of macroeconomics.

## 4–5 SUMMARY

Macroeconomics is built on a framework of economic theory requiring quantitative testing of that theory with evidence from the real world and the abandonment of those theories that do not fit the facts well.

Malthus developed a macroeconomic theory based on a production function, a demand function, and a theory of population (or labour supply) that was internally consistent and implied that population and levels of consumption would be constrained by the limited supply of land.

In fact, significant increases in population and levels of real output have taken place since he wrote during the period of the Napoleonic Wars.

A renewed flurry of interest in the possibility of natural resource scarcity took place in the 1970s, partly in response to OPEC's increases in crude petroleum prices. However, the prices of natural resource products have tended to fall in relation to wage rates over much of the present century.

Natural resources continue to be relatively more important in Canada than in the United States, but they have tended to be a declining share of employment and national income in Canada and other industrialized countries over most of the present century.

## NOTES

1.  T. R. Malthus, *An Essay On The Principle Of Population Or A View Of Its Past And Present Effects On Human Happiness*, 7th ed. (London: Reeves and Turner, 1872) reprinted 1971 by August M. Kelley, New York.

2.  Christopher Freeman, "Malthus with a Computer," and K. L. R. Pavitt, "Malthus and Other Economists," in *Thinking about the Future: A Critique of the Limits to Growth*, S. D. Cole et al. (Toronto: Clarke, Irwin & Company, 1973), pp. 5–13, 137–58; Carl Kaysen, "The Computer That Printed Out W*O*L*F," *Foreign Affairs*, July 1972, pp. 660–68. H. J. Barnett and Chandler Morse, *Scarcity and Growth* (Baltimore: Johns Hopkins Press for Resources for the Future, 1963). Barnett and Morse considered the contributions of the classical economists to this topic and examined the statistical evidence accumulated in previous "Resources for the Future" studies. This excellent study has not had the attention it deserves in the discussion that has emerged a decade or more after its initial publication.

3.  See the statements by W. A. Mackintosh and H. A. Innis in *Approaches to Canadian Economic History*, W. T. Easterbrook and M. H. Watkins, eds. (Toronto: McClelland and Stewart, 1967), pp. 1–19 and additional discussions by A. R. M. Lower, M. H. Watkins, G. W. Bertram, and W. T. Easterbrook in the same volume.

4.  Richard Shaffner, "The Resource Sectors of the United States and Canada: An Overview," in *Natural Resources in U.S.–Canadian Relations*, Carl E. Beigie and Alfred O. Hero, Jr., eds. (Boulder, Colo.: Westview Press, 1980), especially pp. 14–31 and also D. J. Daly, "Mineral Resources in the Canadian Economy: Macroeconomic Implications," in the same volume, pp. 125–35.

5.  Government of Canada, *Economic Development for Canada in the 1980s*, November 1981.

6.  Colin Clark, *The Conditions of Economic Progress*, 3rd ed. (London: Macmillan, 1957), and Simon Kuznets, *Modern Economic Growth: Rate, Structure and Spread*, (New Haven, Conn.: Yale University Press, 1966), especially Chapter 3.

# 5

## Labour and Capital in Economic Growth

After reading this chapter you should understand:

1. The general approach to accounting for the various sources of economic growth that economists now use.
2. Some of the highlights of the changes in the quantity of labour and capital that have taken place historically in the industrialized countries.
3. How the estimates of labour and capital are prepared in Canada.
4. How to quantify the relative contribution of labour and capital to economic growth.
5. The relevance and importance of some of these concepts to business decision making, such as the importance of people in organizations and the role of unions.

## 5–1 AN OVERVIEW OF ECONOMIC GROWTH ACCOUNTING

Chapter 4 pointed out that Malthus and the other classical economists did not incorporate the role of capital and technological change into their analyses of the process of economic growth. Macroeconomic theory has developed significantly since the time when the classical economists were writing, and new developments have taken place on both the theoretical and the quantitative sides. One of the pioneering papers in the latest rebirth of interest in economic growth was published in 1952.[1]

This renewed interest in economic growth on the supply side was partly a response to changes in the North American and world economies, which had operated at quite high rates of utilization for many years (in contrast to the extent of slack during the 1930s). Accumulating evidence showed that economic growth was occurring at a much more rapid rate in North America after World War II than had taken place in the previous eight decades. Furthermore, there were significant differences in the rates of growth of real GDP between countries, as illustrated in Tables 3–1, 3–2, and 3–6 in Chapter 3. It became important to explain these longer-term trends on the supply side in order to predict and plan for the future in both the private and public sectors.[2]

To account for the sources of economic growth, we must separate the contribution of the supply of the factors of production (labour, capital, and land) used in the production process from the other sources of economic growth.

We can describe a simple production function for the economy as a whole as follows:

$$y = AN^wK^{1-w}$$

where

$y$ = real GDP

$A$ = an allowance for technological change over and above the changes in inputs

$N$ = total employed

$w$ = labour share of national income

$K$ = stock of capital

$1 - w$ = share of national income going to capital[3]

This particular form of the production function was developed by Paul H. Douglas in consultation with a mathematician, Charles W. Cobb. Douglas studied production and income distribution with a number of collaborators from 1927 to 1947, primarily at the University of Chicago.[3] He subsequently represented the State of Illinois in the U.S. Senate for many years.

This particular form of the relationship has several implications. First, an increase of 1 percent in both labour and capital inputs implies a 1 percent increase in output, assuming constant returns to scale.

The function also shows $A$ to illustrate the allowance for technological change. (This subject will be discussed further in Chapter 6. A brief illustration will suffice here.) An example of one of these sources of economic growth is the adoption of a modified way of producing some widget (any simple manufactured product) that would permit increased output from the same staff and capital facilities — production in a newsprint plant, for example. A typical plant consists of a number of machines positioned side by side. During each shift, one worker is assigned to look after each machine. During the two eight-hour day shifts, each worker attends his own machine with limited sharing of tasks. The night-shift workers, however, have developed a co-operative system, which allows them to produce significantly more than the day shift and in a shorter period of time. The night shift's co-operative effort was so successful that management studied their superior performance and introduced the same procedures to the day shifts as well, thus initiating technological change over and above changes in input.

This chapter will concentrate on how the contribution of each of the major factor inputs to economic growth can be quantified. Chapter 6 will deal with the other sources of economic growth. This procedure of introducing one topic at a time as part of developing a complete model is the standard partial equilibrium approach that you have been exposed to in your previous microeconomic course. An example is the development of demand and supply considerations separately in the determination of the equilibrium price and production decisions for a particular product.

## 5–2 CHANGES IN THE LEVEL OF CAPITAL PER PERSON EMPLOYED

**Capital** represents goods produced by firms and used in the production of further goods and services. Capital normally includes nonresidential construction (buildings, shopping centres, etc., which have a very long life) and machinery and equipment (a large generator, a machine to stamp out car doors, which wear out or become obsolete quickly). Capital added to the work of an average employee results in more production in a given time period than would be possible without that capital. (Note that we are talking about *real* capital in the sense of buildings, machinery, and equipment rather than *financial invest-ments,* such as the ownership of stocks and bonds by an individual or financial institution.)

The amount of capital per person employed has increased since the industrialization that began in England some centuries ago. Some early examples of capital include the introduction of the spinning jenny in the manufacture of thread. These power machines located in factories replaced the hand-operated machines in individual workers' homes or cottages. Also, the development of synthetics such as rayon and polyester have required much more capital. And more recent developments have involved the use of computers (capital), both in the design of new products and in manufacturing. Japan has installed robots, a form of capital, in the production of manufactured products. The office has also increased its use of capital as the feather quill, the pen, and the manual typewriter were replaced by the electric typewriter which is now being

**TABLE 5–1** Real GDP, Employment and Stock of Capital, Canada (selected years, 1961–1985)

|  | 1961 | 1973 | 1985 |
|---|---|---|---|
| GDP (billions, 1981 dollars) | 136.9 | 264.4 | 389.3 |
| Employed (thousands) | 6,055 | 8,759 | 11,311 |
| GDP per employed (1981 dollars) | 22,609 | 30,186 | 39,418 |
| Mid-year net stock (billions, 1971 dollars) | 79.1 | 145.7 | 282.8 |
| Net stock of capital per employed | 13,064 | 16,634 | 25,002 |
| Rates of change over previous 12 years |  |  |  |
| GDP (1981 dollars) |  | +5.64 | +3.28 |
| Employed |  | +3.12 | +2.15 |
| GDP per employed |  | +2.44 | +1.10 |
| Mid-year net stock (1971 dollars) |  | +5.22 | +5.68 |
| Net stock of capital per employed |  | +2.03 | +3.45 |

SOURCES: Data Resources of Canada, *Canadian Review September 1986,* pp. 70–71; Statistics Canada, *Historical Statistics of Canada,* 2nd ed. (Ottawa: Ministry of Supply and Services, 1983), Series D139; and *Bank of Canada Review,* November 1986, p. S120.

replaced by computers and word-processing machines. These examples of capital have permitted the average worker to produce a larger amount of total output.

There are also large differences in the availability of capital equipment in different countries, with higher levels of capital per person employed in North America than in Japan and Europe, although these differences have decreased since the end of World War II. The industrialized countries also have significantly higher levels of capital in business than the developing countries. We will explore later the question of how important these differences in the availability of capital are in explaining the large differences between countries in output per person employed.

The issues that will be explored in this and the next chapter can be illustrated by Table 5–1. The table shows data on real GDP (using the concepts and data introduced in Chapters 1 and 2), employment, and the stock of capital (the concepts and data sources for these two new terms will be discussed more fully in the next section of this chapter). The rates of change over the two 12-year periods show the key points conveyed by the table. Rates of change in both real output and employment are less since 1973 than in the 12 previous years. The slowdown is relatively greater in real GDP than in employment. The increase in real GDP per employed person was only 1.1 percent from 1973 to 1985, compared to 2.4 percent in the previous 12 years.

On the other hand, the stock of capital increased more rapidly after 1973 than before (in spite of a slowdown in the rate of growth in the stock of capital after 1981). The rate of growth in the stock of capital per employed person was 3.5 percent per year in the period since 1973 compared to 2.0 in the earlier period shown, or about 70 percent higher. Thus the increase in real output per person was less than half as rapid since 1973 than in the earlier period, in spite of a faster increase in the quantity of capital available to the average employed person.

This chapter covers how macroeconomists now explain the effect of changing levels of employment or the stock of capital on the economy's total output. This chapter will deal with the effects of change in the inputs into the production process. However, other factors (such as new technology) can also affect output, and these will be dealt with in Chapter 6.

## 5–3 THE MEASUREMENT OF EMPLOYMENT AND CAPITAL INPUTS

Before continuing the discussion of the contribution of labour and capital to economic growth, it is important to clarify some of the concepts and definitions we will be working with.

We have four main tasks in this section. First, we need to know how the basic statistics on these topics are obtained through the monthly labour-force survey. Second, we need to learn some basic definitions of the labour force categories, relating to employment and unemployment. Third, we should explore a number of additional sources of statistics on both employment and unemployment that can provide more information and detail on some of the developments in the labour market. There are considerable differences within the category of employment reflecting the diverse composition of those employed, based on differences in hours worked, educational levels, and age and sex composition. Finally, a further important input into the function of producing real output for the economy as a whole is the category of capital input, which has increased dramatically in all the industrialized countries over the last four decades. The concept of capital input and how it is measured will be our fourth learning task.

### The Labour Force Survey

The main source of the monthly statistics on employment and unemployment is the *Labour Force Survey,* which is produced and published each month by Statistics Canada. Its statistics are based on a survey of households, chosen in such a way that every household in Canada has an equal chance of being selected. Approximately 56,000 households are surveyed each time, or about 1 percent of Canadian households. The survey was initiated on a quarterly basis in November 1945 and has been conducted on a monthly basis since November 1952.

The process of selecting households for interview is called a random sample. A **random sample** is a small proportion of the population selected for interviewing to obtain useful information at low cost to the collecting agency. Random sampling is a very carefully planned and selected approach. It builds on a geographic area in a city, including families from the city core, the suburbs, and some immediately adjacent nonurban areas (to include new housing developments or small holdings). This process of selection draws on a specialized field of statistical theory, which ensures that the households interviewed provide a basis for drawing reasonably reliable conclusions about the total labour force, even though only 1 percent of them have been interviewed. The method permits you to make a probability statement on the likelihood that the sample falls within a certain percentage of the population total.[4]

This process provides a fairly reliable guide to general economic developments, and these small sample survey results can be produced and released quickly at a fraction of the cost required to do a more comprehensive census, or complete count. With good training and supervision, a small number of interviewers can produce more satisfactory results than the large number of interviewers required to do a census every 10 years.

## The Definitions of Labour Force Categories

The total **labour force** includes all of the adult population 15 years of age and over who are either employed or unemployed. The employed include all those who are at work even if their work is part-time. The survey asks the household members their employment status during the week previous to the survey. The unemployed include those without a job who have been actively looking for work over the previous four weeks.

"Not in the labour force" is a further important category of the adult population and includes housewives, students, and retired persons. This group currently makes up about 35 percent of Canada's adult population.

Much of the adult population falls into one of these three broad categories of employed, unemployed, and not in the labour force. However, other individuals may be at the margin between one category and another, and it may not be easy to place them in a clear-cut fashion. Examples include people with part-time jobs who would prefer to find

**TABLE 5–2**    Labour Force Status of the Population, Canada 1985
(thousands of persons)

| | |
|---|---|
| 1. Civilian labour force | 12,639 |
|    a.  Employed | 11,311 |
|    b.  Unemployed | 1,328 |
| 2. Not in the labour force | 6,733 |
| 3. Civilian noninstitutional population (age 15 and over) | 19,372 |
| 4. Unemployment rate (1*b* as percent of 1) | 10.5% |
| 5. Labour-force participation rates (1 as percent of 3) | 65.2% |

SOURCE: *Bank of Canada Review,* October 1986, p. S120.

full-time work. Another marginal category includes employees who are temporarily laid off or on strike. Such workers would not be looking for a new job and would thus continue to be defined as employed. Another problem in classification occurs when an individual has been looking for a job unsuccessfully for so long that he becomes discouraged and stops looking. Such people would be classified as not in the labour force.

Although some borderline individuals may not be easy to classify into one of the three broad groups (employed, unemployed, and not in the labour force), Statistics Canada has developed conventions so that it treats these cases consistently in successive surveys. Thus, the broad economic trends that are of primary interest to this aggregate economic analysis are not affected, as long as the definitions are applied consistently over time.

The results for Canada for 1985 are shown in Table 5–2. These will give you some impressions of the size of these categories. Note that about 65 percent of the adult population is in the labour force, and the unemployment rate in 1985 was 10.5 percent.

## Other Data on Employment and Unemployment

The Labour Force Survey provides a total for employment and other broad categories, but it cannot provide the detailed industry and occupational data useful for certain types of studies. A regular monthly survey of employment by establishments has been conducted since well before World War II. This survey was expanded in recent years to improve the coverage for small establishments. The individual establishments can provide a greater degree of detail on a finer industry and occupational basis, and such statistics are provided for the major metropolitan areas as well. **Establishment surveys** are based on surveys of individual plants (or establishments), as contrasted to a survey of households such as the Labour Force Survey. Establishment surveys provide some of the data on compensation per hour and total labour income that are part of the income side of the gross domestic product accounts we introduced in Chapter 2.

Canada's Employment Service also provides some additional data on job registrations as part of its administrative operations. A file is set up for all individuals who apply to the placement offices, some of whom may also be registering for unemployment insurance benefits. These figures may not correspond to those produced by the Labour Force Survey. Some of the people who apply for jobs may already be working (or working part-time), they may register in more than one office, and they may obtain a job on their own without reporting that fact to the local office. Their file may thus continue to be listed as active and they may be counted as registered for a job even though they may have already obtained one. These problems have led to reduced publicity and attention to these data, although they may still be available for internal administrative purposes.

For certain purposes of economic analysis, the broad national totals may not be fully satisfactory. Total employment is not a homogeneous category but includes a whole range of individuals with different ages, skills, educational levels, and incomes. Over the last two decades, the composition of these groups has shifted significantly, with a more rapid increase in the number of younger workers (reflecting the large number of labour force entrants from the high birth rates of the 1950s) and the increased participation of women in the labour force.

In many of the studies of economic growth in the United States and Canada conducted over the last two decades, measures of labour input have considered the differences in "quality" of the labour force.

In effect, these measures of labour input are based on the same theories of index number construction that we introduced previously in the discussion of the consumer price index and the Laspeyres-type base-weighted index. Average annual income for the separate labour input categories is used as a weight to produce an index of labour input. The evidence available indicates that the average annual income of young persons and women is considerably below the income of the average adult male. There are also considerable differences in income level between those with only a primary school education, at one extreme, and those with a university degree, at the other.

## Capital Input

It is widely recognized that the average worker in the industrialized countries in the 1980s has a much larger quantity of capital to help in producing higher levels of output per hour and per year than would have been true a few decades ago. This was illustrated for Canada in Table 5–1 earlier in this chapter. Some allowance for this increase in the stock of capital is necessary as part of studying the factors that contributed to the increase in real GDP in total and in relation to employment and labour input.

The **stock of capital** is measured by what is termed *the perpetual inventory method*. There are essentially four steps in preparing such an estimate. First, statisticians consider gross investment in current dollars (distinguishing between construction and machinery and equipment). These are the same data included in the estimates of gross capital formation on the expenditure side of the National Accounts. The second step is to deflate the current dollar estimates of gross investment by the appropriate price index for the categories of investment (the same price indices that are used to deflate the estimates of gross investment on the expenditure side of the National Accounts as described in Chapter 2). The third step is to estimate the depreciation or capital consumption of previous levels of gross investment, based on the average length of life of that type of capital asset. The length of life of buildings is frequently taken as 50 or 55 years, while machinery and equipment may have a length of life of between 5 and 20 years.[5] These estimates of depreciation are prepared in constant prices (such as 1981 for Canada). The deduction of depreciation in constant dollars from the levels of gross investment in constant dollars for the same year yields an estimate of the net investment in that year in constant 1981 dollars. The fourth step is to cumulate all the estimates of net investment for all previous years to give the level of the stock of capital for the year at the end of the period. In order to prepare estimates of the stock of capital for 1985, it is necessary to have data on the levels of net investment in constant dollars for each individual year for the past 50 years (based on 50-year length of life for construction). The derivation of the data on the stock of capital can be shown algebraically as follows:

$$K_n = \sum_{i=1}^{n} I_i - D_i$$

where

$\quad K_n$ = the stock of capital in a particular year, $n$;
$\quad\; I_i$ = gross investment in constant prices in year $i$;
$\quad D_i$ = depreciation in constant prices in year $i$.

Essentially what the perpetual inventory method does is to use data on the flows of expenditures (and capital consumption or depreciation) per year to make estimates of the net changes, and cumulate them to make an estimate of the stock. This distinction between stocks and flows is one you have encountered previously in your microeconomics course, and it will be used again in later parts of this text.

## 5–4 ACCOUNTING FOR THE CONTRIBUTION OF INPUTS TO THE GROWTH IN OUTPUT

Now that we have reviewed the measurement of labour and capital, we will continue the discussion of the contribution of changes in factor inputs to output.

By the latter part of the 19th century, economists were distinguishing three basic **factors of production** — the resources of society used in the process of producing goods and services. They are labour, capital, and land, and all three are still an essential part of current analysis of accounting for economic growth. Over the postwar period, the increases in total real GDP have been accompanied by increases in both labour and capital inputs in Canada (as shown in Tables 3–1, 3–2, and 5–1). As part of analyzing the factors that have contributed to the increase in output, it is clear that increases in the supply and use of the various factors of production are an important part of that story. Macroeconomists working in the area of economic growth accounting have been able to develop workable methods of assessing the contribution of changing inputs to the growth in output by incorporating appropriate theory. We will summarize the methods used to estimate changes in total inputs first. Second, we will estimate what the effect of changing just one of the factor inputs by 1 percent would have on total output. After explaining how these two types of estimates are made, we will explain the assumptions underlying the methods used and discuss their reasonableness.

### Making an Estimate of Total Factor Inputs

At first glance, the task of combining data on changing employment (measured by the average number of persons working each month for a series of years) with changes in stock of capital (measured by the mid-year net stock of capital in 1981 dollars as explained in Section 5–3) looks difficult. It is not that difficult in practice once the basic data are available in a consistent manner. The key step is to make an index of **total factor inputs**, which combines the changes in each of the separate input factors into one single aggregate measure. More specifically, suppose you wanted to assess how much of the increase in total output you could reasonably conclude was associated with an increase in both labour and capital. How could you estimate the increase in labour and capital combined? This process can be illustrated with total manufacturing for Canada.[6] The first step is to obtain data on the rates of change over the period being analyzed for the inputs of labour and capital as shown in the top panel of Table 5–3. Several important points in the table should be noted. First, the rate of increase in the stock of capital was more rapid than the rate of increase in the input of labour

---

**TABLE 5–3**  Canadian Manufacturing, Labour and Capital Inputs, Growth Rates and Contributions to Growth, (1950–73 and 1973–1985)

| Growth Rates | 1950–73 | 1973–85 |
|---|---|---|
| Total hours | +1.17% | −0.29% |
| Mid-year net capital stock (1971 dollars) | | |
|     all components | +7.20 | +3.01 |
| Total output | +5.54 | +1.66 |
| Output per hour | +4.31 | +1.95 |
| Contributions to growth rates: | | |
|     Total hours (.80 weight) | +0.94 | −0.23 |
|     Capital input (.20 weight) | +1.44 | +0.60 |
|     Total factor input | +2.38 | +0.37 |
| Output in relation to total | | |
|     factor inputs | +3.16 | +1.29 |

SOURCE: Statistics Canada, *Fixed Capital Flows and Stocks, 1926–1978,* October 1978, p. 6, and ibid., July 1986, p. 3; and United States Department of Labor, *News,* Bureau of Labor Statistics, June 18, 1986.

---

in both periods. The rate of growth in the stock of capital was also more rapid than the rate of growth of output.[7] A further important development is that total hours worked in manufacturing were actually lower in 1985 than in 1973. Employment and hours dropped sharply in the 1981–82 recession and partially recovered by 1985, but total hours were still not back to the level of the 1970s or the 1981 peak. However, total output was higher in 1985 in spite of the drop in total hours worked. Output per hour increased, but the rate of increase after 1973 was less than half of that experienced in the earlier period.

The bottom half of Table 5–3 illustrates how labour and capital each contributed to output and how an estimate of the change in total factor input (based on labour and capital combined) is prepared.

The key question in theory and practice is how to combine the separate factors of production into a single measure, namely the changes in total factor input over time. The widely used procedure is to prepare an index number. Chapter 2 introduced the consumer price index, which is an index number of prices. The statistical agencies collect prices on individual items each month for such products as loaves of bread, litres of milk, socks, shoes, soap, and litres of gasoline. In combining these individual prices, a statistical agency uses the expenditures on these categories in a historical period. The expenditures by consumers are thus used as weights to combine the individual prices to make a comprehensive measure of the general price level paid by consumers.

Essentially all these same steps are involved in preparing an index of total factor inputs. The expenditures, however, relate to the expenditures by businesses on their purchases of labour and capital from households. Instead of consumer products, the businesses are purchasing the inputs of labour and capital. The preparation of a weighted index number of total factor input is comparable to the preparation of a consumer price index, but the statisticians end up with a measure of total factor inputs.

As a basis of the weights to combine factor inputs, economists use the share that each individual factor receives of total national income. Such shares are a measure of the costs of producing total output from the viewpoint of all business firms, while they are the sources of income from the viewpoint of the income recipients.

The illustration in the bottom half of Table 5–3 is based on these procedures. The contribution of labour to growth for the 1950–73 period, for example, is estimated by multiplying the rate of change in total hours (1.17 percent ) by labour's share of national income (.80 in this example) to obtain the contribution of labour to total factor input (.94 after rounding to two significant figures). The contribution of capital is estimated in a similar manner. The change in total factor input is the sum of the weighted contribution of all the individual inputs.

This procedure is quite general in its application. If significant shifts in the composition of the labour force have taken place in the country, it would be desirable to make an adjustment for the "quality of labour". The **quality of labour** measure, which allows for differences in age, sex, education, and experience, attempts to incorporate broad differences in the contribution of each group to output. Young people, both male and female, (for example, incomes of those under 20) tend to be less than half that of males aged 20 to 64.[8] People with a university degree tend to earn significantly more per year than those with only a primary school education, and the differences become greater at older age levels.[9]

The use of the distribution of costs as a basis for combining inputs can be applied at the industry level as well as for the economy as a whole. At the industry level, purchases of materials from other industries become an important proportion of costs (as interindustry purchases and sales cancel out in estimates of national income and gross domestic product). For example, energy is a cost at the industry level, and a comparable process to that shown in Table 5–1 can be applied to analyze the effects of higher energy prices on input costs and prices.

## 5–5 THE ASSUMPTIONS IN MAKING AN INDEX OF INPUTS

The process of making an index of total factor inputs is a necessary, but interim, step in assessing the contributions of changing inputs to output. This process involves some assumptions about the relations between input and output. An important part of the rationale relates to the marginal productivity theory of income distribution. The **marginal productivity theory of income distribution** is essentially a theory of the demand for a factor of production, developed from the relevant microeconomic theory of production and costs at the level of the firm. An employer who seeks to maximize profits will hire additional units of labour as long as the value of the additional output is greater than the increase in costs from the additional labour. It is thus a theory of the demand for the factors of production, and additional analysis of the supply of the factors of production is necessary to determine the price (and income) of that factor of production. It is the equivalent on the employment side to the condition of marginal costs equal marginal revenues in determining the equilibrium output of a firm.

It is sometimes stated that the marginal productivity theory of distribution assumes **perfect competition**, or a situation of a large number of buyers and sellers of a standardized product. Perfect competition also assumes that new producers can start up producing that product — i.e., that it is easy to enter the industry. However, the marginal productivity theory of income distribution applies also to **monopolistic competition**, which is a situation of differentiated products (such as a variety of models or brand names) and a small number of producers. As long as new producers can begin production (or existing producers introduce new models — such as size and variety of cars or brands of toothpaste), profits are limited to what could be obtained in other industries. If the degree of competition remains about the same over time (or between countries at a point in time), this procedure is appropriate and justifiable.[10]

A second important assumption is that the economy is operating close to a situation of constant returns to scale. **Constant returns to scale** is a situation where an increase of 1 percent in all of the factor inputs will be reflected in an increase of 1 percent in total output. This assumption permits an initial assessment of the quantitative effects of changing inputs to output.

These assumptions permit the analyst to make some conclusions of the effects of changing inputs to output. This can be helpful in analysis of past economic growth and in developing some guides for the future.

## 5–6 CHANGING CANADIAN LABOUR INPUTS IN AN INTERNATIONAL PERSPECTIVE

What can be said about Canada's economic growth over the postwar period in light of the tools and data sources developed in earlier sections of this chapter? One of the key conclusions is that Canada has had the highest rate of increase in labour input of all the major industrialized countries. This can be seen in Table 5–4 for the 1950–84 period.

**TABLE 5–4**   Growth Rates in Employment, Canada and Selected
Industrial Countries, (selected years, 1950–1984)

|  | 1950–1973 | 1973–1984 |
|---|---|---|
| Canada | +2.50 | +2.07 |
| United States | +1.61 | +1.88 |
| Japan | +1.74 | +0.83 |
| Belgium | −0.17 | −0.36 |
| France | +0.38 | −0.05 |
| West Germany | +1.09 | −0.60 |
| Italy | −0.24 | +0.66 |
| United Kingdom | +0.43 | −0.43 |

SOURCE: U.S. Department of Labor, *Comparative Real Gross Domestic Product, Real GDP per Capita and Real GDP per Employed Person, 1950–1984,* January 1986, p. 20.

In this period, the rate of increase in employment was 2.50 percent per year in Canada compared to only 1.61 percent per year in the United States, with Canada having a rate of growth more than 50 percent higher. This was also a more rapid rate of growth than in Japan or any of the countries in Northwest Europe.

The more rapid increase in employment (and the total labour force as well) reflected a higher rate of increase in the adult population, primarily from Canada's higher birth rates. Net immigration also accounted for a higher share of the existing population in Canada than in other countries, especially in the 1950s and 60s. In addition, there was a more rapid increase in the participation rates of women in the labour force.

Canada continued to have a more rapid increase in employment from 1973 to 1984, even though unemployment was still in excess of 11 percent of the labour force in 1984. The increase in employment in Canada of 3.1 million (from 8.8 million in 1973 to 11.1 million in 1984) was larger than the *total* increase in employment of the six European countries shown in Table 5–4 (starting from 100 million persons employed in 1973 in those six countries).

This faster rate of growth in employment and the labour force in Canada than in the other industrialized countries has been well recognized since the mid-1960s. It was a major theme in the first annual review of the Economic Council of Canada.[11]

Adjustments to the growth in total employment are desirable to allow for the changing composition of employment. The growth in employment and total labour force in Canada reflects two important shifts in composition. One change is the higher educational levels of the adult population, reflecting the larger proportion of young people completing high school and going on to university than had been present

---

**TABLE 5–5**   Changes in Labour Quality, Canada,
(selected periods, 1950–1976)

|                                          | 1950–1967 | 1971–1976 |
|------------------------------------------|-----------|-----------|
| Contribution of age–sex composition      | −0.20     | −0.72     |
| Education                                | +0.36     | +0.25     |
| Overall labour-quality change            | +0.16     | −0.24     |

Note: The latter estimates by P. Chinloy show important interactions between age, sex, and education so that components do not add to the total.
SOURCE: Dorothy Walters, *Canadian Growth Revisited* (Ottawa: Queen's Printer, 1970), and Economic Council of Canada, *Strengthening Growth: Options and Constraints,* Twenty-second Annual Review, 1985, p. 130.

historically. These individuals receive higher incomes than those with lower levels of education. Another change is the large increase in employment of younger persons and women, both of whom earn much less per year than an adult male. The net effect of these two changes on an adjustment for labour quality is shown in Table 5–5. In both periods, the contribution of education was a positive factor on the measure of labour quality, while the age–sex composition was negative. In the earlier periods, the contribution of education more than offset the negative effects of the growing share of young persons and women in the labour force, but the effects of the larger numbers of young persons and women in the labour force more than offset the growth in education in the 1970s. The net effect of quality adjustments is a +.16 percent per year in the 1950–67 period and a −.24 percent per year in the 1971–76 period, a fairly large difference.

The quality adjustment partially offsets the large growth in the labour force emphasized previously, but not enough to modify the earlier conclusion that the rate of increase in the input of labour was more rapid in Canada than any of the other major industrialized countries.

## 5–7 THE HUMAN FACTOR IN ORGANIZATIONS

When the distribution of net national income to labour is as high as 80 percent (which is its approximate size in the major industrialized countries), labour income is bound to be a very high share of the internal costs within an individual firm. This phenomenon occurs because anything that is important to the economy as a whole has to be true also for a majority of the individual firms and industries within the economy.

If you look at the costs of labour within the firm, you would initially have to exclude the costs of purchased materials and components, as there would be labour costs in the supplying firms that provide those materials and components. If these purchased materials are excluded from costs, the resulting distribution of costs is sometimes referred to as **value-added costs**. Total labour costs include salaries, wages of hourly paid employees, overtime, and contributions to pension schemes and health programmes.[12]

You might find it interesting to see if you can obtain data for public companies or data on privately held companies to see how these additional benefits in a particular company compare to the national total.

Since labour cost is such a dominant part of cost within the individual firm, management ought to give this area a very high priority in their planning and implementation. However, some evidence indicates that companies sometimes pay more attention to planning for longer-term investment decisions than to planning for personnel. A number of studies indicate that salaries for personnel officers tend to be lower than salaries for other management positions.[13] Very few senior managers in the private sector in Canada have had formal training in psychology, industrial sociology, or the behavioural sciences. This lack of emphasis has begun to change, but personnel recruiting and planning still does not seem to get the same degree of priority in Canada that it does in outstanding U.S. and Japanese companies.

Many programmes in business and public administration include courses in behavioural science and organization to provide future management and executive personnel with greater exposure and understanding of these issues than existing managers have had. Many of Canada's current senior executives got their first exposure to management practice during World War II, and such practices tend to be more authoritarian than is appropriate for the younger members of the labour force who have had higher levels of formal education than those now reaching retirement age.[14]

## 5–8 TWO EFFECTS OF UNIONS

Unions have become an important institution in modern industrialized societies. In Canada, for example, the proportion of union membership as a percent of nonagricultural workers dropped to under 15 percent during the 1930s and was still under 30 percent in 1951. Table 5–6 shows the relative size of union membership in Canada and the United States for selected years from 1951 to 1984. At the start of the period, unionization was somewhat lower in Canada, but the proportion unionized in the United States reached a high point of almost 32 percent in the 1950s and dropped below 20 percent by 1984. In Canada, on the other hand, the proportion has grown fairly steadily since the mid-1950s, and by 1984 the proportion unionized in Canada was almost twice the current U.S. rate. The years shown are representative of the other preceding and following years.

**TABLE 5–6**    Relative Size of Union Membership, Canada and the
United States, Selected Years, 1951–1984 (as a percent of
nonagricultural workers)

|  | 1951 | 1972 | 1984 |
|---|---|---|---|
| Canada | 28.4 | 34.6 | 39.6 |
| United States | 31.7 | 28.8 | 19.4 |

SOURCE: Pradeep Kumar, et al., *The Current Industrial Relations Scene in Canada*, Industrial Relations Centre, Queen's University, November 1986, p. 290.

Recent literature on the effects of unions has dealt with two broad topics, namely the effect of unions on relative wages, and the effect of unions on relative productivity levels in unionized compared to non-unionized sectors.

The extent of the difference in the degree of unionization raises the question of why unionization has declined in the United States while it has increased in Canada. Three institutional differences between Canada and the United States appear to be contributing factors in the difference. One factor is the increased extent of "right-to-work" legislation in the United States. **Right-to-work** laws introduced in a number of U.S. states permit nonunion companies to locate in that state. Legislation in other states permits closed shops, which require workers to be members of the union before they can be hired by a firm. More plants are being established in the states with right-to-work legislation.[15] A second factor is Chapter 11 of the U.S. Bankruptcy Code. This legislation permits the court to impose an agreement on a company and the union (or to remove the right of the union to represent the workers) if the union does not take due note of the financial circumstances of the employer and the employer is being driven to the point of bankruptcy. Under such circumstances, the employer can seek the protection of Chapter 11. These two features of U.S. legislation have led many U.S. unions to negotiate concessions on wages and working conditions during the mid-1980s and have encouraged a moderate stand in wage bargaining. Neither type of legislation is thus far present in Canada.

A further difference in Canada is the greater degree of unionization in public administration than in the United States. Public sector unionization was initiated in the federal government when Lester B. Pearson was Prime Minister, and several large public sector wage increases set a precedent for the private sector. By 1984, about two-thirds of the public sector was unionized in Canada, compared to only 23 percent in the United States a few years ago.[16]

Recently, two of the major unions in Canada have severed their relationships with their American counterparts. Bob White of the United Auto Workers and Jack Monroe, leader of the Woodworkers of

America, have led their members into separate Canadian organizations. Both leaders have made it clear that they intend to take a stronger stand for their members than the American union has been willing to take, and their bargaining postures will reflect an unwillingness to make concessions in Canada. These stronger stands by Canadian union leadership (at a time when unemployment rates have been higher in Canada since 1982 than in the United States) primarily reflect the greater union power in Canada that is encouraged by the differences in the legislative framework.[17]

Such differing developments in the two countries in the extent and policies of unions raises the question as to what effects, if any, the presence of unions has on the performance of wages and productivity in the country. Recent literature on the effects of unions has dealt with two broad topics, namely the effect of unions on relative wages and the effect of unions on relative productivity levels in unionized and non-unionized sectors. This literature will now be summarized.

## Effects of Unions on Relative Wages

There has been considerable research on the effects of unionization on the wage levels in the unionized and nonunionized sectors. Some of this research goes back to the 1940s. The extent of the relative wage difference between the unionized and the nonunionized has varied from one study to another, depending on the state of the business cycle, rate of inflation, industry, and occupational composition of the firms and industries studied. Differences in methodology used to estimate the union–nonunion relative wage difference has also affected the results. Another factor is that many union agreements set wages and other working conditions for a two- or three-year period.

In summarizing an extended period of research on this topic, Greg Lewis put the magnitude of this effect at 10 to 15 percent higher in the unionized sector in the United States, and a comparable study for Canada estimated the difference at 15.8 percent during the 1970s.[18]

## Union and Nonunion Differentials in Productivity

There has been much less research on the effects of unions on productivity, and thus far none for Canada of which we are aware. The research on the United States suggests that the differential in earnings does not lead to a comparable higher level of prices for the unionized firms. There are a number of factors that can reduce and modify the effects of higher wages leading to higher prices. First, the higher wages can lead to some substitution of capital for labour. There may also be additional motivation for management to increase productivity and efficiency to bring the physical output from the unionized workers more in line with the higher wages being paid. The higher wages may also improve morale and motivation of workers by improving job conditions, job content, and workers' perceptions of their jobs. In addition, the presence of unions and the associated information flow from workers to shop stewards and from unions to management may contribute to more effective communication of potential problems and frictions, which can lead to an earlier resolution of these problems.[19]

Studies of unionization's impact on productivity tend to show a positive effect, so the positive effects of unionization on productivity partially offset the effects of unionization on relative wages.

When unions cover about 30 percent of workers in the private sector in Canada, their overall effects on both wage levels and productivity for the economy as a whole are fairly small. For example, if unions cover 30 percent of the labour force and their effect on wages in the unionized sector is 15 percent, the effect on general wage levels for the economy as a whole would only be 4.5 percentage points.[20]

## NOTES

1. J. Schmookler, "The Changing Efficiency of the American Economy, 1869–1938," *Review of Economic Statistics*, August 1952, pp. 214–31.

2. There was a significant increase in interest in and in resources provided for forecasting short-term economic changes during the late 1940s and subsequently. This subject continues to be a major area of interest for many applied macroeconomists reflecting the concern in short-term demand changes that was a heritage of the severe underutilization of resources during the 1930s. The demand side (and the shorter-term cycles around the longer-term, supply-side trends) will be the major area of interest in Part Three and later parts of the book. Longer-term trends continue to get less attention than the shorter-term fluctuations, in spite of their importance.

3. See Paul H. Douglas, "Comments on the Cobb-Douglas Production Function," in *The Theory and Empirical Analysis of Production*, ed. Murray Brown (New York: Columbia University Press for the NBER, 1967), pp. 15–22.

4. Statistics Canada, *Methodology of the Canadian Labour Force Survey 1976*, Catalogue 71–526, October 1977.

5. Statistics Canada, *Fixed Capital Flows and Stocks, 1986* (Ottawa: Ministry of Supply and Services, 1986), pp. xii–xiv.

6. A number of problems prevent a comparison for GDP as this book went to press. GDP includes a number of sectors where labour input is used as a measure of output. For example, estimates of output can be made for only a few sectors of government, but this has not yet been done for all levels of government. In the United States, recent economic growth accounting excludes such sectors from both employment and output to restrict the analysis to the business sector. This has not yet been done for Canada. In addition, the 1986 National Accounts revision has not yet been released for the years before 1961, and a longer series is desirable. The methods illustrated for manufacturing are similar in approach and broad conclusions to a more comprehensive analysis of economic growth based on GDP.

7. A situation in which the ratio of capital to labour is increasing is sometimes referred to as capital deepening. In a growing economy, capital widening would be present if the growth of capital occurred at the same rate as the growth in labour. For most economies, capital deepening has been the dominant tendency in recent decades.

8. Dorothy Walters, *Canadian Income Levels and Growth: An International Perspective* (Ottawa: Queen's Printer, 1968), p. 50.

9. Ibid., p. 20, and Edward F. Denison, *Accounting for United States Economic Growth 1929–1969* (Washington, D.C.: Brookings Institution, 1974), pp. 219–59, especially p. 240. The latter study was able to draw on more direct evidence of age, education, and ability than earlier studies. The effect of higher education on incomes was even larger than had been allowed for in earlier estimates.

10. For a fuller discussion and additional references to the literature see Donald J. Daly, "Combining Inputs to Secure a Measure of Total Factor Input," *Review of Income and Wealth*, March 1972, pp. 27–53.

11. Economic Council of Canada, *Economic Goals for Canada to 1970* (Ottawa: Queen's Printer, 1964, pp. 32–42, and Dorothy Walters, *Canadian Income Levels and Growth: An International Perspective* (Ottawa: Queen's Printer, 1968), p. 17.

12. Pradeep Kumar et al., *The Current Industrial Relations Scene in Canada, 1986,* Industrial Relations Centre, Queen's University, November 1986, pp. 471–74. In 1984, these employee-benefit costs averaged 32.5 percent of gross payroll in Canada, up appreciably from 15.1 percent in 1953, but still somewhat below the comparable percentage of 36.7 in the United States for 1984.

13. Ibid., p. 450, which shows the average salary for selected management groups in Canada in January 1986. A dozen management groups in that salary survey have higher total compensation than the top industrial relations executives and top personnel executives. This reflects the low priority that has traditionally been given to individuals in personnel positions.

14. Donald J. Daly, "Canadian Management: Past Recruitment Practices and Future Training Needs," in *Highlights and Background Studies,* ed. Max von Zur Muehlen (Ottawa: Canadian Federation of Deans of Management and Administrative Studies, 1979), pp. 178–200. There are now many books available dealing with personnel recruitment, training, organization methods, and morale with many comparisons of different countries' approaches to these issues. See some of the references in the selected bibliography in the above study.

15. Henry S. Farber, "Right-to-Work Laws and the Extent of Unionization," *Journal of Labor Economics,* July 1984, pp. 319–52.

16. Kumar, et al., *The Current Industrial Relations Scene,* p. 308, and Bureau of Labor Statistics, *Handbook of Labor Statistics, December 1983* (Washington, D.C.: U.S. Government Printing Office, 1983), p. 159.

17. Michael Walker, "An Important Sleeper," *Fraser Forum,* (Vancouver: Fraser Institute, November 1986), pp. 10–11, and D. J. Daly and D. C. MacCharles, *Focus on Real Wage Unemployment* (Vancouver: Fraser Institute, June 1986), pp. 24–25 and 98–100.

18. H. G. Lewis, *Unionism and Relative Wages in the United States: An Empirical Inquiry* (Chicago: University of Chicago Press, 1963), and H. G. Lewis, "Union Relative Wage Effects: A Survey of Macro Estimates," *Journal of Labor Economics,* January 1983, pp. 1–27, and C. J. Parsley, "Labor Union Effects on Wage Gains: A Survey of Recent Literature," *Journal of Economic Literature,* March 1980, pp. 1–31, and Glenn M. MacDonald and John C. Evans, "The Size and Structure of Union–Nonunion Wage Differentials in Canadian Industry," *Canadian Journal of Economics,* May 1981, pp. 216–31.

19. Richard B. Freeman and James L. Medoff, *What Do Unions Do?* (New York: Basic Books, 1984), especially Chapter 11 entitled "Unionism: Good or Bad for Productivity?" pp. 162–80; and Richard B. Freeman and James L. Medoff, "The Two Faces of Unionism", *The Public Interest,* Fall 1979, pp. 69–93.

20. This result is obtained by multiplying .30 (the percentage unionized) by 15 percent (the effects of unionization on relative wages). Similar conclusions on the effects of monopoly were arrived at by A. C. Harberger.

# 6

# Output per Unit of Input and Economic Growth

Economic growth can come from a variety of sources in addition to the growth of factor inputs covered in Chapter 5. Short-term variations in the strength of the growth in demand can affect both the level of output and the level of employment. Economies of scale refer to changes in output per unit of input made possible by long-run changes in the size of markets that a business serves. Improved resource allocation takes place when labour moves from low-income industries and occupations to higher-income alternatives. Advances in knowledge (both scientific and engineering know-how on the one hand and organizational and managerial knowledge on the other) contribute to more output from given levels of factory inputs.

After reading this chapter, you should understand the relative importance of these key factors to economic growth, how these factors clarify the reasons for changes over time, and differences in growth performance between countries. We want to:

1. Isolate the contribution of changes in demand to both output and input.
2. Clarify the main sources of growth in output per unit of input.
3. Illustrate the extent of these factors to changes in economic growth in the United States since 1929.
4. Compare economic growth in Canada and the United States.
5. Review some of the reasons for the slowdown in economic growth in North America since 1973.
6. Summarize some of Japan's economic growth experiences over the post-war period.

Edward F. Denison has been an active pioneer in economic growth accounting since the early 1960s. He worked in both the National Income Division and the Bureau of Economic Analysis of the Department of Commerce in the United States and so was familiar with the main statistical sources on national income, employment, prices, and capital stock as covered in Chapters 2 and 5. Since 1962, he has published a series of major volumes on economic growth in the United States and comparable studies for the major countries of Western Europe and Japan. In recent years he has been an *emeritus* staff member at the Brookings Institution in Washington, D.C., where he was a Fellow most of the time since 1962.

Denison has gone further in identifying and quantifying the main sources of the increases in output per unit of input than most other students of economic growth accounting. Previous researchers established that only part of the growth in real national income could be explained by changes in the inputs of labour, capital, and land (as explained in Chapter 5). However, over an important quarter of a century of high economic growth in the United States, only about one-fourth of the increase in real potential national income per person employed can be explained by the increase in the factor inputs per person (including increased physical capital and higher levels of education for the average employed person). About *two-fifths* of the total increase in real potential national income in the U.S. over the 1948–73 period came from increases in output per unit of input (as can be seen in Table 6–1).

Differences in output per unit of input are also important in explaining the differences in the levels of real national income per person employed between the United States and such other industrialized countries as Japan and the major countries in Europe. The relative importance of increases in output per total factor input has been even greater in Japan and most of the European countries than in the United States. Some understanding of these factors in economic growth is thus essential to understand the past and assess potentials for the future, not just for each individual country but also for growth and international trade for different countries on a longer-term basis.

As an initial step in quantifying the contribution of some of these sources of economic growth, we will explain how shorter-term fluctuations in output and employment can be allowed for.

## 6–1 ESTIMATING POTENTIAL NATIONAL INCOME AND EMPLOYMENT

It has been recognized for decades that economic growth is not steady and consistent from year to year—rather, it comes in surges or waves. Sometimes economic growth occurs at a rapid rate for a decade or more (such as the 1900–1914 period in Canada), but it can slow down and even decline during other periods (such as the decade of the 1930s).

**TABLE 6–1**  Sources of Growth in Output per Unit of Input to Total
Potential National Income, United States, Selected
Periods, 1929–1982 (contributions to growth rates in
percentage points)

| | Longer Periods | | |
|---|---|---|---|
| *Item* | *1929–1948* | *1948–1973* | *1973–1982* |
| National Income | 2.57 | 3.89 | 2.61 |
| Output per unit of input | 1.01 | 1.66 | 0.08 |
| Economies of scale | 0.22 | 0.32 | 0.21 |
| Improved resource allocation | 0.29 | 0.30 | 0.07 |
| Legal and human environment | 0.00 | −0.04 | −0.17 |
| Advances in knowledge not elsewhere classified | 0.49 | 1.09 | −0.05 |

SOURCE: Edward F. Denison, *Trends in American Economic Growth, 1929–1982* (Washington, D.C.: Brookings Institution, 1985), p. 112.

This variation in output and productivity was recognized some time ago (see W. C. Mitchell's volume *Business Cycles*), and later developments in the United States were documented in several studies by Thor Hultgren and Geoffrey Moore for the National Bureau of Economic Research.[1]

The relationship between changes in unemployment and changes in output became an important tool of analysis for public policy when it was incorporated into the U.S. Council of Economic Advisors' annual reports during the 1960s when Lyndon Johnson was president. This relationship has been referred to as Okun's Law after the late Arthur M. Okun, who first presented it.[2] **Potential output** is a measure of what the economy would produce when the country's labour resources are fully employed (with the level of capital stock then current and the technology then in use). Analysts prepare estimates of potential output in a given period assuming full employment. During a recession or period of slow growth, unemployment would be above the full employment rate, and actual output would be below potential output. A reduction of the gap between actual and potential output from 90 percent to 95 percent of potential output would not be reflected in a drop of 5 percentage points in the unemployment rate but only about 2 percentage points. About three fifths of the increase in output would come from an increase in output per person employed and only two fifths from a reduction in the rate of unemployment.[3]

This approach has been applied in Canada as well in studies prepared by the Economic Council of Canada and the Department of Finance. A recent Bank of Canada study by Gerald Stuber thoroughly documented the cyclical behaviour of labor productivity in Canada. As in previous studies for both United States and Canada, he found that output and labour productivity declined in the three most recent recessions (1974–75, 1979–80, and 1981–82) in both the total for the commercial sector and most of the major component industries. Similarly, labour productivity growth tends to accelerate during the subsequent expansionary phases of the cycle, especially in the early stages.[4]

The recovery from the 1981–82 recession is a good illustration of the extent to which a large increase in GDP in constant prices is necessary to obtain a significant reduction in the rate of unemployment. The 1981–82 recession in Canada was the longest and most severe of any experienced in Canada since the 1930s. The recession trough occurred in December 1982; in the four years after the fourth-quarter low, GDP in constant prices increased about 18 percent. The rate of unemployment, however, declined only about 3 percentage points from a high of about 12.6 percent of the labour force to a bit under 10 percent. Hours of work increased, and productivity increased at a faster rate than over the previous decade. In addition, participation rates went up by about 2 percentage points over that four-year period, so part of the increased level of demand and output encouraged some people to enter or reenter the labour force, and only a small drop in the unemployment rate occurred. The drop in the unemployment rate was only 3 percentage points over four years, while the increase in GDP at constant prices was about 18 percent over the same period, a significant contrast.

The economists and statisticians prepare estimates of the levels of potential employment and potential output before identifying the other longer-term factors that influence the changes in output per total factor input. A variety of methods have been used to prepare potential output, such as extrapolation of the trend from previous periods of relatively low rates of unemployment. Denison prefers a more direct approach based on much greater detail. He defines potential national output as follows:

> I *define* potential national income in 1958 prices in any year as the value that national income (in 1958 prices) would have taken if (1) unemployment had been at 4 percent; (2) the intensity of utilization of employed resources had been that which *on the average* would be associated with a 4 percent unemployment rate; and (3) other conditions had been those which actually prevailed in that year.[5]

Estimates of potential output with levels of unemployment a bit higher and a bit lower than 4 percent make a slight difference on the levels of potential output, but the rates of growth over time are all very similar.

After estimates of both potential output and potential employment have been prepared on a consistent basis, it is possible to explore the factors that have contributed to changes in output per total factor input after allowing for the shorter-term demand variations between actual and potential output.

## 6–2 MAIN SOURCES OF CHANGES IN OUTPUT PER UNIT OF INPUT

Three sources of growth stand out as key among the large number of sources of the increase in output per unit of input that have been identified conceptually and measured in practice. These are:

Economies of scale.
Improved resource allocation.
Advances in knowledge.

A simple definition and brief explanation of each of these three sources will be given initially, before discussing the rough magnitudes of each of them in Section 6–3.

### Economies of Scale

**Economies of scale** refers to the rise in output per unit of input that is made possible by changes in the size of markets that business serves.

Growth of an economy automatically means growth in the average size of the local, regional, and national markets for end products that business serves. Growth of markets brings opportunities for greater specialization—both among and within industries, firms, and establishments—and opportunities for establishments and firms within the economy to become larger without impairing the competitive pressures on firms that stimulate efficiency. Longer production runs for individual products become possible. So, in almost all industries including wholesale and retail trade, do larger transactions in buying, selling, and shipping. This is important, because the length of runs and the size of the transactions in which business deals are major determinants of unit costs. Larger regional and local markets permit greater geographical specialization and less transporting of products. The opportunities for greater specialization, bigger units, longer runs, and larger transactions provide clear reason to expect increasing returns in the production and distribution of many products, and examples of increasing returns are plentiful.[6]

## Improved Resource Allocation

Improved resource allocation comes about primarily from the differences in income level received by labour in different industries at the start of the period of the economic growth analysis. When there are employment opportunities available, employees and individual entrepreneurs can achieve increases in real income by shifting from low-paying alternatives to those that pay more. The signals from the market show a higher level of GDP in constant prices from the same labour input. The two main low-income sectors in North America in the 1920s and at the end of World War II were composed of those engaged in agriculture and those engaged in nonfarm self-employment. With larger income gains possible and expanding employment opportunities (especially from the end of World War II to about 1973), many more individuals shifted from the agricultural to the nonagricultural sector than moved back into agriculture. It is also possible, of course, that if employment growth slows in such high-income industries as basic manufacturing and the alternative opportunities for employment are in the low-paying parts of the service sector, the reverse effect on output in relation to total factor input could take place.

## Advances in Knowledge

The growth in output per person employed and overall economic growth has been heavily influenced by advances in knowledge since the industrial revolution first started. Denison summarizes the concept of advances of knowledge as follows:

> As knowledge relevant to production advances, the output that can be obtained from a given quantity of resources rises. The advance in knowledge is the biggest and most basic reason for the persistent long-term growth of output per unit of input.
>
> The term "advances in knowledge" must be construed comprehensively. It includes what is usually defined as technological knowledge — knowledge concerning the physical properties of things, and how to make, combine, or use them in a physical sense. It also includes "managerial knowledge" — knowledge of business organization and of management techniques construed in the broadest sense. Advances in knowledge comprise knowledge originating in this country and abroad, and knowledge obtained in any way: by organized research, by individual research workers and inventors, and by simple observation and experience.[7]

Such advances in knowledge are only reflected in output as measured in the national income measures after they have been implemented, so it is important that any advances in knowledge actually be

used in production and distribution. There can often be long lags between a basic invention and its implementation in industry, and some
managers and some societies are more open to new ideas and are faster
in incorporating new technologies than others.

Advances in knowledge cannot be measured directly, but rather are
obtained as a residual after all the other factors that can be identified
and measured have been taken into account. Thus the index for advances in knowledge picks up all the errors in all of the other statistical
series that are used in economic growth accounting, insofar as the errors
in the other individual series are not offsetting.

## 6-3 CHANGES IN OUTPUT PER UNIT OF INPUT IN THE UNITED STATES

The main changes in output per unit of input over three major time
periods since 1929 can be seen in Table 6–1. Table 6–1 relates to potential output (as explained in Section 6–1) as did Table 5–1 in the last
chapter.

The contribution of economies of scale amounted to two-tenths or
three-tenths of a percent to the growth in total potential national income
in the United States for each of the three longer periods shown in the
table. Although this was somewhat higher over the 1948–73 period than
the periods before or after that quarter of a century, the differences are
not too great.

Improved resource allocation was approximately as important
quantitatively from 1929 to 1973 as economies of scale, but its importance was sharply lower after 1973 than in the two earlier periods.
By the 1980s, the share of employment in agriculture fell to about 3 percent of total employment from about 20 percent in 1929. There simply
was not enough surplus low-income labour left in farming to allow the
shift from farming to contribute as much as during previous decades to
the growth in national income. As pointed out previously, a shift from
low-income agriculture to higher-income employment in the nonagricultural sector shows up as a higher level of GDP from the same
level of employment. The number of nonfarm self-employed increased
in total from 1929 to the early 1980s but declined in a relative sense to
less than 10 percent of nonagricultural employment by the early 1980s,
well below the 25 percent and higher than existed in 1929. Any further
decline in the share of nonfarm self-employed is not likely to be as
important a factor in the reallocation of resources as took place in the
decades before 1973.

Advances in knowledge were a major source of the increases in
output per unit of input before 1973. In the 1948–73 period, it provided
1.09 percentage points or about two-thirds of the increase of 1.66 per-

centage points of the increase in output per unit of input. Since 1973, however, this source has largely disappeared and was negative from 1979 to 1982. Estimates have been prepared on an annual basis since 1929, and this is the first time that the estimates of the advances in knowledge (including any items not elsewhere classified) have departed so markedly and for such an extended period from the longer-term historical experience. It should be recalled that the evidence thus far has dealt with measures of potential national income, so an allowance has already been made for demand weakness and the existence of unemployment in excess of the 4 percent used by Denison as the basis of his estimates of potential employment and potential output. Such a persistent slowdown in growth since 1973 has led to a reexamination of some of the possible reasons for such a marked slowdown extending over such a prolonged series of years. In Section 6–5 we will look at some of the theories that have been advanced for this marked slowdown.

## 6–4  COMPARISONS OF ECONOMIC GROWTH EXPERIENCE IN CANADA AND THE UNITED STATES

The same factors summarized in this and the preceding chapter on economic growth in the United States are important also in Canada. The timing of the periods of fast and slow growth is broadly similar in the two countries. However, there have been no recent studies of economic growth in Canada completely comparable to those prepared by Denison for the United States. The last comparable study for Canada (by Dorothy Walters) was published in 1970 and ended with the year 1967. There is no later study with the full details on inputs and a variety of the components of output per unit of input on a potential basis as shown for the United States in earlier tables.

However, it is possible to make some comparisons of inputs and output per unit of input between the two countries over the last three decades, but on the basis of total actual national income, without the adjustments to put both output and employment on a potential basis. Because both the United States and Canada had higher unemployment rates in 1982 than in 1973, the extent of the drop in the rate of economic growth over the 1973–82 period is greater in Table 6–2 than shown for the same period in Table 6–1 earlier in this chapter. For the United States, the change in actual output over the 1973–82 period is −.25 points per year (as shown in Table 6–2), as compared to .08 in potential national income for the same period as shown in Table 6–1. In Canada, the unemployment rate was also higher in 1982 than in 1973, with the increase being roughly twice as high in both countries. A summary comparison can be seen in Table 6–2.

**TABLE 6–2**   Sources of Growth of Total Actual National Income,
United States and Canada (selected periods, 1953–1982)

|  | 1953–1973 | 1973–1982 | Change |
|---|---|---|---|
| United States, 1953–1982 |  |  |  |
| Actual national income | 3.46% | 1.85% | −1.61% |
| Total factor input | 1.96 | 2.10 | +0.14 |
| Output per unit of input | 1.50 | −0.25 | −1.75 |
| Canada, 1958–1982: | 1958–1973 | 1973–1982 | Change |
| Actual national income | 5.11 | 2.15 | −2.96 |
| Total factor input | 2.74 | 2.39 | −0.35 |
| Output per unit of input | 2.37 | −0.25 | −2.62 |

SOURCES: Edward F. Denison, *Trends in American Economic Growth, 1929–1982* (Washington, D.C.: Brookings Institution, 1985), p. 111, and Economic Council of Canada, *Strengthening Growth: Options and Constraints* (Ottawa: Ministry of Supply and Services, 1985), p. 125.

Several things about the differences in economic growth between Canada and the United States stand out from these comparisons in Table 6–2. First, the contribution of total factor input to economic growth has been greater in Canada than in the United States, especially in the period up to 1973, as was pointed out in the latter part of Chapter 5. This higher rate of growth in factor input in Canada than in the United States primarily reflects the larger percentage increase in Canada's working age population, a situation that is partly a result of a higher rate of natural increase (reflecting the higher birthrates in Canada during the postwar years) and a higher rate of net immigration. Furthermore, there has been a much larger increase in participation rates of women in Canada than in the United States and a greater increase in the stock of business capital in Canada. All these factors are reflected in a larger contribution of total factor input to Canada than in the United States, and this difference amounted to almost a full percentage point in the period up to 1973. A 1 percent difference in the rate of growth of inputs amounts to about $4.5 billion in 1985 prices, a fairly significant amount. The greater contribution of factor inputs to economic growth in Canada than in the United States shows up in the comparisons of economic growth experience with the eight west European economies and also in comparison with Japan.

The increase in output per unit of input was also greater in Canada than in the United States as shown in Table 6–2, the difference amounting to about .8 percentage points up to 1973. An important part of this difference reflects greater gains from economies of scale in Canada than in the United States. In addition, there was a greater contribution of interindustry shifts in Canada, especially a greater relative shift out of agriculture.

A third important point from the table is that the declines in Canada in ouptut per unit of input have been even greater than in the United States since 1973. The drop in output per unit of input in Canada since 1973 compared to the earlier period amounts to 2.6 percentage points per year compared to a drop of 1.75 percentage points per year in the United States, a difference of almost 1 full percentage point per year. This is a significant difference for economic growth accounting.

This change for both countries is so significant a slowdown in economic growth that some further discussion of this topic is appropriate.

## 6-5 FACTORS IN THE ECONOMIC GROWTH SLOWDOWN IN NORTH AMERICA SINCE 1973

The decline in the rate of growth in output per unit of input in the United States since 1973 compared with earlier periods is a greater change than occurred over a comparable period at any time since the start of the present century.[8] In light of such a dramatic contrast, there has been a considerable discussion of possible factors that could have contributed to such a phenomenon.

Denison has given the greatest amount of attention to possible factors that could explain what happened. In his 1979 study, he examined 17 possible interpretations of these developments and was able to quantify many of them. First, there is no single factor that offers a full explanation for the decline. There is no one culprit, no simple gimmick to enable business and government to put the pieces of the productivity puzzle together and come up with some simple solution to solve the problem. In addition, a full explanation for the productivity slowdown will likely be a puzzle for some time to come. In Denison's comprehensive studies, he compared the difference in the experience since 1973 with the 1948–73 period, where he was able to develop comprehensive estimates for individual years and subperiods within that quarter of a century. The comparisons of potential output per person employed in the later period still left more than half of the shortfall that could not be quantified, and none of the individual items that could be quantified explained more than 10 percent of the shortfall. Thus, some important pieces of the puzzle are still missing.

It might be useful to highlight some of the suggestions that have occasionally been put forth to explain the productivity slowdown, as the available evidence contradicts some of these possible interpretations. We will look at the evidence for the United States to provide some perspective for Canada.

Some observers suggest that weak demand has been a major factor in the productivity slowdown. These analysts believe that the stimulus for more expansionary monetary and fiscal policies is desirable. However, the Denison results in Table 6–1 are based on estimates of potential output and potential employment, so they already allow for the effects of differences in the intensity of demand on potential output and potential employment. Thus, demand weakness can only explain a small part of the slower growth in actual output and actual output per unit of input since 1973. It is unlikely that the situation in Canada could be much different, although no completely comparable study for Canada has thus far been made.

Other observers have blamed a slower pace in business investment and recommend that governments provide greater stimulus to business investment and savings. Denison quantifies the effect of changing capital inputs to economic growth for the United States, but the difference in the contribution of the stock of capital from nonresidential structures and equipment only explains $\frac{1}{10}$ of 1 percent of the slower growth rate since 1973, which is negligible in a very large decline in total potential national income. The argument that lower gross investment in Canada is a major cause for the growth slowdown does not seem appropriate as Canada already has a larger stock of capital per person employed than in the United States, which makes Canada the most capital-intensive country in the world. **Capital intensive** is a measure of the degree to which a country may have a larger stock of capital per person employed. To ensure comparability, this measurement should be made on the basis of common prices of capital goods in the countries being compared. The emphasis on greater capital intensity in Canada than in the United States is clear for both manufacturing and the economy as a whole and does not occur primarily because of a larger share of capital-intensive industries in Canada. Business investment continued to be very strong in Canada from 1973 to 1981 but has weakened significantly since then.

The effect of higher energy prices is another possibility sometimes suggested as an explanation for the slowdown in output per unit of input. The timing of the slowdown in economic growth does correspond roughly with the price increases initiated by OPEC. However, Denison and others conclude that this is not a major factor, although it might explain a slowdown of 0.10 percent per year in the growth rate of output per unit of input for the United States. Furthermore, countries that moved quickly to world energy prices, such as Japan, have continued to achieve larger increases in output per unit of input than all the other major industrialized countries. Canada has kept energy prices below world levels through the 1970s, but still experienced a more marked slowdown in productivity change than most other industrialized countries. Energy price increases do not explain the differing international productivity performance of the 1970s.

Decreased spending on research and development is another factor sometimes suggested as a reason for the decline in the rate of increase in output per unit input. However, Denison concluded that a reduction of 0.10 is all that can be explained by this factor. Some declines in the share of research and development to sales and gross national product took place in Canada during the 1970s, but increases have taken place during the 1980s. However, with increased specialization and longer runs, Canada could achieve high productivity growth even if companies decrease their expenditures on research and development. Furthermore, because the amount of new technology obtained abroad is far larger than that produced domestically, the key problem for Canada is the speed at which new technology is implemented rather than where it was initially produced. About 95 percent of the new patents issued in Canada are issued to nonresidents, reflecting the heavy dependance on imported technology. This heavy reliance on imported technology is also reflected in large payments for such technology. In addition, although Canadian subsidiaries have access to all the latest technology and managerial practices of the parent,[9] they are sometimes slow to adopt new practices.

There is a further factor that has begun to be more important quantitatively as a factor in the productivity slowdown since 1981 than previously. This is the effect of interindustry shifts mentioned as a positive factor in both the United States and Canada for the period prior to 1973, arising primarily from the shift from the low-income agricultural sector to the higher incomes in the nonagricultural sector. In the 1981–85 period, the more rapid growth in the share of employment in the lower-productivity service sector (retail trade and business, personal, and community services) reduced the aggregate productivity growth compared to the 1970s. Growth of output per hour in the private sector was *reduced* in absolute terms by about 0.4 percentage points per year in Canada relative to what would have occurred if the 1981 employment shares had prevailed throughout the period. In the United States, the comparable figure was about 0.6 percentage points per year.

Much of the shortfall in real income growth was borne by workers who suffered real income losses when they lost jobs in the high-productivity, high-wage, goods-producing industries and ended up employed in low-productivity, low-wage, service-producing industries. This change in the scope of intersectoral shifts from a positive factor in economic growth for some decades up to 1973 to a negative factor in the 1981–85 period reflects new economic developments.[10]

There is an additional interpretation that Denison considers important but is unable to quantify—the impairment of efficiency by inflation. To make rational decisions about production, investment, borrowing, cash management, and international trade, businesspeople must use information from the price system. It is easier to detect changes in relative prices when the general price system is stable than when all prices are going up, and a high average rate of inflation normally involves greater variation in individual price changes. Higher rates of inflation in goods prices are also normally associated with higher interest rates. There are also larger differences in the rates of price changes internationally, and the differential experience in prices and interest rates among countries is reflected in significant exchange-rate changes. Market prices become less effective as a guide in decision making and in the co-ordination of economic activity. Senior business leaders spend more time analyzing the economy and so have less time to manage other key aspects of their business effectively. Denison concludes that inflation impairs productivity, especially since 1973, but is unable to say by how much.

This possibility can be looked at internationally. Eight major industrialized countries had an average increase of 2.8 percent in unit labour costs in manufacturing in domestic currencies from 1950 to 1973; this cost rose to 10.7 percent from 1973 to 1980, almost a fourfold increase. Every single country had higher cost increases after 1973 than during the previous quarter of a century. Each country also experienced a productivity slowdown both for GDP and output per hour in manufacturing after 1973. In addition, the two countries with the smallest increases in costs domestically (Japan and Germany) also had the smallest decline in productivity in the later period compared to the experience from 1950 to 1973.

## 6–6 THE JAPANESE POSTWAR PERFORMANCE

The Japanese economic growth has been so high in the postwar period that it deserves some discussion. Table 3–1 showed that Japan's real GDP per employee increased at an annual rate of 7.6 percent from 1950 to 1973 and 2.8 percent from 1973 to 1986. For both periods, Japan's rate of growth was higher than that of any other industrialized countries. A variety of factors contributed to this higher increase in output per person employed in Japan than in North America.

Japan has a much higher rate of business investment and personal savings as a share of GDP than other industrialized countries. This has been reflected in a more rapid increase in the stock of capital per person employed in Japan than in any of the other industrialized countries. However, the stock of capital per person employed in Japan was so much below the other countries at the start of the period that Japan is still well below the North American levels in this category.

Japan also had a very high contribution of output per factor input. There was a significant shift of labour out of agriculture and other areas of self-employment. Income levels in the self-employed sector have persisted well below those attainable in the more modern sectors of the economy, such as in large-scale manufacturing plants. Advances in knowledge were also a very important source of growth. During this period, both business and government put a high priority on the importance of catching up to the levels of technology in the larger industrialized countries. The high rates of growth from this variety of sources permitted more transactions in the average establishment (both manufacturing and retail) encouraged by a further increase in the degree of urbanization. All of these developments permitted very important economies of scale in Japan, resulting in more output in relation to labour and capital inputs. In summary, there were a number of very positive factors in economic growth in Japan, and there were no areas of particular weakness.

There are some significant differences in productivity levels between individual Japanese industries and the comparable ones in North America. For example, Japanese agriculture has levels of output per person employed well below North American levels. This difference also appears to hold true for important parts of the retail trade and restaurant sectors, especially small-scale establishments. On the other hand, manufacturing has begun to approach the levels of the countries in Western Europe and North America and deserves further discussion in the light of the importance of manufacturing trade as a growing share of world trade.

The changes in output per hour in manufacturing for Japan compared to the United States can be seen in Figure 6–1, which covers an extended period from the 1960s to the middle of the 1980s. In 1955, the level of output per hour in Japanese manufacturing was about one-sixth of the U.S. level. Over the last 30 years, however, the rate of increase in manufacturing in Japan has been so rapid that the Japanese began to exceed the Canadian levels in the 1980s. In the 1950s, the level in Japan was lower than the level in any of the European countries, but by the middle of the 1980s, Japan moved ahead of all the European countries except West Germany — clearly a very impressive performance.

The relative levels of output per hour for selected years from 1955 to 1984 can be seen in Table 6–3. Notice that Japan moved up from well below Canada and the United States in 1955 to about halfway between Canada and the United States by 1984. Such changes can be important for changing market shares in the world market for manufactured products.

A number of key factors in the decision-making process of individual Japanese manufacturing firms influence the results summarized in Table 6–3 and Figure 6–1.

One factor is the relative importance of fixed costs in a Japanese firm compared to a North American firm. Another is the concept of permanent employment, which is more important in Japan than in North America. After a three-year probationary period, many Japanese companies regard employees as permanently employed. There is a mu-

**TABLE 6–3** Output per Hour, Manufacturing, United States, Canada and Japan, Selected Years, 1955–1984 (United States = 100)

|      | United States | Canada | Japan |
|------|---------------|--------|-------|
| 1955 | 100.0         | 56.2   | 16.1  |
| 1970 | 100.0         | 72.3   | 46.7  |
| 1984 | 100.0         | 72.2   | 87.2  |

SOURCE: D. J. Daly and D. C. MacCharles, *Focus on Real Wage Unemployment* (Vancouver: The Fraser Institute, 1986), Appendix Table A–1, p. 65.

**FIGURE 6–1** Output per Hour in Manufacturing, United States, Canada and Japan, 1965–1984

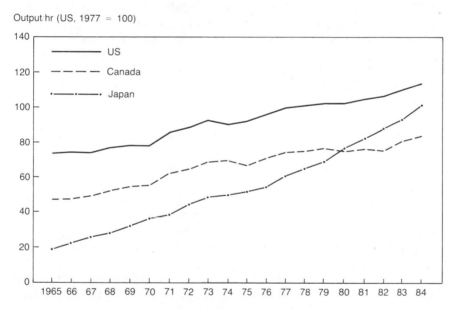

Output hr (US, 1977 = 100)

SOURCE: D. J. Daly and D. C. MacCharles, *Focus on Real Wage Unemployment* (Vancouver: Fraser Institute, 1986), Appendix Table A–1, p. 65.

tual obligation between the employer and the employee to stay together until the normal retirement age of 55. This arrangement is not completely foreign to the North American experience in practice, as many male employees after about age 35 stay with one employer for the balance of their working lives. However, the implied employer obligation is not as widespread or as formally accepted. Since payroll costs are such a large part of value-added costs in all countries, permanent employment is quite an important consideration as an element of fixed costs in Japan. **Value-added costs** are the costs of a company less the purchased materials and services. Purchased materials are a large and growing part of total costs in many companies. From the viewpoint of Japanese managers, about the only way to reduce costs per unit is by significant increases in production volume. This consideration is an important source of pressure on Japanese management.

It is significant that in a number of Japanese industries, individual plants have been able to achieve levels of output broadly comparable to those of North American plants, but with a plant area and a total plant cost just a fraction of the North American size and cost. In the case of automobile assembly, the Japanese use a completely different plant layout and supply system. The supplying assembly plants deliver components to a large number of delivery bays located around the plant. The standard of quality on these components is so high and so well established that they are put immediately into the assembly line without checking for quality or count. In North America, on the other hand, the deliveries are all made to a central receiving area where they are then stored until needed. Plants must be much larger to allow parts and materials to be moved from the shipping and storage area to the assembly line when and where they are needed. The different plant layout and delivery system permits the Japanese plant to operate with about two hours of inventory on hand, while the North American plant has about two weeks of inventory on hand. Thus, a Japanese plant has lower inventory, plant, and capital costs per unit than a broadly comparable North American plant, even though total car production may be approximately the same. Under these circumstances, the levels of car production per worker are higher in Japan than in North America even though the levels of fixed capital and inventories are lower. North American companies are currently implementing some of the same types of inventory control and plant-layout systems presently in use in Japan.

There has also been a significant difference in the approach to the production and diffusion of new technology. In the early postwar years, Japanese industrialists made an important decision to put high priority on purchasing new technology in the world market. The Japanese Productivity Agency initiated and coordinated many visits by Japanese industrialists to plant locations in the rest of the world. For a total expenditure of about $5 billion U.S., the Japanese were able to get access to most of the major technological developments of the West. That amount is just a fraction of what U.S. firms spend on research and development each year. The Japanese, however, did not just incorporate the technology as developed elsewhere. They gave a great deal of attention to how products could be produced with high engineering standards of precision and quality, but at low cost. This trend has continued to the present. Rather than putting priority on basic research and development, the Japanese put a high priority on fast adoption of new technology, no matter where it had been developed. In some cases, they were able to bring new products and new technologies to the stage of commercialization more quickly than manufacturers in the countries where the technologies were initially developed.

## SUMMARY

The reasons for calculating estimates of potential output were explained, as were the methods used to prepare such measures. These adjustments are necessary as changing levels of unemployment are reflected in even larger changes in actual output.

The three main sources of change in output per unit of total factor input were then defined and explained. These key sources are economies of scale, improved resource allocation (based on interindustry shifts from low- to high-paying alternatives) and advances in knowledge.

The relative importance of these three main sources of growth were illustrated by discussion of three major periods of economic growth in the United States.

Some comparisons of economic growth between Canada and the United States over the postwar period were made. A key difference is that Canada has had a larger contribution to economic growth from increased inputs of labour and capital than the United States. In addition, larger increases in output per total factor input took place in Canada up to 1973, but since then growth in Canada has slowed down significantly.

It has not been possible to make a full explanation of the reasons for the productivity slowdown in the United States and Canada since 1973, and a number of popular interpretations of possible reasons are inconsistent with the available evidence. Greater inflation is probably an important factor in many of the industrialized countries, but this important factor cannot yet be quantified.

The postwar economic growth performance of Japan has been impressive. Performance in manufacturing is particularly striking. Japan has moved from the lowest of the major industrialized countries in the 1950s, as measured by levels of output per hour, to higher levels than in Canada and most of the countries in Northwest Europe by the middle of the 1980s. High fixed costs pressure management to achieve higher volumes to obtain lower overhead costs per unit and thereby reduce other costs as well. In addition, Japan has been very effective in incorporating new technology quickly, sometimes even more quickly than in the countries where the technology was initially developed.

## NOTES

1.   Geoffrey H. Moore, "Productivity, Costs and Prices: New Light From an Old Hypothesis," *Business Cycles, Inflation and Forecasting* (Cambridge, Mass.: Ballinger Publications, 1980), Chapter 14, pp. 275–91; Thor Hultgren, *Changes in Labor Cost During Cycles in Production and Business* (Ann Arbor, Mich.: University Microfilms, 1960); and Thor Hultgren, *Costs, Prices and Profits: Their Cyclical Relations* (New York: Columbia University Press, 1965).

2.   Arthur M. Okun, "Potential GNP: Its Measurement and Significance," reprinted in *The Political Economy of Prosperity* (Washington, D.C.: Brookings Institution, 1970), pp. 132–45.

3.   This estimate is based on an updating of Okun's initial work to allow for a lag in the response of the unemployment rate to an increase in actual output. See Robert J. Gordon, "Inflation, Flexible Exchange Rates, and the Natural Rate of Unemployment," in *Workers, Jobs and Inflation*, Martin J. Bailey, ed. (Washington, D.C.: Brookings Institution, 1982), p. 94.

4.   Gerald Stuber, *The Slowdown in Productivity Growth in the 1975–83 Period: A Survey of Possible Explanations*, Bank of Canada Technical Report No. 43, 1986, pp. 38–51.

5.   Edward F. Denison, *Accounting for the United States Economic Growth 1929–1969* (Washington, D.C.: Brookings Institution, 1974), p. 86.

6.   Ibid., p. 71.

7.   Ibid., p. 79.

8.   Moses Abramovitz, "Welfare Quandaries and Productivity Concerns," *American Economic Review*, March 1981, pp. 1–17.

9.   D. J. Daly, "Technology Transfer and Canada's Competitive Performance," *Trade and Investment in Services: Canada/U.S. Perspectives*, Robert M. Stern, ed. (Toronto: University of Toronto Press, 1986), pp. 304–333.

10.   Andrew Sharpe, "The Impact of the Growth of the Service Sector on Aggregate Productivity Trends," Department of Finance, December 1986, presented to the Annual Meeting of the Allied Social Science Association, New Orleans, Louisiana.

# PART THREE

# Consumption, Investment, and Business Cycles

In Part Two, we developed the supply side of the macroeconomic system, emphasizing the determinants of potential output when the economy is operating with a low rate of unemployment. Now in Part Three, we shift emphasis to develop the underlying theory for the variations in demand that will influence the actual level of output (and any gap between actual and potential output). This theory will lay the basis for the variations in production and national income that were among the questions posed for macroeconomic theory in the historical material in Chapter 3.

Chapter 7 will provide an overview to demand and a bridge between the determinants of national income on the supply side and the longer-term developments on the demand side. This chapter will also provide an overview of the modern theory of aggregate demand.

Chapter 8 will develop the theory and evidence relating to consumption and the determinants of the consumption function. This chapter will look at the evidence on longer-term trends in consumption and savings, as well as the effects of shorter-term fluctuations in income on consumption. The cross-section behaviour of consumption (for families with different levels of annual income) will also be examined.

Chapter 9 will explore the determinants of business investment and the effects of changes in interest rates on the level of business spending in both the business capital investment and housing areas. This chapter will explore the interrelations between investment and consumption in the determination of gross domestic product via the multiplier. This chapter will also discuss in a preliminary manner the effects of changes in investment on national income and the stability of the private sector.

Chapter 10 will consider the evidence on instability in the economy, including a review of the evidence on the timing and severity of business cycle fluctuations in the U.S. and Canadian economies. The role of lags in a number of key economic sectors and processes will be introduced, together with the influence of unanticipated shocks from outside the private sector.

# 7

## The Demand Side: An Overview

After reading this chapter, you should understand:

1. That the general priority of the classical economists was understanding the growth in the long-term potential supply of the economy (to put their ideas into modern terminology).
2. An important theme from J. B. Say and other classical economists that technological change does not lead to a persistent increase in unemployment for the economy as a whole or for a majority of the individual industries.
3. A simplified theory of aggregate demand, which was macroeconomists' primary area of interest for many decades.

A key issue of demand-side economics is studying how the personal sector responds to higher real income in terms of consumer expenditures on goods and services. The subject of **consumer expenditures on goods and services** covers current expenditures on all goods (both durables and nondurables) and services. Durables include such items as new cars, refrigerators, television sets, and personal computers, while nondurables include such items as bread, milk, fresh vegetables, and clothing. Services consist of such things as laundry and dry cleaning services, residential rent, beauty parlours and barber shops, and financial services. Consumer expenditure on goods and services is the most important demand sector in the economy. These expenditures amount to about 60 percent of gross domestic product in Canada in recent decades. The proportion was even higher in the 1950s and 1960s. Similar high proportions prevail in all the major industrialized countries.

## 7–1 THE CLASSICAL VIEW

Classical economists' interest in what we would now term macro-economics concerned the performance of national economies over long historical periods and the reasons for the persistent differences in nations' real income. Thus, classical economists were principally interested in the longer-term developments on the supply side that were discussed with contemporary economic methods in Chapters 4, 5, and 6. The classical economist who discussed the relationship between supply and demand most fully was J. B. Say.

Jean-Baptiste Say published his most celebrated writing, *Traité d'économie politique,* in 1803. Although Say made a number of contributions to economic theory, for our purposes, we will emphasize his *loi des débouchés,* or law of markets, which has come to be known as Say's Law. He wrote, "It is production which opens a demand for products."[1] This phrase is widely summarized as "supply creates its own demand." Products "can never be too abundant, since some provide the means of purchasing the others."[2]

This theme had also been present in Adam Smith's *The Wealth of Nations* when Smith stated that savings are always invested and spent. James Mill was influenced by Say and had a similar idea which appeared in his major work *Elements of Political Economy,* published in 1848. He expressed the idea that production generates purchasing power of a comparable amount. In simple terms, the more an economy produces, the more it has the means to consume. Moreover, Mill stated that in total it is always possible to sell total output at cost-covering prices for the economy as a whole. These early economists rejected the idea that increased production would lead to unemployment, an issue that continues to generate concern in the popular press.

## 7–2 TECHNOLOGICAL CHANGE AND UNEMPLOYMENT

The idea that increased capital equipment and technological change lead to unemployment has been around for a long time. The most widely publicized illustration was the Luddites in the early part of the 19th century. This group of masked roving workmen operated at night, destroying textile machinery in the textile cities of England. The group was named after a leader Ned Ludd, who may have been a mythical or imaginary rather than actual person. The Luddites assumed that the new machinery installed in textile plants would lead to widespread unemployment. Long before, in the Middle Ages, workers opposed the introduction of the wheelbarrow to move bricks around at construction sites. The word *sabotage* comes from the French and Belgian word *sabot* or wooden shoe, which workmen would on occasion drop into the machinery to disrupt production. The basic concern in all these cases was that new capital and new technology would lead to a loss of jobs. Such concerns tend to appear more frequently during recessions, especially if they are severe.

We have examined the importance of technological change on potential output on the supply side. Now let's examine the impact of technological change on the demand side. For example, there was a fourfold increase in real GDP per capita in Canada from the late 1920s to the mid-1980s; however, there was also a fourfold increase in real consumption per capita over the same period. This increase is what you would expect when personal income and personal consumption are a dominant part of total output. Increased productivity need not lead to an increase in unemployment for the economy as a whole, and increases in unemployment result from quite different economic and social factors.

It is clear from the historical evidence that periods of unemployment tend to occur during business cycle recessions when productivity increases typically *slow down*, rather than during business cycle expansions when productivity increases are more vigorous. High rates of unemployment typically occur during periods of slow productivity increase rather than fast — the exact opposite of the implications suggested by a number of newspaper articles during the early part of the 1980s. The common problem in these stories is the tendency to overlook the important positive contribution to the demand side of productivity growth from the supply side for the economy as a whole. These stories seem to have popular appeal even though they are not based on evidence or on a tested body of theory.

Japan's postwar experience provides further evidence that economic growth, technological change, and low unemployment can occur together. Economic growth and technological change have taken place there at a more rapid rate than in any of the countries in North America and Europe. During the length of time it has taken for real GDP per capita to double in North America, the Japanese have experienced roughly an eightfold increase (with a doubling in real GDP per capita every eight years between 1950 and the mid-1970s). The increase in consumption and other demand sectors in Japan has been roughly in line with the increase in supply. The unemployment rate in Japan has been consistently below North American levels (based on comparable definitions of unemployment and the labour force).

We might ask whether technological changes could lead to employment reductions and unemployment at the industry level, even if this does not happen for the economy as a whole. This phenomenon could occur when there are significant differences from one industry to another in the rate of technological change or the rate of change in output per hour. Differences in the rate of change in output per hour are reflected in changes in relative costs and prices. Industries with *high* rates of productivity growth tend to experience relative *declines* in the costs and prices of their products. W. E. G. Salter has made one of the few studies of the relationships between productivity growth and the distribution of employment and output by industry in the United States. He found that the lower prices for products with high productivity increases tend to be reflected in *higher* levels of employment and output rather than reduced employment, as so much current public discussion seems to assume. A quotation illustrates Salter's conclusions:

> Industries which have achieved substantial increase in output per head have, in general, been successful in other respects: their costs have risen the least, the relative prices of their products have fallen, output has expanded greatly, and in most cases employment has increased by more than the average. On the other hand, industries with small increases in output per head are generally declining industries — at least in relative terms. Their costs and selling prices have risen the most, output has increased much less than average (or even fallen), and increases in employment are below average.[3]

Although evidence suggests that high rates of productivity at the industry level lead to increases in employment in a majority of the individual industries, there can be exceptions.

The introduction of the factory system using power-driven machinery into the British cotton textile industry between 1770 and 1850 was one of the most important technological developments of the past few centuries. Hand-spinning in India in the 18th century was a cottage industry. It required more than 50,000 operator hours of labour per hundred pounds of cotton. Crompton's mule required water or steam power and thus production was centralized in factories. Labour requirements were reduced to about 2,000 hours per 100 pounds of cotton by 1780. Automatic mules required only about 135 operator hours for the same input of cotton. In England, increased production and export made possible by cost reductions in the spinning of cotton thread led to increased employment in the weaving of the thread into cloth. In India, however, there was a loss of livelihood for many thousands, resulting in poverty, political reaction, and eventually the drive to independence. Gandhi made hand-spinning the symbol of his crusade.

Technological changes took place in weaving also. Power looms replaced hand looms with a resultant eightfold increase in output per worker and higher-quality, more regular cotton cloth. Real wages of hand loom weavers (one of the highest-paid British occupations in the early years of the 19th century) fell in the early decades of that century. Employment in handloom weaving in homes dropped so dramatically in the second quarter of the 19th century that it could not be offset by increased employment in power weaving in factories. Both employment and real wages fell with the technological changes in the British cotton textile industry. And both the geographic location of production and the demand for skills changed too.

This example illustrates the possibility that technological change can have adverse effects on specific occupations and industries. These changes led to declines in relative prices of cotton textiles and increases in consumers' real incomes. Consumers gained more from the new technology than workers in the industry that used the new technology. Adjustment problems in real incomes and employment were more severe when the work force lived in areas lacking other employment opportunities.[4]

Another important and more current example is the situation in agriculture in this century. Increases in productivity have been above the average for the economy as a whole for much of the present century in both the United States and Canada, but significant reductions in employment have now taken place. Agriculture employed about 45 percent of the Canadian labour force at the start of the present century. But the number of workers employed in agriculture has dropped about 60 percent since 1946 while real GDP per person has increased to almost five times the level that it was at the start of the century. During the 1980s, agricultural output has been almost double the level of the late 1940s, but it has been produced by only a fraction of the number of farmers. Increases in output per person have been higher in agriculture than in the commercial nonagricultural industries for decades, but there has been no comparable increase on the demand side in Canada and elsewhere to match the increase in the supply side. What has happened is that there has been a very low income elasticity of demand for agricultural products, as reflected in the fact that the consumption of food on a per capita basis (as measured both by pounds of food or consumption of total calories) has been roughly unchanged since before World War I until well into the 1980s. The price elasticity of the demand for agricultural products has also been low. So declines in the prices of agricultural products relative to nonagricultural products have not led to comparable increases in consumption of agricultural products.

**Price elasticity** refers to the percentage change in purchases for a small percentage change in price, a concept you will have encountered before in your microeconomics course. **Income elasticity** is a similar concept, referring to the percentage change in purchases for a small percentage change in incomes. The price elasticity is negative, and the income elasticity is normally positive. The changes in national income and agricultural prices have led to persistently lower incomes in agriculture than in the nonagricultural sectors, and a significant net outward movement of people from agriculture. These problems arise primarily because of the low income and price elasticities on the demand side, rather than the rapid productivity increases on the supply side.

The 19th-century cotton textile industry and the 20th-century developments in agriculture are exceptions. In a typical situation, high productivity increases are associated with increased employment at the industry level rather than declines.

## 7–3 AN OVERVIEW OF THE THEORY OF AGGREGATE DEMAND

The classical economists were primarily interested in explaining the longer-term changes in potential output and the reasons for persisting real income differences between countries. They recognized that economic crises, financial panics, and business cycles occurred, but these developments and problems were not the centre of their interests or their writings.

The severity and duration of the depression of the 1930s in North America (and similar problems in Europe) led to a major shift in emphasis of a high proportion of the economists in the industrialized countries with an interest in macroeconomics. A central part of that shift was a refocussing of interests of macroeconomists from the longer-term supply developments in the economy (the types of topics covered in Part Two using contemporary theory and evidence) to the shorter-term developments on the demand side. This shift in the area of interest was reflected in the introduction of new theoretical tools that continue to play a central part in the analytical framework used by both academic and applied economists up to the present day. This theory will receive a major emphasis in the balance of the book, with recognition of some differences in interpretation (some major and some minor) that continue to exist within the mainstream of economic thinking.

The way to look at the shift in emphasis that we are now beginning is to recognize that Part Two was dealing with the longer-term trends while we will now try to explain the central causal factors in the shorter-term fluctuations around potential output. Since 1945, such business cycles have averaged about 56 months in the United States, longer than the average cycle before World War I. These shorter-term periods require that economists study monthly and quarterly series to detect the ebbs and flows in the economic system, especially when some of the recessions since World War II have been so short and mild.

This shift in interest was reflected in new economic tools to analyze and predict the performance of the economy over time and to assess the appropriate public policies to deal with such changes. This section will provide an overview of that theory so that you can see the central elements. Later chapters in Part Three will develop the theory and the related evidence for individual areas of demand more fully.

The theory will be developed in a manner similar to what you have already experienced in microeconomics, namely, what is called a partial equilibrium approach. **Partial equilibrium** involves concentrating on one narrow and specific part of the economy at a time and ignoring the other parts of the economy for the time being.

At this stage in the text, we will be following this standard approach to examine three other economic issues. First, we will deal with a simplified situation of a closed economy and no government. This will permit us to see the essential minimum elements of the theory as it relates to the private sector. Later parts of the text will introduce the role of government and the international aspects (which you all recognize as being crucial for Canada).

Second, we will deal with the *real* parts of the economy but ignore any changes in the general price level. The **real parts** of the economy refer to the constant-dollar estimates of gross domestic product that were defined and explained in Chapter 2. Such an approach will permit us to study these demand aspects of the economy without the additional complexity of changes in the general price level. (We will relax this limiting assumption in Part Four.)

Third, we will concentrate on a model in which there is no change in technology, and the supply of labour (i.e., the total labour force) and the supply of capital are kept fixed. In other words, all the factors identified as important in the determination of potential output in Part Two will now be ignored.

These three important abstractions will permit us to concentrate on two major groups of participants in the economic process—namely, business units and households. These components have already been introduced in the circular-flow diagrams in Chapter 2. The business units hire factors of production (principally labour of all kinds— blue-collar, white-collar, full-time, part-time, both male and female) and use these factors in the production of business services. The products produced include manufactured products (television sets, computers, clothes, and processed food), fresh fruit and vegetables, and the whole range of personal services (haircuts and styling, insurance, legal services, entertainment, and air travel). These goods and services are then purchased by households and paid for out of the incomes they receive, reflecting their individual tastes and preferences. Such household expenditures are termed personal expenditures on consumer goods and services, a major part of GDP (as illustrated in Chapter 2 and again at the start of the current chapter).

A further important expenditure sector in this simplified model is business investment, consisting of nonresidential construction, machinery, and equipment (which would be a part of the stock of capital used by businesses in the production of goods and services). Another form of business investment is residential construction, consisting of owner-occupied homes, condominiums, and apartments.

The income received by households is primarily spent on consumer goods and services, but part of it is saved. In some instances, the personal sector might use their savings by directly investing them in a newly constructed, owner-occupied home or condominium, or in a new tractor or combine for the family farm. In other situations, they might save in financial assets (deposited with a bank or other financial institution, or by buying shares or bonds in a company), thus facilitating a corporation's investment in new machinery or a retail outlet in a shopping centre.

Thus far we have simplified a complex situation by assuming that the savings and investment decisions are done independently by different institutions, with the financial system, in effect, providing a matching of the savings and investing by different final borrowers and lenders. A company that puts up a new building in a shopping centre makes the decision to construct new physical assets. That investment may be partly financed by a bank loan, and that bank loan may be made possible by many individual families leaving individually small accounts on deposit with the bank. Many individuals and financial institutions may be involved in the indirect financing of that business investment, and the individual depositors would not be aware of the total process. The detailed sources of financing of individual projects cannot be identified from the available statistics.

In some instances, an established company can finance a new project from undistributed corporate profits and the associated cash flow. **Undistributed corporate profits** are the net profits of the company after paying taxes and any dividends to shareholders. In the situation described above, the saving and the investment decisions are done simultaneously by the same business unit. During the earlier post-war years, undistributed corporate profits could finance an important part of the post-war investment done by businesses in North America. However, the proportion financed this way through internal funds has fallen, and companies have had to finance a higher proportion of new investment by borrowing from the capital market. **Capital market** refers to the raising of funds by selling stocks and bonds through the specialized financial institutions that provide such services. A corporation investing in new plant equipment may also borrow from banks and other financial institutions.

Another situation in which the investing and the saving decision are made by the same economic organization occurs when a family has a new house built and puts up a down payment as part of their own equity in a new owner-occupied home. However, a major part of new residential construction is financed by new mortgages, and the saving decisions by many individual households are involved indirectly in the financing of residential construction.

The theory of aggregate demand that has emerged from the Keynesian contribution emphasizes the stability of the consumer and the key impact of an unstable and volatile level of business investment in leading to the fluctuations in national income that were described in Chapter 3. This section will provide a graphical introduction to the theory of aggregate demand that will be discussed in more detail in subsequent chapters.

The basic model that we will be describing consists initially of only investment and consumption as the two main sources of demand, which in total add up to aggregate demand for the economy as a whole. We defined both consumption and investment expenditures in Chapter 2, with emphasis on how they were measured after the period had passed. Our interest in this and the next two chapters is rather on how their levels are determined.

We will start with the determinants of consumption, the most important single component of aggregate demand. In Keynesian theory, the basic model emphasized the key role of current income to the household sector in a particular year as the determinant of consumption in the same period. This theory played down the role of changes in interest rates or the influence of wealth in the determination of current consumption. Time series data on current consumption (in constant prices) and personal disposable income in real terms (i.e., deflated by an appropriate price deflator) would look as depicted in Figure 7–1. Disposable income (the independent variable) is shown on the horizontal axis, and consumption expenditure (the dependent variable) is shown on the vertical axis. Observations for individual years are scattered in a random fashion along the line $CC$ in Figure 7–1, which illustrates the line of best fit in a linear regression. For an income level $OA$ on the horizontal axis, the corresponding consumption level would be $AB$ (reading vertically). For a higher level of personal disposable income $OD$, the corresponding level of consumption would be $DE$. The increase in consumption would be $EF$, for an increase in personal disposable income $AD$ (which equals $BF$ as these two points are directly above the points $AD$ on the horizontal axis). The **marginal propensity to consume** is the relative change in consumption compared to a change in disposable income. In Figure 7–1, the marginal propensity to consume is $EF/BF$.

The same diagram also shows the saving function. The **saving function** is the change in saving for a given change in disposable income, and its value falls between 0 and 1. On Figure 7–1, saving is the vertical distance between consumption and the 45-degree line shown on the

**FIGURE 7–1** The Consumption Function

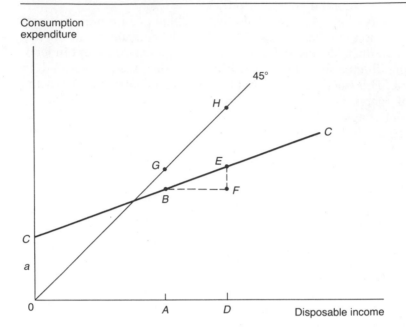

chart. With an income level $OA$, $BG$ would be saved, while at an income level $OD$, $EH$ would be saved. At low levels of disposable income, consumption exceeds income, meaning that dissavings would be occurring at such low levels of disposable income. Dissavings occur when individuals run down their existing assets or borrow. However, neither of these options would be available to the chronically poor.

Figure 7–1 shows the consumption function as a straight line. In these circumstances, the marginal propensity to consume ($EF/BF$, for example) is a constant and the same at both high and low levels of personal disposable income. However, the average propensity to consume ($AB/AG$ or $DE/DH$) would vary, being equal to unity (1) at the crossover point of $CC$ with the 45-degree line (where $C = Y_D$) and in excess of 1 at low-income levels to the left of the crossover line.

The consumption function is a necessary but insufficient amount of information to determine the level of aggregate demand. It is also necessary to introduce business investment to provide a complete explanation. In mathematical terms, the consumption function consists of two independent variables (consumption and disposable income), but that is only one mathematical equation.

Suppose that the survey of business investment intentions (done twice a year by the federal government in Canada) indicated that the level of business investment was going to be $I$ (the distance shown on the vertical axis in Figure 7–2). Once the level of business investment in a given year was determined, the equilibrium level of national income could be determined. The **equilibrium level of national income** is a level of national income that, if attained, could be maintained without any unintended building up or running down of business inventory. In equilibrium, the level of personal savings in the personal sector just equals the amount of investment done by business units that is injected back into demand. This relationship is shown in Figure 7–3 by adding the amount of investment anticipated as shown in Figure 7–2 to $a$ (the vertical distance on the $X$ axis) where the consumption function would intersect the $X$ axis if the straight-line regression through the observed points was extended back to the $X$ axis. A new line of aggregate demand $(C + I)$ would cut the 45-degree line at $G$. At this point, personal savings $(EG)$ just equals business investment, and the new equilibrium level of national income is $OD$. Only at this point does business investment equal personal savings, leaving consumption in line with the estimated underlying consumption function.

This theoretical framework implies that it is the shifts in investment that create the instability in aggregate demand. Psychological factors and changes in business attitudes could be important in the variability in business investment, and the resulting fluctuations in national income raise the possibility of government acting to play a contracyclical role (by operating against the cyclical tendencies in the private sector)

---

**FIGURE 7–2**  Investment at a Constant Level

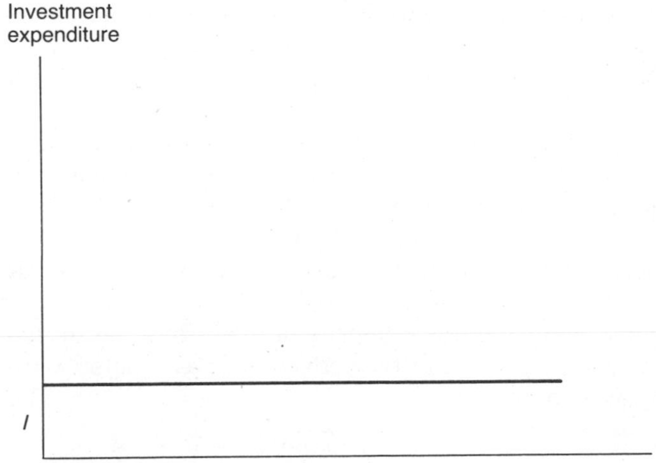

---

Investment
expenditure

**FIGURE 7–3**   Equilibrium Level of Investment and Consumption

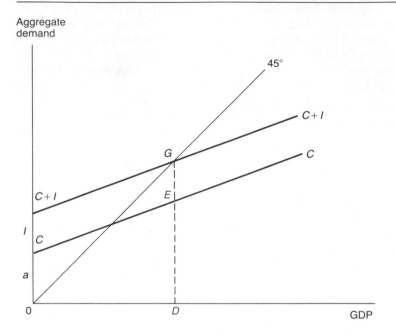

in offsetting the fluctuations in private demand in order to maintain greater stability in national income.

## SUMMARY

The classical economists were primarily interested in the determinants of longer-term potential output and were less interested in the determinants of actual output (to use contemporary terminology). They also recognized that increases in potential output permit increased actual demand for that output.

The evidence suggests that high rates of productivity increase occur during periods of low unemployment and that significant increases in demand occur, and are indeed made possible, by increases in supply. Japan provides interesting and important evidence that economic growth, technological change, and low unemployment can occur together.

This tendency also shows up in a majority of the individual industries, where above average productivity increases are associated with above average increases in employment.

The English textile industry during the Industrial Revolution and agriculture are examples of the exceptions to that general tendency, but these exceptions can be explained.

The chapter also introduced the concepts of consumption, savings and investment, and how the level of investment and the consumption function provided sufficient information to determine the equilibrium level of national income in that simplified but basic model of the demand side of the economy.

The next three chapters in Part Three will be devoted to further extensions and development of this basic model and to testing the reliability of the predictions that can be and have been made of models of this type. Later parts of the book will further extend the basic model to deal with price changes, the role of government, and the interdependence with the rest of the world, topics which have been set aside by assumption in Section 7–3.

## NOTES

1. Jean-Baptiste Say, *A Treatise on Political Economy or The Production, Distribution and Consumption of Wealth*, trans. C. R. Prinsep (Philadelphia: Claxton, Remsen, and Haffelfinger, 1880; reprint, New York: Augustus M. Kelley, Bookseller, 1964), p. 133.

2. Quoted in Thomas Sowell, *Say's Law: An Historical Analysis* (Princeton, N.J.: Princeton University Press, 1972), p. 20.

3. W. E. G. Salter, *Productivity and Technological Change* (Cambridge, Mass.: Cambridge University Press, 1972), p. 20.

4. This illustration draws on Robert C. Allen, "The Impact of Technical Change on Employment, Wages, and the Distribution of Skills: A Historical Perspective," in *Adapting to Change: Labour Market Adjustment in Canada*, W. Craig Riddell (Toronto: University of Toronto Press, 1986), Collected Research Studies, Royal Commission on the Economic Union and Development Prospects for Canada, vol. 18, pp. 82–88.

# 8

## Consumption

In the last chapter, we provided an overview of the theory of aggregate demand. This chapter will develop the theory and evidence on one particular demand sector of that complete system — namely, consumption and its major determinants.

After reading this chapter, you should understand:

1. The contribution made by the late Lord John Maynard Keynes to the discussion of the determinants of consumption with his emphasis on current income as the key determinant.
2. The extent to which the early evidence on consumption and savings raised questions about the stability and adequacy of the initial theory.
3. How the permanent-income hypothesis and the life-cycle hypothesis introduced new ideas that were more consistent with the available evidence.
4. The extent to which factors in addition to income, such as wealth, interest rates, and the distribution of personal income, affect consumption.

## 8–1 KEYNES'S *GENERAL THEORY*

John Maynard Keynes (1883–1946) was an influential economist, who spent most of his adult life teaching economics at Cambridge University in the United Kingdom. He was the principal representative of the Treasury at the Paris Peace Conference after World War I and criticized the size of reparations imposed on Germany. Most of his writings related to monetary theory and policy. His teaching was interspersed with time spent advising on public policy. He was a member of the Macmillan Committee on Finance and Industry (1930), an adviser in

Treasury during World War II, and an active participant at the 1944 **Bretton Woods Conference** that established the International Monetary Fund (which acts as a co-ordinating body for international financial questions for the participating governments). He was thus actively involved in the development and application of macroeconomic theory to the analysis and solution of practical problems of public policy.

John Maynard Keynes contributed to a major shift in the emphasis in macroeconomics away from the long-term supply side, which had dominated the interests of economists for centuries, toward an emphasis on the short-term demand side. His book *The General Theory of Employment, Interest, and Money* published in 1936 (after some half-dozen years of high unemployment and economic slack in the United States, Canada, and a number of the European economies) explicitly assumed no change in technology and a fixed stock of capital in the short run. He also developed the basic core theory on the assumption of a closed economy with no government receipts or expenditures, placing emphasis on the demand-side developments for the private sector. The resulting simplified model (as summarized in Section 7–3) emphasizes the fluctuations in private investment in combination with a stable consumption function as key in the determination of actual output in the private sector.

Subsequent work by a wide range of economists in following decades extended the assumptions in *The General Theory* to cover the international dimensions of demand instability and the role of government to offset the instability in the private sector which was a central tenet of Keynes's contribution.

His basic logic in *The General Theory* argued that consumption responded in a stable manner to changes in investment or other sources of instability on the demand side. A key part of his thinking was that the marginal propensity to consume was positive but less than unity (1). His central explanation was as follows:

> The fundamental psychological law ... is that men are disposed, as a rule and on the average, to increase their consumption as their income increases, but not by as much as the increase in their income.[1]

The **consumption function** is a schedule showing the relationship between aggregate consumption expenditures and income. The relationship is positive, meaning that a higher level of personal disposable income (for example) would be reflected in a higher level of consumption. The general form of the consumption function followed by most economists in the Keynesian tradition specifies:

$$C = a + bY \qquad\qquad (8\text{–}1)$$

where

$C$ = total consumption in a given year
$Y$ = total income in that year
$b$ = the marginal propensity to consume (the proportion
  of an increase in the income that is consumed)
$a$ = the distance on the vertical axis above the origin

Economists have made many estimates of relationships using this equation over various time periods since then and for many different countries. Those made for the periods covering the severe depressions of the 1930s tended to show a significant positive value for $a$, and the relationship was fairly close to linear because of the difference between a stable marginal propensity to consume and the average propensity to consume for an individual year. For low values of income (such as for the 1930s), there could be net dissavings for the economy as a whole or for the personal sector in particular. **Dissavings** occur when the personal sector as a whole spends more on consumption in a given year than it receives as income (for instance, personal disposable income after direct taxes and transfers). This comes about when people with existing assets sell some of them to maintain a level of consumption closer to the style to which they had been accustomed. For these years, the average saving ratio was negative, and average consumption exceeded income. On the other hand, at high levels of income, the average savings ratio increases, and the average consumption ratio declines, even when the marginal propensity to consume is a constant. (This topic was introduced in Section 7–3 and Figure 7–1. This discussion is designed to amplify and reinforce the topic. The consumption function shown in Figure 8–1 is similar to Figure 7–1 in the last chapter, which explained the consumption function and the marginal propensity to consume.)

The saving function is shown in Figure 8–2, which can be derived from Figure 8–1 above it. A 45-degree line has been drawn through the origin, and all points on that line are equidistant from both the vertical and horizontal axes. At point $B$ (the break-even point), consumption equals income, and savings are 0. At point $A$ (to the left of $B$), consumption is greater than disposable income, and savings are negative. At point $C$ (to the right of $B$), consumption is less than disposable income, and savings are larger at higher levels of personal disposable income (both in total and as a percentage of personal disposable income).

The saving function can be derived from the consumption function, as consumption plus savings are defined to be always equal to unity. Similarly the **marginal propensity to save** is the proportion of an in-

**FIGURE 8–1**   Illustrative Consumption Function (millions of dollars at constant prices)

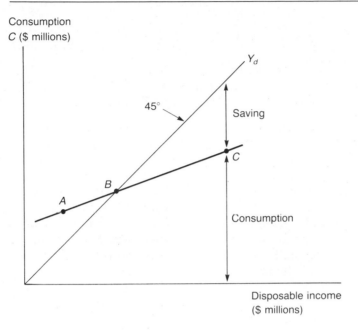

**FIGURE 8–2**   Illustrative Saving Function (millions of dollars at constant prices)

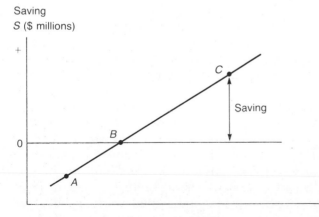

crease in personal disposable income that is saved. In mathematical notation:

$$MPS \ = \ \frac{\Delta S}{\Delta Y_d} \tag{8–2}$$

where

$MPS$ = the marginal propensity to save
  $S$ = the total amount of personal savings
  $Y_d$ = personal disposable income (as defined in Chapter 2).

This can be seen in Figure 8–2.

Both the marginal propensity to consume and the marginal propensity to save are shown as straight lines, which means that both are constant proportions of the *changes* in personal disposable income. However, the *average* portion of consumption to personal disposable income falls as you move to higher income levels, and the average ratio of savings to personal disposable income increases at higher income levels. At income levels to the left of B, personal savings are negative (i.e., dissaving occurs), and the consumption ratio to personal disposable income is greater than unity. Thus, the average ratio of consumption and savings to personal disposable income varies over different levels of income even though both the marginal propensity to consume and the marginal propensity to save is constant.

## 8–2 EARLY EMPIRICAL EVIDENCE

In light of the consumption function's importance to Keynesian theory, a number of estimates of the consumption function were produced by his followers. This was partly made possible by the production of national income estimates for a number of the major industrialized countries beginning in the late 1930s. The construction of these accounts was influenced by and certainly encouraged by *The General Theory* itself. This interest in the national accounts was also accelerated by World War II and the recognition that the National Accounts and the emphasis on demand-side analysis could also be applied to the problems of war finance.

During World War II, personal savings zoomed up, based on high levels of personal income made possible by increased government expenditures associated with the war effort. Expenditures were limited by the incomplete availability of some items of consumer expenditure (including cars and gasoline) and rationing of some food items. The personal sector held a part of that increased savings in the form of Victory Bonds. It was recognized that those high wartime levels of personal savings were not sustainable, so most estimates of the consumption function made in the immediate postwar years usually excluded the wartime experience. However, estimates of the consumption function from the late 1920s and 1930s experience ended up showing rather low values of the marginal propensity to consume and an estimate of $a$ (the vertical intercept on the X axis of Figure 8–1) that was significantly different from 0. This difference implied that an increase in personal disposable income would be reflected in a large absolute increase in the savings ratio and in total savings. Consumption expenditures would also grow, but they would tend to become a smaller percentage of personal disposable income.

The evidence for Canada for the years 1926 to 1939 can be seen in Figure 8–3, which shows that personal savings were negative in such

**FIGURE 8–3**   The Consumption Function, Canada, 1926–1939 (millions of dollars at 1971 prices)

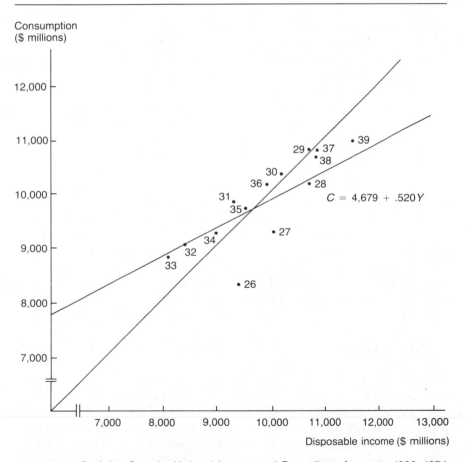

SOURCE: Statistics Canada, *National Income and Expenditure Accounts, 1926–1974* (Ottawa: Information Canada, 1976), pp. 8–11.

severe depression years as 1932, 1933, and 1934. The estimate of the marginal propensity to consume was .52, implying that for an *increase* in personal disposable income, only 52 percent of that increase would be spent on consumption, and 48 percent would go into personal savings — a relatively flat consumption function for that period.

When these initial estimates of the consumption function based on the prewar years were extrapolated to the postwar period, they implied quite high savings rates. It was widely expected that once government war expenditures were sharply curtailed after the cessation of hostilities in both Europe and the Far East, a significant depression would ensue. It was not anticipated that private investment could recover enough to maintain a high level of employment.[2]

Some Keynesians also expected that the U.S. economy would return to a period of secular stagnation comparable to that experienced during the 1930s. **Secular stagnation** is the hypothesis that the North American economy would return to a period of persisting inadequate private investment and high personal savings at the end of World War II. Many economists were convinced that there would not be much need for additional accumulation of capital at the end of the war, while savings would rise even faster than income, based on the evidence on consumption and savings relationships of the 1920s and 1930s. The growth in savings would outstrip the "need" for capital, and the economies would return to the stagnation of the 1930s. These views of the "stagnationist" school, prominent in the 1940s and early 1950s, were popularized by Alvin H. Hansen, who thought that the opening of the western frontier in North America and the adoption of new technology had contributed to historical economic growth to a degree that he did not expect to see repeated after World War II.[3]

About the same time, Simon Kuznets completed a historical study of the U.S. national income. His data indicated that the savings rate was stable over many decades of historical experience. Edward F. Denison reached similar conclusions using later data for the United States. His conclusions have sometimes been referred to as "Denison's Law."[4] This evidence was inconsistent with the evidence that the savings rate varied over the business cycle, which was an important part of the early Keynesian thinking.

The marginal propensity to consume for the postwar years in Canada looks quite different than Figure 8–3. For the postwar years (1961 to 1985) the marginal propensity to consume is .73, significantly higher than the .52 estimated for the 1926 to 1939 period.

The failure of the initial postwar forecasts and the evidence of long-term stability in the savings rate led to a basic reexamination of the theory of the consumption function. If a theory led to incorrect predictions outside the range of the period for which it had been developed,

**FIGURE 8–4**  The Consumption Function, Canada, 1961–1985 (millions of dollars at 1981 prices)

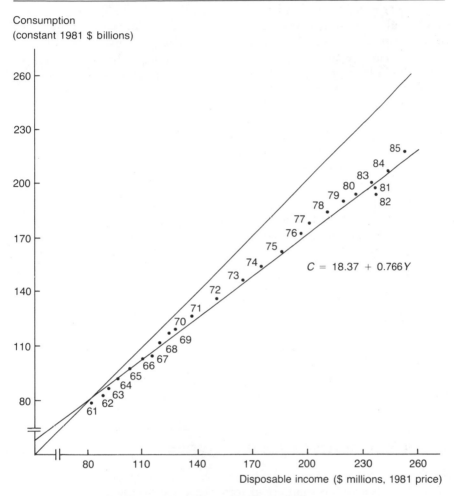

Consumption
(constant 1981 $ billions)

$C = 18.37 + 0.766Y$

Disposable income ($ millions, 1981 price)

SOURCE: Statistics Canada, CANSIM tapes, Sept. 1986.

it either had to be revised or an alternative theory had to be developed that could better describe developments. Several of these later developments will now be described.

## 8–3 THE PERMANENT-INCOME HYPOTHESIS

Milton Friedman provided a new interpretation that reconciled the long-term stability of the savings ratio with a decline in savings during business cycle recessions or depressions. He emphasized that annual data on income were a measure of short-term developments, but that people decided how much to spend (consume) based primarily on longer-term views about income, which he termed *permanent income*. During a recession, individuals could maintain their consumption levels by either depleting their existing assets or by borrowing. They could only borrow, of course, if they had good earnings prospects or assets and their incomes were low only temporarily. Some individuals, such as farmers, entrepreneurs, or authors, experience considerable year-to-year income variability.

How could individuals form a view about their permanent income? Friedman suggested that they would form their views about their permanent income levels on the basis of their own personal experience. This would be based on a weighted average of past income levels, with a heavier weight for the most recent years. If individuals experienced significant increases in their incomes on a long-term basis, they would revise their estimates of permanent income up significantly. On the other hand, if their income increases were modest, the estimates of permanent income would be changed only slightly. If their incomes dropped, and they expected to be reemployed soon, their estimates of permanent income might not be revised, and their consumption levels would be retained close to previous levels. In this and other areas, Friedman was rather skeptical that individuals could forecast their own future income with any degree of confidence and would thus adjust their views only on the basis of their own personal experience. This view has tended to be termed *adaptive expectations*, based on the individual's own learning.[5]

Such an interpretation reconciles the longer-term stability in the savings ratio with considerable variability during periods of recession or depression.

## 8–4 THE LIFE-CYCLE HYPOTHESIS

In the early 1950s, Franco Modigliani and a number of associates provided an alternative theoretical formulation to explain the long-term stability in the saving ratio and the shorter-term variation in the saving ratio during recessions and depressions. These studies emphasized the role of wealth in addition to income in the determination of annual (and quarterly) levels of consumption. By wealth they meant the level of personal income over a lifetime, physical wealth (owner-occupied homes or physical facilities in a business or farm), and financial assets (savings in pension schemes, money, bonds, and stocks after adjustment for price changes).

In the simplest version of the life-cycle hypothesis, it was assumed that consumption would be relatively constant over a person's lifetime.

However, income was earned over a person's working life until retirement, but then declined. This implied a growth in people's (or family) wealth during their working life and dissaving on retirement as they maintained consumption by depleting their accumulated assets. Such a framework suggests a fairly constant rate of saving in the central age groups, but lower saving or even dissaving among the very young and retired persons. Income levels, rate of growth in income, length of working life, length of retirement, and age distribution of the population would thus all become relevant factors in analyzing consumption.[6]

This theory has some important implications for a growing economy. One is that productivity growth in an economy implies that younger people and families will have larger lifetime resources than older people. Their savings will be larger than the dissaving of the older retired individuals and families. When real incomes per capita double in 25 or 30 years (roughly the North American experience from 1950 to the early 1970s), younger people could receive lifetime incomes roughly double their parents' on average. They could buy televisions, freezers, cars, and homes much earlier in their careers than their parents and still have higher levels of savings.

This theory can also help explain the differences in saving rates between countries. Countries with low rates of growth in real per capita disposable income (such as the United States, Canada, and the United Kingdom) would have a much lower savings rate than the faster-growing countries such as Japan, France, West Germany, and Italy.[7]

Thus, the life-cycle hypothesis could reconcile the long-term stability of the saving rate with its cyclical instability, explain the patterns of savings and consumption over a person's lifetime, and throw light on the differences in saving rates between countries. It was thus richer in its implications and less inconsistent with some of the evidence than the simpler Keynesian consumption function out of which it developed. It also raised potential future problems of lower savings rates when the elderly become a higher proportion of the population, which is predicted for the end of the present century.

## 8–5 THE ROLE OF WEALTH AND INTEREST RATES

Both the permanent-income hypothesis and the life-cycle hypothesis put much more emphasis on all forms of wealth in the consumption and saving relationships and much less emphasis on quarterly and annual estimates of national and personal disposable income in real terms. Increases or decreases in income (or taxes) that were regarded as temporary and not likely to persist would not have as great an impact on consumption as changes in income that were expected to persist. Although this interpretation is plausible, it is not easy in practice to distinguish between temporary and permanent changes in income for individuals or the economy as a whole. Economists have struggled with how to measure such differences in practice for decades without developing procedures that would be satisfactory and fully accepted. For some questions and policy issues, this is not too serious, but for others it is.

Interest rates were not identified as a factor in the consumption and savings functions in Keynes's *General Theory.* Although interest rates can have some influence on some areas of consumption expenditures (such as cars and consumer durables), later research has been unable to find any significant impact of interest rates on aggregate consumption. Rising interest rates can lead to either larger or smaller savings depending on the motives of individuals and some of the underlying institutional behaviour characteristics of the economy. We will follow the widespread practice of ignoring any possible effects of interest rates on consumption, and most empirical work suggests this will not mislead us.

## 8–6 CROSS-SECTION EVIDENCE AND INCOME REDISTRIBUTION

Most of the empirical work on consumption and savings has used time-series data for individual countries. However, a number of countries have conducted surveys of the income, consumption, assets, and savings of families and individuals in individual income groups. These data can throw light on an additional dimension of theory and policy raised by *The General Theory.*

One portion of *The General Theory* suggests that fiscal policy can be used to encourage a more equal distribution in incomes, and such redistribution would increase the propensity to consume.[8] By transferring income from high-income consumers to lower-income consumers, the aggregate level of consumption would increase and the level of savings would decrease out of the same level of total income after taxes, making the distribution of income a further necessary variable to analyze in predicting consumption. The issues of income redistribution, progressive taxation, and social security become important topics for macro policy.

A consumption function for different income groups can be prepared similar to that shown from time-series data in Figure 8–1 earlier in this chapter. Figure 8–5 is based on the assumption that the marginal propensity to consume can be represented by a straight line, indicating that the marginal propensity to consume by high-income and low-income individuals is the same and that income redistribution would

**FIGURE 8–5**   Consumption Function from Cross-Section Data

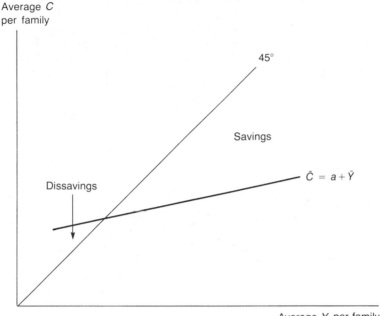

not affect total consumption and savings out of a given level of personal disposable income. On the other hand, a downward-curving line at higher-income levels would indicate that higher-income groups had a higher marginal propensity to save as well as a higher average saving ratio. Under these circumstances, income redistribution from high-income to low-income groups would reduce total savings and increase total consumption out of a given personal disposable income.

A number of studies have explored the linearity of the consumption function over the last four decades, particularly the possibility that the consumption function would curve downward at higher income levels. One of the earliest studies, conducted by Harold Lubell, examined the effects of income redistribution on consumption.[9] He concluded that income redistribution would not greatly change the size of con-sumption and savings and would thus not affect aggregate demand.

A. S. Blinder examined U.S. time-series data for the years 1947 to 1972 with income and consumption data broken down into quintiles. He concluded that "equalizing the income distribution will either have no bearing on or (slightly) reduce aggregate consumption". Further studies have examined the data on income distribution across countries

---

**TABLE 8–1**   Average Income after Direct Taxes and Average
Consumption Expenditures for All Families and
Unattached Individuals (Canada, 1982)

---

| Income Bracket | Average Income | Average Consumption Expenditure |
|---|---|---|
| 0–9,999 | 7165.3 | 7451.6 |
| 10,000–14,999 | 12,289.2 | 11,676.5 |
| 15,000–19,999 | 16,352.2 | 15,257.1 |
| 20,000–24,999 | 20,073.5 | 17,806.8 |
| 25,000–29,999 | 23,762.9 | 20,475.3 |
| 30,000–34,999 | 27,704.1 | 23,140.6 |
| 35,000–39,999 | 31,497.9 | 25,373.2 |
| 40,000–49,999 | 36,808.3 | 28,754.6 |
| 50,000+ | 53,090.9 | 36,857.8 |

---

SOURCE: Statistics Canada, *Family Expenditures in Canada, 1982* (Ottawa: Ministry of Supply and Services, 1985), pp. 2.8 and 2.9.

in a number of developed and developing countries, although some of the results are contradictory or not statistically significant.[10]

The data for Canada for nine income classes for disposable income and consumption are shown in Table 8–1.

A number of regressions were done by the author on this Canadian data, and the results suggest that income redistribution would have only a minor effect on the levels of consumption and savings out of a given level of personal disposable income. These results for Canada were thus similar to the earlier studies by Lubell and Blinder.

There may be some broader social goals that can be achieved by income redistribution, but you should not expect to find any significant influence on the level of aggregate demand from income redistribution. In the light of this evidence, we can ignore the effects of income redistribution on the aggregate consumption function.

## SUMMARY

Keynes made a stable consumption function and a stable marginal propensity to consume a key part of *The General Theory*. However, the size of the marginal propensity to consume was lower for the 1930s than for the postwar years, and the possibility of the continuation of a high rate of unemployment at the end of World War II did not materialize.

The permanent-income hypothesis and the life-cycle hypothesis fitted the interwar and postwar experience in a more satisfactory manner than the initial simpler formulations.

Other variables, such as interest rates and the distribution of income, are not important factors in the total level of consumption and savings.

## NOTES

1. John Maynard Keynes, *The General Theory of Employment, Interest and Money* (New York: Macmillan, 1936), Book III.

2. L. R. Klein, "A Post Mortem on Transition Predictions of National Product," *Journal of Political Economy*, August 1946, pp. 289–308; and J. R. Beattie "Some Aspects of the Problem of Full Employment," *Canadian Journal of Economics and Political Science*, 1944, pp. 328–42.

3. Alvin H. Hansen, "Economic Progress and Declining Population Growth," *American Economic Review*, 1939, reprinted in *Readings in Business Cycle Theory*, (Philadelphia: Blakiston, 1944), pp. 366–84.

4. Simon Kuznets, *National Income and Its Composition* (New York: National Bureau of Economic Research, 1941); Paul A. David and John L. Scadding, "Private Savings: Ultrarationality, Aggregation, and 'Denison's Law,' " *Journal of Political Economy* 82 (March/April 1974).

5. Milton Friedman, *A Theory of the Consumption Function* (Princeton, N.J.: Princeton University Press, 1957).

6. For convenient recent summary of this literature, see Franco Modigliani, "Life Cycle, Individual Thrift, and the Wealth of Nations," *American Economic Review*, June 1986, pp. 297–313. This article was based on the author's lecture when he received the Nobel Prize in Economics.

7. Ibid., pp. 302–3.

8. Keynes, *General Theory*, p. 95.

9. Harold Lubell, "Effects of Redistribution of Income on Consumers' Expenditures," *American Economic Review*, 1947, pp. 163 and 169.

10. A. S. Blinder, "Distribution Effects and the Aggregate Consumption to Function," *Journal of Political Economy*, 1975, pp. 447–75; P. A. Della Valle and N. Oguchi, "Distribution, The Aggregate Consumption Function, and the Level of Economic Development: Some Cross Country Results," *Journal of Political Economy*, December 1976, pp. 1325–34; and P. Musgrove, "Income Distribution and the Aggregate Consumption Function," *Journal of Political Economy*, June 1980, pp. 504–25.

# 9

# Investment and the Multiplier

After reading this chapter, you should understand:

1. The general determinants of business investment spending.
2. The role of changes in interest rates on the extent of change in both business and housing investment.
3. How changes in income affect business investment.
4. How changes in investment can have a multiplier effect on the equilibrium levels of national income, both in a simple model and a more realistic model including government and foreign transactions.
5. How quantitative econometric models are prepared.
6. That the results from such models indicate a high degree of stability in the modern economies.

The whole area of investment has received an increased amount of attention in economic theory, economic forecasting, and public policy in light of the contribution of John Maynard Keynes. He emphasized the changing attitudes in the business community and how such psychological attitudes could affect the community's willingness to expand capacity through additional investment.

This chapter emphasizes how changes in investment are determined and how such changes influence the overall level of demand and national income for the economy as a whole. This involves a shift in emphasis from Chapter 5 in Part Two, where we showed how changes in investment influenced the size of the capital stock, and thereby the supply of national output.

The areas of investment expenditures to be discussed in this chapter include gross private investment in plant, machinery, and equipment and housing (including individual owner-occupied homes, apartments, and condominiums). The concepts and their measurements were introduced in Chapter 2.

## 9–1 BUSINESS INVESTMENT — AN INTRODUCTION

Business investment will be dealt with first. There are three general factors that influence the level of gross private investment in a particular year. A key factor is the level of national income. Variations in the level of national income can have an important impact on the size of any gap between actual and potential national output (as defined and explained in Section 6–1). When the level of actual output is high and the gap between actual and potential output is small, many plants (especially in the commodity-producing industries such as manufacturing and the related transportation facilities of trucking and railway-freight business) operate at high rates of capacity. Some plants may have to introduce overtime or extra shifts to meet the strong demand. Such strong demand pressures (such as occurred during some of the years in the 1945–73 period when the gap between actual and potential output was small) are reflected in high levels of profits and undistributed corporate profits. This, in turn, can lead to a justifiable increase in optimism on the part of business managers, their boards of directors, and their bankers. Such developments can also cause higher prices for shares in the stock market. All of these developments on the demand side encourage business firms to initiate new plans to expand their existing capital facilities through new investment in construction, machinery, and equipment.

On the other hand, a low level of national income will be reflected in a lower rate of utilization of capital facilities, lower profits, and lower corporate cash flow and undistributed corporate profits after tax. There will be very little incentive for business managers to expand their capital facilities when they are not using the existing facilities fully, and the lower rates of utilization will lead them to a more pessimistic assessment of the economic future. We have seen this effect in the business cycle recession of 1981–82, which had a significant impact on business investment spending. The hesitant subsequent recovery in Canada has meant that the volume of business investment in 1986 is still well below the levels of 1981 in real terms. This is almost the first time during the postwar period that business investment has been so slow in recovering to the levels of the previous business cycle peak. The level of national income and the associated levels of demand thus have an important positive impact on the level of business investment spending.

A second consideration concerning the level of business investment is the rate of interest, which directly influences the cost factor in business accounts but also has another important effect. Suppose that a business firm is planning to modernize or expand capacity, but the income made possible from that investment decision will only be realized at some stage in the future. For some investment decisions, relating to long-life business assets, the future incomes could be influenced even some decades down the road. Interest rates are an important part of the calculations carried out by a firm to determine if an investment being made now is likely to be justified by adequate future profits. If the future profits are expected to be sufficiently high, the company would go ahead with the investment decision. On the other hand, if future profits are not expected to be adequate, the company might instead concentrate on how to modify the existing facilities to further reduce costs per unit, to increase productivity, or take other steps to improve profitability. There is always some degree of risk in making such assessments of the future, and the company may do even better (or worse) on future profits than expected, depending on the response of the market, new products, new sources of competition, and so on.

Later in this chapter, we will consider further the extent of influence that alternative levels of interest rates would have on business spending. For the time being, it is sufficient to note that higher rates of interest lead to lower levels of business investment spending; in other words, the relationship between interest rates and investment is negative.

A third influence on the level of business investment spending is the size of the existing stock of capital (which was defined and explained in Section 5–3). If the producing units already have a large stock of capital facilities, they would find it less necessary to expand their capital facilities further, and thus the amount of new business investment could be low. On the other hand, if their capital facilities are limited, they would normally want to have more capital facilities, and this would involve a higher level of business investment than the previous situation. Thus, a high level of the stock of capital tends to *depress* new net investment, while a low level of the stock of capital *encourages* new net investment (for a given level of actual output and interest rates). The stock of capital thus has a negative influence on the rate of current investment.

In summary, the level of national income has a positive influence on the level of business investment spending, while the influence of interest rates and the stock of capital are negative. These relationships can be shown mathematically as follows:

$$I = c + dY - eK - fi \qquad (9–1)$$

where

$I =$ the amount of business investment in a given year

$d$ = the extent to which a higher level of actual national income
($Y - GDP$ in fixed prices) will encourage more business
investment

$e$ = the extent to which a large existing stock of capital ($K$) will make
further new investment less necessary

$f$ = the extent to which a higher rate of interest ($i$) would reduce the
attractiveness of a high rate of investment by making it less
profitable

$c$ = a constant. Look at it as the amount of investment required to keep
the existing capital facilities modernized by replacing worn out
and obsolete capital facilities

These same relationships can be partially shown in Figure 9–1,
which indicates the influence of interest rates and national income for
a given stock of capital. The figure shows that at a low level of actual
national income ($Y_0$), the level of investment would be much lower than
at a higher level of national income for any given level of interest rates.
Furthermore, for any given level of national income, (say $Y_0$), the level
of investment per year would be higher at low rates of interest than at
higher interest rates. For any given level of national income, the equilibrium level of investment will change down or up depending on the
level of interest rates in the market. However, the whole investment

---

**FIGURE 9–1**  Investment Spending as Influenced by National Income
and Interest Rates

---

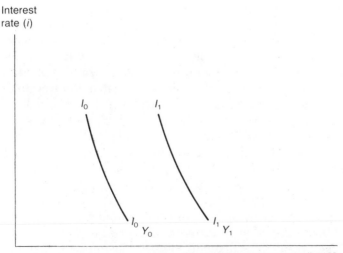

Interest
rate ($i$)

$I_0$        $I_1$

$I_0$ $Y_0$        $I_1$ $Y_1$

Planned investment spending ($I$)

schedule would shift to the right at a higher level of national income. (Be careful to distinguish between movements along a given curve and shifts of the curve. You will have seen these same distinctions between movements along a given curve and shifts of the curve, such as the price effects and income effects in the demand for a given product in earlier exposure to microeconomics.)

## 9–2 INTEREST RATES AND BUSINESS INVESTMENT DECISIONS

In Keynes's *General Theory* (Chapter 7) considerable emphasis was given to the influence of interest rates on business investment decisions. In fact, this was the only expenditure area that reflected any influence of interest rates at all. His work generated studies of the quantitative relationship between interest rates and investment decisions.

The extent of the influence of changing interest rates on the amount of business investment is important. This is one of the areas of ongoing debate about the relative scope for monetary policy, on the one hand, and fiscal policy, on the other, to influence the level of demand in the economy. It is also important to understand the extent of the influence of interest rates as part of the planning process for business investment decisions within the firm. How much attention in the planning process should be given to alternative interest rates and how much to other investment determinants such as prospective sales, alternative competition (both domestic and international), cost reductions with existing facilities, etc., is a question for business managers to consider.

One of the major studies done for the Royal Commission on Banking and Finance in Canada in the early 1960s examined the question of the effects of interest rates on business investment. A number of periods of monetary restraint occurred during the 1950s which provided further evidence for this debate. The Royal Commission study was designed to avoid some of the criticisms of earlier studies in this area. For example, all the large companies in Canada were personally interviewed. In addition, a sample of both medium-sized and smaller companies were sent a mail questionnaire, with follow-ups to nonresponding companies. Emphasis was also placed on the magnitude of the responses, if any, to the changes in interest rates.

The most striking conclusion of this survey was that the results were essentially similar to those that had been arrived at previously by earlier studies in the United Kingdom and the United States. Similar conclusions had been arrived at in different countries and at different time periods. A key result was that the interest elasticity of business capital expenditures on nonresidential construction and equipment was −0.1.[1] (Recall that elasticity is the percentage change in a dependent variable for a given small percentage change in the independent variable. In this case, a 10 percent change in interest rates would be associated with a 1 percent decline in business spending.)

Similar conclusions on the small negative influence of interest rates on investment decisions has also been arrived at in a number of econometric studies of investment spending. Such results have appeared in major studies in the United States and Canada. This same result was recently published by the Economic Council of Canada in their Economic Review for 1985. In that study, the influence of interest rates was −0.14, only slightly different from the survey results done for Canada two decades earlier.[2]

These results raise as many questions as they answer. One area is the whole question of the potential scope for monetary policy and the related changes in interest rates. If business investment is the only expenditure area influenced by interest rates and the effects are relatively minor (as both survey and econometric results suggest), monetary policy could not be expected to have any significant impact in either stimulating the economy during a period of high unemployment or in restraining the economy in a period of inflation. Under these circumstances, the primary scope for economic policies to influence economic activity would have to fall on fiscal policy, direct controls, and wage and price guidelines.

**Monetary policy** refers to changes by the central bank (Bank of Canada here) that influence the supply of money and interest rates and the related effects on the private sector. **Fiscal policy** refers to changes in government expenditures and taxes (and their difference — budget surpluses and deficits) and their effects on the private sector. These two areas will be developed more fully in Parts Four and Five, respectively.

A further question was whether the results of the survey and econometric studies were plausible in light of corporate decision making. This question will be addressed in the next section.

## 9–3 THE RATIONALE FOR THE LIMITED EFFECT OF INTEREST RATES ON BUSINESS SPENDING

During the earlier postwar years, a significant amount of the investment programme in Canadian industry could be financed by internal funds (undistributed corporate profits and depreciation reserves). In the 1960s and 1970s, interest costs were just a fraction of 1 percent of total costs (including purchased materials) for both manufacturing and the non-financial corporate sector. During the 1970s and early 1980s, a growing share of new business investment was financed by external funds. In addition, interest rates on long-term corporate bonds rose from about

10 percent in the 1970s to 16 to 20 percent in the early 1980s, although much of the long-term corporate debt outstanding had been incurred at earlier lower rates. During the early 1980s, the combination of higher interest rates and more external borrowing was reflected in interest costs moving up to about 1.5 percent of sales. This ratio is likely to increase further in the 1980s, but it is a key point that interest rates are not a large factor in costs for manufacturing. For example, for total Canadian manufacturing in 1979, salaries and wages were 10 to 15 times larger than interest costs, and the costs of purchased materials were about 40 times interest costs.

A further consideration is the tax treatment of interest charges for business organizations. Interest costs are a deductible expense for companies in calculating corporate profits for tax purposes. In those circumstances, higher interest costs lead to lower corporate profits and lower corporate profit taxes. For example, if the corporate profits tax was 45 percent, 45 percent of the higher interest charges would be paid for in the form of lower taxes to the federal and provincial governments.

This analysis suggests that the empirical results summarized previously were quite plausible, in light of the cost and tax considerations in the operating environment of corporations.

## 9–4 INTEREST RATES AND HOUSING INVESTMENT

Developments in interest rates have a far bigger impact on housing investment than on business investment. Let's examine the impact for individual homes. For individual home buyers, a house and its financing are a major factor in their balance sheets, both on the asset side and the liability side. Interest and mortgage amortization costs are an important expense in family financing, especially on the first housing purchase. Owner's equity has provided only a small proportion of the funds for new housing over the postwar period, and the proportion of owner's equity has fallen from over 20 percent of the source of funds in the 1960s to just over 10 percent by early in the 1980s. The lending institutions and Central Mortgage and Housing provide a major source of the funding for new residential construction. This heavy reliance on mortgage debt is reflected in large amortization payments in relation to family income, although there is considerable diversity depending on the age of the household head and the asset position of the family, as shown in Table 9–1. For example, older couples with large equity are in a radically different position when buying a new house than a young couple considering the first purchase of a home. If a family has undertaken a mortgage with a heavy debt-servicing charge in relation to income, it can be in an acute financial position if the mortgage comes up for renewal in a period in which going mortgage interest rates are

**TABLE 9–1**   Ratio of Gross Debt Service to Income (new housing loans approved under the National Housing Act, 1985)

| Percentages | |
|---|---|
| 0.0–15.0 | 10.4 |
| 15.1–18.0 | 12.9 |
| 18.1–20.0 | 11.7 |
| 20.1–23.0 | 19.0 |
| 23.1–27.0 | 23.9 |
| 27.1–30.0 | 14.5 |
| 30.1 + | 7.6 |
| | 100.0 |

SOURCE: Canada Mortgage and Housing Corporation, *Canadian Housing Statistics,* March 1986, p. 85.

appreciably higher. This situation became common with the shift in the 1970s and 1980s to much shorter mortgage interest rate commitments by lenders.

The construction of rental units can also be affected significantly by changing mortgage interest rates, especially when many apartment owners are highly leveraged, with a high debt-to-equity ratio. Interest costs and amortization can be an important element in the total costs of operating an apartment, normally a far higher proportion of costs than in the manufacturing and the commodity-producing industries. In a period of rising interest rates, new apartment construction typically falls sharply. This situation is intensified in several provinces (including Ontario) where a form of rent control limits the extent to which rising costs for existing apartments can be passed along to potential tenants. Such situations can occur even when strong demand and low vacancy rates are also occurring.

A tax consideration can also affect the influence of changing interest rates on housing investment. In Canada, interest costs are not deductible as an expense in calculating an individual's income for tax purposes. Under these circumstances, an increase in interest rates would be borne entirely by the individual homeowner. This is a contrast to the tax situation in the United States, where interest costs on housing are deductible in calculating taxable income under the individual income tax law. In both countries, interest expenses are deductible in calculating corporate profits.

In light of the high ratio of mortgage debt to new housing costs, the high ratio of interest and principal costs to income (for both individual homeowners and apartment owners), and the tax treatment for individuals, interest rate changes have a far bigger impact on housing construction than they do on plant and equipment investment.

**TABLE 9–2** Impacts of Interest Rate Changes, Based on 1985 Expenditure Levels (billions of dollars)

| Expenditures | 1985 Levels | Interest Elasticities | Effects of 10 Percent Increases in Interest Rates |
|---|---|---|---|
| Business capital expenditures on nonresidential construction and equipment | 55.5 | −0.14 | −0.78 |
| Residential construction | 25.4 | −2.00 | −5.08 |
| Personal expenditure on durables | 40.0 | −0.40 | −1.60 |
| | 120.9 | | −7.46 |

SOURCE: Elasticities are developed from data and studies in D. J. Daly, "The Impact of Monetary Policy: A Synthesis," in *Conference on Stabilization Policies* (Ottawa: Queen's Printer, 1966), pp. 1–51, updated with expenditures from *Bank of Canada Review,* October 1986, p. S114; and Economic Council of Canada, *Strengthening Growth: Options and Constraints* (Ottawa: Ministry of Supply and Services, 1985), p. 91.

## 9–5 SUMMARY OF INVESTMENT SPENDING RESPONSES TO INTEREST RATE CHANGES

The effects of interest rate changes on some of the key expenditure areas in the National Accounts can be seen in Table 9–2, which shows the levels for the three main areas of final expenditures that appear to be influenced by changes in interest rates. The expenditure areas shown are business capital expenditures, residential construction, and consumer durables. Canadian estimates of interest rate elasticities are shown for each expenditure area. The effects of a change in interest rates of 10 percent are shown. For example, an initial interest rate level of 10 percent would increase to 11 percent. An aggregate effect on expenditure is also shown in the table. Remember that there is an inverse relationship between interest and expenditure. An interesting point is that the absolute size of the effects on housing are almost six times as large as on business capital expenditures, even though housing investment expenditures were less than one-third the size of business capital expenditures that year. Similarly, the effect of higher interest rates on consumer durable spending was about twice the size of the effect on business capital spending even though it was initially only half the size. The aggregate elasticity in total of these three expenditure areas to interest rate changes was about −0.62 (based on an absolute change of −$7.46 billion on an initial level of $120.9 billion for investment and personal expenditure on durables), as shown in Table 9–2.

The much larger responsiveness of expenditures on housing investment and purchases of consumer durables to changes in interest rates mean that such changes can have an important *indirect* effect on sales and demand in other industries, even though the direct effects of interest rates on costs are normally small.

This evidence on the responsiveness of the various expenditure areas to changes in interest rates has important implications for monetary policy. The key point is that interest rates have a much larger impact on the level of final expenditures than you would conclude from looking at the small degree of responsiveness in business capital expenditures. Thus, this evidence is fairly important in assessing the continuing debate between the Keynesians and monetarists on the relative effectiveness of monetary and fiscal policy.

## 9–6 INCOME AND ACCELERATOR EFFECTS ON BUSINESS INVESTMENT

Section 9–1 introduced the effect of alternative levels of actual national income on investment, and Figure 9–1 showed how a higher level of national income encouraged a higher level of business investment. This is sometimes referred to as the accelerator principle. The **accelerator principle** is the theory that net investment depends on the expected change in output in the economy, with higher expected output leading to higher planned investment. A recent Annual Review of the Economic Council of Canada summarized the effects of the demand for final product on investment decisions.

> Both in econometric models and in real life, the demand for the final product turns out to be among the most important factors in investment decisions. In the surveys about investment intentions conducted by the Department of Regional Industrial Expansion, expected sales were often the most important factor affecting current and expected investment spending. For the respondents who had modified their plans, the most important reason for doing so was a change in domestic market demand.[3]

Their research concluded that a 1 percent increase in the growth rate of output would lead to a 1.3 percent increase in investment, or an elasticity of investment with respect to national output of 1.3. This is substantially larger than the interest rate elasticity of business investment shown in Table 9–2 from the same study.

However, it has not been easy to isolate how quickly business firms will respond to a change in demand with changes in business investment. Lags in that response occur, but there are a variety of theoretical interpretations for the timing of the response, and none of them adequately explain the changes in business investment in the 1970s.[4]

## 9-7 THE MULTIPLIER IN A SIMPLE MODEL

One of the important contributions of Keynes's *General Theory* was the notion of the multiplier. The **multiplier** is defined as the change in the equilibrium level of national income for a given change in investment. (You may recall that the *equilibrium* level of national income is a value that, if attained, would be maintained.) If investment *changes* by a certain amount (say $5 billion in 1981 prices), there would be a larger *change* in the equilibrium level of national income. Such a change can be either up or down, and Keynes's view was that the change would have a larger impact on national income than just the change in investment in isolation, but it would also have some indirect effects on personal consumption as well.

Incidentally, actual changes in business investment can be quite large, as illustrated by the declines in the 1981–82 recession, the most severe in Canada since the 1930s. Business fixed-capital investment in nonresidential construction, machinery, and equipment reached a peak of $56.6 billion (1981 prices) in the second quarter of 1981 and fell to $46.0 billion (1981 prices), a drop of about 20 percent, by the third quarter of 1983, more than two years later. In addition, nonfarm business inventories accumulated at an annual rate of $4.4 billion in the second quarter of 1981, and inventory investment shifted to a peak rate of inventory liquidation in the fourth quarter of 1982 reaching $9.9 billion (all in 1981 prices). The total swing in business inventory investment was thus $14.3 billion in addition to the drop in fixed-capital investment. Such large changes are bound to have an impact on other spending sectors of the economy, unless they are offset by changes elsewhere.

We will initially develop the notion of the multiplier in a simplified mathematical model of the economy and will then discuss its probable size. Let's explore the concept of the multiplier for the relatively simple situation of a closed economy and no government transactions. This will permit us to see the essential issues, while in later sections we can incorporate the additional degrees of realism associated with an open economy and the existing structure of government tax rates, the associated government revenues.

The essential ideas can be seen for this simple situation of an economy consisting of a business sector that does the investing and a personal sector that receives income, which is then either spent on consumer goods or saved. In the following mathematical presentation, all of the variables are measured in the prices of a base period, and the following notation is used:

$Y$ = total national income

$C$ = total personal expenditure on consumer goods and services

$I$ = business investment

$b$ = the marginal propensity to consume (as discussed in Chapter 7)

$a$ = the vertical intercept in the consumption function

Beginning with the basic definition of national income and the consumption function as previously developed, we can make a relatively simple algebraic substitution as follows:

$Y = C + I$ (definition of equilibrium national income)

$$(9–1)$$

$C = a + bY$ (simple consumption function) $\qquad$ (9–2)

$Y = a + bY + I$ (substitution of two above equations)

$$(9–3)$$

$Y - bY = a + I$ (grouping of terms involving $Y$) $\qquad$ (9–3)

$Y(1 - b) = a + I$ $\qquad$ (9–4)

$Y = \dfrac{a + I}{1 - b}$ (dividing both sides by $[1 - b]$) $\qquad$ (9–5)

A change from one level of investment to another will be associated with a change in the equilibrium level of national income which can be derived from Equation (9–5), but $a$ will disappear when a *difference* is derived because it is common to both the initial and final positions of equilibrium.

$$\Delta Y = \frac{1}{1 - b} \Delta I \qquad (9–6)$$

(showing the *change* in equilibrium level of national income

for a *change* in investment)

Equations (9–5) and (9–6) are what are referred to in the econometrics literature as reduced forms of an economic system. A **reduced form** of a model is one where all the endogenous variables to be explained in the system are on the left-hand side of the equation, while the exogenous variables (determined outside the model) are shown on the right-hand side. In this simple model, the level (and changes in) business investment determine the level (and changes in) the equilibrium level of national income.

The key determinant of the multiplier is the marginal propensity to consume. This is the fundamental concept, and the multiplier is derived from it. If the marginal propensity to consume is stable, then the derived multiplier will also be stable.

The key question on the application of this model to the economy is whether such a change in business investment will have a large or a small impact on the equilibrium level of national income. In this illustration, the size of the multiplier depends on the size of the marginal propensity to consume. If the marginal propensity to consume is a high value (such as 0.90), the multiplier is also high. For this example, the multiplier would be 10.0, implying that a small change in investment in our closed economy would lead to a large change in the equilibrium level of national income. On the other hand, if the marginal propensity to consume is lower (such as 0.66), the multiplier is also lower. For this example, it would be 3.0, which implies a much smaller change in the equilibrium level of national income than was implied with a larger value of the marginal propensity to consume.

The discussion in the last chapter showed that the marginal propensity to consume out of personal disposable income in Canada in recent years was about 0.75, implying a fairly large multiplier. The implication for government policy is that if a small change in government expenditure or taxes were introduced, the result would be a large impact on the equilibrium level of national income.

However, if it were this easy, and the government wanted to use discretionary changes to achieve broad economic and social goals, why have most of the industrialized countries had high rates of inflation and occasional periods of fairly high unemployment?

## 9–8 GOVERNMENT AND THE FOREIGN SECTOR AND THE SIZE OF THE MULTIPLIER

In the last section, the ideas of the simple multiplier were developed on the assumption of a closed economy with no government. In this section, these two key assumptions will be relaxed, and a more realistic situation will be outlined in which government revenues and imports are incorporated into the model. The key result from this extension will be that part of the stimulus to the economy from an increase in government expenditures (or exports or investments) is reflected in an increase in government revenues and imports, the net effect of which is to reduce the size of the multiplier significantly.

The value of the multiplier for this more realistic model can be derived algebraically in a manner similar to that used in the last section. This result can be shown as the following:

$$\Delta Y = \frac{1}{1 - b + bt + m} \Delta I \qquad (9-7)$$

where

>   $b$ = the marginal propensity to consume
>   $t$ = the marginal tax rate in relation to GNP
>   $m$ = the marginal propensity to import[5]

Reasonable values of these parameters for Canada in the 1980s would be approximately:

>   $b$ = 0.8
>   $t$ = 0.3
>   $m$ = 0.25

For these values of the parameters, the value of the multiplier would be roughly 1.45, a drastic reduction from the illustrative multiplier for the simpler model outlined in the last section. Part of the potential stimulus to the economy is deflected into higher tax collections, so that there is less disposable income available after taxes for consumers to spend on consumption. In addition, part of the stimulus to domestic demand spills over into an increased level of imports, so that not all of the stimulus to domestic demand accrues to domestic suppliers.

A further important implication is that the private sector would be fairly stable in response to exogenous shocks from outside the system, rather than unstable as suggested by the simple model with a high marginal propensity to consume. This possibility is sufficiently important to justify further discussion and explanation. However, the evidence to assess this point draws heavily on the results from econometric models of the economy for the industrialized countries, so a brief explanation of this type of model may be helpful to the reader.

## 9–9 ECONOMETRIC MODELS FOR THE ECONOMY

An **econometric model** for the economy is a statistical summary of the of the behaviour of the economy, based on the historical experience of that country as captured in its statistical records. It assumes some historical continuity between the past and the future.

Preparing econometric models of the contemporary economies of the industrialized countries involves a number of steps. For our purposes, two initial stages can be distinguished.

The first step in the construction of an econometric model is to build on the basis of economic theory for the economy as a whole, much along the lines developed and presented in this book, although normally in much greater detail.

The second step is to develop statistical estimates of the individual equations that are part of the complete macroeconomic system. A production function and a consumption function along the lines already introduced illustrate some of the structural relationships that would have to be estimated. The estimates are prepared using multiple-regression methods of a kind that are developed in most of the standard courses in statistics. Once a complete system for the economy has been prepared based on a large number of individual structural equations, the resulting complete model can be used for economic forecasting, economic policy analysis, or simulations. We will consider some simulations in the next section.

A number of factors have increased the feasibility of building such models and lowering their costs. First, the development of faster and more powerful computers has reduced the cost of computing such models. As a rough guide, it appears that the cost of doing particular operations on a computer has dropped about 20 percent per year compounded—a significant contrast to the increase in wages and salaries that occurred over the last several decades. In addition, an important part of the cost of developing these models in the past has been the cost of collecting the data from public sources and then inputting it to the computer by hand, by card, or by magnetic tape. Nowadays, this material is available from Statistics Canada, the Bank of Canada, and some private statistical research groups in machine-readable form, thus lowering costs and reducing the risk of error in the data. More years of observation in both annual and quarterly data have also increased the number of observations available for statistical estimates, leading to an improvement in the quality and reliability of the estimates so obtained.

However, there are continuing practical problems in the development and use of these models which should be noted. First, the basic statistical methods were initially developed in the areas of biology and the physical sciences where experiments could be made under controlled conditions, thus limiting or controlling the influence of secondary variables. In economic problems, however, such controlled experiments are rarely possible, and the resulting observations on the economy reflect many simultaneously occurring relationships. Special statistical methods have been developed to deal with such problems of simultaneity in economic relationships, but the methods are complex and expensive. Another significant problem is that a significant amount of variation in the historical experience of some independent variable must be observed in order to obtain reliable estimates of a change in that variable on the rest of the economy. In practice, such variations may not have occurred frequently enough in the historical experience to provide reliable estimates. For example, prior to the 1950s, interest rates varied little historically; thus there was little opportunity to observe the effects of alternative levels of interest rates on the economy. The developments of the 1970s and 1980s have given us a much wider range of experience of changes in nominal interest rates to analyze statistically.

Another example of a variable that was of interest to policymakers was the exchange rate. The range of variation in the exchange rates among the major industrialized countries has been fairly narrow, apart from special problems associated with wars and depressions. However, since 1971, far wider swings in the exchange rate have occurred among the major industrialized countries, so we are now beginning to see a growing number of different exchange rate levels.

## 9–10 IS THE ECONOMY INHERENTLY UNSTABLE?

The development of econometric models for a number of countries has permitted us to form conclusions about the stability of the economy as a whole. This is essentially premised on developments in the private sector—an environment that can be influenced by developments in the public sector (including both fiscal and monetary policy) and in the world economy.

Irma and F. L. Adelman studied the dynamic properties of a medium-sized econometric model for the United States developed initially by L. R. Klein and Arthur Goldberger. They simulated the model for 100 years into the future, based on a number of assumptions about future developments in population, labour force, productivity, and government expenditures and taxes. In the initial base case, they assumed steady growth in government expenditures and some of the other independent variables. They then examined what the effects would be on the dynamic performance of the economy, for many years into the future, of a different pattern of exogenous shocks, such as a sudden and large increase in government expenditures, which then return to their initial level. What emerged was that the economy fairly quickly settled down to a level of growth not too different from what the initial base case had shown. In other words, the model as estimated was inherently quite stable, and significant shocks did not throw the economy into either severe depression or extreme inflation. It required a combination of exogenous shocks to the system as a whole and random disturbances in the individual subparts of the economy to replicate results closer to what had been observed historically in the United States.[6] These results did not correspond to what many Keynesians would have expected in light of the emphasis on the instability in private investment that had been a central part of Keynes's *General Theory*.

It is significant that this result was similar to what Jan Tinbergen found in his study of business cycles in the United States first published in 1939 for the League of Nations. His model was based on a model containing 70 variables designed to be a complete business-cycle system.[7] Simulations of an abbreviated model of the system yielded a *highly damped cycle*. A **damped cycle** is a cyclical fluctuation that decreases in amplitude (the extent of change from the peak to the trough of the cycle) over time. In other words, the economy would return to a growth around potential supply when subjected to an initial shock. Changes in a variety of individual coefficients usually had only a small effect on the extent of dampening in the Tinbergen model.

Simulations of econometric models of Canada give results quite similar to those summarized above for the United States. A study done by S.J. May in 1966 showed values of the multiplier for Canada even lower than those for the United States, which implies a high degree of stability. The effects of a change in government expenditures of GNP five years later was 1.71 for Canada, compared to over 2.0 for changes in nondefence expenditures in the United States.[8] The lower multipliers for Canada reflect the high revenue elasticity of the Canadian tax structure and the higher marginal propensity to import for Canada than the United States.

Similar results are also obtained from the series of econometric models developed and published by the Bank of Canada. The 1980 version, for example, showed a peak impact on domestic production in about two years, but by the end of six years, the change in domestic and foreign demand was roughly equal to the increase in government expenditures. Thus, the multiplier was down to about 1.0 six years after the initial shock.[9]

Similar results were obtained in a number of econometric models for other countries of roughly the same size as Canada with the same degree of openness. These were surveyed by Bert Hickman in the volume *Is The Business Cycle Obsolete?*.[10]

Evidence from a number of econometric studies for different countries done over a period of more than four decades by different research groups all suggest that the private sector is inherently fairly stable in response to exogenous shocks. This raises a different question. What factors have contributed to the business cycles that have been observed in the industrialized countries throughout the present century? This topic will be explored further in the next chapter.

## SUMMARY

Business investment is determined by the level of national income (in a positive direction). It is negatively affected by the existing size of the capital stock and the level of interest rates.

The level of national income and changes in the level of national income are important influences on the level of business investment, but changes in interest rates have a relatively small, but not zero, influence on business investment.

Interest rates have a much larger impact on housing investment, partly because mortgage interest and principal repayment costs are much larger in relation to income for most homeowners and landlords than business investment is to business income.

Econometric models for the economy are prepared using economic theory and statistical methods. The costs of preparing such models have been reduced by the use of computers and machine-readable data.

Simulations from such models over many decades and for a number of countries show a high degree of stability in the private sector of the economy, rather than inherent instability.

## NOTES

1.  J. H. Young and J. F. Helliwell, "The Effects of Monetary Policy on Corporations," Royal Commission on Banking and Finance, *Appendix Volume* (Ottawa: Queen's Printer, 1964), pp. 305–435; and D. J. Daly, "The Impact of Monetary Policy: A Synthesis," in *Conference on Stabilization Policies* (Ottawa: Queen's Printer, 1966), pp. 1–51.

2.  Economic Council of Canada, *Strengthening Growth: Options and Constraints* (Ottawa: Ministry of Supply and Services, 1985), p. 91.

3.  Ibid., p. 90.

4.  Peter K. Clark, "Investment in the 1970s: Theory, Performance and Prediction," *Brookings Papers on Economic Activity*, 1979, pp. 73–113.

5.  Equation 9–7 is another example of a reduced form of a system of equations similar in principle to those shown in Equations (9–5) and (9–6) in the last section. This is a derivation of a larger (but still simple) model of the economy that contains a tax function and an import function. The following expanded definition of GDP (national income) is basic:

$$Y = C + I + G + XP - IMP$$

where

$C$ and $I$ = consumption and investment as defined before

$G$ = government expenditures on goods and services (at constant prices)

$XP$ = exports of goods and services (at constant prices)

$IMP$ = imports of goods and services (at constant prices)

The measurement of all these variables was explained in Chapter 2. Investment ($I$) and exports of goods and services ($XP$) are treated as exogenous, while imports of goods and services ($IMP$) and federal tax collections are treated as endogenous. The import function could be shown as

$$IMP = g + my$$

and

$$T = h + ty$$

where

$m$ = the marginal propensity to import

$t$ = the marginal propensity to tax with a given structure of tax rates.

If these linear equations are substituted into the definition of national income and the terms are grouped to have all the terms involving $Y$ on the left-hand side of the equal sign and all the exogenous and constant terms on the right-hand side, Equation (9–7) is obtained in a procedure similar to that shown in Equations (9–1) to (9–6) in the simpler multiplier shown earlier in Section 9–6. For those of you with a mathematical bent, derive Equation (9–7) on your own.

The values of $t$ and $m$ shown in the text are both based on statistical research, and the explanation of their size will be developed in later parts of this text.

6.   Irma Adelman and Frank L. Adelman, "The Dynamic Properties of the Klein-Goldberger Model," in *Readings in Business Cycles,* ed. R. A. Gordon and L. R. Klein (Homewood, Ill.: Richard D. Irwin, 1965), pp. 278–306.

7.   J. Tinbergen, *Statistical Testing of Business-Cycle Theories II, Business Cycles in the United States of America, 1919–1932* (Geneva: League of Nations, 1939), reprinted in *Statistical Testing of Business Cycle Theories* (New York: Agathon Press, 1968), pp. 136–79.

8.   Sydney May, "Dynamic Multipliers and their Use for Fiscal Decision-Making," in *Conference on Stabilization Policies* (Ottawa: Queen's Printer, 1966), p. 127.

9.   *The Structure and Dynamics of RDXF, September 1980 Version* (Ottawa: Bank of Canada, 1982), pp. 213–35.

10.  Bert G. Hickman, "Dynamic Properties of Macroeconometric Models: An International Comparison," in *Is The Business Cycle Obsolete?* ed. Martin Bronfenbrenner (New York: Wiley-Interscience, 1969), pp. 393–435.

# 10

## Business Cycles and Demand Instability

The last chapter suggested that the private sector in the industrialized economies reflects a good deal of inherent stability. This raises the question of why business cycles occur and persist. After reading this chapter you should understand:

1. The main approaches to research on business cycles.
2. The role of external shocks as an initiating factor in business fluctuations or cycles.
3. The role of lags in the economy.
4. Some of the main features of the historical experience with business cycles in the United States and Canada.
5. The main reasons recessions have become milder in North America since World War II.
6. The extent to which the fluctuations in actual demand affect the rate of change in productivity (or output per hour).

## 10–1 RESEARCH ON BUSINESS CYCLES

The evidence summarized in the last chapter indicated that a theory based entirely on the inherent instability of the private sector was an incomplete explanation of the persistence of business cycles over many decades. Such a theory, termed an **endogenous theory**, states that business cycles are caused entirely by inherent problems within the market-oriented industrialized economies. An **exogenous theory** of business cycles, on the other hand, emphasizes the role of shocks or disturbances from *outside* the system as central to the recurrence of cycles.

Although you can distinguish such alternative interpretations of the causes of business cycles on the basis of theory, deciding which interpretations best stand the tests of historical experience and which are more helpful in forecasting is essentially an empirical question.

Two approaches to empirical business-cycle research have been applied in the United States, Canada, and other countries. One approach is an outgrowth of the business-cycle research initiated by Wesley Clair Mitchell at the National Bureau of Economic Research in the United States. W. C. Mitchell (1874–1948) helped organize the National Bureau of Economic Research and was its director of research until 1945. His early research examined the period of inflation during and after the U.S. Civil War; the study of money, prices, and business cycles was a continuing area of interest throughout his career. Mitchell taught economics at Columbia, and his lectures on economic theory and its history were highly regarded by students and other economists. The research on business cycles that he initiated led to the selection of a smaller group of series to help identify changes in economic conditions (peaks, troughs, and intermediate slowdowns during expansions) that are widely used in analyzing current developments and short-term forecasts. Such a selection has been published monthly since 1961 in the United States by the Department of Commerce in *Business Conditions Digest*. The selection of series is convenient, well presented graphically, and includes some international economic indicators as well. Some private organizations also provide similar material, sometimes on a monthly and even on a weekly basis.

A similar publication is produced by Statistics Canada, but it is more technical and less widely publicized and used. The Royal Bank produces a briefer *Trendicator* on a monthly basis, and a private organization produces a regular publication using a short list of indicators similar to the ones developed in the United States. Japan produces a monthly publication based on statistical indicators, and Geoffrey Moore has been developing and circulating international economic indicators since the 1970s.

The main alternative approach is the development and use of econometric models, along the lines sketched in Section 9–10. By the mid-1970s about 30 percent of forecasters in the United States used econometric models as the most important forecasting method. A leader in the development of econometric models for forecasting and analysis of policy options is Laurence R. Klein, who has taught at the University of Pennsylvania for many years and received the Nobel Price for Economics in 1980. He helped develop the Wharton Econometric Forecasting Model for the U.S. economy, and he helped initiate similar work in Canada (a short-term forecasting model for the Department of Trade and Commerce in 1947), the United States, and Japan. He has also been active in the co-ordination of models in different countries.

Econometric models for forecasting are currently used in Canada by the Economic Council of Canada, the Bank of Canada, the Department of Finance, the Conference Board in Canada, the University of Toronto, and such private organizations as Informetrica in Ottawa and Data Resources of Canada. Many of these forecasts are summarized regularly by the Conference Board in Canada (about 15 for 1987, for example), and many organizations have regular meetings on the economic outlook.

There are many major areas of similarity between econometric models and statistical indicators. They both start from a basis in economic theory of the types of economic processes to study and the most promising area of the causes of economic change. They both use the available statistics for the past to try to identify the direction and timing of the main economic forces in the future. They both assume a good deal of historical continuity, although both must watch for the possible emergence of new factors or changes in the importance of various economic forces. If there are a small number of major influences present in the economy, these forces should emerge in the basic data no matter what methods of statistical analysis are used.

Econometric models can have an advantage in analyzing the result of alternative public policies. The decreasing costs of doing statistical analysis on computers and the lower costs of obtaining current and accurate statistics in machine-readable form have encouraged a greater amount of econometric research. On the other hand, the forecasting record of econometric models has not been entirely successful, and many forecasters continue to use a combination of methods.

Section 9–8 in the last chapter indicated that the private sector contains a good deal of inherent stability, which raises the question of what additional factors are necessary to explain the persistence of fluctuations in the major economies of the Western world. Some of the simulations from a variety of models for different countries indicate that exogenous shocks (from outside the private sector) and random disturbances were both necessary and sufficient to explain why business cycles persist. This conclusion is much in line with that suggested by Milton Friedman in summarizing the contribution of W. C. Mitchell to the understanding of business cycles historically:

> At the very broadest level of generality, persistent self-generating fluctuations in economic activity can occur only in a world characterized by both uncertainty (in the sense of unpredictable change) and lags in response (in the sense of different timing of response).[1]

We will return to this concept after we examine some examples of both exogenous shocks and lags in response.

## 10–2 ILLUSTRATIONS OF EXOGENOUS SHOCKS

One important historical example of an exogenous shock is the effect of a war. During World War II in Canada, for example, defence and war expenditures increased from $70 million in 1939 (1 percent of GNP—the concept of national income then used) to $4.3 billion in 1944 (40 percent of GNP). Such a major increase in government expenditures was necessary to purchase weapons and support the armed forces in Europe and on Atlantic convoys. Defence and war expenditures dominated federal expenditures on goods and services, both current and capital. This was a dramatic shift in the composition of demand, but the increase in defence expenditure stimulated output in the economy to such an extent that personal expenditure on consumer goods and services per capita (on a constant-dollar basis) increased more than 20 percent from 1939 to 1944.[2] Increases in defence expenditures are often accompanied by an associated monetary expansion to finance the budget deficits likely to occur during wartime periods.

Another example of the effect of war expenditure was the curtailment of defence orders in the first half of 1953 in the United States when President Eisenhower assumed office. The cut in orders and expenditures was so sharp that it contributed to the recession from July 1953 to May 1954 (as shown in Table 3–4 earlier). The change in defence expenditures combined with a swing in business inventories from inventory accumulation to inventory disinvestment were the key shifts on the expenditure side of U.S. national accounts. Such changes also contributed to a Canadian recession of about the same duration.

A less dramatic example of an exogenous shock was the increase in world petroleum prices initiated by the OPEC countries in 1973 and again in 1978. These price increases were reflected in the United States and Canada, although changes in federal policy in Canada kept wellhead returns below world levels for some years. The increase in petroleum prices shifted resources and incomes from energy users to energy producers and, in the process, increased pressures to conserve energy in light of the dramatic price increases. These pressures for conservation were felt in most countries and affected decisions by consumers and some areas of investment expenditures as well.

Before the introduction of central banks in the major industrialized countries, exogenous shocks occasionally occurred in the financial system. Some of the private commercial banks experienced runs on their banks (when depositors withdrew their funds and held their financial assets in bank notes), and some of them went bankrupt. What we now describe as recessions within full business cycles were once called financial crises. They occurred because of the prevalent weaknesses in the financial system, including poor and even dishonest managers in some of the financial institutions.

Exogenous shocks of the kinds illustrated above create impacts on the private sectors—such as the increases and decreases in defence expenditures mentioned above. Increases in petroleum prices encouraged the shift to smaller cars in North America, improved insulation in homes and offices, and development of new sources of petroleum and natural gas. These changes had a major impact on Alberta (as reflected in rapid population increases in such cities as Calgary and Edmonton, downtown office construction, high home prices, and expensive rental accommodation). The subsequent drop in petroleum prices led to layoffs, especially in exploration and development areas, and a sharp drop in real estate prices.

In the United States, widespread bankruptcies of commercial banks were an important factor contributing to the severity and duration of the Great Depression of the 1930s. These serious problems in the banking system led to further bankruptcies of individuals and businesses that held deposits in the banks that failed, and many companies and individuals had to curtail expenditures to survive. These difficulties occurred in spite of the Federal Reserve System, which had been established before World War I.

Exogenous shocks can create practical problems for business forecasting, especially if they occur frequently. Forecasts can be wrong if some unexpected development occurs.

## 10–3 THE ROLE OF LAGS

**Lags** occur when decisions or developments in one time period influence other economic variables not in the same time period but in some later period. Lags can occur in many parts of the economic system. Two examples will be introduced in this section, and further examples will be explored in later chapters.

Lags in private investment in plant and equipment occur because of the length of time from initial planning decisions to peak expenditures on a particular project. A major project could require decisions on the optimum location of a plant in relation to markets, sources of supply, and access to transportation facilities. After a site has been located and purchased, time is spent planning the project. Architects and associated specialized engineers and draftsmen must prepare detailed plans for the facility, including specifications for plumbing, heating, and electrical systems. The project then goes out for tender by construction contractors, and a contract is eventually awarded. Months may pass before the contractor can start work, and only after the excavation, foundation, and basement have been completed can the girders, exterior concrete work, and other construction steps be initiated. Later stages of the project are frequently labour intensive and expensive as the interior finishing, decorating, elevators, and furnishings are completed. Considerable time elapses between the decision to build a plant and the time when the plant's investment project has an impact on the economy. The lags are normally longer for large projects than for small ones.

Similar trends occur in the housing industry, both for individual homes and multiple units. Such projects normally require approval by municipal and provincial governments. Delays in obtaining decisions have been an important source of frustration and cost to builders. In addition, builders are not normally willing to progress very far, or even commence construction, until mortgage financing is assured. The peak value of the work put in place per month is normally higher in the last stages of construction than during the earlier stages.

These differences in timing over the business cycle can be seen in a number of the major indicators of fixed-capital investment, with some indicators beginning to decline in advance of business-cycle peaks, while other indicators continue to increase. Examples can be seen in Table 10–1.

The timing shown in each of the three vertical columns is the timing of each particular economic series in relation to the business cycle for the total economy. For example, contracts and orders in 1972 dollars have reached a peak eight months before the business-cycle peak on average for the eight full business cycles from 1945 to 1982. The lead at troughs averages much less, and there are some recoveries that start in housing or with a swing from inventory liquidation during the recession to inventory accumulation in the expansion phase of the cycle. Contracts and orders for plant and equipment might not begin to recover until other spending areas have laid the basis for increased profits and higher rates of utilization of existing capacity. The average for all turns is based on the combination of the timing differences for both peaks and troughs.

Another important source of lags in North America comes from the presence of a significant amount of seasonal variation in many economic processes. Business management is always aware of seasonal highs and lows and their timing. In assessing recent developments business managers compare individual months in the current year with the same months in the previous year and assume they have a correct picture of the most recent developments. In fact, this comparison only provides them with a perspective on what has happened over the intervening 12-month period and *not* what has happened in the last six months.

To illustrate, suppose incoming orders in your company have increased at a steady rate on a seasonally adjusted basis. Then a recession begins that leads to a decline in incoming orders at the same rate they had been rising before. It will take six months of decline before an individual month's sales will drop below the same month's sales of the

**TABLE 10–1**  Cyclical Indicators of Fixed-Capital Investment, Median Timing at Peaks, Troughs, and All Turns (United States, 1947–1982)

| Series Title | Peaks | Troughs | All Turns |
|---|---|---|---|
| Contracts and orders for plant and equipment in 1972 dollars | −8 | −1 | −3½ |
| Manufacturers' new orders in 1972 dollars, nondefence, capital goods industries | −9 | −2 | −4½ |
| Construction contracts awarded for commercial and industrial buildings | −4 | +2 | 0 |
| Business investment expenditures: Expenditures for new plant and equipment by U.S. nonfarm business | +1 | +4 | +1 |
| Gross private nonresidential fixed investment in 1972 dollars, structures | −2½ | +3 | +1 |
| Gross private nonresidential fixed investment in 1972 dollars, producers' durable equipment | 0 | 0 | 0 |
| Residential construction commitments and investment: New private housing units started | −13 | −2 | −9½ |
| Gross private residential fixed investment in 1972 dollars | −10 | −3 | −6 |

SOURCE: U.S. Department of Commerce, *Handbook of Cyclical Indicators, 1984* (Washington, D.C.: Bureau of Economic Analysis, 1984), pp. 172–73.

year before. This means that with a year-to-year comparison, management normally won't recognize a change in new orders until six months after it has begun. The individual firm can handle this problem if it prepares a seasonally adjusted series for new orders, which can now be done on computers quickly and inexpensively. When encouraging business managers to prepare seasonally adjusted data for their firm and industry, it is technically correct to ask them if they would like to know what is happening in their industry six months earlier than their competitors. This method frequently leads businesses to convert to seasonally adjusted data.[3]

The advantages of using seasonal adjustments can be seen in Figure 10–1. The data relate to the production of roofing paper, a seasonal item widely used under asphalt shingles in individual home construction. The top portion of the figure shows the actual production data on a monthly basis. The second line shows the seasonally adjusted

**FIGURE 10–1** Illustration of the Gains from Seasonal Adjustment, Production of Asphalt Shingles (original data, moving average of seasonally adjusted and seasonal-adjustment factors monthly, 1970–86, Canada)

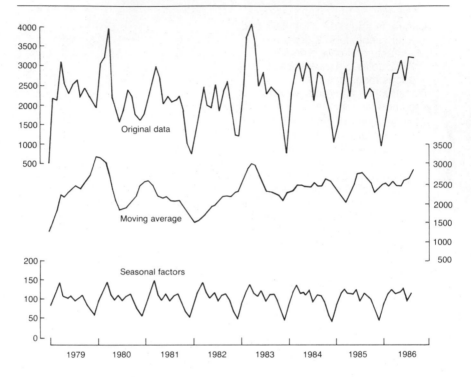

series. It is much easier to identify the changes in the second line. The lower line shows the seasonal factors. The whole process of figuring the seasonal adjustment was done on a main-frame computer, using what is termed the Census X-11 programme. This programme does a high-quality seasonal adjustment in minutes at a fraction of the cost of computing a seasonal adjustment by hand on a desk calculator and using a system of graphs to estimate the seasonal factors for each month.

Even among large firms in Canada, only a small minority prepare seasonally adjusted data for their own particular organizations. Part of the reason for this is that many of the standard statistics texts for business students discuss how to do a seasonal adjustment, but few explain adequately *why* they should be done.

One way to test whether business firms recognize changes in their own business only with a lag is to check the reliability of the many surveys of short-term business expectations made regularly in the

United States and Canada. Some of these surveys have been conducted regularly since the 1920s. Their forecasting accuracy has
been appraised by comparing the surveys with actual developments
as reflected in seasonally adjusted data. The striking result is that such
surveys consistently miss business-cycle turning points at both
peaks and troughs. They also tend to underestimate the vigour of
expansions while they are underway and the severity of recessions.

Such a consistent lagged recognition of turning points in individual
businesses is bound to lead to faulty business decisions. At business-
cycle peaks, companies are likely to continue producing even after
orders and sales have begun to decline, leading to an unintended accumulation of business inventories. Reducing inventories will subsequently require cuts in production and, perhaps, layoffs of employees.
Similarly, at lower turning points, a pick-up in orders and sales that
is not correctly identified early will lead to an unplanned rundown
of business inventories, and an acceleration in production through increased overtime and extra shifts. The prevalence of this practice has
been insufficiently recognized by some economists. They have tried to
develop a theory of the business cycle based on the assumption that
businesspeople had correct and unbiased expectations about future
developments in their own organizations.

The more widespread use of seasonally adjusted data would
shorten the existing recognition lags within business organizations. The
shortening of the lag would moderate the prevalence and extent of
inventory swings of both unplanned and undesired accumulations and
liquidations.

One important practical problem is that smaller companies frequently experience a significant degree of irregular developments. Thus
it is more difficult for them to estimate the appropriate seasonal factors
for the past and for the current year.

To recapitulate the last two sections, evidence of the last three
decades is consistent with Friedman's assessment of Mitchell's work on
business cycles that shocks and lags continue to be important characteristics of business cycles.

## 10–4 BUSINESS CYCLES IN THE UNITED STATES

Table 3–4 summarized the timing of business cycles in the United
States since the middle of the 19th century. One point that emerged
there is that since 1945 the average duration of contractions has been
11 months, compared with almost twice that over the period of nearly
a century from 1854 to 1945. There has been some tendency toward the
shortening of recessions since World War II, since the longest recessions
have lasted only 16 months each (November 1973 to March 1975 and

July 1981 to November 1982). There is also some evidence that recessions have become milder. During the six recessions between 1948
and 1975, the average decline in the index of industrial production was
12.3 percent, and the extent of the increase in the average unemployment rate was 3.5 percentage points from the business-cycle
peak to the trough in the case of industrial production and from the low
month to the highest month in the case of the unemployment rate.

Geoffrey Moore has researched business cycles since the 1950s,
initially as director of business cycle research at the National Bureau
of Economic Research. He also served in government as commissioner
of Labor Statistics in the U.S. Bureau of Labor Statistics from 1969 to
1973. He is a leading international authority on business cycles in North
America and elsewhere. He has summarized some of the secular
changes in business cycles as follows:

> Perhaps the most obvious change is that business recessions —
> periods of actual decline in economic activity — have become less
> frequent, shorter, and milder. Interruptions to a steady rate of
> growth are more often simply slowdowns rather than actual de-
> clines in aggregate economic activity. This kind of shift can be
> observed in the business recessions identified by the National
> Bureau of Economic Research. On the whole, the five recessions
> of 1948–1970 were shorter than the five recessions of 1920–
> 1938; produced smaller declines in output, income, and employ-
> ment; and were less widespread in impact. But recent recessions
> have been accompanied by higher rates of unemployment than
> might have been expected in view of other evidence attesting to
> their mildness.[4]

We will discuss some of the reasons for these secular changes later
in this chapter.

## 10–5 BUSINESS CYCLES IN CANADA

A number of studies of business cycles in Canada have been published,
including some during the 1980s. Some of the more recent studies have
used different concepts to date the business-cycle peaks and troughs
than those developed by the National Bureau of Economic Research that
continue to be published and updated by the U.S. Department of Commerce. However, a number of points can be made about timing and
severity of business cycles in Canada compared to the experience in the
United States.

With respect to timing, the evidence is quite clear that there never
has been a recession in Canada unless one was occurring at about the
same time in the United States. Over a period of almost 100 years,

80 percent of the business-cycle turns in Canada have occurred within three months of a comparable turn in the United States. *There is no general tendency for Canada to either lead or lag the United States.* Thus, there is no empirical basis for the view that continues to reappear that what happens in the United States happens in Canada with a lag in timing.

Essentially Canada can be considered part of a common North American economy, with largely common factors in both private decision making and public policy. There are common patterns in commodity prices (especially for sensitive internationally traded raw materials), interest rates, and stock prices. Exports from Canada are increasingly sold in the U.S. market. Foreign ownership is also a factor that leads to similarity in corporate decision making for those firms, although the proportion of foreign ownership and control reached its peak in the 1960s and has tended to decline modestly since. Essentially, one should expect similar timing of business-cycle expansions and contractions in the two countries, and if any differences emerge, it is the task of the analyst to explain why that particular situation is different from historical experience.

There is one important contrast in the severity of business-cycle recessions in the two countries. In every business-cycle recession in Canada from 1900 to 1980, the extent of the drop was smaller in Canada than in the United States as shown in the index of industrial production, factory employment, freight car loadings, and most other economic processes relating to production, employment, and money income. There is no empirical basis for the view that an open economy like Canada is so vulnerable to conditions elsewhere that the business-cycle declines are more severe than in the United States.[5]

A key reason for this difference relates to the large quantitative importance of imports. Imports of goods and services are now approaching almost 30 percent of GDP in Canada, and merchandise imports are even more important in relation to output in the commodity-producing industries. During recessions an important part of the drop in domestic demand falls on foreign producers, rather than on producers and production within Canada. During every recession, the drop in the volume of imports has been greater than the drop in industrial production. This pattern shows up both in aggregate and for such broad categories as machinery and equipment, producers' durable and nondurable production, and imports. In technical terms the marginal propensity to import is quite high. This point was noted in Section 9–8 relating to the lower size of the multiplier in Canada than in the United States.

The one exception to the generalization that recessions in Canada are milder than in the United States is the 1981–82 recession in Canada, which was two months longer and more severe than in the United

States. We will consider the possible reasons for this unusual situation later in this text.

## 10–6 WHY HAVE BUSINESS-CYCLE RECESSIONS BECOME MILDER?

A number of factors have contributed to the milder nature of business-cycle recessions in North America since World War II.

In Table 3–5 in Chapter 3 it was noted that there are significant differences in the changes over business cycles in different expenditure areas reflecting their differing cyclical sensitivity. Differences between individual industries also occur over business cycles. A key difference is that fluctuations in employment in manufacturing, construction, and other commodity-producing industries is greater than in the service sectors. Such a difference can be seen in the varying extents of the declines in employment during five recessions in the United States from 1948 to 1970. This is particularly important in light of the significant shift in employment away from the commodity-producing industries and toward the service sector which has taken place over the postwar period. The extent of the average decline in employment, together with the changed distribution of employment for the same industries between 1955 and 1985, can be seen in Table 10–2.

Table 10–2 shows the distribution of employment in 1955 and a prediction for 1985 of the distribution of employment by industry in the two right-hand columns. The top left section of the table shows the industrial sectors that have had significant percentage declines in employment in the five postwar recessions from 1948 to 1970. For example, the employment declines in durable manufacturing have averaged 12 percent over those recessions, as shown in column 1. The middle panel shows that employment actually *increased* in most of the service industries during these five postwar recessions. A key interrelation shown in the table is that the industries that typically experience the greatest reduced employment during recessions have declined from 53 percent of total employment in 1955 to only 37 percent by 1985. On the other hand, industries that experience employment increases (or only small declines) during recessions have increased from 47 percent of total employment in 1955 to about 63 percent in 1985. The bottom panel shows a calculation that the 1985 distribution of employment would typically be associated with a decline of only 1.4 percent in recessions, roughly half of that on the basis of the 1955 distribution of employment. The changing industrial distribution of employment over the last three decades has thus tended to reduce the severity of employment reductions during recessions in the United States.

**TABLE 10–2**   Estimated Effect of Employment Trends to 1985 on Cyclical Stability of Employment (United States)

| | Annual Percent Change in Employment During Five Recessions, 1948–1970 | Percentage Distribution of Total Employment | |
| --- | --- | --- | --- |
| | | 1955 | 1985 |
| Sectors with substantial percentage declines in employment during recessions: | | | |
| Durable manufactures | −11.9 | 14.9 | 13.2 |
| Mining | −9.6 | 1.3 | 0.6 |
| Transportation and utilities | −4.5 | 6.6 | 5.0 |
| Agriculture | −3.8 | 9.8 | 1.8 |
| Nondurable manufactures | −3.5 | 11.5 | 8.7 |
| Contract construction | −3.1 | 5.4 | 4.8 |
| Federal government | −3.0 | 3.3 | 2.6 |
| Total | | 52.8 | 36.7 |
| Sectors with small percentage declines or with increases in employment during recessions: | | | |
| Wholesale and retail trade | −0.8 | 20.1 | 20.8 |
| Services | +1.8 | 15.9 | 22.2 |
| Finance, insurance and real estate | +2.4 | 4.0 | 5.5 |
| State and local government | +4.5 | 7.2 | 14.9 |
| Total | | 47.2 | 63.4 |
| All sectors | −3.0 | 100.0 | 100.0 |
| Estimated percent change during recession for all sectors: | | | |
| based on 1955 distribution of employment | −2.7 | | |
| based on 1972 distribution of employment | −1.7 | | |
| based on 1985 distribution of employment | −1.4 | | |

NOTE: Some totals may not equal 100.0 due to rounding differences.

SOURCE: Geoffrey H. Moore, *Business Cycles, Inflation, and Forecasting* (Cambridge, Mass.: Ballinger Publishing, 1980) p. 68.

Similar shifts in the industrial composition of employment have taken place in Canada and in the other industrialized countries as well. These shifts can be seen for Canada for the years 1961 and 1985 in Table 10–3. The share of employment in the commodity-producing industries in Canada has fallen from about 45 percent in 1961 to about 30 percent in 1985, with the largest declines taking place in manufacturing and agriculture, the two most important of the commodity-producing industries historically. On the other hand, the service industries have increased from 55 percent of the total to almost

**TABLE 10–3**   Percentage Distribution of Total Employment by Industry (Canada, 1961 and 1985, annual averages)

| Industry | 1961 | 1985 |
|---|---|---|
| Goods industries: | | |
| Agriculture | 11.2 | 4.6 |
| Forestry, etc. | 1.7 | 0.6 |
| Mines, etc. | 1.3 | 1.7 |
| Manufacturing | 24.0 | 17.5 |
| Construction | 6.2 | 5.2 |
| Utilities | 1.2 | 1.1 |
| Subtotal — goods | 45.6 | 30.7 |
| Service industries: | | |
| Transportation, etc. | 8.1 | 6.7 |
| Trade | 16.9 | 16.7 |
| Finance, etc. | 3.9 | 5.6 |
| Community, etc. | 19.4 | 32.3 |
| Public administration | 5.9 | 7.1 |
| Subtotal — services | 54.2 | 69.3 |
| All industries | 100.0 | 100.0 |

NOTE: Totals may not equal 100.0 due to rounding.

SOURCES: Statistics Canada, *Historical Statistics of Canada, Second Edition* (Ottawa: Ministry of Supply and Services, 1983), Series D 290 to 316, and Pradeep Kumar et al., *The Current Industrial Relations Scene in Canada, 1986* (Kingston, Ont.: Industrial Relations Centre, Queen's University, 1986), pp. 128–29.

70 percent by 1985, with the largest increase in the large and diverse category of community, business, and personal services.

Most observers expect this decline in the importance of the commodity-producing industries and the increased importance of the service industries in Canada to continue in the future (as in the other industrialized countries). These factors can be important for economic stability since the commodity-producing industries tend to be more volatile over the business cycle and experience greater relative reductions in employment during recessions, as shown in Table 10–2 for the United States. This greater degree of fluctuation in the commodity-producing industries is partly related to the fact that commodities can be stored in inventories. Commodities don't necessarily have the immediate connection between production and consumption that exists in the services, which tend to be produced and consumed on a local basis.

Unfortunately, no comparable table on the severity of employment reductions by industry during recessions has thus far been prepared for Canada. However, Table 10–3 for Canada shows the same shifts between the commodity-producing and the service industries that occurred for the United States. The industries that have historically been most cyclically sensitive have declined in relative importance, while the more stable industries have increased in relative importance in both countries.

A second important development has been an increase in the quantitative importance of the built-in stabilizers associated with the relative size of the public sector and the tax structure. **Built-in** (or automatic) **stabilizers** are institutional factors that reduce the amplitude of cyclical fluctuations (both up and down) without any direct, discretionary action by governments. One of the most important of these is the progressive personal income tax, which leads to a prompt reduction in personal income tax collections at the source when personal incomes decline during a recession. Such built-in stabilizers reduce the size of the multiplier, as pointed out in Chapter 9 (Section 9–8). In both Canada and the United States, the tax structure tends to emphasize the cyclically volatile areas of income and cyclically volatile industries. These changes are reflected in an increase in the marginal tax rate. For example, in Canada, the short-term marginal tax rate at the federal level in 1929 was 13.0 percent. In recent decades this rate has roughly tripled to about 42 percent, meaning that for a given change in an exogenous variable like exports, about 40 percent of the change is offset by an entirely automatic change in the opposite direction in federal government revenues. The extent of the built-in stabilizers appears to be somewhat greater in Canada than in the United States. A fuller explanation of the reasons for these differences is included in Chapter 14 on fiscal policy.

A third important development has been a change in the institutional side of the banking system. During the 19th century and again in the United States in the 1930s, bankruptcies of commercial banks were an important contributing factor to the occurrence and severity of business-cycle recessions and the associated financial crises. In the 1930s in the United States the deposit liabilities of chartered banks that went bankrupt amounted to about one third of total deposit liabilities. Individuals and corporations who had deposits in these banks experienced severe liquidity problems, and some of them in turn went bankrupt. Their spending decisions were definitely affected.

In light of the importance of bankruptcies in commercial banks in the United States during the 1930s, the government introduced a system of federal deposit insurance that insured individual depositors up to a specific maximum amount. The costs of such insurance were borne by the banks and their depositors. A similar system of federal deposit insurance was introduced by the Canadian government in the late 1960s and was subsequently extended to trust companies. All three of these developments helped reduce the severity and perhaps the duration of recessions in the period since World War II.

There have also been a number of changes intended to reduce the hardship on individuals and families in periods of unemployment. In the United States a system of state-administered unemployment compensation was developed during the 1920s. A constitutional amendment was needed in Canada to ensure that the federal government had the necessary constitutional authority to introduce a national system of unemployment insurance. This system was initiated during World War II. The Canadian system provides benefits based on income earned while the wage earner was contributing. The duration of benefits is related to the period of contribution. For both countries the income provided after a short waiting period helps to sustain wage earners until they obtain other employment. However, the benefit period can be exhausted, especially if few employment alternatives are available.

During the 1920s and 1930s only the male head of the household was normally gainfully occupied. In the postwar period, many married women and teens have entered the work force thus providing families with a greater number of potential income earners and thereby greater stability for total family income than was typical before World War II.

One area of uncertainty, however, involves the effects of continued slower growth since 1973 in the United States, Canada, and other industrialized countries. Continued slow growth may lead to longer and more severe business-cycle recessions in spite of the factors that contribute to short and mild business-cycle recessions and less individual and family hardship.

## 10–7 BUSINESS CYCLES AND PRODUCTIVITY CHANGE

Economic growth and productivity change do not occur at a uniform rate from year to year and over the varying stages of the business cycle, as pointed out in Section 6–1. Rather, there is considerable short-term variability in productivity change over the various stages of the business cycle. The sharpest increases in productivity occur in the early stages of a business-cycle expansion, partly because of the slack in operating rates at the recession lows. As the economy moves into the later stages of a business-cycle expansion, the rate of productivity tends to slow down and perhaps even cease. In the early stages of a recession, production is frequently cut back more sharply, while total employment may be maintained. There may be some reduction in hours worked, but companies are frequently reluctant to lay workers off, perhaps assuming that the period of weakness may only be temporary. Costs of recruiting and training employees are high, and companies may be unwilling to lay people off until it becomes essential to maintain corporate survival. The retention of employees even though there has been a drop in orders and sales is bound to have a negative effect on corporate profits in those circumstances.

The net effect is that not all of the impact of a drop in real output is reflected in an increase in the unemployment rate, but part of the drop in output is reflected in a drop in productivity. Similarly, when there is a pick-up in economic activity, there can be a much bigger increase in output while the extent of the recovery in the employment rate may be less pronounced. This phenomenon was emphasized by Arthur Okun, economic adviser to the Kennedy and Johnson administrations, and it has subsequently been referred to as Okun's Law. Okun's Law states that each 1 percent increase or decrease in unemployment results in a corresponding 3 percent increase or decrease in real economic growth; or, conversely, each 3 percent increase or decrease in real economic growth results in a 1 percent decrease or increase in unemployment.

Similar patterns of change in real output and the unemployment rate can be observed in Canada. For example, after the business-cycle trough in the fourth quarter of 1982, GDP in constant prices had increased about 18 percent by the end of 1986, but the seasonally adjusted rate of unemployment had only dropped about 3 percentage points over that four-year period.

## SUMMARY

Both econometric models and statistical indicators contribute to our knowledge of business cycles for the past and the prospects for the future.

Exogenous shocks from outside the private sector have been important factors in cyclical changes in the past, and this trend is expected to continue in the future.

Lags are also important in perpetuating cycles. Recognition of lags is important to the process of making business investment plans and changes in levels of investment spending.

The presence of seasonality makes it hard to identify recent developments, and many companies continue to recognize changes with a lag due to the limited use of seasonally adjusted data in their own operating decisions.

Business-cycle recessions have become less frequent, shorter, and milder since World War II.

Business cycles in Canada have been very similar in timing to those in the United States, and recessions from 1900 to 1980 have tended to be milder in Canada than those occurring at about the same time in the United States.

Recessions have become milder due to the decreased importance of cyclically sensitive industries and the increased importance of the service industries. In addition, built-in stabilizers have become quantitatively more important since the 1920s. The introduction of deposit insurance in both countries has reduced the risk of losses by depositors due to bank failures (an important source of instability in the past).

Productivity varies over the cycle, tending to increase more rapidly in the expansion phases, slow down in the later stages of the expansion, and even decline in the early stages of recessions, especially the more severe ones.

## NOTES

1.  Milton Friedman, "The Economic Theorist," in *Wesley Clair Mitchell: The Economic Scientist*, ed. Arthur F. Burns (New York: National Bureau of Economic Research, 1952), p. 259.

2.  These comparisons are based on Statistics Canada, *National Income and Expenditure Accounts, Volume 1, 1926–1974* (Ottawa: Information Canada, March 1976), pp. 7, 99, 106, and 328.

3.  D. J. Daly, "Seasonal Variations and Business Expectations," *Journal of Business*, July 1959, pp. 258–70.

4.  Geoffrey H. Moore, "Some Secular Changes in Business Cycles," in *Business Cycles, Inflation and Forecasting* (Cambridge, Mass.: Ballinger for the NBER, 1980), p. 65.

5.  See Derek A. White, *Business Cycles in Canada* (Ottawa: Queen's Printer, 1967), p. 48; and D. J. Daly, "Business Cycles in Canada: Their Postwar Persistence" in *Is the Business Cycle Obsolete?* ed. Martin Bronfenbrenner (New York: Wiley-Interscience, 1969), pp. 45–66. The evidence to support this view has been in the public domain for more than 20 years, but the earlier incorrect view occasionally reappears.

# PART FOUR

# Money, the Price Level, and Interest Rates

Chapter 3 highlighted two important developments since 1970 that economic theory and analysis should explain. First, inflation was more widespread among the major industrialized countries than it had been in any other peacetime period in history. Second, interest rates in the late 1970s and early 1980s reached all-time highs for the present century. The central aim of Part Four is to develop the theory relevant to these two developments and to show some of the side effects on the performance of the North American economies and the policy routes to achieve improved performance in future.

Chapter 11 will provide an overview of the determinants of the rate of interest in financial markets, based on the interrelationships between the supply of money and the demand for money. This chapter will include an initial discussion of the causes of inflation and illustrate the theory with some examples of inflationary experience.

Chapter 12 will emphasize the determinants of the supply of money and the role of the major participants in that process, namely, the central bank, the commercial banks, and the final borrowers and lenders. This chapter will also develop the orders of magnitude for a quantitative determination of the money supply multiplier. An appendix will provide a diagramatic presentation of the IS and LM curves to show the interrelations between the goods markets and financial markets in a complete system.

Chapter 13 will discuss inflation more fully in light of the tools developed in the previous chapters, including some development of the role of demand pull, cost push, and profit margins in the timing of price changes over the business cycle. The importance of price changes on the level of interest rates will also be explored. Some discussion of the effect of inflation on some of the participants in the economic system will be included. Inflation also has an impact on corporate profits as reported to shareholders for tax purposes, so the use of inflation accounting will be explained. Some alternative monetary strategies to deal with inflation and demand instability will be set out as a basis of assessing both the historical experience and the policy options for the future.

# 11

## Money and Interest Rates:
## An Overview

After reading this chapter you should understand:

1. What money is and its role in the whole price system.
2. The theory that interest rates reflect the combined influences of the demand for money and the supply of money, and Keynes's clarification of the various motives for holding money.
3. The definitions of the money supply in Canada.
4. What alternative measures of domestic inflation are available in Canada and elsewhere.
5. The evidence suggesting that both mild and severe inflations have been preceded by sustained increases in the money supply.

The whole process of industrialization is based on increased specialization in the production of a wide range of goods and services by corporations and other economic units, and the exchange of the goods produced by one economic participant for the goods and services produced and sold by other economic participants. A central part of this specialization and exchange is the use of money. A wide variety of items have been used for money in primitive societies, including shells, cattle, and coins, both wood and metal. Initially, some of these coins were composed of such precious metals as silver and gold; the value of the metal minted into each coin was equal to the coin's face value.

In current industrialized societies, coins and notes make up a decreasing share of the total money supply (as usually defined). The major part of the money supply is now made up of deposit liabilities of commercial banks. **Deposit liabilities** of chartered banks are the deposits of both individuals and businesses with the chartered banks. They are liabilities from the banks' point of view, but these same accounts are assets from the depositors' point of view. Deposit liabilities of the Canadian chartered banks are the dominant part of the comprehensive measure of the money supply, amounting to more than 90 percent of total $M_2$ (to be more fully defined in Section 11–5 of this chapter). **Currency outside banks** are the notes (produced on behalf of the Bank of Canada by two specialized printing plants) and coin (minted primarily by the Royal Canadian Mint in Ottawa). Currency outside banks held by the public in Canada was 8.6 percent of the money supply in Canada at the end of 1985, down from 13.5 percent in 1960.[1]

It is interesting that currency held by the public in the United States in 1867 was about 45 percent of the comparable broad definition of the money supply (including currency and both demand and time deposits). The comparable proportion had dropped to about 14 percent by 1960,[2] about the same as the comparable proportion for Canada in that year. The higher proportion of currency held by the public in the 19th century in the United States reflected the greater importance of rural life, the distance to banks, and some distrust of banks (because of bankruptcies). The increased importance of bank deposits and the associated more widespread use of cheques reflects the increased importance of payments at a distance, the development of new and faster methods of transportation and communication, and increased confidence in bank solvency.

## 11–1  WHAT IS MONEY?

The standard current definition of **money** in economics refers to a unit of account that is broadly acceptable by other participants in the economic process as payment for something bought or sold, or as payment of a debt. The standard bank note in Canada states "This note is legal tender." In the United States the wording on federal reserve notes is "This note is legal tender for all debts, public and private." People accept notes primarily because they know the notes will be accepted by others in turn. The pieces of various-coloured paper are transferred between individuals and companies, with really no thought as to why they are accepted so readily.

In North America, almost 90 percent of the money supply is now based on deposits with commercial banks. Funds are transferred through a system of clearing that moves cheques back and forth within individual cities, and between cities in the individual countries. As long as the accounts on which they are drawn have sufficient funds, cheques reduce deposits in one bank and increase deposits in another. This movement of funds is accompanied by a corresponding exchange of goods or services, or settlement of debts. A fuller definition of money, the various components of the money supply, and the factors that contribute to changes in it, will be provided in Chapter 12.

## 11–2 THE ROLE OF MONEY IN THE PRICE SYSTEM

In primitive societies or in an economy whose monetary system has collapsed (as it does in the extreme situation of hyperinflation), individuals and organizations must resort to exchange by a system of barter. An individual who wants a loaf of bread or a dozen eggs has to find another individual who has those commodities, but wants the goods or the services the other individual can provide. It can be a time-consuming process to try to match up the goods and services one individual has to sell with those another individual has to offer. The major advantage of a monetary system is that bank notes or cheques are accepted by all the participants, thus avoiding the high transaction costs of a barter economy. The increased specialization and division of labour that is a central part of the process of industrialization would not have been possible without the development and reasonably effective operation of a monetary system. As long as the monetary system is operating effectively, the whole process is taken for granted. It is only after the system experiences serious problems and acute instability that its full value becomes recognized and appreciated.

## 11–3 MONEY AND INTEREST RATES

Interest rates reflect the net interaction of the demand for money and the supply of money. It is thus a price much like any price you have already encountered in a course in economic principles or microeconomic theory. This chapter will develop some of the underpinnings for the demand for money, and the next chapter will concentrate on the supply of money.

The classical theory of the **demand for money** emphasized the level of the money value of national income (as defined in Chapter 2, Sections 1–4) on the demand side. If the level of the money value of national income is high, it would take a larger amount of bank notes, for example, to sustain that level of national income than would be necessary at a lower level of the money value of national income. The Cambridge theory of interest rates emphasized that the demand for money would be approximately a constant proportion of the money value of national income. The Cambridge theorists used the symbol $K$ as a constant, as in Equation (11–1):

$$MD = K \times Y \qquad (11–1)$$

where

$K$ = a fairly stable constant

$Y$ = the money value of national income

This theory is premised on the notion that the main reason for holding money is to store purchasing power until it is needed for purchasing goods and services. This is usually termed the *transactions motive* for holding money.

Irving Fisher (1867–1949) made important contributions to monetary theory and the construction of price indexes. He defined and estimated the velocity of circulation of money, using the definitions of money national income in Chapter 2 (Section 2–4) and the money supply (Section 11–1). The **velocity of circulation of money** is defined as the level of national income divided by the value of the stock of money. This concept was developed by Fisher as part of the **quantity theory of money**. He stated the theory in the following form:

$$MV = PT \qquad\qquad (11\text{--}2)$$

where

$M$ = the stock of money in the economy at a point in time

$P$ = the price level in the economy at a point in time

$T$ = the real volume of transactions in the economy, including both the level of real national income and the number of financial transactions in the economy (such as sales of stocks, bonds, and real estate)

$V$ = velocity which is derived by dividing the value of $(P \times T)$ by the stock of money

Fisher regarded $V$ (velocity) as a fairly stable relation, with its value being determined by the institutional framework and the types of payments used in that society. He recognized that shocks or disturbances from outside the system could lead to a short-term departure from its longer-term value, but it would soon return to its equilibrium value after any temporary departures. $T$ would be based on such longer-term considerations as labour force, technology, and other factors related to potential output (to use the terminology of Chapter 6). Under these circumstances, significant increases in the supply of money would lead to increases in the general level of prices.

There is an arithmetic relationship between the velocity of money as developed by Fisher and the Cambridge demand for money approach, as one is the mathematical reciprocal of the other.

$$V = \frac{1}{K} \qquad\qquad (11\text{--}3)$$

It is important to recall that both of these theories emphasized the levels of money national income (and any related transactions in stocks, bonds, and real estate in the Fisher version of the demand for money) in the determination of the demand for money, with no explicit emphasis on the rate of interest in the demand for money.

## 11–4 MONEY DEMAND — KEYNES'S *GENERAL THEORY*

An important contribution of John Maynard Keynes's 1936 volume *The General Theory of Employment, Interest and Money* was the recognition of two further motives for holding money, namely, the precautionary and speculative motives. The **precautionary motive** recognized that all individuals and organizations face some degree of uncertainty in the timing of their receipts and expenditures, or individuals face the risk of illness or accident. Under these circumstances individuals would be willing to hold some proportion of the stock of money against the possibility of an accident, a chance to buy some item at a favourable price, or to cover any other eventuality. However, the amount of money that they may want to hold for these precautionary purposes could be affected by the rate of interest. If the rate of interest was high, they would hold relatively less cash in such idle balances, but if the rate of interest was low, they would be willing to hold larger balances in this precautionary form.

A further motive for holding money is the **speculative motive**. This motive is particularly relevant to attitudes and expectations about future developments in financial markets, particularly related to expected or possible changes in stock prices and interest rates. Individuals and corporations would be willing to hold cash balances in expectation of being able to buy stocks or bonds at a lower price in the future.

The total demand for money reflects the combined influence of all three motives, namely, the transactions, the precautionary, and the speculative motives. The net effect of all three of these motives can be shown diagrammatically (see Figure 11–1). The demand for money is shown as being influenced by the level of national income. If that was the *only* influence on the demand for money, it would be shown as a vertical line for a given level of national income (such as $Y_0$). However, the precautionary and speculative motives can also influence the demand for money. These motives for holding money as a stock are influenced by the rate of interest, with a larger stock of money being held at low rates of interest rather than at high rates of interest. A higher level of national income (such as $Y_1$) is shown on the right side of Figure 11–1. Remember to be careful about distinguishing between movements along a *given* demand curve at one level of income, and

---

**FIGURE 11–1**   Demand for Money

---

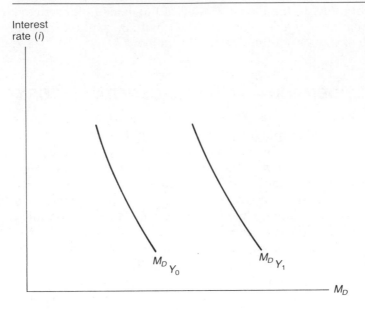

shifts of a curve (as from $Y_0$ to $Y_1$) as you have learned from a previous exposure to microeconomics.

Economists continue to differ on the general slope of these money demand curves. In *The General Theory*, Keynes tended to emphasize the idea that at the rate of interest in the United Kingdom at that time and in the economic circumstances of the period, the demand-for-money curve became quite elastic. Under these circumstances, further increases in the demand for money would not necessarily lead to any further decline in the rate of interest but would primarily lead to a larger stock of money being held for precautionary and speculative purposes, with no further declines in the rate of interest. A Keynesian view of the demand for money in the 1930s is shown in Figure 11–2. During the period of the depression with quite low rates of interest, the demand curve for money became close to horizontal. In Canada, for example, three- to five-year Government of Canada bond yields dropped to under 2 percent. The relatively horizontal slope of the money demand curve in Figure 11–2 is sometimes referred to as the liquidity trap. The **liquidity trap** is a situation in which individuals hold larger money balances without using them to buy bonds, stocks, or goods.

**FIGURE 11–2**   Keynesian View of the Demand for Money

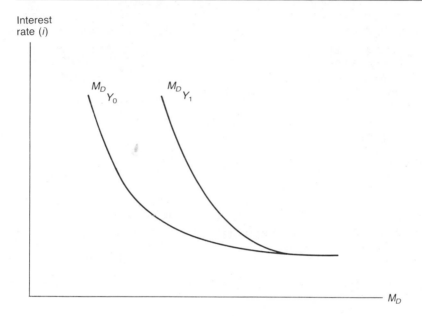

## 11–5 THE MONEY SUPPLY IN CANADA

The money supply in Canada consists partly of the currency and coin held outside the banking system (roughly $14 billion at the end of 1985). A far larger part of the Canadian money supply (more than 90 percent) consists of deposits with the Canadian chartered banks in Canadian funds. The currency outside banks had been about 12 percent of the total money supply in 1913, but this amount fell to below 10 percent by the latter part of the 1970s and to 8.6 percent at the end of 1985. Table 11–1 shows the money supply in Canada at the end of 1985.

The narrow definition of the money supply in Table 11–1 ($M_1$) is about 20 percent of the more comprehensive measure of the money supply ($M_2$), which includes all privately held chartered bank deposits. $M_2$ excludes the significant amount of deposits which the Canadian chartered banks now hold in foreign currency (primarily U.S. dollars). These foreign currency deposits are excluded because they are not legal tender for payment within Canada. $M_2$ also excludes the deposits with the trust companies, although data on this are published regularly in the *Bank of Canada Review*. In the next chapter we will discuss the factors

**TABLE 11-1**   Money Supply, Canada, End 1985 (billions of dollars, rounded)

| Money Supply Component | Amount |
|---|---|
| Currency outside banks | $ 13.9 |
| Demand deposits (less float) | 17.8 |
| $M_1$ (currency and demand deposits) | 31.7 |
| Notice deposits, term deposits and daily interest chequable | 131.0 |
| $M_2$ (currency and Canadian dollar privately held chartered bank deposits) | 161.7 |

SOURCE: *Bank of Canada Review*, January 1986, p. 878.

that contribute to changes in the money supply and the significant shifts in the composition of the money supply that have taken place over the last 15 years — an important issue in the implementation and assessment of monetary policy.

## 11-6 MEASURES OF INFLATION

There are a number of possible measures of inflation available. Chapter 2 (Section 2-4) introduced the consumer price index (CPI) and the implicit price index for gross domestic product. A number of special factors have emerged in Canada over the last 15 years that make it both necessary and important to consider this topic again here.

One of the questions in assessing inflation in Canada is the degree to which price increases within Canada have been directly related to price increases in the rest of the world (especially the United States) and the degree to which the price increases primarily reflect increases in costs and prices domestically. Two developments are important in this respect. First, exports and imports of both goods and services have increased relative to GNP over the postwar period, and the proportion of Canadian trade (particularly exports) with the United States has increased. Second, the value of the Canadian dollar has declined significantly since 1975, and by late 1986 it reached its lowest level relative to the value of the U.S. dollar during the present century.

The consumer price index is a readily available and widely used measure of domestic inflation. However, it has some limitations if you are trying to disentangle the relative direct influence of changes in prices abroad and in Canada. The CPI reflects not only costs of goods and services within Canada, but is also affected both directly and indirectly by changes in prices internationally and by changes in the Canadian exchange rate. Even if foreign prices remained unchanged, a drop in the value of the Canadian dollar would influence the level of consumer prices within Canada. When the decline in the Canada–U.S. exchange rate exceeded 30 percent over the last decade, this influence was felt. In addition, the CPI only covers about 55 percent of total GNP in Canada, and price changes in these other expenditure categories can also be important.

If you just wanted to measure the extent of price increase in Canada, the CPI is a perfectly adequate measure of what it was designed for — namely, to measure the change in prices for a wide range of goods and services purchased by the average urban consumer. The CPI is also useful to compare with money weekly earnings (or another measure of earnings) to obtain a measure of real weekly earnings.

However, it is also useful and important to try to isolate the domestic sources of price increases from the direct impact of price increases internationally. The consumer price index reflects the net result of *both* domestic and international influences on prices (direct and indirect). The separate contribution of each source cannot be isolated.

The implicit price index for GNP is a preferable price index to use rather than the CPI for two reasons. First, it is more comprehensive, covering not only consumer expenditure, but also domestic investment, government expenditures, and exports and imports. In addition, the way in which the index is calculated excludes the direct effect of changes in import prices (whether associated with price changes abroad or changes in the value of the Canadian dollar).

During the 1970s, increases in petroleum prices and in prices of fresh fruits and vegetables were reflected in both the CPI and in the GNP deflator. Two measures that exclude the effects of such special influences as petroleum prices, food prices, price inflation abroad, and exchange rate changes are compensation per hour in manufacturing and unit labour costs in manufacturing. The former is a comprehensive (but partial) measure of factor prices, while unit labour costs viewed over time measure the extent to which the increases in compensation per hour differ from the increases in output per hour. Both of these measures avoid the direct effects of international and other price changes. When comparisons are made of these measures between countries (both between countries at a point in time and changes between countries over time), they can be useful summary measures of the difference in domestic inflationary pressures and useful measures of differences in the international competitive position in manufacturing.

These various measures of inflation provide a general guide to the differing rate of inflation over time. Rates of increase in comprehensive price measures of less than 10 percent would be regarded now as mild rates of inflation. Rates of increase of 15 or 20 percent would be regarded as intermediate degrees of inflation. However, there have been a number of documented studies of hyperinflation. A dividing line developed by Phillip Cagan to designate periods of hyperinflation occurs where the rates of price increase began to exceed 45 percent, *not* per year, but *per month*.[3] Rates of inflation this high, however, do not usually continue for very long without economic, social, and political pressures to correct the underlying problems. In Germany in the 1920s, hyperinflation created an atmosphere in which the Nazi Party could sow the seeds for its rise to power.

## 11-7 IS INFLATION A MONETARY PHENOMENON?

One of the generalizations about inflation that Milton Friedman has made is that "inflation is always and everywhere a monetary phenomenon."[4] This generalization is based on the quantity theory of money, modified and extended to incorporate more recent developments in monetary theory and the empirical work relating to inflation that was initiated at the Money Workshop at the University of Chicago. This theory recognized a number of influences by which money and financial developments would affect the demand for goods and services and the price level at which exchanges of those goods and services took place. Some influences could work through movements in interest rates, which would have an influence on the demand for goods and services such as housing. If individuals begin to experience an increase in the ratio of their holdings of money relative to their incomes, they may begin to increase their spending and reduce their saving out of a given level of personal disposable income. This asset effect may occur in addition to the short-term effects of a reduction in interest rates on the demand for housing and consumer durables. There could be other effects and other channels as well, although some of this empirical work tended to emphasize the overall result, rather than the detailed mechanisms in theory and practice through which these influences could work.

This theory of inflation is a demand-oriented theory of expansion in the sense that it emphasizes the role of an increase in effective demand when the economy has begun to operate close to potential output. A key element in this framework of analysis is that the initiative for the increase in the demand for goods and services comes from an increase in the supply of money. A monetary expansion that leads to inflation can only come about if the rate of monetary expansion exceeds the growth in potential output (as explained in Chapter 6, Section 6–1). **Monetary expansion** is the rate of increase in the supply of money (as defined in Section 11–5 in this chapter). The model is as follows:

$$\dot{P} = \dot{M}_s - \dot{y} \qquad\qquad (11-4)$$

(where the dots above the variables indicate compound rates of growth)

$\dot{P}$ = rates of change in a comprehensive measure of prices
$\dot{M_s}$ = rates of increase in the money supply in earlier periods
$\dot{y}$ = the rate of increase in GDP at potential output in prices of a base period

This work emphasized that increases in the money supply need not have an immediate effect on price levels — that it might take a series of years even before participants in the economic process became fully aware of what was happening to the price level and thereby the general purchasing power of their monetary and financial assets. Lags in the process are thus emphasized. Friedman and others also emphasized that these lags, as well as being long, were also variable from one economic situation to another. For example, if the level of financial assets was initially lower than the level the participants in the economic process desired, they might be willing to let their levels of financial assets build up for a while before changing their spending patterns. If the rates of *monetary expansion* were quite high, the participants might recognize the developments more quickly and respond faster than if the rates of monetary expansion were more moderate. They might also recognize that institutional constraints could affect the lags. For example, if a high proportion of the labour force was unionized, and there were a fair number of two- and three-year wage contracts, the lags would be longer than if a high proportion of the wage contracts were made at about the same time of the year and were normally only one year in duration.[5] The latter situation approximates the situation in recent years in Japan, where most labour contracts are set in the spring wage offensive for a one-year period. The Japanese also allow for significant mid-year and end-year bonuses to employees, depending on the company's financial success, which gives an additional element of flexibility to their wage system. On the other hand, in North America the proportion of two- and three-year contracts is more widespread than in Japan, leading to longer lags in the process of wage determination.

The generalization that "inflation is always and everywhere a monetary phenomenon" is a statement that is subject to empirical testing. Data on money supply and price levels are widely available for many countries, and we can test whether the rates of increase in the money supply were high before periods of inflation took place. A variety of studies have now been done for a large number of countries and a large number of time periods. In all of these, an increase in money supply preceded a period of inflation, and none of the studies has yet disproved Friedman's hypothesis.[6]

The particular circumstances that led to the expansion in the money supply have varied considerably. For example, the price inflations in Spain and Portugal in the 16th and 17th centuries were initiated by an inflow of gold from the explorations in Central and South America. Many of the wartime inflations (the Napoleonic wars, the U.S. Civil War, and World Wars I and II) were associated with war finance, in which the increase in expenditures for military purposes exceeded the increase in revenues with the tax structures then prevailing in those countries. The governments resorted to financing part of the increased expenditures by increases in the money supply (the institutional details of which vary from one situation to another, of course).

The examples of hyperinflation have been particularly interesting, as they were all preceded by very rapid increases in the money supply for a series of years. One typical development in the later stages was complete collapse of confidence in the value of the currency. There are reports that inflation in Germany following World War I was so great that workers would be paid twice a day. Their wives and children would come to the factory gate at lunchtime to get the family paycheck and spend it because prices would go up appreciably if they waited to shop at the end of the day! Debtors were reported to have run down the streets with wheelbarrows full of currency chasing their creditors who were running away, as the currency was essentially worthless to use for anything but paying debts. During the U.S. Civil War, a country storekeeper would be unwilling to sell a bolt of cloth for currency, but would insist on a side of pork or some butter and eggs instead. Most of these periods of hyperinflation involved an increased degree of barter, and productivity frequently declined with the collapse of the price system. Resolution of the forces that led to hyperinflation was often followed by spectacular recoveries in productivity, and any deflationary results from the shift from an inflationary situation to price stability were relatively short and temporary.

## 11–8 PRICE INFLATION IN CANADA SINCE 1970

From 1951 until late in the 1960s, the rate of price increases in Canada, as in the United States and a number of the European economies, was fairly moderate. However, after about 1970 the rate of price increase began to accelerate, moving up into the 10 to 12 percent per year range until about 1982. During this period, the rate of price inflation for Canadian currency was significantly more pronounced than the rate for U.S. currency. This tendency is illustrated in Table 11–2. The measures shown in that table relate to hourly compensation and unit labour costs in manufacturing, both of which reflect only domestic cost considerations, and exclude the direct effects of higher petroleum prices, higher prices for agricultural products, and the first effects of the ex-

**TABLE 11–2**  Measures of Domestic Inflation (United States and
Canada, ratios, 1985/1970)

|  | Canada | United States | Canada/ United States |
|---|---|---|---|
| Hourly compensation in manufacturing, domestic currency | 4.12 | 3.08 | 1.34 |
| Unit labour costs in manufacturing, domestic currency | 2.74 | 2.05 | 1.34 |
| Hourly compensation in manufacturing, U.S.-dollar basis | 3.13 | 3.08 | 1.02 |
| Unit labour costs in manufacturing, U.S.-dollar basis | 2.10 | 2.05 | 1.02 |

SOURCE: U.S. Department of Labor, *Output Per Hour, Hourly Compensation and United Labor Costs in Manufacturing, Twelve Countries, 1950–1985,* Bureau of Labor Statistics, December 1986.

change rate depreciation since 1975. As can be seen from the table, the price increase in Canada was about one third higher in both measures of domestic costs and factor prices.

The two top rows and two left-hand columns in the table show the ratios in 1985 to those in the same country in 1970. "Domestic currency" means that the measures are changes over time in Canadian currency for Canada and U.S. dollars for the United States. Both measures show increases for Canada about one third higher than in the United States. The bottom two rows show the same measures for each country, but the Canadian data are converted to U.S. dollars on the basis of the average exchange rate between Canada and the United States for the years 1970 and 1985. It is significant and interesting that the drop in the value of the Canadian dollar from 1970 to 1985 (largely concentrated in the years since 1974) is roughly comparable to the greater increase in the two measures of costs for Canadian manufacturing. We will explore the forces affecting exchange rate changes in Part Six.

This period of greater price inflation in Canada is consistent with the other studies of price inflation, which show a higher rate of increase in the money supply. For Canada the rate of increase in $M_2$ (the comprehensive measure of money supply) was 13.0 percent from 1968 to the end of 1975 (a seven-year period), but it was almost identical at 12.9 percent per year compounded over the nine years from 1975 to the end of 1985. Such rates of increase were well in excess of the rates of increase in real GNP over the period as discussed in Chapters 5 and 6. The increase in the narrower definition of the money supply, $M_1$, was 11.3 percent from 1968 to 1975 and had accelerated to 13.9 percent over the period from 1975 to 1985; the increases were even more rapid after 1981.

Both of these measures of the money supply tended to show higher rates of increase in Canada than the comparable measures in the United States, although some special institutional developments in the financial institutions in both countries have made the situation difficult to sort out. In light of the importance of these developments, they will be examined more fully in Chapter 12.

## SUMMARY

Money was defined. Money has important advantages over the barter system of exchanges. Money has permitted increased specialization and exchange, which have led to higher real incomes.

The role of the demand for money and the supply of money in the determination of interest rates was explained.

The relative size of currency outside banks, $M_1$ (the narrow definition) and $M_2$ (the broad definition), were explained as components of the money supply.

A number of measures of inflation were introduced and explained.

The monetarist interpretation of inflation was summarized, but no studies of inflation have thus far been found that do not show a rapid increase in the supply of money for a time before inflation began.

Some measures of costs for Canadian manufacturing show much more rapid increases in Canada over the last 15 years than in the United States. The drop in the value of the Canadian dollar is roughly of the same magnitude as the greater increases in costs in domestic currency.

## NOTES

1. Statistics Canada, *Historical Statistics of Canada, Second Edition* (Ottawa: Ministry of Supply and Services, 1983), Series J1 and J8 and *Bank of Canada Review*, November 1986, p. S78.

2. Milton Friedman and Anna J. Schwartz, *A Monetary History of the United States, 1867–1960* (Princeton, N.J.: Princeton University Press, 1963), pp. 704 and 722.

3. Phillip Cagan, "The Monetary Dynamics of Hyperinflation," in *Studies in the Quantity Theory of Money*, ed. Milton Friedman (Chicago: University of Chicago Press, 1956), pp. 25–117. This essay was based on Cagan's doctoral dissertation at the University of Chicago.

4. Milton and Rose Friedman, *Free to Choose* (New York: Harcourt Brace Jovanovich, 1980), p. 254.

5. W. Craig Riddell, "The Responsiveness of Wage Settlements in Canada and Economic Policy," *Canadian Public Policy*, March 1983, pp. 9–23.

6.  See the reference to Cagan in Note 3 above, and other studies in Milton Friedman, ed., *Studies in the Quantity Theory of Money* (Chicago: University of Chicago Press, 1956); Milton Friedman, *The Optimum Quantity of Money and Other Essays* (Chicago: Aldine Publishing, 1969), especially pp. 157–187; see Chapter 9 in Milton and Rose Friedman, *Free to Choose*, pp. 257–261 for charts for a number of individual countries on the rates of change in prices and the supply of money.

# 12

## The Supply of Money

The last chapter introduced the supply of money and its importance as a causal influence on inflation. This chapter will discuss the participants in the money supply process and the influence of Bank of Canada on the total money supply.

After reading this chapter you should understand:

1. The interaction between money supply, money demand, and interest rates.
2. The role of the three major participants in the determination of the money supply, namely, the Bank of Canada, the chartered banks, and the general public.
3. The money multiplier, which is a measure of the quantitative influence of the Bank of Canada's open-market operations on the money supply in Canada.
4. The functions of the other financial institutions in Canada.
5. The role of U.S. monetary policy in the depression of the 1930s.

The Appendix will develop a diagrammatic presentation of the interactions between financial markets, on the one hand, and the goods and services markets on the other, in the determination of interest rates and national income.

## 12–1 AN OVERVIEW OF MONEY SUPPLY AND DEMAND AND INTEREST RATES

Before considering the determinants of the supply of money in any detail, it may help to outline the determination of interest rates in financial markets. Chapter 11, Section 11–4 has provided a perspective on the demand for money and explained why the demand for money was influenced by both the level of national income and the rate of interest. This chapter will develop an explanation of how the supply of money is determined.

For the moment, let's assume that the Bank of Canada can determine the supply of money. We will treat the supply as a vertical line. The rate of interest that would achieve equilibrium in the financial markets would occur where the demand function for money intersected the vertical supply curve as in Figure 12–1. At a low level of national income ($Y_0$), the equilibrium interest rate would be $i_0$. On the other hand, at a higher level of national income ($Y_1$) but with the same level of the money supply, the equilibrium rate of interest would be higher, as can be seen in Figure 12–1. The plausibility of this curve is apparent if you recognize that at higher levels of national income there will be a greater demand for funds, for instance, for mortgage borrowing, auto loans, and consumer durables purchased on credit. This greater demand for funds in relation to a fixed supply of money would push interest rates up to $i_1$. $Y_1$ involves a demand curve for money up and to the right of the demand curve at the lower level of national income $Y_0$.

This same type of diagrammatic presentation can be used to show the effect of a change in the supply of money. Suppose the level of national income is assumed to be unchanged for the time being at $Y_0$,

---

**FIGURE 12–1**   Interest Rate Effects of Different Income Levels and Given Money Supply

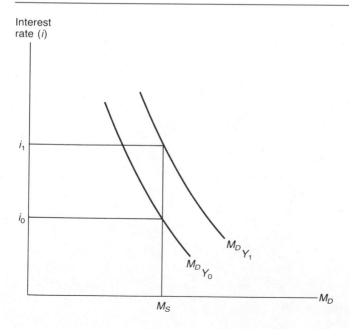

but the Bank of Canada modestly increases the supply of money and then keeps it at that new and higher level. This change in supply would be reflected in a shift of the money supply curve $M_{s0}$ to the right to $M_{s1}$ along the given demand curve for money at $Y_0$. The result would be a lower rate of interest. This is reasonable, of course, as the demand for funds would be the same at all points on that demand curve, but the increased supply from the change in Bank of Canada policy would mean that some financial institutions would offer lower rates of interest on mortgages and automobile financing, thus forcing market rates down. Banks could earn more on a mortgage loan (even at lower rates of interest) than by leaving cash balances idle in their vaults on which they would earn zero. This can be seen in Figure 12–2.

Remember that the demand curves in Chapter 11 and this chapter and the supply curves here both relate to the stock of money at a point in time. A **stock of money** refers to its value at a *point in time* (such as December 1986). An **income flow**, on the other hand, is the level of national income over a *period of time*, such as the calendar year 1986. This difference between stocks and flows is a common distinction in economics, both micro and macro.

**FIGURE 12–2**   Interest Rate Effects of Different Money Supplies and Given Income Levels

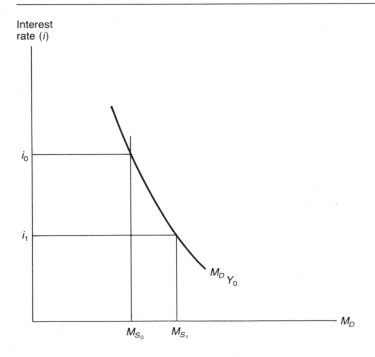

We can now turn to a fuller discussion of how changes in the money supply come about.

## 12–2 THE PARTICIPANTS IN THE MONEY SUPPLY PROCESS

There are essentially three groups of participants in the whole process of the determination of the money supply. The Bank of Canada has a central role in this process, both as a participant in the evolution of the legislation and the longer term rules and regulations for monetary policy, and also in the day-to-day implementation of those policies. A second major group of participants is the chartered banks. A third group of participants is the final borrowers and lenders, who keep a large part of their cash reserves on deposit with the chartered banks but may also borrow from them, either on a long-term or a temporary basis. We will discuss each of these three groups of participants, looking at their goals, the choices and options they may have, and the instruments by which they try to achieve their objectives.

An important aim of the Bank of Canada (as specified initially in the first legislation establishing the bank in 1935 and reflected in the most recent legislation) is to try to provide a broad framework of economic stability relating to both the price level and the general level of employment, insofar as that may be possible within the scope of monetary policy.

Although the Bank of Canada has a number of ways by which it can try to attain these broad objectives, the most important instrument currently used is open-market operations. **Open-market operations** are sales or purchases of government securities by the Bank of Canada. These purchases and sales are made through one of the larger investment dealers. **Investment dealers** issue new bond and stock issues for their clients, and also buy and sell outstanding securities for them. The ultimate seller or buyer does not and need not know that a particular transaction being handled by an investment dealer was on behalf of the Bank of Canada. In that sense it is an "open market" as contrasted to a closed market where the Bank of Canada deals on a one-to-one basis in the transaction.

The Bank of Canada accepts deposits from the chartered banks and occasionally makes loans to them. However, it does not make loans to the general public nor does it accept deposits from the public.

The management of the Bank of Canada consists of a governor, a senior deputy governor, and a board of 12 directors, providing some regional representation. Mr. John W. Crow became governor in February 1987, succeeding Mr. Gerald K. Bouey, who retired after 14 years as governor. The deputy minister of finance is an ex-officio member of the board of directors and provides the necessary information link to help coordinate monetary and fiscal policy. During the 1980s, for example, the large borrowing requirements of the federal government to finance the large budget deficit were an important and essential element for assessing economic developments and the borrowing needs of the federal government, both in terms of size and composition of planned debt issues.

The Bank of Canada can also influence the general views about the economy (including fiscal policy, interest rates, and exchange rates) by its statements and annual reports and the rare speeches of the governor of the Bank of Canada and the deputy governors and other senior staff of the bank. The Bank of Canada publishes a monthly *Review* containing discussions of domestic economic developments, international financial developments, credit markets, and a regular set of charts and statistics on financial and economic developments. Officials of the Bank of Canada also make regular presentations (using their very effective sets of charts on the current economic situation in Canada and the rest of the world). These presentations can have an influence on public thinking.

The second major participant in the money supply process is the chartered banks. Canada has a highly concentrated banking system. The three largest banks have a very large part of the total banking business in the country.

However, the chartered banks have been experiencing increased competition. Changes in legislation in the 1970s permitted more foreign banks to be established in Canada, but they cannot accept deposits. Thus they can only operate in a part of the total financial market, but they have clearly become important in corporate lending. In addition, trust companies, which have become similar to banks in many respects, have also become relatively more important in competition for deposits.

A major objective of the chartered banks is to make a profit on the activities that they are permitted to carry out under the Bank Act. Their major function is to accept deposit liabilities from depositors (both corporate and personal) and to make loans, mortgages, and investments. Their profit is derived from the spread between interest paid on deposits and the interest and other investment income received from their loans and other assets. Their expenses of operation (staff, telephones, computers, offices, and furniture) are paid out of that gross spread between interest paid and interest received.

The third major group of participants in the process is composed of final borrowers and lenders. Since anyone who has a bank account falls into this category, the number of participants is enormous. Depositors are interested in liquidity, cheque-writing privileges, and earning interest on some of their deposits. Individuals and corporations borrow from and deposit with the chartered banks. They are interested in establishing lines of credit and hope to obtain low interest rates on any loans needed. Nonfinancial corporations have a range of options for raising funds for expansion or corporate buy-outs. These can raise long-term funds in the equity and long-term capital market, but they also frequently rely on loans from the chartered banks, sometimes for seasonal or short-term reasons. In some cases, they may remain indebted to a bank for extended periods. Although they frequently establish a line of credit with a bank, they may have loans outstanding well below that limit. They may be charged for that service, but it gives them a degree of flexibility to deal with unexpected cash requirements. The existence of significant lines of credit in excess of current loans can limit the ease with which a commercial bank can reduce loans during a period of monetary restraint that may develop in the banking system, since a line of credit is a guarantee that the bank will make a specified amount of money available to such customers on request.

All three of these participants in the financial system can influence the overall changes in the money supply. The next section will set out these influences in a more specific manner.

## 12–3 THE MONEY MULTIPLIER

A key determinant of the supply of money that can be provided by the banking system is its customary or legal cash reserve ratio. The legal **cash reserve ratio** is the ratio of cash that the chartered banks are required to keep in their vaults and tills or on deposit with the Bank of Canada. No interest is paid on such deposits. For example, suppose the government and the Bank of Canada required the chartered banks to keep a cash reserve ratio of 10 percent of their total deposits. Since no interest is paid on these legal cash reserves, whether held in the tills of the chartered banks or left on deposit with the Bank of Canada, the chartered banks try to keep their actual cash reserves as close to the minimum level required as they can achieve administratively. Interest is received on all loans and investments that the banks can make on the balance of their assets. Because the interest they pay on deposits is well below what they receive on loans and investments, the more they keep on deposit and can reinvest, the higher their total profits will be. Under these circumstances, an increase in their cash reserves of, say, $100 million would permit an increase in their total deposits (and the corresponding level of assets on the assets side of their balance sheet) of $1 billion.

One complication is the public's desire to hold some of their liquid assets in the form of notes and coin. If the public withdraws some of their deposits in the form of notes, they will reduce the cash reserves of the banking system to the same extent. This occurrence is usually referred to as the **internal cash drain**. It was a crucial factor in earlier periods when notes and coin were about half the comprehensive money supply. Currently, however, the currency has fallen to less than 10 percent of the total money supply in both Canada and the United States.

Our initial simple example of the money multiplier was based on a uniform cash reserve ratio for all types of deposits. Such a uniform cash reserve ratio has been the standard practice in the United Kingdom for most of the last two centuries. For many years the Canadian chartered banks followed the British practice of a uniform cash reserve ratio for all deposits. Such cash deposit ratios were first based on accepted banking and business conventions and later on Bank of Canada regulations. It is one of the duties of the Bank of Canada and the government to set the level of cash reserves that must be followed by the chartered banks. The Bank of Canada continued to follow the British practice of uniform cash reserve ratios for all types of deposits until the 1963 report of the Royal Commission on Banking and Finance recommended a lower legal cash reserve ratio for savings deposits (with lower turnover of cheques in relation to deposits) than for chequing deposits (which normally have a much higher turnover).[1]

The money multiplier is defined as the change in the equilibrium level of the money supply for a given change in the cash reserves of the banking system. (The wording is similar to that used for the Keynesian multiplier in relation to a change in the equilibrium level of money national income.) In other words, the money supply multiplier is 10. Such a large multiplier permits a significant increase in the money supply for a relatively small increase in the cash reserves of the banking system.

If the cash reserve ratio was only 5 percent, the money supply multiplier would be 20. An increase in the cash reserves of the commercial banks of $100 million would permit an increase in total deposits and total assets of $2 billion. One of the effects of this differential cash reserve ratio is that the size of the money multiplier could be influenced by the degree to which deposit liabilities were kept in one type of deposit as compared to another.

It may be useful in the light of this initial discussion to provide a more formal statement of the money supply determinants. We will use the following notation:

$M$ = the money supply (or money stock)
$HP$ = high-powered money (the cash reserves of the banking system)
$cd$ = the ratio of currency to total deposit liabilities (broad definition)
$rd$ = the ratio of cash reserves to deposit liabilities (broad definition)
$mm$ = the money multiplier

$$mm = \frac{1 + cd}{rd + cd} \cdot HP \qquad (12\text{--}1)$$

The money multiplier will be large if the cash reserve ratio (rd) is low. The money multiplier will also be high if the ratio of currency to deposits (cd) is low. It is significant that the major trends in the composition of the total money supply have moved in the direction of a higher money multiplier with current legal requirements and business practice than would have been true a century ago or even as recently as the 1960s in Canada.

For October 1986, the ratio of currency to $M_2$ was 0.0282(cd) and the ratio of cash reserves to $M_2$ was 0.0860(rd). Substituting these values in Equation (12–1) gives a value of the money multiplier for late 1986 of 9.0. This is a much larger value for the money multiplier in Canada for late 1986 than the value of the fiscal multiplier of 1.45 derived in Chapter 9, Section 9–8 and the related discussion in Section 9–10.

The legal cash reserve ratio in Canada has been changed on several occasions since the current differential cash ratio was first introduced in the latter part of the 1960s. Currently the legal cash reserve ratio on demand deposits (accounts from which customers can withdraw money immediately at any time) is 10 percent. However, the cash reserve ratio on term deposits (money can only be withdrawn after a specified amount of time) is only 3 percent — significantly lower. The banks have an incentive to encourage depositors to keep as high a proportion of their deposits in term deposits as possible.

The introduction of computerized teller operations and a proliferation in the types of deposits available has led to changes in the composition of deposits. These changes have permitted a much higher level of the total money supply for a given level of cash reserves with the banks than would have been true a decade or more ago. Thus it is more difficult to predict the effects of a given increase in the cash reserves of the banking system than would have been true with a uniform cash reserve ratio for all types of deposits because the form in which deposits are held affects the size of the total cash reserve ratios.

The nonuniformity of reserve requirements between different classes of deposits can influence the required reserves of the banking system. If the general public switches deposits with higher reserve requirements into deposits with lower reserve requirements, the money supply can expand for a given level of cash reserves. This phenomenon has been recognized in a Bank of Canada study.[2]

## 12–4 OTHER CANADIAN FINANCIAL INSTITUTIONS

A number of financial institutions are important parts of the financial system in Canada. These are trust companies, insurance companies, and investment dealers.

**Trust companies** provide regular banking services and can clear cheques through the Canadian Payments System. They are the only corporations that act as executors, trustees, and administrators of wills, and they are active in the total mortgage market. They can be incorporated under federal or provincial charter and are regulated by the Department of Insurance in Ottawa or by comparable provincial bodies.

The **insurance companies** provide life, car, and fire insurance. Insurance involves an agreement between the insured (who pays a premium) and the insurer (who promises to reimburse the insured against financial losses for the specified risks). Mutual insurance companies are owned by the insurer, and any excess of income over claim settlements and expenses is returned to the insured in the form of dividends or reduced premiums. Stock insurance companies are owned by shareholders and are profit oriented. The Federal Department of Insurance is concerned with the ability of the companies to meet their obligations to policyholders.

The **securities dealers** provide a service to companies and governments who want to issue new securities (either bonds or stocks) to the public, and also assist in the purchase and sales of outstanding stocks and bonds. They provide advice to corporate and individual clients and customers.

The **four pillars of the financial system** are the commercial banks, the trust and loan companies, the insurance companies, and the securities dealers. Traditionally they had rather separate specialized functions, but there has been a move to reduce the regulatory barriers and increase competition between these institutions. Trust companies, for example, can now clear cheques through the Canadian Payments System and have been termed *near banks*. Federal proposals for reform of the financial sector released in December 1986 will remove unnecessary regulatory barriers and allow common ownership while retaining separate institutions for supervisory services. The Office of the Inspector General of Banks supervises the chartered banks, while the Department of Insurance supervises the trust, loan, and insurance companies. The Canada Deposit Insurance Corporation acts as deposit insurer for the banks and trust companies. The failure of the Canadian Commercial and Northland banks in mid-1985 (the first bank failures in Canada since 1922) has made the solvency and government inspection and supervision of financial institutions topics of importance in Canada.

## 12–5 U.S. MONETARY POLICY IN THE GREAT DEPRESSION

The **Federal Reserve System** was established in 1913 to provide the functions of a central bank and a strengthened system of regulatory control over the commercial banking system. It has a federal structure composed of 12 Federal Reserve District Banks. The Federal Open

Market Committee has a key role in forming monetary policy. The chairman and the Federal Reserve Board governors are appointed by the president, but the system has achieved a considerable degree of independence in its own policy decisions and in its comments on broader economic events and policies.

The evidence summarized in Chapter 11, Section 11–7 indicated that monetary policy and the supply of money has been an important factor in historical periods of inflation. This raises the important question of whether changes in the money supply can also play a contributing factor to severe depressions. A well-documented study of this period was provided in a major chapter in the Friedman and Schwartz volume.[3]

One important element in monetary policy was the concern within the Federal Reserve System about the extent of speculation that developed in both the New York stock market and in the real estate markets in a number of the major cities and metropolitan areas. There was also some concern about international capital flows and some of the vulnerabilities in the international financial system as an outgrowth of reparations and war debts that were a heritage of World War I.

The Federal Reserve System moved to restrain the money supply. There were several banking crises in 1930 and 1931 and, of course, the spectacular stock market crash begun in October 1929. These symptoms of problems were followed by a major banking panic in 1933, and over a period of a few years about one third of the commercial banks in the United States went into bankruptcy. Some of these bank failures occurred in states in which drops in farm income and cutbacks in mineral production led to delays in payment on loans to banks, and frequently, personal and corporate bankruptcies that also affected the solvency of individual banks. From August 1929 to April 1933 the money stock declined by about 35 percent.[4]

The large number of bank failures encouraged the public to withdraw cash (and hide it under mattresses!). The ratio of currency to deposits increased from under 10 percent in 1929 to about 20 percent in early 1933.

This large a decline in the money supply and the related large number of bank insolvencies had a significant impact on the private sector. Stock market and real estate prices collapsed. The commodity-producing industries operated at well below capacity, and many experienced losses. With unemployment rates running between 20 and 25 percent of the labour force, consumer expenditures were also depressed. Under these circumstances there was very little incentive for corporations to expand investment when they were not using their existing capital facilities fully and profits and rates of return were close to all-time lows. Even when monetary policy became more expansionary in the latter part of the 1930s, companies still had very little incentive to increase investment, and sales of cars and houses were slow.

One of the important institutional changes during the latter part of the 1930s was the introduction of Federal Deposit Insurance in 1934 with very extensive coverage. This change was described by Friedman and Schwartz as the structural change that was most conducive to monetary stability since the United States Civil War.[5]

Although the Great Depression is an important illustration of the effects of a reduction in the money supply on aggregate economic activity, the evidence suggests that all the severe depressions since the 1860s in the United States have been preceded by large reductions in the money supply. Similarly, mild recessions had been preceded by smaller declines in the money supply.[6]

We have now examined the determinants of both the demand for money, in the last chapter, and the supply of money, in this chapter. An equilibrium condition in financial markets exists when the demand for money as a stock is in line with the supply of money. This interpretation emphasizes that interest rates are determined in financial markets. However, the demand for money is also influenced by the level of national income, which is determined in the market for goods and services. It is necessary to bring together these two markets to permit the equilibrium conditions in both markets to be determined simultaneously. This is done in the diagrammatic presentation usually termed the IS–LM curves. Information about the curves is presented in the accompanying appendix.

## SUMMARY

This chapter has provided a framework to explain the determination of interest rates and national income.

The three major participants in the determination of the money supply are the Bank of Canada, the chartered banks, and the final borrowers and lenders.

The determinants of the money multiplier (the change in the equilibrium level of the money supply for a given open market operation) were explained. Its value in late 1986 was about 9.0 in Canada.

The functions of the trust companies, the insurance companies, and the securities dealers were explained.

The monetary policy developments in the United States in the 1930s were explained, including the role of bank failures and the drop in the money supply on the private sector. One of the important institutional changes in the 1930s was the introduction of Federal Deposit Insurance that insured depositors against loss (to a certain maximum).

The Appendix develops a diagrammatic presentation of the *IS–LM* curves, and discusses the differing perspectives of the Keynesians and monetarists on these points. The framework was used to illustrate changes in monetary and fiscal policy.

## NOTES

1. Royal Commission on Banking and Finance, *Final Report* (Ottawa: Queen's Printer, 1964), pp. 390–94.
2. Kevin Clinton and Kevin Lynch, *Monetary Base and Money Stock in Canada*, Bank of Canada Technical Report No. 16, 1979, and Peter Howitt, *Monetary Policy in Transition: A Study of Bank of Canada Policy, 1982–85* (Scarborough, Ont: Prentice-Hall Canada for C. D. Howe Institute, 1986), pp. 54–57.
3. Milton Friedman and Ann Jacobson Schwartz, *A Monetary History of the United States 1867–1960* (Princeton, N.J.: Princeton University Press, 1963), Chapter 7, pp. 299–419. This study was reviewed in a number of economic journals, and all the reviews commented on the soundly documented and important analysis in this chapter.
4. Ibid., p. 333.
5. Ibid., p. 434.
6. M. Friedman and A. J. Schwartz, "Money and Business Cycles," *Review of Economics and Statistics*, February 1963, reprinted in *The Optimum Quantity of Money and Other Essays*, Milton Friedman (Chicago: Aldine Publishing, 1969), pp. 189–235.

---

## APPENDIX: *IS–LM* DIAGRAMMATIC PRESENTATION AND KEYNESIAN/MONETARIST DIFFERENCES

Sir John Hicks developed a presentation for the interrelations between the markets for goods and services, on the one hand, and the financial markets, on the other, in an article entitled "Mr. Keynes and the Classics: A Suggested Interpretation"[1] that has been termed the *IS–LM* framework. It will be summarized here to draw together some of the relationships developed in previous chapters. There are four pieces of the puzzle to bring together, namely, the investment demand and the saving function from Part Three (where both the level of national income and the rate of interest are present), the demand for money (where both the level of national income and rate of interest are present), and the supply of money discussed in Part Four. All four parts *jointly* determine national income and interest rates simultaneously. We will follow Hicks's procedure of assuming that the price level is stable, which avoids undue complication.

One of the important advantages of this system of presentation is that it draws together the four interrelationships developed thus far and presents them in a two-dimensional diagram. The *IS* curve was given its name by John Hicks to emphasize the equality of investment (*I*) and savings (*S*). The **IS curve** shows all the combinations of income and interest rates in the economy where desired investment and saving are equal. It is a schedule that is downward sloping, reflecting the relationship introduced in Chapter 9 (Sections 9–4 to 9–5) that a higher level of investment will take place at a low rate of interest than at a high rate of interest (especially in housing). The *IS* curve also incorporates all the secondary effects of changes in investment on the equilibrium level of national income. Here, as elsewhere in this book, a condition of equilibrium means a situation that if attained would be maintained. It shows the direction in which economic forces are moving the economy.

The conditions of equilibrium in the money or financial markets are summarized in the *LM* curve. The **LM curve** shows all the combinations of income and interest rates in the economy where the demand for money equals the supply of money. The term *LM* reflects the importance of *liquidity* and *money* in such a market, and any given *LM* curve is based on a given and fixed supply of money. It is an upward-sloping curve, as contrasted to the *IS* curve, which is downward sloping. It is easy to see that the curve has to be upward sloping if you recall Figure 11–1 from Chapter 11 showing the demand for money (the three motives for holding money combined) at different interest rates and a given level of national income. For a given supply of money, the rate of interest has to be higher at a high level of national income (such as $Y_1$) than at a lower level of national income to have the demand for money in equilibrium with the given supply of money. Thus the relationship between the level of interest rates and the level of national income is positive in the financial markets.

The only position that can maintain equilibrium in both the goods markets *and* the financial markets is where the downward-sloping *IS* curve for the goods market intersects the upward-sloping *LM* curve for the financial markets. This can be seen in Figure 12 A–1.

Any point off the intersection point between the *IS* and *LM* curves would not be a position of continuing equilibrium. For example, a point *Q* that was on the *LM* curve, but to the right of the *IS* curve, would be in a condition of disequilibrium where the current position of national income was not sustainable. The level of national income would be temporarily high based on a level of inventory investment in which the level of output and national income exceeded the areas of final demand (such as consumer spending and investment in durable physical assets). Such inventory investment might be unplanned and not sustainable, and companies would soon have to curtail production and employment to get output back down to a level that was sustainable on a longer-term basis.

It is not of much value to know that some condition of equilibrium could be attained in both markets. The main gain from the *IS–LM* presentation is to be able to predict what will happen to interest rates and the equilibrium level of national income if some new development occurs to change the economic situation from that present in the initial position of equilibrium. The *IS* curve (and its slope) is designed to show the relative impacts on the equilibrium position of both interest rates and national income *if* conditions change in the financial markets. A typical factor contributing to such a change in financial markets would be an *increase* in the supply of money, which would be designed to show how changes in the market for goods and services would be reflected in changes in the equilibrium levels of both interest rates and national income. A typical factor contributing to such a change in the market for goods and services would be an increase in government expenditures, which would be reflected in a shift in the initial *IS* curve upward and to the right.

## Fiscal Policy

To simplify the exposition initially, let's assume that the initial position of equilibrium in Figure 12 A–1 is a condition of a balanced budget for the federal government. A shift in fiscal policy (as defined in Chapter 9, Section 9–2) will be illustrated by an increase in government expenditures on goods and services. (Other changes in fiscal policy would have a similar stimulative effect. For example, a cut in the personal income tax or an increase in personal transfer payments would have a similar expansionary effect, reflected in a shift of the *IS* curve upwards and to the right.) We will deal only with a one-time increase in government expenditures — in other words, a shift to a new level of expenditures that is then maintained at the new and higher rate. Any increase in the level of expenditures (or decrease in taxes) will involve a budget deficit for the federal government, as contrasted to the budget balance that was present initially in Figure 12 A–1. To keep the analysis simple, we will consider that the new budget deficit is financed by a sale of bonds to the general public. This will mean that there will be no change in the money supply from its initial position.

The point that a budget deficit financed by sales of bonds to the general public will involve *no* change in the money supply is often misunderstood, so this point will be expanded on briefly. The sale of bonds to the general public will provide cash to the government, and the cheques from the sale of bonds to the general public will be deposited in the chartered banks. However, the cash so obtained would immediately be paid out again to finance the new federal deficit. The deposits of those who bought the bonds will now be lower, while the bank

**FIGURE 12 A–1** Initial Equilibrium in Both Markets

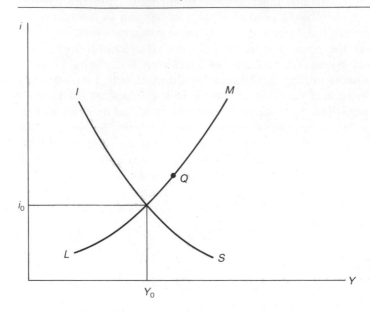

deposits of those who received payments from the federal government would be higher by the same amount. There will be a redistribution of deposits from one group of customers of the chartered banks to another group of customers of the chartered banks, but there will be no change in the total supply of money.

The next effect of such an **expansionary fiscal policy** (one that involves a government deficit and an increase in the government debt) is shown in Figure 12 A–2. The increase in government expenditures and the associated shift to the right in the IS curve will be reflected in an increase in the equilibrium levels of both interest rates and the level of national income. The extent to which the increase in the federal deficit will be reflected in interest rates, on the one hand, and national income, on the other, will depend on the relative slopes and positions of the IS and LM curves.

## Monetary Policy

We will begin again with an initial position of equilibrium in the financial markets and the markets for goods and services as in Figure 12 A–1 with a budget balance for the federal government. A shift in monetary policy can be illustrated by an increase in the supply of money initiated by the Bank of Canada. The normal way that the Bank of Canada increases the supply of money is by open-market purchases

**FIGURE 12 A–2** Effects of Shifts in the *IS* Curve

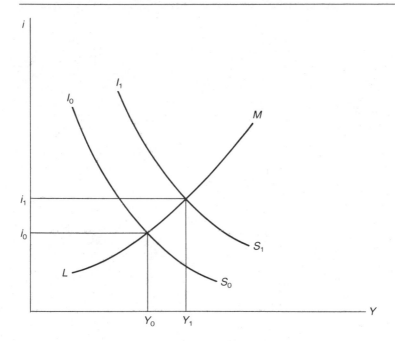

of government debt. An **open-market purchase** is conducted by the central bank in the open market (i.e., by buying from existing holders of government bonds in the private sector rather than directly from the government). When the cheques are received by the sellers of the bonds, they will be deposited in the chartered banks. This action will lead to an increase in the supply of money that can be much greater than the size of the initial open-market purchases for the reasons discussed in the body of Chapter 12. This will lead to a shift in the *LM* curve to the right as shown in Figure 12 A–3. It can be seen that this one-time increase in the money supply will lead to an increase in the equilibrium level of national income and a drop in the equilibrium level of interest rates. An **expansionary monetary policy** (one that increases the money supply) will thus lead to a *drop* in interest rates, while an expansionary fiscal policy, as discussed previously, will be reflected in an increase in interest rates.

Several points about this example of a shift in monetary policy should be made. First, we are illustrating the effects of one single open-market purchase that will lead to a shift in the money supply from the initial level to a new and higher level where the money supply will then be maintained at this new and higher level. The longer-term effects of

---

**FIGURE 12 A–3**   Effects of Shifts in the *LM* Curve

---

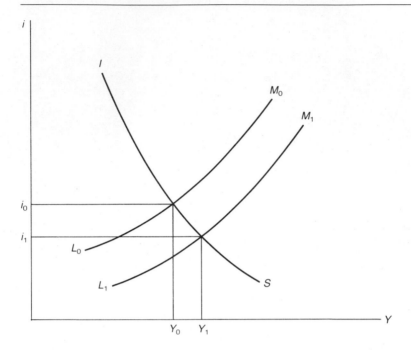

a continuous and high rate of increase can be quite different. (We will consider this possibility later in this appendix.) Second, it is important to recognize that the central bank can initiate an increase in the supply of money even if the federal government has a balanced budget initially. The holdings of cash and government bonds by the central bank are sufficiently large that it can easily buy bonds from the public no matter what position the federal government's budget is in. In fact, the higher level of national income from the stimulative effects of an increase in the money supply will lead to increased tax collections by the federal government at a given structure of tax rates, which would be reflected in the development of the budget surplus at the federal level.

## A Keynesian View of the *IS–LM* Curves

There has been an ongoing debate for decades about the relative scope for fiscal and monetary policy in initiating changes in equilibrium in the economy. This difference in views can be depicted using the *IS* and *LM* curves. It is important to realize that these differences in views are not really differences in economic theory, as both schools can be represented by the same theoretical apparatus using the *IS–LM* curves. The differences in views reflect differences about the real world, and it should be possible at least to narrow these differences by examining empirical evidence from the real world.

A key continuing emphasis by Keynesians is that an increase in the money supply (and the associated shift to the right in the *LM* curve) would be reflected in only a *small* increase in the equilibrium level of investment. This implies a steep downward slope to the *IS* curve as illustrated in Figure 12 A–4. Such a view by the Keynesians was based on the slight responsiveness of business investment spending to changes in interest rates (based on the evidence and rationale in Chapter 9, Sections 9–2 and 9–3). On the other hand, they feel that an increase in the budget deficit (and the associated shift in the *IS* curve to the right) would be reflected in a *large* increase in the equilibrium level of national income and only a small increase in interest rates. You can visualize the *IS* and *LM* curves intersecting at a right angle. A Keynesian view of the effects of an increase in the budget deficit can be seen by a shift in the *IS* curve to the right. You can see that the new position of equilibrium involves a significant increase in national income, but only a small increase in interest rates.

## A Monetarist View of the *IS–LM* Curves

Monetarists can use the same *IS–LM* curves to analyze changes in equilibrium, but they make quite different predictions about the relative impacts of changes in fiscal and monetary policy than those predicted by the Keynesians. One reason for the difference in predictions comes about because of the greater elasticity in the investment schedule with respect to interest rates. They put more emphasis on the effects of interest rate changes on investment in housing and consumer durables as discussed in Chapter 9, Sections 9–4 and 9–5, and other potential secondary effects. They expect that an increase in the budget deficit would be reflected in a *larger* increase in interest rates and a smaller increase in national income than the Keynesians. Their reasoning emphasizes that with a steeper upward slope in the *LM* curve, the enlarged deficit would lead to a higher rate of interest than is predicted by the Keynesians with a more horizontal slope in the *LM* curve. The *IS–LM* curves that they feel portray the real world would be as shown in Figure 12 A–5. Think of starting off with the Keynesian curves from Figure 12 A–4 and rotating both of them *counterclockwise*, still keeping them at a 90-degree angle to one another.

Figure 12 A–5 shows why the Monetarists put more emphasis on the "crowding out" of private investment by an enlarged federal deficit. If interest rates had stayed at the initial level, a higher level of national

**FIGURE 12 A–4**    A Keynesian View of the *IS–LM* Curves

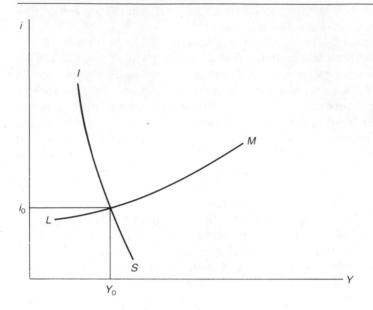

**FIGURE 12 A–5**    A Monetarist View of the *IS–LM* Curves

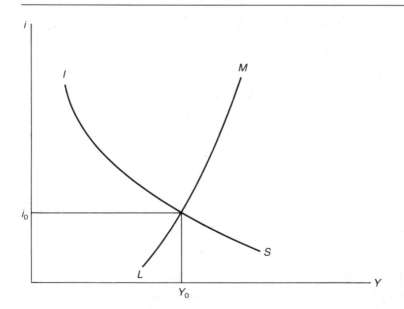

income from the expansionary fiscal policy would encourage a higher level of investment. However, this would *not* be a position of sustainable equilibrium, and the new *IS* curve would intersect the unchanged *LM* curve at a much higher equilibrium rate of interest than would emerge with the flatter *LM* curve of the Keynesians in Figure 12 A–4. At this new and higher equilibrium level of interest rates, some investment spending would be curtailed. In light of the evidence presented in Chapter 9, Section 9–4, housing investment would be the key area affected rather than business spending on fixed business investment, which is much more interest-inelastic than housing. In other words, the large federal deficit would be partially offset by a curtailment in housing investment. A larger deficit would *not* have the large stimulative effect predicted from the Keynesian analysis. Thus the Monetarists have always given more emphasis to crowding out of private investment by an enlarged budget deficit rather than the greater stimulus from the budget deficit predicted by the Keynesians. **Crowding out** refers to the effect of a larger government deficit (and its financing) has in reducing private investment or consumption. The mechanism through which such crowding out occurs is higher interest rates. Such crowding out could occur even if the economy was operating at less than full employment.

## Money Supply and Inflation

In the discussion of the effects of a change in the money supply and the associated shift in the *LM* curve, we have considered an increase in the money supply to a new and higher level, with the money supply then staying at that new level. We have assumed unchanged prices, the convention introduced by Hicks and still widely used. The short-run effect is a lower rate of interest than the initial equilibrium position. The situation of a persistent increase in the money supply over an extended period is quite different, however. In that case, a persistently high rate of increase in the money supply leads to a shift in the *IS* curve to the right, as the general price level rises for the reasons set out in Chapter 11, Section 11–7.

One of the reasons that this appendix presents the *IS–LM* curves with the assumption of no change in the price level initially is that the central bank can influence, and even determine, the supply of money in nominal terms, but it *cannot* determine the general level of prices. It is much simpler to present and understand this framework in the simpler case (but it is recognized to be an unrealistic assumption for the 1970s).

The persistent increase in the price level will become recognized by economic agents, and there will be upward pressures on interest rates, as lenders will be unwilling to see a continued drop in their rate of interest income in real terms and the drop in the real value of their bond holdings. Thus the long-term effects of persistent increases in the money supply will be an *increase* in interest rates, the reverse of the short-term effect of a one-time increase in the money supply.

## NOTES

1. John Hicks, "Mr. Keynes and the 'Classics': A Suggested Interpretation," *Econometrica* 1937, pp. 147–89.

# 13

## The Price Level, Interest Rates, and Monetary Policy

Chapter 11 developed the key determinants of the demand for money, and Chapter 12 emphasized the determinants of the supply of money, including the interaction among the major participants and the quantitative size of the money multiplier for Canada. This chapter will develop some aspects of the interactions between the demand for money and the supply of money. The chapter will also look at some of the major effects in the economy of changes in the supply of money. Some of these illustrations will build on the IS and LM curves developed in the appendix of the last chapter.

After reading this chapter you should understand:

1. How changes in the money supply affect economic activity.
2. How increases in the general price level lead to increases in nominal interest rates.
3. How inflation affects accounting reports even after the price increases have stopped.
4. That prices, costs, and profits differ in their response timing over the business cycle.
5. That profit margins are a good basis of distinguishing between demand-pull and cost-push inflation, but cost-push is not an independent factor for the economy as a whole.
6. That there are important lags in using monetary policy.
7. That there are a variety of monetary strategies available with different implications for stability of employment and output and the rate of inflation.

## 13–1  CHANGES IN THE MONEY SUPPLY AND ECONOMIC ACTIVITY

Let us assume that the Bank of Canada increases the money supply from an initial position of equilibrium to a new and higher level that is then maintained. The economic effects of that change can be seen using the diagramatic presentation developed in the appendix of Chapter 12. An increase in the money supply will shift the *LM* curve down and to the right as shown in Figure 13–1. The economy will find a new position of equilibrium at a lower level of nominal interest rates and a higher level of money national income than was present initially. The precise extent of the decline in interest rates and the magnitude of the increase in money national income will depend on the relative positions and elasticities of the *IS* and *LM* curves.

 An important source of the increase in money national income would come about from the stimulus to investment in housing that would result from the lower rates of interest. You will remember (see Section 9–4) that the stimulus in the housing area is greater than in investment in plant and equipment. There may be some possible further

**FIGURE 13–1**   Money-supply Shift and *IS* and *LM* Curves

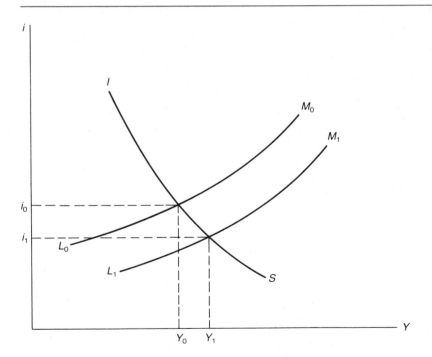

effects on spending from the higher level of money supply in relation to income that would result from expanding the money supply. Such initial increases in expenditure could have further effects in the economy (partially offset by the leakages associated with higher tax collections and increased imports as explained in Chapter 9, Section 9–8). The economy would thus settle down to a new position of equilibrium, unless disturbed by further shocks from outside the private sector.

The conditions that have just been described apply to a one-time increase in the money supply, followed by stability at a new level. The situation would be quite different if continuous increases in the money supply took place year after year. The analysis would no longer be appropriately represented by a shift in the *LM* curve moving along a given and fixed *IS* curve. Instead, the economy would begin to experience price increases, especially once it approached full capacity. Eventually, further increases in the money supply would no longer lead to increases in real national income, but would be reflected in higher prices for the economy as a whole, resulting in shifts of the *IS* curve to the right as well. Under these circumstances the long-term effects of persistent increases in the money supply would be an *increase* in nominal interest rates, the exact opposite of the short-term effects dealt with initially. This effect can be seen in Figure 13–2 which contrasts to the short-term effect in Figure 13–1.

**FIGURE 13–2**  Prolonged Money-supply Expansion (*IS* and *LM* curves)

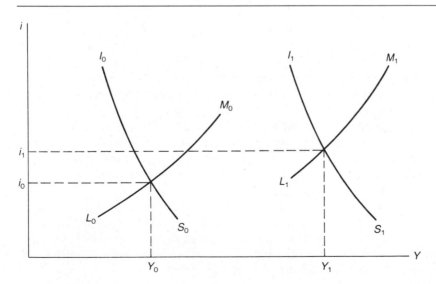

Once the economy approaches full capacity, further increases in the money supply are reflected in increases in the general price level. This can be shown algebraically as follows:

$$\dot{P} = \dot{M}_s - \dot{y}$$

where

$\dot{P}$ = the rate of change in the general price level (e.g., the GDP deflator)

$\dot{M}_s$ = the rate of change in the nominal money supply

$\dot{y}$ = the rate of change in real national income (real GDP)

A high rate of increase in the money supply need not necessarily be reflected immediately in an increase in the price level to the extent shown in the previous equation. It may take as long as a year before the effects of lower interest rates have a large impact on housing investment. There may be a further lag before all of the secondary repercussions have spread through the economy. Furthermore, householders and business firms may not be initially aware of the increases in the money supply. Initially, they may let their cash balances accrue (i.e., become more liquid) without any immediate adjustments in their spending patterns — in effect, the velocity of circulation of money could drop. Persistent increases in the money supply in excess of the increases in real national income will be reflected in increases in the general price level.

## 13–2 MONEY AND REAL INTEREST RATES

The development of persistent price increases in the economy would eventually lead to effects on the general level of interest rates. Individuals and businesses, the net holders of cash balances and financial assets, would find that the higher level of prices would lead to a reduction in the real purchasing power of those liquid assets. You could think of the reduction as the equivalent of a tax on the holders of monetary and financial assets with the rate of tax proportional to the rate of price increase. On seeing the real purchasing power of their assets declining, these individuals and businesses would want to shift the compositions of their portfolios into assets less affected by price increases, such as houses, antiques, or art (recognizing, of course, that there are costs in the holding of such assets).

Irving Fisher, a famous American economist, suggested that in situations of perfectly anticipated inflation, a long-term equilibrium could be achieved in the level of nominal interest rates. Money interest rates would be established on the basis of "real" interest rates plus the rate of change in the general price level.

$$i = r + \dot{P}$$

where

$i$ = the money rate of interest

$r$ = the real rate of interest (after allowing for general price increases)

$\dot{P}$ = the rate of change in the general price level (the GDP deflator)

Fisher thus provided a basis for understanding why the high rates of price increase that emerged during the 1970s were eventually reflected in high levels of money interest rates. In 1981 and 1982, the interest rates in North America reached their highest level of the present century.

The experience of the 1970s and 1980s provides a basis for considering whether the real rates of interest are stable. Estimates of the real rates of interest are made by subtracting the rate of price increase from the money rates of interest. The rates of increase over several years rather than a shorter time period have sometimes been used. The resulting estimates of the real rates of interest were low during the 1970s, but increased in the mid-1980s, when the rates of price increase slowed down.

Let's also consider the tax implications of these changes in interest rates and the general price level. Personal income tax is paid on interest income. If the marginal tax rate of the holder of financial assets is high, the real rate of return on financial assets after taxes can be quite low.

## 13–3 INFLATION AND CORPORATE ACCOUNTING PRACTICES

Inflation leads to higher nominal interest rates (as discussed in Section 13–2). It also affects the reporting of corporate profits and the valuation of physical assets (plant, equipment, and inventories) on the balance sheet.

The accounting information used by managers for financial reporting for corporation profits tax purposes and for other decisions on pricing, investment, and dividend policies is usually based on historical costs in Canada rather than replacement costs. This policy of using historical data from the market has a long tradition in accounting practice because it reflects the principles of objectivity and conservatism considered to be important. These historically determined values reflect cash payments for values that have been determined independently in competitive markets.

The use of such historical costs is good practice when there has been general price stability over extended periods of time. However, when prices are rising significantly, historical cost data do not provide reliable information for managerial decision making and can affect the ability of a firm to survive over the longer term. It is important that firms recognize the impact of inflation on their valuation of some costs and assets. With persistent price inflation (whether consistent or erratic), the provisions for depreciation based on historical costs are insufficient because the eventual replacement costs of the assets would be higher than the original costs. Also, materials and goods valued in inventories at historical cost would be charged to cost of goods sold at a value less than replacement costs. In the longer run, firms using historically determined costs in an inflationary era for managerial decision making would overstate profits available for distribution as dividends (perhaps even paying out capital rather than current earned income); overstate rates of return on investment; set aside insufficient cash to replace assets; and value physical assets and inventories at below current market replacement costs.

Such historical valuation of profits and assets could even threaten a company's continuation as an ongoing entity. Such distortions from misstating the depreciation of physical assets would continue even after the rate of inflation ceased because some capital assets are carried on company books for 40 and 50 years. Furthermore, in Canada, firms pay corporate profits taxes on the overstated portion of reported profits. The firms and their accountants are not well enough informed and concerned to seek revisions from the government on this point, as was done in both the United Kingdom and the United States some years ago.

The extent of this effect is quite significant. By 1985, the GDP deflator was roughly four times its 1961 level and more than double the 1974 level. The increases in the price deflators for construction, machinery, and equipment are broadly comparable. Furthermore, partial information on corporate accounting practices suggests that perhaps only 5 or 10 percent of the companies listed on the Toronto Stock Exchange are using inflation adjustments for their operating statements and balance sheets even in their internal operating records.

Adjustments to put manufacturing profits and balance sheets on a replacement cost basis have been made for Canada. These results are included in Figure 13–3 for the years 1966 to 1985. The vertical scale is rate of return on total capital on a percentage basis. The top line is based on historical cost. A lower line reflects inflation-adjusted rates of return (with both profits and the balance sheet revalued to current replacement cost for that year). The difference in the 1960s was less than 2 percentage points, but that difference widened to almost 10 percentage points by the 1980s. To provide a basis of comparison with market interest rates, the long-term corporate bond rate for the individual years is also included. (Some tax effects are recognized, but they do not modify the marked differences in the movements over time.) In the mid-1960s, corporate rates of return in manufacturing were well above the long-term corporate bond rate. Both rates of return dropped drastically in the 1981–82 recession, but even by 1985, the inflation-adjusted rates of return had recovered to about 7 percent—still only

---

**FIGURE 13–3**  Return on Total Capital before Tax, Historical Cost, Inflation Adjusted and Long-term Corporate Bond Rate (Canadian manufacturing, 1966–1985)

---

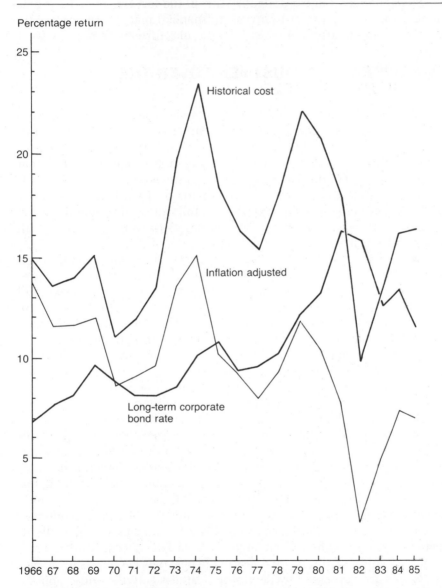

SOURCE: D.J. Daly and D.C. MacCharles, *Focus on Real Wage Unemployment* (Vancouver: Fraser Institute, 1986), p. 34.

half the 1966 rate. The 1984–85 inflation-adjusted rates of return were about 5 percentage points *below* the corporate bond rate. This figure had been about 5 percentage points *above* in 1966.

Such changes show a dramatic shift in the last two decades. Some manufacturers may prefer to invest in financial markets rather than in more plant and equipment when the rates of return are so much lower.[1]

## 13–4  SPEED OF ADJUSTMENT OVER THE BUSINESS CYCLE

In Chapter 10, we introduced the importance of lags in the economy's adjustment process. Section 10–3 examined lags in business investment spending in relation to contracts and orders. We also examined delayed recognition of lags that can occur in seasonal industries that use year-to-year comparisons. This section introduces the topic of differing speeds of adjustment in various parts of the pricing system. By the pricing system we mean the prices of the factors of production such as profits and wages, as well as the prices of finished products (both goods and services).

Evidence suggests that there are significant differences in the speed of adjustment in various parts of the pricing system. For example, producer prices for sensitive materials tend to lead at both peaks and troughs by 10 and 7 months, respectively. In Table 13–1, leads are shown as (−) and lags as (+). Corporate profits also tend to lead, with a longer lead at business cycle peaks than at troughs. The business community frequently speaks of "profitless prosperity" in the later stages of business cycle expansions, reflecting an awareness of this long-term tendency for profits to begin to decline before physical activity and the business cycles have reached a peak.

On the other hand, some of the cost measures continue to go up even after a business cycle peak has been passed. For example, unit labour costs tend to lag by about 8 to 10 months at both peaks and troughs in business cycle activity. Union wage settlements have an effect on relative wages (as pointed out in Chapter 5, Section 5–8), but wages can only affect the general price level if monetary policy permits (or encourages) this to happen. Interest rates (such as the prime rate charged by banks or mortgage interest rates) tend to lag, especially at business cycle troughs. When such costs as labour costs and interest costs keep going up after a business cycle peak has been passed, corporate profits are depressed by declining business activity, and corporate profit margins are further squeezed. These cost pressures can lead to dramatic drops in corporate profits, which then have an effect on business decisions on inventory investment and longer-term investment. Some of the evidence regarding these changes in prices and costs over the postwar period can be seen in Table 13–1 for the United States. No

---

**TABLE 13–1**  Cyclical Indicators of Prices, Costs, Profits, and Interest
Rates (median timing at peaks, troughs, and all turns)

| | Peaks | Troughs | All Turns |
|---|---|---|---|
| Changes in producer prices for 28 sensitive materials | −10 | −7 | −7.5 |
| Corporate profits after taxes 1972 dollars | −11 | −2 | −5 |
| Profits after tax per dollar of sales, mfg. corps. | −10 | −2 | −5 |
| Index of unit labour cost, business sector | +10 | +9 | +9 |
| Index of labour cost per unit of output, mfg. | +8 | +10 | +9 |
| Secondary market yields on FHA mortgages | +2 | +9 | +3.5 |
| Average prime rate charged by banks | +3.5 | +15 | +5.5 |

SOURCE: U.S. Department of Commerce, *Handbook of Cyclical Indicators, 1984*
(Washington, D.C.: Bureau of Economic Analysis, 1984), p. 173.

comparable data have been assembled for Canada, but similar patterns prevail here for the comparisons that have been made.

The leads (−) and lags (+) are the timing differences in relation to the business-cycle peaks and troughs (as in Table 10–1).

## 13–5 DEMAND-PULL AND COST-PUSH INFLATION

Public discussion frequently makes a distinction between demand-pull inflation and cost-push inflation. **Demand-pull inflation** is inflation caused by too much demand relative to potential output at full employment. The only outcome is rising prices. **Cost-push inflation** is said to come from excessive wage and cost increases reflecting market power rather than excess demand.

How can you distinguish in practice between demand-pull and cost-push inflation? A useful criterion that has been used for many years in the analysis of the current economic situation is to look at corporate profit margins in manufacturing or the commodity-producing industries (the industries that are most cyclically sensitive, as pointed out in Chapter 10). If corporate profit margins are widening during a period of inflation, demand-pull is an important factor in the price increases. On the other hand, if corporate profit margins are narrowing, the economy is in a period of cost-push. However, there have been no periods of cost-push inflation that have not been preceded by demand-pull inflation. The presence of cost-push pressures is more a matter of the typical timing differences in the speed of response rather than any new and independent causal factor.

It is sometimes argued that if inflation occurs because of cost pushes, the use of monetary and fiscal policy to check such inflationary pressures would be inappropriate. This type of interpretation is usually premised on the view that cost-push pressures can occur independently of demand pressures. We have just seen that this situation does not actually happen.

Inflationary pressures essentially originate from prior increases in the money supply in excess of the increases in real national income, extending over a series of years. This theory is essentially a demand-initiated theory of inflation. However, this theory also recognizes significant differences in the speed of adjustment of different parts of the pricing system, as reflected in Table 13–1. That table demonstrates that unit labour costs and interest costs lag at both business cycle peaks and troughs.

The price system also provides a system of incentives, by encouraging the producers and the sellers of factor services to move resources into areas that provide them with a higher rate of return. It is not necessary for all participants to move, but there will be more moving from weak areas to strong areas than the other way around.

The third function of the price system is to provide a mechanism for the distribution of the economic system, reflecting the number and quality of the factors of production that an individual or a family have to provide to the market and the price at which those factors of production are made available.

A typical experience during inflation is greater year-to-year variability in the rate of price change when the rate of price increase is higher over a number of years than during a period of greater price stability. Thus the problems associated with the differences in timing discussed in the two previous sections and as shown in Table 13–1 are further intensified, forcing business managers to spend a large proportion of their time identifying the movements in the price system and adjusting wages, fringe benefits, catalogues, and selling prices. On one occasion the author participated in a round-table luncheon with representatives of a personnel association during a period of inflation, and the major topic of conversation was the problem of trying to update the appropriate mileage allowances for personal cars used for business purposes. Participants also related the problems of trying to entice senior staff to move from Winnipeg to Toronto, when the differences in house prices were so great that it would have involved a substantial increase in the carrying costs of an enlarged mortgage. The individual ended up staying in Winnipeg.

An additional problem arises with the increased importance of international trade and the interconnections in the price level and price structure between countries. The period of the 1970s witnessed significant differences in the rates of inflation and a significant increase in exchange rate volatility among the major industrialized countries. This development was pointed out in Chapter 3 and will be explored more fully in Part Six. The greater exchange rate volatility since 1972 has increased the degree of uncertainty related to this major price in the economic system.

The incomplete evidence available suggests that inflation has an adverse effect on productivity performance. This is clearest in periods of hyperinflation, when the usual forms of money are no longer acceptable in exchange, and people resort to barter and all its related inefficiencies. During the period since the 1970s, the rates of productivity increase have continued at higher levels in the countries experiencing low rates of inflation, such as Japan and West Germany. However, the rates of productivity increase have been slower in such countries as the United Kingdom and Sweden during the 1970s.

## 13–6 INDICATORS OF MONETARY POLICY

Before considering monetary policy and the optional strategies that the Bank of Canada can follow, it would be useful to consider how to assess whether monetary policy is easy or tight (most popularly judged on the basis of low or high interest rates). The rate of interest reflects the net interaction between the supply conditions and the demand conditions in financial markets for the stock of money. An increase in interest rates can reflect a shift in the demand curve to the right as well as a shift in the supply curve to the left. Thus it is an ambiguous indicator of monetary policy. The only clear and unambiguous indicator of monetary policy is the transactions of the Bank of Canada. We can look at these to see what the bank is doing to the cash reserves of the banking system and the total supply of money. When there are institutional changes in the banking and financial system and a variety of cash reserve ratios and types of deposit liabilities, even that indicator is not always easy to evaluate.

## 13–7 LAGS IN MONETARY POLICY

It has been widely recognized for some decades that lags in monetary policy (as in fiscal policy) occur between the time that it is first recognized that a change in policy may be desirable, and the time the new policy has been in operation long enough to have a significant impact on production, employment, and the price level.

Three types of lags have been distinguished in economic literature. The first lag is a recognition lag, the time it takes to realize that some change in monetary policy is required. A second lag is a policy lag while the Bank of Canada and the government are considering the appropriate responses. A third lag is the outside lag during which the private sector responds to the changes in policy that have been implemented. Each of these lags will be briefly discussed, with application to the area of monetary policy.

The recognition lag occurs because of the delay in the collection and publication of statistical data relating to the current economic situation and short-term prospects. The quarterly national accounts data only become available about two months after the quarter to which they relate, and the fourth quarter is even later because many corporations make their year-end adjustments to corporate profits during the final quarter of the year. There are also delays in the release of such monthly series as the labour force survey, employment and payrolls, prices, inventories, and international trade. Sometimes these series experience irregular movements due to strikes, adverse weather, or the shifting dates of holidays. All these factors contribute to a delay in recognizing changing economic circumstances. Such delays in recognition affect all types of policy decisions and can affect decisions in the private sector as well as in public policy.

Once the evidence from current economic developments suggests that the economy is deviating from what the government and the Bank of Canada would like to achieve, there is a delay before a change can be implemented. The supporters of discretionary monetary policy emphasize the flexibility and short internal lags of monetary policy. Bank of Canada staff are meeting continually to review the latest developments in Canada and the rest of the world and have continuing contacts with officials from other countries and central banks. Meetings occur regularly with the IMF and at the Bank of International Settlements in Basel, Switzerland.

The recognition lag and the policy lag are both described as inside lags, since they occur within the government. The outside lag refers to the response in the private sector.

The outside lags of monetary policy appear to be fairly long but variable from one situation to another. Evidence before the Porter Commission during the 1960s indicated that prolonged lags could occur within the commercial banking system before changes were made. In some instances, it was almost a full year from the time that the Bank of Canada began to move to a position of restraint until instructions went out from the head offices of the chartered banks to their local offices to tighten up on their lending policies. With greater experience with periods of monetary restraint and improved economic information and analysis within the chartered banks, these lags have now been reduced appreciably. However, even when interest rates begin to increase, it may be several months before they have an effect on the number of new mortgages approved. The delay may be even longer before the increase in interest rates begins to be reflected in a slowdown in residential construction investment. Further delays would occur before additional responses take place in the industries supplying residential construction materials and other areas of business capital spending and inventories. Under these circumstances, the long outside lag in monetary policy can largely offset the short inside policy lags.

Since the total length of these lags can be as long as two years, you can appreciate how serious the lags are for those who plan monetary policy. The duration of business cycle recessions since World War II has averaged only about 12 months in North America.

## 13–8 ALTERNATIVE MONETARY STRATEGIES

In light of the existence of lags, what are the alternative strategies that could be followed in setting general guidelines for monetary policy? Let us consider three broad policy options for a rate of change in the money supply. The first possibility is a high but variable increase in the money supply from quarter to quarter. The rates of increase in the money supply could range from −5 percent, at one extreme, to +25 percent at the other, but average 15 percent over a series of years. A second possibility is the same 15 percent increase over an extended period, but with a steady rate of increase. A third possibility is a rate of increase of 5 percent in the money supply, with a steady rate of increase from year to year. In all three situations, let's assume that the rate of increase in real national income is 5 percent a year.

What would you expect to see happen to the price level and the rate of change in employment and output in response to these three possible scenarios for monetary policy? With a high but erratic increase in the money supply you might expect a rate of price increase of about 10 percent per year, but with considerable variability from year to year. You would also expect to find erratic growth in employment and output, with declines occurring some quarters after the more marked reductions in the money supply, followed by renewed acceleration after more rapid increases in the money supply.

The steady rate of increase in the money supply of 15 percent per year would be reflected in a rate of price inflation of about 10 percent per year, but with steady growth in employment and output. This could be a stable system if the participants expected that rate of inflation to continue and wages and interest rates to adjust to those developments.

A steady rate of increase in the money supply of 5 percent per year (in line with potential output) would be associated with rough stability in prices and steadier growth in employment and output.

The conclusion of many classes of students over the years has been that the third situation would be the most desirable strategy for a closed economy. In fact, the movements in the money supply from about 1960 to 1982 were much closer to the first alternative, which led to a great amount of instability in the economy, both in terms of variations in production and employment, and in variability in the rates of inflation.

## SUMMARY

Changes in the money supply affect economic activity through their influence on the nominal interest rate, housing investment, and other economic variables.

Prolonged increases in the money supply in excess of the increase in potential GDP eventually lead to higher prices and interest rates through the Fisher effect.

Inflation affects the valuation of reported profits and physical assets on the balance sheet, when most Canadian companies report on the basis of historic costs. When adjustments are made for Canadian manufacturing, the inflation-adjusted rates of return in the mid-1980s are well below the rates of two decades ago, and much less attractive relative to the long-term corporate bond rate.

Prices, costs, and profits vary in timing in relation to business cycle peaks and troughs, with corporate profit margin tending to lead, while wage rates, unit labour costs, and interest rates tend to lag.

Profit margins are a good basis of distinguishing between demand-pull and cost-push, with costs responding with a lag to prior demand-pull rather than having a major independent role for the economy as a whole.

There are important lags in the implementation of discretionary monetary policy, namely a recognition and policy lag (both inside lags) and outside lags (which continue to be quite long for monetary policy).

A number of alternative monetary strategies were explored, but a steady rate of increase in the money supply approximately in line with the increases in potential output (at fixed prices) was the most promising strategy to achieve reasonably steady growth and price stability.

## NOTES

1.  See D. J. Daly and D. C. MacCharles, *Focus on Real Wage Unemployment* (Vancouver: Fraser Institute, 1986), pp. 33–35; D. J. Daly, "Inflation, Inflation Accounting, and Its Effect, Canadian Manufacturing, 1966–1982." *Review of Income and Wealth,* December 1985, pp. 355–74; and D. J. Daly, "High Costs and Low Productivity Erode Profits," *The Canadian Business Review,* Spring 1984, pp. 6–10. Don MacCharles assisted in updating the material and did a first draft of this section. His help is appreciated.

# PART FIVE

# The Role of Government

This part of the text will concentrate on the potential for fiscal policy to contribute to the future stability of the Canadian economy. We will see that the decentralized nature of the federal system of government in Canada and the lack of flexibility in expenditures at the federal level hampers the use of fiscal policy.

Chapter 14 will concentrate on the structure of the expenditure and revenue system. This chapter will study ways in which the federal system and other aspects of the structure of government can help to either achieve or thwart the attainment of broader social and economic goals. The chapter will show how economic growth and business cycles are reflected in variations in tax collections with a given structure of tax rates.

Chapter 15 will explore some aspects of federal deficits, the associated growth in public debt, and the increased importance of interest payments to service that enlarged public debt. This chapter will examine the economic effects of deficits and options to reduce deficits. It will also consider the scope for discretionary changes in fiscal policy to further moderate the effects of recessions.

# 14

# Government Expenditure and Taxes

After reading this chapter, you should understand:

1. How the Canadian economy has performed since World War II in terms of economic growth, unemployment, and inflation.
2. Some of the major characteristics of government expenditures in Canada, including those of the federal-provincial divisions, growth in government expenditures, and flexibility to vary expenditures to offset changes in the private sector or those originating from international forces.
3. Some of the major characteristics of government revenues in Canada, including the distribution of revenues between the federal government and the provinces and how federal revenues respond to changing circumstances in the private sector (both in response to long-term growth and over business cycles).

Can we use deliberate changes in government expenditures and revenues to offset changes in the private sector so that we can achieve broad social and economic goals? The topic of government expenditures and taxes is so large and complex that it is not feasible or desirable to cover all the aspects in two chapters. Rather, we will concentrate on the effects of changes in the public sector on the total economy and the potential scope for changes in the private sector to affect the public sector, especially revenues. As an essential part of that assessment, we will initially summarize the postwar performance of the Canadian economy, recapitulating some of the conclusions of Chapter 3.

## 14–1 THE POSTWAR PERFORMANCE OF THE CANADIAN ECONOMY

Any assessment of how well a particular economy functions requires a view of what broad social and economic goals are appropriate and desirable for that economy. This section will summarize the broad goals that seem to be accepted in Canada and compare these goals to actual performance, especially in the private sector, for the period since 1950. Let's begin by examining the Economic Council of Canada. The **Economic Council of Canada** (ECC) was established in 1963 as an independent body to provide projections of the medium-term growth prospects for Canada and advice to governments, business, and labour on how Canada's broad economic goals could be achieved. It is composed of three full-time members (a chairman and two directors) and up to 25 other members from business, labour, agriculture, and the general public (although labour representatives have not participated in this or other federal advisory bodies for some years).

One of the important contributions of the Economic Council of Canada was to develop a statement of broad economic goals for Canada. The ECC went further than many independent advisory bodies in other countries and many governments in suggesting specific quantitative goals for each of the broad objectives. A further contribution was the emphasis that these goals be achieved simultaneously (since individual goals can sometimes conflict; that is, the achievement of one goal may prevent the achievement of another.[1]

Although it may be desirable to set goals, the experience of the last two decades suggests that it can be very difficult to achieve them. For example, the ECC proposed a target rate of unemployment of 3 percent, but the unemployment rate for the 1980–86 period, for example, averaged about 11.5 percent of the labour force, well above the 3 percent proposed by the council in their 1964 report. This higher level of unemployment partly reflected the persistence of business cycle fluctuations in Canada. These fluctuations contributed to high unemployment in 1981–82 which has persisted in spite of the recovery of the early 1980s.

Research since that time has concluded that a more realistic and potentially attainable rate of unemployment stands in the range of 6.5 to 8 percent of the labour force, based on the "nonaccelerating inflation rate of unemployment." The **nonaccelerating inflation rate of unemployment** is the unemployment rate not expected to be associated with accelerating inflation.[2]

The most severe postwar business cycle recession in Canada occurred in 1981–82, but it was less severe than experienced in the 1930s. The unemployment rate reached a postwar peak in excess of 12.7 percent of the labour force seasonally adjusted in late 1982. Regionally, the unemployment rate exceeded 16 percent in the Atlantic provinces and 14 percent in Quebec and British Columbia for a period during the first half of the 1980s. The unemployment rates for both sexes in the 15- to 24-year age group exceeded 20 percent for about a year between mid-1982 and mid-1983.[3]

Another ECC goal is reasonable stability of prices and, certainly, a rate of increase in prices not higher than that of our closest competitors in international trade. The council proposed a rate of price increase averaging 2 percent per year in the GDP deflator as a longer term goal, but it recognized that some moderate year-to-year variation around such a low rate had occurred in the past and would probably continue in the future. The actual rate of increase in the revised GDP deflator was 9.9 percent per year over the four-year period from 1978 to 1982. It was 7.6 percent for the 15-year period from 1970 to 1985. These high rates of price increase did not lead to hyperinflation, however, as some economists had predicted.

The council also proposed an equitable distribution of rising real income, meaning some narrowing of the regional differences in incomes on a per capita and a per-person-employed basis. A significant improvement in real incomes for Canadians has taken place both on a per-person-employed basis and on a per capita basis since the 1920s and the 1950s. However, the growth in real GDP per employee dropped from 2.6 percent annually in the 1950–73 period to 0.5 percent annually from 1973 to 1984. This latter rate of increase for Canada was the lowest of the seven countries shown in Chapter 3, Table 3–1.

It is clear that Canada is not meeting the economic objectives established by the ECC. The key question raised by this evidence on recent performance in the Canadian economy is whether modifications in the implementation of fiscal policy can be made to achieve better performance in the future. If not, what options are open to policymakers in the broad areas of stabilization and economic growth in Canada?

## 14–2 THE FEDERAL SYSTEM IN CANADA

The federal system of government in Canada is an important element in fiscal planning. A **federal system of government** is one where the central government has some areas of responsibility (on both functions of government and sources of revenue), while the provinces and municipalities have different areas of responsibility and sources of revenue. Much of the discussion of fiscal policy was developed in the United Kingdom and the United States, where the institutional frameworks of government are different. The United Kingdom has a unitary form of government, where the central government is the major layer of government in relation to total expenditures and revenues, and the municipal governments have a much more limited area of responsibility, primarily related to those established for them by the central government. The United States has a federal system as well, but the central government spends a much higher proportion of total government funds than in Canada. The U.S. system tends to be more centralized and stronger at the national level than in Canada, where regional, language, and religious differences are relatively more important. Australia and West Germany are federal countries as well, but both of these are much stronger at the national level and weaker at the lower levels of government than Canada.

The division of responsibilities between the federal government and the provinces is set out in Sections 91 and 92 of the Constitution Act of September 1981 (previously the British North America Act enacted in 1867). The most rapid growth in expenditures since the 1920s (reflecting the preferences of the electorate) has been in such areas as roads, highways, education, and health expenditures—all functions that are the primary responsibility of the provinces (and the municipalities which they have created and to which they have delegated the implementation of some of these functions, such as primary and secondary education and hospitals and other health costs). The provinces and municipalities have some limitations on their taxing powers, while there are no limitations whatsoever on the tax powers of the federal government. Both the federal government and most of the provinces levied both personal and corporate income taxes during the 1930s. But as part of the Wartime Tax Agreements and a series of further tax collection agreements negotiated since that time between the federal government and the provinces, the federal government administers the personal and corporate tax collections for all the provinces except Quebec. Provincial tax rates tend to be a fixed additional proportion of federal taxes, but there is some variation from province to province. With the major reliance on the personal and corporate tax collections at the federal level, the federal government has had a much more buoyant source of revenues up to the mid-1970s than the provinces and municipalities.

This tendency for the federal government to have access to the major sources of revenue from the personal and corporate tax collections while the provinces and municipalities have had the primary responsibility for the most rapidly growing areas of expenditure has had important implications for federal-provincial relations for decades. The provinces pushed aggressively (and successfully) to obtain a larger share of personal income tax collections, the most buoyant revenue source.

Our primary interest is examining this pattern of expenditure and revenue powers for the possibility of operating a discretionary stabilization policy to see if Canada could achieve more of the potential economic goals in the future than it has in recent decades.

The Royal Commission on the Economic Union and Development Prospects for Canada, chaired by Donald Macdonald, held numerous meetings across Canada and submitted a three-volume report, together with 72 volumes of studies prepared by a large research staff. After reviewing these issues in a comprehensive study of economic development prospects and the political and economic aspects of economic union, the Royal Commission Report assessed the federal and provincial roles for economic management as follows:

> We must all recognize that both federal and provincial governments have legitimate and important functions in managing the economy, and that these functions are not identical: there is a real division of labour between the two orders of government, partly as a result of our constitutional tradition and partly as a result of our needs. The federal government must concern itself first and foremost with the needs of the whole national economy. This responsibility derives both from its political mandate as the only government elected by all Canadians and also from its powers and resources. The provincial governments, in turn, will focus on the needs of their own economies.
>
> First the federal government is, and must be, primarily responsible for Canada's presence in the international world, and for mediating between that world and domestic economic and political life. This requires a predominant federal role in the negotiation and ratification of treaties, in co-ordinating federal and provincial activities abroad, and in managing the domestic adjustments that follow from international activities. Secondly, the federal government must be the advocate and catalyst for the effective functioning of the economic union. It must minimize the effects of federal and provincial barriers to interprovincial trade, and maximize the benefits of the economic union. Thirdly, the federal government is primarily responsible for redistribution between regions and provinces, between social and economic interests, and among individual citizens.[4]

With the existing distribution of responsibilities between levels of government, the changing priorities of the public are reflected in a major role for the provinces and municipalities on expenditures. In 1985, for example, provincial and local governments spent $66.9 billion on goods and services (both current and capital expenditures) or 14.4 percent of GDP. The comparable federal expenditures on goods and services were $26.1 billion or 5.5 percent of GDP, or only about two-fifths of provincial and local expenditures on goods and services.[5]

## 14–3 STRUCTURE OF GOVERNMENT EXPENDITURES

The discussion of government expenditures in Canada will deal with three broad and important topics, namely:

> The over-all growth in the size of government expenditures historically.
> The current distribution of federal expenditures.
> Flexibility in expenditures.

**Flexibility in government expenditures** is the possibility of adjusting some types of expenditures in response to changes in the economic situation to try to offset any instability in the economy coming from international forces or changes in the domestic private sector.

### The Historical Growth of Government Expenditures

During the century since Confederation, there has been a significant growth in the range of government activities, a development that has taken place in many other countries as well. Federal, provincial, and municipal government expenditures on goods and services were only 4.6 percent of GDP in 1870. This expenditure increased to 8.1 percent in 1910, 11.1 percent in 1929, and 22.3 percent in 1985, reflecting government's direct use of resources, including payments to civil servants, the armed forces, capital construction, and purchases of equipment, stationery, and supplies. Government purchases for selected years from 1950 to 1985 are shown in Table 14–1. The table illustrates that government expenditure on goods and services has increased from less than 14 percent of GDP in 1950 to more than 20 percent in the 1970s and 1980s, with all of the increases occurring in government current expenditure on goods and services.

There has also been a growth in the payments made by governments to certain groups in the population, such as family allowances and old-age pensions. These are payments for which no direct service is provided by the recipients to the government and are thus transfer payments as explained in Chapter 2, Section 2–5. At the start of the present century, such transfer payments were insignificant. By 1929 they were still only about 2 percent of personal income. With the introduction of family allowances, old-age pensions, and unemployment insurance, transfer payments increased to 14.6 percent of personal income by 1985. All of these payments continue irrespective of the state of the economy, and unemployment insurance payments increase during recessions.

The increase in relative size and importance of the government sector has contributed to a greater degree of stability for the economy

---

**TABLE 14–1**   Direct Use of Resources by All Levels of Government
(percent of GDP, current dollars, 1950, 1973, and 1985)

|  | 1950 | 1973 | 1985 |
|---|---|---|---|
| Government current expenditures on goods and services | 10.7 | 17.9 | 19.9 |
| Government capital expenditure | 2.9 | 3.3 | 2.4 |
| Total, current and capital | 13.6 | 21.2 | 22.3 |

SOURCE: Statistics Canada, *National Accounts, Income and Expenditure, 1926–1974*
(Ottawa: Information Canada, 1976) pp. 161, 163, 261, 263; and Statistics Canada, CANSIM
Tapes.

---

as a whole, as these expenditures continue to grow, while the cyclically sensitive sectors have declined (as discussed in Chapter 10, Section 10–6).

## Distribution of Federal Expenditures

Our analysis of government expenditures will concentrate on the national accounts presentation of government expenditures (and revenues). The **national accounts presentation of government transactions** refers to the payments and receipts that relate to the general public. This consolidates the extra budgetary funds (such as the Unemployment Insurance Fund and the Canada and Quebec Pension Plan) and excludes bookkeeping transactions (such as writing off of bad debts).

A key point about the current distribution of total federal government expenditures is that federal expenditures on goods and services are only about one-fifth of total federal expenditures. Each of three other expenditure areas are almost as large, namely, transfers to persons, transfers to other levels of government (primarily the provinces), and interest on the public debt (a large and growing share of federal expenditures). The federal expenditures in 1985 and the percentage distribution of those expenditures are shown in Table 14–2. About two-fifths of government expenditures on goods and services are for purchases of services provided by the business sector, such as capital facilities, telephone, and travel services. Only about 14 percent of federal expenditures are for wages, salaries, and supplementary labour income for civil servants, members of the Senate and House of Commons, and members of the armed forces. It usually comes as a surprise to most students and the general public to learn how small a proportion civil service payrolls actually are of total federal expenditures.

**TABLE 14–2**   Percentage Distribution of Federal Expenditures, 1950, 1973, and 1985

|  | 1950 | 1973 | 1985 |
|---|---|---|---|
| Goods and services |  |  |  |
| Capital | 3.4 | 3.1 | 2.0 |
| Current | 36.9 | 26.9 | 20.5 |
| Transfers to persons | 26.8 | 31.3 | 27.4 |
| Interest | 18.6 | 11.3 | 21.8 |
| Transfers to provinces and municipalities . | 11.0 | 21.5 | 18.8 |
| Transfers to nonresidents | 0.6 | 1.4 | 1.4 |
| Subsidies | 2.6 | 3.3 | 5.5 |
| Capital assistance | 0.0 | 1.3 | 2.6 |
| Total | 100.0 | 100.0 | 100.0 |

SOURCE: Statistics Canada, *National Accounts, Income and Expenditures, 1926–1974* (Ottawa: Information Canada, 1976), pp. 169, 171, 173, and 175; and Statistics Canada, CANSIM Tapes.

## Flexibility in Expenditures

The evidence on the distribution of expenditures in Sections 14–2 and 14–3 is crucial in assessing how much flexibility the federal government has in trying to achieve greater stability in the economy. The highly decentralized nature of the federal system in Canada means that about three-fifths of government expenditures on goods and services are spent at the provincial and municipal levels. Some of these expenditures are related closely and positively to growth in the private sector (such as roads, sewers, and schools related to the shift to the suburbs in the construction of individual homes, apartments, and shopping centres) and cannot be deferred when private investment is strong. The provinces and municipalities guard their areas of responsibility and decision making and often resent and oppose advice from the federal government on the timing of their expenditures.

Even for expenditures that are the federal government's responsibility, flexibility is severely limited. Capital expenditures are only 2 percent of federal expenditures. Current expenditures on goods and services are about 20 percent of federal expenditures, and part of those expenditures are for purchases from the private sector closely related to the current operations of government. Interest on the public debt has been a large and growing share of federal expenditures, having almost doubled as a share of federal expenditures since early in the 1970s. (The declines in interest rates since 1981 will slow the growth in interest payments, but the size of the federal debt outstanding has continued to grow). There is little opportunity to limit the growth and size of the debt on which interest payments must be paid. Payments to the provinces have been the subject of active negotiations between the federal government and the provinces for decades, and any proposals for change (especially downward) are the subject of long and active debate and negotiation between the various levels of government. Transfer payments are also a large item, but federal proposals to modify old-age pensions and unemployment insurance schemes led to an active public outcry. (Prime Minister Mulroney referred to these programs as a "sacred trust.") They can be modified only in the face of a great deal of political pressure.

Almost the only expenditure area that can be modified slightly is the size of the federal government civil service, and some growth in that category in line with increased growth in the number of people being served is necessary. It would take a major effort on the part of the government with support from wide areas of the public to move federal expenditures on goods and services up or down by even 2 percent of GDP over a five-year period. It is these types of considerations that led Auditor General Kenneth Dye to say in one of his annual reports in the early 1980s that federal expenditures were out of control. The **auditor general** reports directly to parliament rather than the government in power and has the responsibility not only to audit the financial records of government departments and agencies, but also to comment on aspects of expenditure policy that he feels are inappropriate or poorly managed. His annual reports are awaited eagerly by the press and the Opposition for evidence of new examples of government waste, extravagance, wrongdoing, and mismanagement.

## 14–4 STRUCTURE OF FEDERAL REVENUES

This discussion of federal revenues will be organized into three steps, namely:

> The main historical development and present distribution of federal revenues.
> The growth in federal revenues as the economy grows at potential output with a given structure of tax rates.
> The cyclical variability in federal revenues over the business cycle.

The main changes in the sources of federal revenues can be seen in Table 14–3 for selected years from 1950 to 1985. As the top line of the table shows, the major change has been an increase in the share of direct taxes on persons (primarily the personal income tax) from about 27 percent of federal revenues in 1950 to over 50 percent in 1985. On the other hand, corporate profits taxes have fallen from 28 percent of federal revenues in 1950 to less than 14 percent in 1985. Indirect taxes

**TABLE 14–3**    Federal Government Revenues, Percentage Distribution (national accounts basis, 1950, 1973, and 1985)

|                              | 1950  | 1973  | 1985  |
|------------------------------|-------|-------|-------|
| Direct taxes, persons        | 26.7  | 47.6  | 50.7  |
| Direct taxes, corporations   | 28.1  | 16.0  | 13.9  |
| Direct taxes on nonresidents | 1.8   | 1.4   | 1.3   |
| Total indirect taxes         | 36.9  | 25.6  | 22.6  |
| Investment income            | 4.4   | 8.1   | 10.0  |
| Capital consumption          | 1.9   | 1.4   | 1.5   |
| Total                        | 100.0 | 100.0 | 100.0 |

SOURCE: Statistics Canada, *National Accounts, Income and Expenditure, 1926–1974* (Ottawa: Information Canada, 1976), p. 159; and Statistics Canada CANSIM Tapes. Some totals may not equal 100.0 due to rounding.

have also declined, from much more than direct taxes on persons in 1950 to less than half of direct taxes on persons in 1985. Changes in other revenue sources have been smaller.

## Growth in Federal Revenues in a Growing Economy

This section will deal with revenue changes in response to long-term economic growth (such as growth at potential output as explained in Chapter 6, Section 6–1) and rising prices. A major point in this section is that tax revenues grew much more rapidly than the rate of growth in GDP up until 1974.

The growth in federal revenues is the net result of two factors — the growth in incomes and the tax base, and the structure of federal tax rates. We will deal with growth in incomes first.

Most of the individual federal taxes are levied on specific income and expenditure categories of the national accounts. For example, the personal income tax of taxpayers is levied on personal income and the corporation profits tax on corporation profits before tax. Customs collections are levied on certain categories of imports, and gasoline, liquor, and tobacco taxes are levied on those areas of personal expenditures. Over the 20-year period from 1950 to 1970, the increase in the taxable components of GDP was roughly equal to the increase in total GDP. Changes in the relative size of the taxable components in relation to GDP is not an important factor in the growth in federal revenues over the long run.

A key factor in the growth in federal revenues is the long-term growth in personal income tax collections. Personal income tax collections from the early 1950s to the 1970s grew much more rapidly than personal income (even after allowing for any changes in tax rates over that period). An important reason for this greater increase comes from the system of personal exemptions for dependants and other deductions, such as charitable contributions. If the income for one taxpayer is increased by 1 percent, the increase in his taxable income is much greater on a percentage basis, because of the constant amount of his personal exemptions. In addition, the increase in income can shift some individuals into higher marginal tax rates and thus increase their taxes even more than their increase in taxable income.

During the 1970s, we saw an increase of about 1.7 percent in personal income tax collections for each 1 percent increase in GDP, a much more rapid rate of increase than in GDP. This is an example of tax elasticity. **Elasticity** is the percentage change in a dependant variable (tax collections, in this instance) for a 1 percent change in an independent variable (personal income, here). This is the same concept you have encountered in your microeconomics, in the discussion of the price elasticity of demand for a particular product.

The long-term revenue elasticity for the tax structure in the early part of the 1970s was about 1.26, slightly higher than the elasticity prevailing in the 1960s. The tax elasticity at the federal level is substantially higher than the comparable elasticities at the provincial and municipal levels; these were about 1.02 and 1.00, respectively.[6]

An important part of the buoyancy of the federal tax revenues comes from the personal income tax during periods of inflation. The increase in personal income (closely related to the increase in prices of the products produced in the economy) leads to a much larger increase in incomes after personal exemptions (i.e., taxable income) than in incomes before tax. Over the years from the 1940s to the early 1970s, a good rule of thumb was that a 1 percent increase in average income per taxpayer led to a 2 percent increase in taxable income per taxpayer. This led to a significant buoyancy in personal income tax collections.

This buoyancy implied a long-term elasticity of 2 in personal income tax collections for a given structure of tax rates (in which we include personal exemptions and increases in the marginal tax rate as taxpayers move from lower income levels to higher levels of taxable income). As inflation became more pronounced during the late 1960s and 1970s, this buoyancy in personal income tax collections began to create more public concern and debate on two points. One concern was that the growth in federal revenues was so rapid that it could siphon off income from the personal sector and potentially prevent the Canadian economy from achieving close to full employment with growth in step with potential output. This concern has been termed fiscal drag. **Fiscal drag** is a situation in which the growth in tax revenues could cause a dampening effect on the rate of growth of economic activity. A second concern was that the effect of rising prices and average incomes per taxpayer would lead to an increase in the average tax rate. The opposition argued that this was, in effect, an increase in actual tax rates on average incomes that had not been approved by parliament. The debate led to a proposal in favour of indexation of the personal income tax structure.

**Indexation of personal income taxes** is the process of adjusting personal income tax allowances and tax brackets (the upward steps in marginal tax rates at specific higher income levels) upward in step with increases in the general price level. The federal government in Canada introduced indexation of the personal income tax in 1974 and is now committed to index these allowances each year in line with the increase in the consumer price index over the past year. Indexation is one of the most important structural changes made in the personal income tax in Canada in recent decades. I estimate that if the 1974 structure of exemptions and tax rates were applied to the 1985 level and distribution of personal income, the federal personal income tax collections would have been about $75 billion in 1985 instead of the $42 billion actually collected that year. Indexation was thus equivalent to a tax reduction of about 40 percent from the 1974 structure of rates and exemptions. The size of the tax reduction from indexing the personal income tax is roughly the size of the federal budget deficit in 1985!

## Variability in Federal Revenues during Business Cycles

The economy does not always grow steadily in line with potential output, as discussed in the previous section, but variations in the rate of growth take place in a recurrent manner over the short-term business cycle. In response to the changing demand pressures (for some of the reasons considered in Part Three, especially Chapters 9 and 10), some of the key items in the tax base in the Canadian federal tax structure undergo marked changes, which have a significant impact on federal revenues. Corporation profits, for example, undergo marked declines during business cycle recessions and recover very sharply in the early stages of a business cycle expansion. Merchandise imports also fluctuate more markedly than domestic production of comparable items.

The author has prepared estimates of tax collections for alternative levels of GDP, reflecting a typical response during business cycles. The short-term elasticity of federal tax collections was estimated to be roughly 2.2, markedly higher than the long-term value of 1.26 before indexing, and an even lower figure after indexing was introduced. A key reason for the much higher cyclical volatility in tax collections is the marked volatility in corporate profits, imports, and to some extent, manufacturing shipments in response to the shorter-term changes in

**TABLE 14–4**   Summary of Short-term, Revenue-Yield Changes, 1929
and 1985

|  |  | 1929 | 1985 |
|---|---|---|---|
| 1. | Federal taxes (dollars in millions) | 399 | 82,417 |
| 2. | GDP at market prices (dollars in millions) | 6.134 | 476,361 |
| 3. | Average federal tax rate to GDP | | |
|  | (Line 1 ÷ Line 2) | 6.5% | 19.3% |
| 4. | Short-term elasticity | 2.0 | 2.2 |
| 5. | Short-term marginal tax rate | 13.0% | 42.5% |
|  | (Line 3×Line 4) | | |

SOURCES: Lines 1 and 2 from Statistics Canada, *National Accounts, Income and Expenditures, 1926–1974* (Ottawa: Information Canada, 1976), pp. 4 and 58 and Statistics Canada, *National Accounts, Income and Expenditure Accounts, Second Quarter 1986* (Ottawa: Ministry of Supply and Services, October 1986), pp. 5 and 23. The estimates of elasticity for 1929 are from D. J. Daly, "Fiscal Policy—An Assessment," in *Canadian Perspectives in Economics,* John Chant, ed. (Don Mills, Ont.: Collier-Macmillan Canada, 1972), Chapter A–6.

GDP over the business cycle. Thus we can calculate the short-term marginal tax rate, based on the definition of tax elasticity as the ratio of the marginal tax rate to the average tax rate. The **marginal tax rate** is the share of an increase in GDP that is collected by the federal government. For 1985, this amounts to 42.5 percent, significantly higher than the percentage of federal tax collections to GDP of 19.3 percent for the same year. This amount is significantly higher than a comparable estimate for 1929. To demonstrate the importance of this point, Table 14–4 shows the short-term, revenue-yield changes in 1929 and 1985. The top line shows federal taxes in 1929 and 1985, with the levels of GDP on Line 2. Line 3 shows the average federal tax rate in relation to GDP. Line 4 shows the short-term revenue elasticities calculated on the basis of the typical movement in the taxable components of GDP during the business cycle. Line 5 shows the short-term marginal tax rate as derived by multiplying Line 3 by Line 4.

Line 5 shows that the short-term marginal tax rate increased from 13.0 percent in 1929 to 41.5 percent in 1985, more than triple. This is one of the three major changes in the institutional environment that have contributed to the moderate nature of recessions in Canada since World War II (discussed in Chapter 10, Section 10–6).

These quantitative results for Canada indicate that the structure of the federal tax system provides a significant degree of stability to moderate the cyclical volatility in the economy that could otherwise take place, but the much lower, longer-term revenue elasticities indicate that the risks of fiscal drag are not a particularly serious threat to long-term economic growth.

## SUMMARY

Canada has not been able to achieve the goals of an unemployment rate of 3 percent and price stability proposed by the Economic Council of Canada in the First Annual Review. Later research has indicated that a more appropriate goal would be in the range of 6.5 to 8.5 percent of the labour force.

The federal system of government involves a decentralized distribution of expenditures, with the provinces and municipalities having the larger share of expenditures on goods and services.

Only about one-fifth of federal expenditures are spent for goods and services. The major expenditures include transfers to persons, transfers to the provinces, and interest on the federal debt, giving the government very little flexibility to offset any change in the external sector or domestic developments in the private sector.

Federal revenues grew rapidly due to unchanged tax rates during past periods of high economic growth and price increase, but indexation has sharply reduced the buoyancy in the personal income tax collections with inflation.

Federal tax collections vary markedly throughout business cycles and partially offset any fluctuations that might otherwise occur. They thus provide an important degree of built-in stability to the economy. This stability is quantitatively more important in Canada in the 1980s than in the 1920s, which is a factor in the mildness of postwar recessions.

## NOTES

1. Economic Council of Canada, *Economic Goals for Canada to 1970* (Ottawa: Queen's Printer, 1964), especially Chapter 2, pp. 7–30. An example of the possibility of conflict between goals would be a low rate of unemployment versus reasonable stability of prices. One problem with the goals proposed in the first review is that they have not been achieved since they were proposed.

2. Royal Commission on the Economic Union and Development Prospects for Canada, *Report, Volume Two* (Ottawa: Ministry of Supply and Services, 1985), p. 276.

3. *Bank of Canada Review,* December 1986, pp. S10–11.

4. Royal Commission on the Economic Union and Development Prospects for Canada, *Report, Volume Three* (Ottawa: Ministry of Supply and Services, 1985), p. 149.

5. Statistics Canada, *National Income and Expenditure Accounts, Second Quarter 1986* (Ottawa: Ministry of Supply and Services, 1986), pp. 3, 23, 25, and 27.

6. These paragraphs draw on D.J. Daly, "Fiscal Policy—An Assessment" in *Canadian Perspectives in Economics,* John Chant, ed. (Don Mills, Ont.: Collier-Macmillan Canada, 1972), pp. Chapter A–6.

# 15

# Government Deficits, Debt, and Financing

A new dimension in fiscal policy in the 1980s in Canada has been the development of the first large federal deficit as a percent of GDP in peacetime since the 1930s. All projections indicate this deficit will continue for at least the balance of this decade. There was fairly broad agreement among economists on the subject of deficits in the 1950s and 1960s, but this broad agreement has disintegrated during the 1980s. This chapter will incorporate deficits, debt, and financing into the framework that we have been developing. The chapter will also summarize some of the evidence supporting various macroeconomic policies relating to debt.

After reading this chapter you should understand:

1. The main factors that have contributed to the growth in federal deficits since 1977.
2. The main effects of deficits and how their financing influences the performance of the economy in terms of output and prices.
3. The effect of higher interest costs on federal expenditures.
4. The possibility for reducing the deficit.
5. The possibility for discretionary changes in fiscal policy when the next business cycle recession occurs.

## 15–1 A REVIEW AND EXTENSION OF THE FRAMEWORK

The effects of a budget deficit can be analyzed using the $IS-LM$ framework introduced in the appendix to Chapter 12. Let us assume that the government budget is balanced as we begin our analysis (approximately the condition that prevailed from 1962 to 1974 in Canada). Let us explore what would happen with a budget deficit of $30 billion a year, based on federal expenditures of $105 billion and federal revenues of $75 billion. The deficit would thus be 40 percent of revenues and a little less than 7 percent of GDP. The federal deficit would be approximately one third of the size of fixed-capital investment. (These numbers are for purposes of illustration but are close to the actual experience in 1984 and 1985.)

A deficit of this size would be reflected in the *IS–LM* curves by a shift in the *IS* curve to the right. We would see an increase in national income and nominal interest rates. The degree to which the deficit is reflected in higher national income, on the one hand, and nominal interest rates, on the other, would depend on the slopes of the curves, one of the topics on which there has been a continuing difference of view between the monetarists and the Keynesians, as discussed in the Appendix to Chapter 12.

The next step is to determine what effect, if any, the budget deficit may have on the *LM* curve. Let us suppose that *all* of that deficit is financed by sales of bonds to the general public. Under these circumstances, the government would find its bank balances increased by the sales of the bonds. However, those bank balances would immediately be used to pay for the expenditures being made in excess of current federal revenues. At the end of the year, the government has the same level of cash holdings as at the beginning. There may be some reduction in bank balances of those who bought government bonds, and some increase for those who received cheques from the government as part of federal expenditures (on goods and services, interest payments, and transfer payments); however, the point is that *no increase in the money supply* would occur if the sales of bonds to the public equaled the size of the budget deficit. In other words, there would be no shift in the *LM* curve.

The new situation can be shown as a shift in the *IS* curve to the right, moving along a given *LM* curve (see Figure 15–1).

Figure 15–1 represents a simplified, but not a distorted, view of Canadian developments in the early 1980s. The budget deficit increased from a rough balance in 1974 (a surplus of less than 5 percent of expenditures) to a deficit of $32 billion in 1985, with expenditures about 40 percent higher than revenues. The deficit has averaged $27 billion a year over the four years from 1982 to 1985. However, the increase in the money supply $M_2$ was 7.7 percent per year over the four-year period from late 1982 to late 1986 (when the federal deficit was large), substantially less than the increase of 14.7 percent per year over the seven-year period from December 1974 to December 1981.[1] Monetary expansion (as measured by the comprehensive measures of the money supply) need not be an inevitable result of a federal budget deficit. It makes a

---

**FIGURE 15–1**   Effects of a Budget Deficit Financed by Bond Sales to the Public

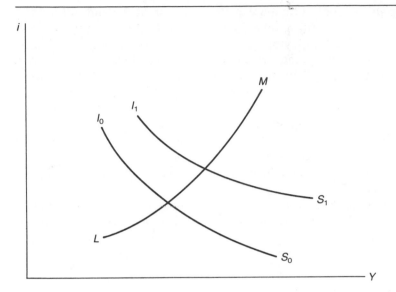

major difference whether the budget deficit is financed largely by sales of bonds to the general public, or whether even a small share of the deficit is financed by purchases of bonds (either new or outstanding issues) by the Bank of Canada.

We will be using some new terms in this chapter, so we will explain their meaning here. A **federal budget deficit** occurs when current and capital expenditures exceed current tax collections. It is thus a *flow* of expenditures in excess of revenues. **Outstanding debt** is the accumulated overall deficit since Confederation. It is thus a *stock*, and it will continue to increase each year as long as the budget deficits continue. The federal government also has some recorded assets—about $38 billion in the mid-1980s. On March 31, 1985, these assets were deducted from the gross public debt (all debt and other liabilities) to calculate the **net public debt**, or the total accumulated indebtedness after deducting the recorded assets. **Interest on the public debt** comprises the annual payments to holders of the federal debt outstanding. It has been growing in recent years as the size of the debt has grown, but its growth has also been supplemented by the interest paid on new issues, which was higher than that paid on bonds issued in the 1960s and early 1970s. In 1985, for example, the average rate of interest paid on the federal debt outstanding was 11.3 percent, well above the 4 percent paid in 1960 or the 6 percent paid in 1970.[2]

## 15–2 FACTORS IN THE EMERGENCE OF FEDERAL DEFICITS

The net public debt in Canada was $12.7 billion at the end of the 1947 fiscal year, after having grown in the 1930s (with increased federal expenditures for relief payments and assistance to the provinces, some of which were in desperate financial straits) and during World War II (when defence expenditures increased to 40 percent of GDP and deficits occurred). Over the next 30 years the net public debt grew at a rate of 1.6 percent per year with a few more years of federal deficits than surpluses. With the dramatic growth in the national income, the net public debt fell from 106.6 percent of GDP in 1947 to 17.5 percent at the end of the fiscal year 1974–75. By then, the net public debt to GDP was about one sixth what it had been 28 years earlier. These changes can be seen in Figure 15–2.

A number of new developments emerged after 1975 that led to larger federal deficits (both absolutely and as a ratio of federal expenditures and of GDP).

One factor was the growth in federal expenditures, which began to increase more rapidly than GDP as shown in Table 15–1. The most

---

**FIGURE 15–2**   Government of Canada: Net Public Debt as a Percentage of GDP

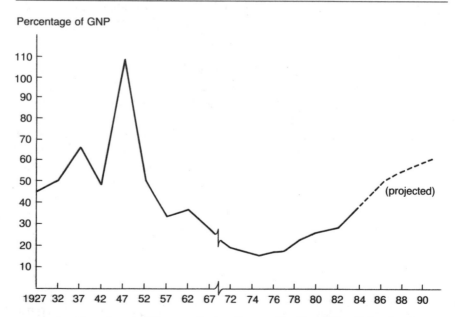

SOURCE: Department of Finance, *Budget Papers, The Fiscal Plan*, Feb. 26, 1986, and projections calculated from Minister of Finance, Gov't of Canada, *A New Direction for Canada*, November 1984.

**TABLE 15–1**  Growth in GDP (current dollars), Federal Expenditures, and Revenues (selected periods, 1961 to 1985)

|  | 1961–73 | 1973–81 | 1981–85 |
|---|---|---|---|
| GDP, current dollars | 9.93% | 13.71% | 7.55% |
| Federal expenditures, current dollars | 9.91 | 15.80 | 12.52 |
| Federal revenues, current dollars | 10.68 | 13.97 | 6.49 |

SOURCE: Statistics Canada, *National Income and Expenditure Accounts, Volume I, 1926–1974* (Ottawa: Information Canada, 1976), pp. 204, 205, 258–261.

rapid increase was in interest on the public debt. Interest on the federal debt increased from $3.7 billion in the calendar year 1975 to $25.3 billion in 1985 (almost a sevenfold increase in a decade). This is an annual rate of increase in excess of 20 percent per year and partly reflected the growth in the net federal debt over the period. It also reflected an increase in the average rate of interest from about 7.25 percent in 1975 to 11.3 percent in 1985, an increase of more than 50 percent.

The growth in interest payments was so large that the share of all other federal expenditures fell as a share of total federal expenditures (refer to Table 14–2). In 1985, transfers to persons (such as Unemployment Insurance payments), transfers to provinces, and current expenditures were all between 2.5 and 3.0 times their 1975 level, roughly the same as the increase in GDP over the same period (2.8 times the 1975 level).[3]

The growth in federal revenues from 1973 to 1981 was slightly slower than the growth in federal expenditures, as shown in Table 15–1. From 1981 to 1985, however, federal expenditures grew at a rate of 12.5 percent per year, while federal revenues grew at 6.5 percent per year. The rate of growth in revenues from 1981 to 1985 was less than half the rate of growth from 1973 to 1981.

This slowdown in the rate of growth in federal revenues primarily reflected three important developments. First was the slowdown in the growth in GDP in constant prices in the economy, reflecting the severity of the 1981–82 recession and the sluggish nature of the early stages of the recovery. In a second development, the rate of price increase also slowed, with the increase in the GDP deflator dropping below 5 percent per year after 1982, well below the increases of the 10 years before 1982. A third factor in the declining rate of growth in federal revenues was the introduction of indexation of personal income tax in 1974. Indexation sharply reduced the revenue buoyancy that had occurred during previous inflationary periods. The combination of all three factors resulted in a slower rate of growth in federal revenues during the 1981–85 period than had occurred for some decades. The size of the budget deficit was partly a result of the severity of the 1981–82 recession and the automatic decline in federal revenues, which would have been much greater if the economy had been operating closer to potential output in those years.

The net result of a significant slowdown in the rate of growth of revenues and a high rate of increase in expenditures was the emergence of a large federal deficit, reaching a peak of $37.7 billion at an annual rate, in the first quarter of 1982, of 8.1 percent of GDP.

This deficit was higher than any experienced since World War II, when the deficit reached a peak of 22.8 percent of GDP. The federal deficit was a higher proportion of GDP in Canada than in the United States.

The Department of Finance predicts a continuation of a high deficit over the balance of the decade. It also predicts that the net public debt at the federal level will exceed $400 billion in 1990–91, compared to $200 billion on March 31, 1985, $100 billion in 1982, and only $48.3 billion in 1978. This is more than an eightfold increase from 1978 to 1991, or almost 18 percent a year during that period. This projection by the Department of Finance estimated annual net public debt charges of $20 to $30 billion a year from 1985 to 1990.[4]

## 15–3 EFFECTS OF FEDERAL DEFICITS

For many years, economists agreed on many aspects of economic developments and fiscal policy (although full agreement was still lacking on some important points). This broad consensus of the 1960s and 1970s has tended to disintegrate during the 1980s, with differences of view and emphasis emerging on two topics.

One issue involved differing views on the reasons for the severity of the recession and the persistence of a high rate of unemployment in the winter of 1986–87, some four years after Canada's business cycle trough in December 1982. Some economists attribute this performance primarily to a policy of monetary restraint. They point to the fact that the comprehensive measures of the money supply were all increasing at less than the rate of inflation after about 1982. This is a condition that could be fairly easily remedied, recognizing that quick solutions could not be expected due to existing lags. On the other hand, some economists suspect more deep-seated and structural problems that contribute to the persisting higher level of unemployment in Canada than in the United States. The higher level of Canadian unemployment has persisted for much of the period since 1982, the first time in the postwar period that such divergences have occurred. One of the puzzles is why unemployment has stayed so high in spite of a large federal deficit by peacetime standards.

A second issue involves the differing views and emphasis on the effects of the budget deficit and its financing on economic performance, including physical activity, interest rates, prices, and investment in business plant and equipment and housing. A brief review of these differing views will illustrate how some of the tools developed in earlier chapters can clarify the issues, but will also reveal some of the issues that economists do not yet agree on, and perhaps do not fully understand.

Three hypotheses can be suggested to explain how the larger federal debt and deficits affect the performance of the economy. These three alternative hypotheses can be described as the monetization hypothesis, the net wealth hypothesis, and the Ricardian hypothesis.

The **monetization hypothesis** emphasizes the risk that the existence of public debt (or its potential increase) results in economic and/or political pressure to increase the money supply, an action that is more politically acceptable than raising taxes or cutting expenditures. If that increase occurs, it would promote increases in the price level. The concern in this hypothesis is more with the possibility of monetary expansion and inflation than with the size of the debt itself.

The **net wealth hypothesis** emphasizes that an increase in the supply of government debt leads to an increase in real interest rates (assuming the money supply to be constant) because private borrowers would compete with government for investment dollars. Nominal interest rates would increase faster than the price level. The increase in interest rates could lead to some "crowding out" of private investment and the possibility that the reduction in private investment could partially offset the stimulative effect of the enlarged deficit.

The **Ricardian hypothesis** maintains that the government debt has no influence on the economy, either through the money supply or through other channels. People would view as equivalent a tax of a certain amount and a current deficit of the same amount.[5]

There has now been sufficient experience with varying combinations of growth in debt and money supply to test some of these hypotheses. Analysts examined 10 industrialized countries for the 1952–83 period (and some subperiods within those three decades).[6] One such test was done by two American economists for the Federal Reserve Bank of Philadelphia. Their data suggest that monetary growth is a strong influence on inflation, but a large debt is often, but not always, related to an increase in the money supply. It is the growth in money supply that is a key factor in inflation, rather than the excess growth in debt.

Other studies by Paul Evans suggest that there is no evidence that interest rates are related to current, past, and future deficits. Periods of war finance and large deficits and growth in the public debt have not led to high interest rates in the past.[7]

There has not been sufficient exploration of the theory and evidence for either Canada or the United States to resolve these differences in view of the effects of government deficits. No clear consensus has as yet emerged.

## 15–4 OPTIONS ON THE DEFICIT

The Progressive Conservative Government came to power in 1984 with expressions of concern "that the cupboard was bare" and that they had inherited serious problems with the size of the deficit and the projected growth in interest costs and the public debt. The Department of Finance produced a comprehensive document that identified continuing budget deficits as a key factor in the high interest rates of the early 1980s. They also expressed the view that such high interest rates were critical to the extent of the drop in business investment in Canada and its sluggish recovery after reaching a low point in early 1983. There were more than 20 references to high nominal and real interest rates in the first 20 pages of that study.[8] (The drop in business investment was much sharper in Canada than the United States. Business investment continued well below the 1981 peak in constant prices right through to the end of 1986.) The Finance position favoured a reduction in the size of the deficit, a view favoured for the United States by President Ronald Reagan and a number of his key advisors.

There were two problems with the analysis in that study, however. First, it ignored the evidence that has been in the public domain in Canada for 20 years, namely, that interest rates are a relatively small influence on business investment, although they are a much greater influence on housing investment (see Sections 9–2 to 9–4). Second, the study emphasized large budget deficits as the key factor in high interest rates, but made no reference at all to the effects of inflation on interest rates, a critical part of Irving Fisher's contribution to economic theory (see Section 13–2). Since the Department of Finance study was published, there has been a marked drop in long-term interest rates, even though the budget deficit has continued to be large.

A more important influence on interest rate developments in Canada has been the slowdown in the rate of increase of all the monetary aggregates. After 1982, this change was reflected in a significant slowing in the rate of price increase (encouraged by the degree of under-utilization as the economy operated with a level of actual output below potential), and eventually a drop in interest rates. This is consistent with Fisher's theory of interest as explained in Section 13–2. Such a development had been predicted publicly in 1981 by Michael Parkin of the University of Western Ontario using a monetarist-type model as a basis of his analysis.[9]

The issues raised by Michael Wilson and the Department of Finance study were reviewed at the National Economic Conference in Ottawa in March 1985. The conference had been called to provide an opportunity for a dialogue about such economic problems as high unemployment, high interest rates, and the budget deficit, with representatives of business, labour, and the general public in attendance. However, no consensus emerged regarding the sources of the problems or possible policy solutions. Representatives of the business and financial community were concerned about the size of the deficit and the public debt and generally favoured a reduction in federal expenditures. They also tended to be supportive of the possibility of freer trade to achieve increased access to the large U.S. market.

Union representatives, on the other hand, advocated more stimulative fiscal and monetary policies to reduce the high levels of unemployment. They also viewed the gains from freer trade skeptically, and emphasized the serious problems in transition to freer trade and the potential problems of political independence.

The conference produced no strong consensus that would permit the government to move forward with aggressive measures to reduce the budget deficit. Proposals to modify the indexation of old-age pensions or to reduce some of the most costly features of the Unemployment Insurance System led to a vocal public outcry. The government was forced to reconsider, even though the government had a large majority in the House of Commons.

## 15–5 DISCRETIONARY CHANGES IN FISCAL POLICY

What is the possibility of discretionary change in Canada's fiscal policy in the future? What can the federal government do if a new recession takes place? This section will deal with the magnitudes of changes that may be necessary to achieve broad goals, and the limited responses available to the federal government to make large changes.

Earlier discussion has shown that postwar recessions have been shorter and milder than earlier recessions. (The reasons were given in Section 10–6.) But it is also clear that lags in response in the private sector are continuing. It is also likely that the private sector in Canada will continue to be subjected to shocks from developments in the world economy and changes in domestic public policy.

Two basic factors diminish the scope for the federal government to act in any aggressive manner to stimulate the economy by taking an initiative on its own. One problem is the low values of the fiscal multipliers in Canada. These were described in Sections 9–8 to 9–10. As we saw, it would take massive changes to increase expenditures, and cut taxes, to achieve any large impact on the economy.[10]

The second problem is that the federal government can influence only a small part of total government expenditures due to the key role of the provinces and municipalities. Even at the federal level, expenditures are dominated by interest on the public debt, transfers to persons, and transfers to the provinces. None of these areas are likely to change. (See Sections 14–2 and 14–3 for the evidence on these points.) Federal expenditures are inflexible, and there are active supporters of many individual expenditures that limit the government's ability to bring about reductions.

In addition to factors inherent in our economic system, the federal government is constrained by a large budget deficit when the economy is still in the expansion phase of a business cycle. A renewed recession would create future growth in the budget deficit.

The federal government is facing a dilemma. On one hand, the low values of the fiscal multipliers mean that large expansionary changes are necessary to stimulate the economy to move closer to potential output. On the other hand, the government has very little scope to modify expenditures due to limited flexibility and the size of the deficit. A further issue concerns the timing of discretionary changes in fiscal policy (which will be explored in the next section). There are no easy answers.

## 15–6 LAGS AND THE TIMING OF FISCAL POLICY

Simple static economic models are adequate to deal with large and persisting inflationary or deflationary situations. However, the postwar experience in North America has been characterized by relatively mild and temporary fluctuations around a high rate of long-term economic growth. This fact, together with the evidence from a range of empirical studies and the experience with discretionary changes in fiscal policy since World War II, suggests that much more attention must be paid to the whole area of *dynamics*, including lags in response in the private sector of the economy and the appropriate timing of discretionary policy, whether fiscal or monetary.

Discussions of the lags in stabilization policy usually distinguish among three distinct ways in which lags in timing can occur. These are the *recognition lag*, the *action lag*, and the *outside lag* or *response lag*. The recognition and the action lags together are sometimes called the *inside lag*. It should be recognized that the total length of the lag is additive, or the cumulation of the three individual timing lags.

The **recognition lag** refers to the time during which a change in the economy begins to take place before the basic data for that period become available. It takes time to assemble the basic monthly data from companies, customs ports, and tax collection agencies, which are then tabulated and published by Statistics Canada. Monthly series are typically irregular, and there are frequently conflicting tendencies in the economy, especially in the neighbourhood of cyclical turning points. It sometimes takes a few months before symptoms of change become evident, especially if the changes are mild, as they have been throughout the postwar period. The range of monthly series available and the increased number available on a seasonally adjusted basis has improved the knowledge and understanding of current economic conditions considerably since the early 1950s, and thereby shortened the recognition lags.

Even when it becomes apparent that serious consideration should be given to shifts in fiscal policy, considerable time may elapse before such shifts can be implemented. It is sometimes difficult to determine what changes in policy might be most appropriate and to get agreement within the cabinet on these changes. Changes in expenditure ordinarily require considerable advance planning. This process is referred to as the **action lag**.

The timing of capital expenditures is relatively inflexible, and changes cannot be made quickly. Changes in tax rates are usually made at the regular budget time, although tax changes have been made in Canada on a number of occasions in the fall, when changes related to indexation are announced. If unexpected economic events occur just after the usual budget period, the cabinet may be unwilling to revise policy until the next normal budget period. These delays in decision making within the administration and the cabinet are a major source of the delay in implementing discretionary fiscal policy. There is no regular pattern in the length of the lags. They depend on the expected severity and duration of economic difficulties; a consensus of economic goals in the public and the cabinet; the degree of public knowledge, awareness, and concern; the extent of support or opposition in the House of Commons; and the imminence of an election. A major source of lags in discretionary stabilization policy involves interrelations between public opinion and the political-administrative process.

There does not seem to be much indication of a shortening in the lags in this area comparable to improvements in analysis and forecasting. A populist government will want to consult its electorate before making policy changes, and consultation takes time. The sheer size of tax collections and expenditures at the provincial and municipal levels and the lack of co-ordination between the three levels of government cause further delays in initiating discretionary stabilization policy in the Canadian institutional framework.

Even after policy changes have been made and the resultant changes in tax rates and expenditure changes have become effective, there can be a further lag before the full impact on GDP is felt. This delay is referred to as the **outside lag** or **response lag**. Some effects on certain expenditure sectors may be felt right away. Industries supplying goods and services to the expanding departments and agencies and some consumer sectors responding to the increased incomes related to a personal income tax cut would receive immediate benefits. Other secondary effects take time to work through the system as part of moving to a new equilibrium. Business investment, for example, may remain depressed after a period of decreased profits and low rates of utilization and only begin to expand after a number of quarters of increased profits and higher rates of utilization provide more assurance that the market will justify the output from new capital facilities.

These three lags are sequential. As long as 24 months may pass from the time that trends requiring correction begin to occur in the economy until a majority of the changes implemented have influenced GDP and employment. The major source of uncertainty is the duration of the inside lag associated with the political-administrative, decision-making process.

The over-all length of lags is very long in relation to the duration of the postwar recessions in Canada and the United States. The methods developed by the National Bureau of Economic Research, if applied to Canada, would indicate that postwar recessions have lasted about 10 or 12 months, certainly much less than the total duration of the lags outlined in the previous pages. It seems that discretionary changes in aggregative economic policy are likely to have their major effect *after* the economic problems they were designed to offset have largely passed. For example, measures designed to stimulate the economy (growing out of the short recessions typical of the postwar period) are likely to have their major stimulating effect during the next expansionary period, accentuating demand and price pressures. This evidence suggests that discretionary measures of stabilization policy are more likely to *increase*, rather than reduce, instability in the private sector. A further implication of this evidence is that postwar recessions have not been ended by the policies adopted by governments, but by the inventory corrections and the recovery in housing investment which have been the prime characteristics of the early stages of postwar recoveries in Canada.

Attempts to adjust stabilization policy to offset changes in the levels of demand in the private sector would require fairly frequent changes in policy. The duration of business cycle expansions and contractions in North America suggests that about five changes in policy direction would be required each decade. It is doubtful that there would be political support for such frequent changes in direction, especially if the cycles continue to be relatively mild and largely self-correcting.

Although this chapter has emphasized fiscal policy, it should be noted that these same questions about lags in response have been raised and discussed in relation to monetary policy. The flexibility of monetary policy is important to scrutinize because the inside lags are shorter for monetary than for fiscal policy. However, the evidence summarized in Section 13–7 suggested that the outside lags on monetary policy were quite long, reflecting the lags within the chartered banks and the timing of response in housing and other expenditure sectors. The outside lags in monetary policy are clearly *longer* than for fiscal policy, and the total length of lags for monetary and fiscal policy seems to be comparable.

Under these circumstances, I have come to a pessimistic view on the possibility of using discretionary stabilization policy to offset changes in demand in the private sector. Such attempts are more likely to *increase*, rather than reduce, instability, as long as the North American cycles continue to perform as they have in the past. This conclusion is based on many years of experience in the federal government conducting short-term forecasts partly as background for monetary and fiscal policy. This conclusion is supported by a large volume of applied research by economists in North America.

## SUMMARY

Three factors contributed to the emergence of a series of annual budget deficits beginning in 1977. One factor was a rapid increase in federal expenditures, especially in interest payments on the growing federal debt. A second factor was the introduction of indexing personal income tax in 1974, which reduced the buoyancy in federal revenues caused by rising prices in previous years. The third factor was the severity of the 1981–82 recession and the slower growth in the early stages of the expansion that led to increased expenditures on unemployment insurance and a decline in revenues with the drop in corporate profits and indirect taxes. The resulting deficits were larger in relation to total federal expenditures and GDP than any experienced since World War II.

The effects of federal deficits are still debated among economists. The monetarists are concerned that the size of the deficit may cause economic and political pressure to finance part of the deficit by monetary expansion through increased holdings of the public debt by the Bank of Canada. Others, following Keynesian models, have predicted that the larger federal debt would lead to higher interest rates (both nominal and in excess of the rate of price increase). Still others, in the tradition of David Ricardo, suggest that the effects of a budget deficit are equivalent to a tax increase and have no significant effect on interest rates or on economic activity.

This chapter raised the possibility of the emergence of another recession as a basis for considering the scope for discretionary fiscal policy. The low fiscal multipliers require enlarged budget deficits to keep unemployment low, but the federal government has little ability to reduce expenditures, due to the importance of provincial and municipal expenditures.

Other difficulties are intensified by long lags in the decision-making process within the government. When recessions are as short as we have experienced during the postwar years, attempts by the government to offset these recessions are more likely to stimulate the next expansion than to check the increase in unemployment while it is occurring.

The importance of lags and shocks makes the implementation of discretionary fiscal and monetary policy much more difficult to implement in practice than is conveyed by many static models.

## NOTES

1. *Bank of Canada Review*, February 1986, p. S 161. Lower rates of increase for the years 1982–85 can also be seen in the six other monetary aggregates charted in Peter Howitt, *Monetary Policy in Transition: A Study of Bank of Canada Policy* (Scarborough, Ont.: Prentice-Hall Canada for the C.D. Howe Institute, 1986), pp. 42–43. Only $M_1$ shows a markedly different pattern over time than the seven other measures.

2. For concepts and data see Canadian Tax Foundation, *The National Finances: An Analysis of the Revenues and Expenditures of the Government of Canada, 1985–86*, (Toronto: 1986), pp. 300–311.

3. Data Resources of Canada, *Canadian Review*, September 1986, pp. 33 and 53.

4. Department of Finance, *A New Direction for Canada, An Agenda for Economic Renewal*, Nov. 8, 1984, pp. 16 and 20.

5. See Robert J. Barro, *Macroeconomics*, (New York: John Wiley & Sons, 1984), pp. 380–83.

6. Aris A. Protopapadakis and Jeremy J. Siegel, *Is Money Growth and Inflation Related to Government Deficits? Evidence from Ten Industrialized Countries*, Federal Reserve Bank of Philadelphia, May 1986.

7. Paul Evans, "Do Large Deficits Produce High Interest Rates?" *American Economic Review*, March 1985, pp. 68–87; and Paul Evans, "Interest Rates and Expected Future Budget Deficits in the United States," *Journal of Political Economy*, February 1987, pp. 34–58.

8. Department of Finance, *A New Direction for Canada: An Agenda for Economic Renewal*, November 8, 1984.

9. Michael Parkin, "Watch Out for Falling Inflation," *Canadian Business Review*, Autumn 1981, pp. 18–23.

10. These paragraphs draw heavily on material included in D.J. Daly, "Fiscal Policy: An Assessment" in *Canadian Perspectives in Economics*, John Chant, ed. (Don Mills, Ont: Collier-Macmillan Canada, Ltd. 1972), Chapter A–6.

# PART SIX

# International Trade and Exchange Rates

Chapter 3, Section 3–5, highlighted two important developments in the international area that economic theory and analysis should try to explain. One development was the changing historical composition of world trade, especially the falling share of trade in natural resource products (agricultural and mineral products) and the increased importance of trade in manufactured products. The second development was the collapse of the system of stable exchange rates, and the emergence of greater volatility in exchange rates for the major industrialized countries in the world economy. The central aim of Part Six is to develop the relevant theory for these occurrences and to relate them to the recent performance of the North American economies.

Chapter 16 will deal initially with the distinction between traded and nontraded goods and services and explain the reasons for the changing composition of world trade. The chapter will next deal with the concept of comparative advantage, which helps explain the interrelations between resources and the effectiveness of their use, industrial structure, and the broad composition of exports and imports. This part of the chapter will build on the concepts of economic growth developed in Part Two. The theory of comparative advantage will be used to explain the differences in the structure of exports between Canada and Japan. Some of the developments in the trade of manufactured products will be related to the concept of economies of scale. An appendix to that chapter discusses the theory and evidence related to economies of scale.

Chapter 17 will extend the demand model introduced in Part Three to the international sector and show how the interrelations between developments abroad and domestically affect the movements of exports and imports over time. International capital flows can also affect the demand and supply of foreign exchange, and some of the factors affecting such capital flows will be examined in the context of a single country.

Chapter 18 will emphasize the international financial system and some of the major reasons for the abandonment of the system of stable exchange rates, a key part of the world economy since the middle of the 19th century (apart from periods of war and severe depression). Some of the changes in exchange rates can be related to the differential rates of inflation explored in Part Four, but changes in capital flows have also been important either in sustaining some exchange rates and in precipitating exchange rate appreciations or depreciations in other situations.

One of the important developments in North American economies in the 1970s and 80s is the increased importance of international competition in manufactured products. Chapter 19 will discuss these issues in light of the theory and evidence on both exchange rate changes and the micro discussion of costs and international comparisons in this part. Consideration will be given to the positions of Japan, Europe, and the developing countries.

Chapter 19 will discuss changes in international trade in manufactured products, for decades the most rapidly growing area of world trade. This area, however, has been an area of comparative disadvantage for Canada historically. On the other hand, it has been an area of comparative advantage for Japan, which has been able to obtain a growing market share of world trade in manufactured products.

# 16

# International Trade and Comparative Advantage

After reading this chapter, you should understand:

1. The differing relative importance of exports of goods and services in the major industrialized countries.
2. That primary products have been a falling share of world trade since before World War I, while manufactured products have been a growing share of world trade.
3. The main theories of comparative advantage and the evidence on Canada's position in that framework.
4. Some of the evidence on Japan's rapid emergence as a major competitor in the growing world market for manufactured products.

There is an increasing economic interdependence among countries. An increasing share of production as measured by GDP is exported. This has been true for most developed and developing countries since World War II. A similar interdependence appears in financial markets. Price levels and the structure of relative prices in the world economy show evidence of the close interdependence among economies.

It is important to understand the structure of trade, before turning to the aggregates of exports, imports, and the balance of payments, which will be examined in the two subsequent chapters.

## 16–1 IMPORTANCE OF INTERNATIONAL TRADE

Almost all major countries have experienced an increase in the ratio of exports to GDP throughout the postwar period, as reflected in Table 16–1. As the table shows, the United States and Japan have low ratios of exports to GDP, but smaller countries such as Sweden and

**TABLE 16–1**  Exports of Goods and Nonfactor Services to GDP
(selected industrial market economies, 1960 and 1981)

|  | 1960 | 1981 |
|---|---|---|
| United States | 5 % | 10 % |
| Japan | 11 | 15 |
| France | 15 | 22 |
| Italy | 14 | 27 |
| Canada | 18 | 28 |
| United Kingdom | 21 | 28 |
| Germany | 19 | 30 |
| Sweden | 23 | 31 |
| Belgium | 33 | 65 |
|  | — | — |
| Industrial market economies (weighted by GDP) | 12 % | 20 % |

NOTE: Exports of goods and nonfactor services include merchandise, freight, and insurance but exclude investment income and workers' remittances from abroad.

SOURCE: World Bank, *World Development Report, 1983* (New York: Oxford Univ. Press, 1983), p. 157.

Belgium have much higher ratios of exports to GDP. This situation is to be expected because countries with large populations and large national incomes can achieve a significant degree of specialization within their large domestic markets. However, countries with smaller populations and a lower total level of national income must trade to take greater advantage of economies of scale.

Canada has a higher ratio of exports to GDP than larger countries such as the United States, Japan, and France, but lower than in a much smaller country like Belgium.

With the formation of the European Common Market and the achievement of essentially free trade in industrial products within that large market, the ratio of trade to GDP of most of the European countries has increased significantly. We used a weighted average in Table 16–1 because the countries vary markedly in size of their GDPs. These developments make it increasingly important to give greater attention to the topic of international trade in economics texts.

There are a number of reasons for the widespread increase in the importance of exports to GDP. One reason is the improvement and relative cost reductions that have taken place in transportation and communication. The information on product availability and prices has improved with faster and cheaper means of communication, including the use of computers and improved automatic telephone exchange systems. Faster and cheaper air transportation has permitted high-value merchandise and perishable products to be shipped by air between countries. In the 1930s and at the end of World War II, international trade was significantly impeded by high tariffs and nontariff barriers to trade. **Tariffs** are taxes imposed on goods imported into a country, frequently as a percentage of the value of the import (an ad valorem tariff). **Nontariff barriers** are limitations on imports (but not in the form of a tax). Quotas are the most prevalent nontariff barrier, but there are many other varieties of nontariff barriers such as "voluntary" export controls — for example, Canada's pressure on the Japanese to limit their exports of automobiles to Canada.

These tariff and nontariff barriers have been reduced appreciably by a series of multilateral tariff negotiations that have taken place under the General Agreement on Tariffs and Trade. The **General Agreement on Tariffs and Trade**, which came into effect in 1948, provides a forum for negotiations between countries on the gradual reduction or elimination of tariffs and other barriers to trade, and also sets out rules of conduct for international trade relations. Also, a number of regional free-trade associations have been formed, the most important of which is the **European Economic Community (EEC)**. The EEC covers countries with a total population of more than 300 million people, including associated European countries.

Table 16–1 is an aggregative table, but it is also important to recognize that a very large proportion of output in the major industrialized countries is produced and consumed on a relatively local basis. Local consumption applies to a large part of the service sector of the economy, covering such broad industrial groups as government services, health, education, wholesale and retail trade, restaurants, and many parts of the personal service sector such as barbershops and beauty parlours. These sectors have become a growing share of total employment and GDP by industry, which means that trade in commodities has grown even more rapidly than the totals in Table 16–1 suggest. This raises the important distinction between traded and nontraded goods and services. The distinction between **traded and nontraded goods and services** recognizes that many services are produced and consumed on a local basis by residents, while other goods (such as wheat, copper, and newsprint) are transported and traded between countries.

The importance of the service sector for Canada can be seen in Table 16–2. In 1985 merchandise exports were about 85 percent of the value of gross domestic product in the goods-producing industries, while receipts from foreign sales of nonmerchandise were only 5 percent of the value of GDP in the service-producing industries.[1] This is a dramatic illustration of the extent to which international influences are important to the commodity-producing industries. However, services are domestic in orientation, produced and consumed by residents of Canada.

---

**TABLE 16–2** Services and Goods-producing Industries (as a proportion of Canadian GDP at factor cost, 1980)

| | |
|---|---:|
| Services | |
| Transportation, storage, and communications | 8.5 |
| Electricity, gas, and water | 3.5 |
| Wholesale trade | 4.7 |
| Retail trade | 6.3 |
| Finance, insurance, and real estate | 10.6 |
| Public administration and defence | 7.5 |
| Business and personal services | 9.8 |
| Education and related services | 5.3 |
| Health and welfare services | 5.5 |
| Total services | 61.7 |
| Goods-producing industries: | |
| Agriculture | 3.3 |
| Forestry, fishing, and trapping | 1.1 |
| Mines, quarries, and oil wells | 6.5 |
| Manufacturing | 21.6 |
| Construction | 5.8 |
| Total goods-producing industries | 38.3 |

SOURCE: Economic Council of Canada, *The Bottom Line, Technology, Trade and Income Growth* (Ottawa: Ministry of Supply and Services, 1983), p. 12.

---

In summary, this section has shown that international trade has increased in relative importance in most of the industrialized countries. Canada is more dependent on exports than are many other industrial market economies. There is a major difference in the relative importance of exports in the commodity-producing industries compared to the large and growing service sector (the differences being 85 percent in the goods-producing industries, but only 5 percent in the service-producing industries, as measured by GDP at 1981 prices).

International trade is such a major part of the output of commodity-producing industries that it deserves extended treatment in a text designed for use by Canadian students of business and accounting. It has an important influence on the macroeconomy.

## 16–2 TRENDS IN WORLD TRADE

There have been important changes in the composition of international trade throughout the present century. This fact can be seen in Table 16–3, which shows the changes since before World War I to 1960. An important point shown in the table is that the growth in the volume of primary produce (a major area of Canada's historic strengths) has been slower than the growth in trade in manufactured goods since before World War I.

---

**TABLE 16–3**   World Levels of Trade Volume, Selected Years, 1911 to 1960 (index numbers, 1913 = 100)

| Period | Manufactures | Primary Produce |
|--------|--------------|-----------------|
| 1911–13 | 94 | 97 |
| 1936–38 | 100 | 125 |
| 1948–50 | 132 | 116 |
| 1960 | 297 | 208 |

---

SOURCE: David W. Slater, *World Trade and Economic Growth: Trends and Prospects with Applications to Canada* (Toronto: University of Toronto Press for the Private Planning Association of Canada, 1968), p. 8.

---

**TABLE 16–4**   Development of World Exports, Commodity Output, and Gross Domestic Product (indices 1970 = 100)

|  | 1950 | 1960 | 1973 | 1984 |
|--|------|------|------|------|
| World exports (volume) | | | | |
| Total | 21 | 44 | 130 | 180 |
| Agricultural products | 42 | 68 | 110 | 157 |
| Minerals* | 23 | 50 | 119 | 102 |
| Manufactured goods | 16 | 37 | 137 | 238 |
| World commodity output | | | | |
| total | 34 | 56 | 119 | 154 |
| Agricultural products | 58 | 78 | 108 | 138 |
| Mining | 38 | 59 | 114 | 119 |
| Manufacturing | 26 | 49 | 123 | 167 |
| World real GDP | 38 | 59 | 119 | 157 |

---

*Includes fuels and nonferrous metals.
SOURCE: General Agreement on Tariffs and Trade, *International Trade, 1984/85* (Geneva: 1985), p. 201.

Table 16–4 shows the development of the volume of world exports and the volume of world commodity output for selected years from 1950 to 1984. This table shows that trade in primary products has continued to grow at a slower rate than the volume of world trade in manufactured goods. The declining share of international trade in agricultural products is primarily a reflection of the relative decline in agricultural employment and output that has occurred in all the major industrialized countries over the present century. You will recall that Section 7–2 discussed low-income elasticity in the demand for agriculture products and the declining importance of agriculture that resulted. These same tendencies have been reflected in international trade. A further consideration that limits international trade in agricultural products is the widespread use of agricultural subsidies and price-support systems in many countries and the associated tariff and nontariff barriers to trade that have persisted through many years of international negotiations for tariff reductions in the industrial products area. Trade in minerals (including fuels and nonferrous metals) also shows a falling share of total world trade, in spite of the importance of international trade in petroleum products. The major declines in relative shares have occurred in the minerals and nonferrous metals area. Some of the reasons include the development of new materials (such as plastics) that are substitutes for metals and the increased importance of reclaimed materials from scrap.

International trade in manufactured products has grown much more rapidly than the output and the consumption of manufactured products. Trade in manufactured products increased 15-fold between 1950 and 1984, while manufacturing production increased sixfold. On a worldwide basis, there has been an increased specialization of individual plants and firms in manufacturing and an associated increase in purchased materials and components as a part of total output. **Specialization** is the practice of producing only a small number of products or models in a particular plant. Specialization has developed in many countries, as reflected in a growth of purchased materials as a share of manufacturing costs for many individual countries. Specialization is also reflected in an increase in the two-way flow of trade in manufactured products, a tendency illustrated in the trade statistics for many countries.[2]

Increased specialization is taking place in many multinational firms, with individual plants specializing in certain models or products and distributing those products through the marketing channels of the parent. For example, IBM produces electrical conductors for world distribution in its plant near Montreal. Ford and General Motors produce particular models in their Canadian plants and provide the North American market with them, but they import other models from their U.S. plants. There is a large Canadian-U.S. two-way flow of trade in automobiles and trucks.

Similar tendencies toward specialization have occurred in small Canadian-owned plants and firms as well.

## 16–3 THEORIES OF COMPARATIVE ADVANTAGE

The theory of comparative advantage clarifies the interrelations between the structure of exports and imports in international trade, on the one hand, and the related supplies of the basic factors of production and the effectiveness with which they are used in individual industries within a particular economy, on the other. Comparative advantage has been a part of the discussion of international trade theory for more than a century and a half, since initially proposed in 1817 by the British economist David Ricardo. Much of the discussion of comparative advantage has followed the Ricardian method in the sense that it is primarily deductive and is based on some initially simplifying assumptions about the behaviour of individual consumers and producers (such as, companies prefer higher profits to lower profits). This chapter will follow the broad theoretical lines developed in the literature and will apply this framework to Canada in the next section.

Most pure theories of international trade emphasize that trade takes place between countries because relative prices of individual products differ between the countries concerned. Trade tends to equalize the relative prices of commodities, although the presence of tariffs and transport costs can prevent this equality from fully occurring in practice. For example, cotton goods and some consumer durables are more expensive in Canada than in the United States, after allowing for differences in the exchange rate.

Despite the established acceptance of the concept of comparative advantage, there are important differences in the explanations provided in the literature. The modern theory of comparative advantage finds the source of the differences in the relative prices of goods produced in different countries in the inequalities of supplies and prices of the main inputs into the production process (labour, land, and capital). It is maintained that low land prices in Australia, for example, encourage the production and export of grain, wool, and mutton. This theory originates with the Swedish economists Eli Heckscher and Bertil Ohlin. In the Heckscher-Ohlin model, the relative supplies of various factors of production are assumed to vary between countries, as reflected in the different relative prices of factors between countries, or differences in the elasticities of supply of the factors. Paul Samuelson, Harry Johnson, and others have since explored and applied many aspects of this framework. There is an extensive literature in this field, but it is somewhat tangential to our main themes here.[3]

The Heckscher-Ohlin-Samuelson tradition assumes similar production conditions and constant returns to scale in individual industries in different countries.

The Ricardian tradition, on the other hand, emphasizes differences in labour productivities between industries as the major source of differences in comparative costs and comparative advantage between countries. The evidence from a large and growing number of published intercountry comparisons of productivity by industry is inconsistent with the assumptions made by the modern theorists. Significant intercountry differences in productivity levels exist for agriculture, mining, and manufacturing. Within manufacturing, the differences are even more pronounced, with finer levels of disaggregation. We will return to this point in the next section when we look at the factors affecting Canada's comparative advantage.

Two key assumptions traditionally made in the modern theory are the existence of similar production conditions in different countries and constant returns to scale. The differing relative use of the various factors of production in different countries and differing relative supplies of factors in the various countries are regarded as crucial in determining the difference in the structure of relative prices. International specialization emerges as a result of specialization in each of the various countries in those industries that involve more intensive use of the factors that are relatively more abundant (and thereby less expensive) in that country.

Central to the earlier alternative theory of the source of differences in relative prices is an emphasis on differences in production conditions between industries in different countries. Ricardo initially emphasized such differences in relative labour productivities between countries. This idea has continued to be a central part of the Ricardian tradition since, although more recognition than Ricardo initially allowed for is now given to factors of production other than labour (such as capital) and their costs. In light of the importance of labour income in net national income (as pointed out in Section 5–4), the emphasis on the importance of labour productivity makes the Ricardian approach still relevant, especially when *all* the intercountry comparisons of productivity by industry continue to show large differences.

Both of these theories of comparative advantage (i.e., both the Ricardian and modern theories) are static, rarely allowing for changes in technology or for nonprice elements in trade. Recent theoretical work has attempted to extend the boundaries of the models to include the role of research and development, new technology, and other factors.

Each of these three theoretical approaches to comparative advantage will be examined for their applicability later.

## 16–4 EVIDENCE ON CANADA'S COMPARATIVE ADVANTAGE

This summary of the evidence on Canada's comparative advantage will draw on the framework for intercountry comparisons of real income levels and growth experience developed by Edward F. Denison, initially introduced in the discussion of economic growth over time in Chapters 5 and 6. That conceptual framework permits the distinctions made in international trade theory to be summarized in quantitative terms for a number of the major industrialized countries. The countries studied include the United States, Canada, Japan, and eight European countries (Belgium, Denmark, France, Germany, Italy, the Netherlands, Norway, and the United Kingdom).

**TABLE 16–5**  Land Area and Mineral Production per Person
Employed, 1960 and 1970, Relatives (U.S. = 100)

| | Arable Land Area per Person Employed | Value in U.S. Dollars of Major Mineral Production per Person Employed |
|---|---|---|
| Canada (1970) | 218 | 222 |
| United States | 100 | 100 |
| Northwestern Europe (1960) | 20 | 26 |
| Japan (1970) | 5.2 | n.a.* |

*n.a. = Not available
SOURCE: D. J. Daly, *Canada's Comparative Advantage,* Economic Council of Canada Discussion Paper No. 135, 1979, p. 13.

Let us begin the discussion by examining those factors of production with which Canada is relatively well endowed. The data on factor inputs has been standardized between countries on a per-person-employed basis to permit ready comparisons between countries with quite different employment numbers.

Canada is clearly better endowed with natural resources than any other country or group of countries shown in Table 16–5. The quantity of arable land per person employed in Canada is more than twice the U.S. level and more than 40 times the level in Japan. However, these comparisons are only part of the picture. Climate and rainfall are less favourable than in other countries for the production of fruits, vegetables, and livestock, and thus Canada is a net importer of a wide range of agricultural products. The availability of land is reflected in radically different types of agriculture. Japan, for example, now grows about as much rice as it consumes due to very intensive use of small plots of land. Farm production per agricultural worker in Canada was consistently below that of the United States well into the 1960s, and any subsequent narrowing of the gap has been insufficient to modify that condition. Mineral production is relatively more important in Canada than in any other country studied. On the basis of an expanded list of major mineral products, mineral production was about 120 percent greater in 1960 on a per-person-employed basis than in the United States, about seven times greater than in Europe, and almost 50 times greater than in Japan (all comparisons valued at U.S. prices). However, the qualities of Canadian ore are not outstandingly favourable in relation to other countries, and some studies indicate that output in mining has fallen relative to labour and capital in recent decades; that is, we are getting less return for each hour of work and dollar of investment.

The evidence for Canada indicates that significant differences in the levels of output per worker-hour in manufacturing relative to the United States have persisted for decades. Since about 1970, the average level has run 25 to 30 percent below the United States. There are, of course, a number of manufacturing industries in Canada where the levels of output per hour are higher than in the United States, but these are offset by the much larger number where the levels are lower. Why have differences of this kind between countries physically close, with easy flows of information and considerable foreign ownership, persisted? Such differences can only persist over decades with the continued presence of important tariff and nontariff impediments to trade. Significantly, tariff reductions in both directions (or complete industry-free trade as in the Canada-U.S. automotive agreement) have narrowed the productivity differences from those that prevailed in the 1950s. The presence of some remaining tariff and nontariff barriers to trade prevent individual firms from achieving all the potential benefits of economies of scale.

The term **economies of scale** refers to reductions in the average cost of producing a given product made possible by an expanded level of output. Canadian plants typically produce a wider range of products than plants of the same size in the same industry in the United States, and the length of run of each product variety is inevitably short, leading to high unit costs. The resulting high costs limit sales to the smaller domestic market behind a tariff wall. The high Canadian costs and U.S. tariffs reduce the opportunity for Canadian firms to be competitive even when large American population concentrations are physically close to Canadian plants. The shorter Canadian runs and frequent down-time required to make adjustments to production specifications when changing product runs are reflected in higher unit costs for goods produced in Canadian factories. Some plant sizes in Canada are less than minimum efficient scale — for example, some continuous process plants in chemicals and plastics and in beer (where provincial preferences are examples of nontariff barriers within the domestic market).

The two latest rounds of multilateral tariff reductions took place under the auspices of the General Agreement on Tariffs and Trade (GATT). The Kennedy Round (named after the late President J. F. Kennedy) was fully implemented by 1973 and reduced the average level of world industrial tariffs by approximately one third. The Tokyo Round was completed in 1979, and further industrial tariff reductions of 25 to 30 percent will have been implemented by 1987.

With the reduction in tariffs under the Kennedy and Tokyo Rounds, and the Canada–U.S. Automotive Products Trade Agreement of 1965, the extent of the productivity differences between Canada and the United States have narrowed over the last three decades. Increased specialization has taken place within individual manufacturing industries.[4]

Refer once again to Table 3–6. You will see that the Canadian relative levels of output per hour have slipped compared to other countries such as Japan and some of the countries in Europe. In the mid-1960s, Canada was second only to the United States in levels of output per hour. Since then, output per hour has continued to grow in North American, but at a slower rate, especially since 1973. Growth in Japan and the European countries has been more rapid than in the United States and Canada, and by the mid-1980s Canada was surpassed by Japan, Belgium, France, West Germany, and Sweden. Lower levels of output per hour in Great Britain and Italy still keep the average for the four major European countries (France, West Germany, Italy, and the United Kingdom) slightly below Canada. This information translates as a comparative disadvantage for Canada when it competes in the world market for manufactured products.

The evidence on Canada's comparative advantage is important in the context of the changing trends in world trade described in Section 16–2 above. Canada has a comparative advantage in natural resource products, but these products have been a falling share of world trade since before World War I. On the other hand, Canada has a comparative disadvantage in manufactured products as summarized above, and this area has been the major growth area in world trade since World War II.

## 16–5 JAPANESE MANUFACTURING PERFORMANCE

Japan provides a significant contrast to Canada and the United States in terms of natural resource availability. Japan imports a very high proportion of its natural resource requirements in such products as oil, coal, and minerals.[5] Japan must export a significant volume of manufactured products to pay for these natural resource imports. Dramatic increases in the levels of output per hour in Japanese manufacturing have helped to achieve this. Table 16–6 shows that the increases in Japan have been so much more rapid than in other industrialized countries that the levels of output per hour by 1984 are only about 10 percent below the United States, while in 1950 they were almost 90 percent below the United States! The table also shows that Japan actually surpassed Canada during the 1980s.

There is much more variation in the levels of the value of output per employee and per hour between large and small plants within Japan than in North America, reflecting what is called a "dual economy." A **dual economy** refers to any economy that contains a mixture of large, modern, and highly mechanized plants and some small, old, and more labour-intensive plants. This mixture continues to be important in Japan. The large plants have levels of value added per employee about 50 percent above the national average, while the small plants are about half the national average. Thus the large plants have levels of output per

**TABLE 16–6**   Output per Hour in Total Manufacturing, United States, Canada, and Japan, Selected Years, 1955–1984 (United States, 1977 = 100)

| Year | United States | Canada | Japan |
|------|---------------|--------|-------|
| 1955 | 56.4 | 31.7 | 9.1 |
| 1965 | 74.6 | 47.8 | 19.9 |
| 1975 | 93.4 | 67.9 | 51.4 |
| 1980 | 101.7 | 76.0 | 77.4 |
| 1984 | 115.6 | 83.5 | 100.8 |

SOURCE: D. J. Daly and D. C. MacCharles, *Focus on Real Wage Unemployment* (Vancouver: Fraser Institute, 1986), p. 65.

hour about one third above North American large-plant levels. This distinction is important for international trade since Japan's large plants play a dominant role in world exports.[6] For example, Japanese manufacturers export Japanese cars to North America and elsewhere.

These developments in Japanese manufacturing are important for two reasons. First, Japanese manufacturers have been able to attain a significant increase in their share of the world market for manufactured products, partly made possible by their high productivity levels and related low costs. This is also important in their increased share of domestic markets within Canada and the United States and the related competition with domestic producers.

The second reason is the question of whether the production methods and organizational practices being implemented by Japanese firms have relevance and applicability to North American firms. One extreme is the Rudyard Kipling view that "east is east and west is west and never the twain shall meet," which implies that cultural and attitudinal differences are too great to be bridged. Another view is the convergence hypothesis, that management practices in different countries will become more similar with industrialization. There has been an explosion of interest in Japanese management practices in North America. Some of these practices are very similar to those already followed by the excellent companies in North America.[7]

## SUMMARY

International trade has been a growing percentage of GDP in the major industrialized countries for some decades.

Trade in natural resource products has been a falling share of world trade since World War I, while trade in manufactured goods has been a growing share of world trade.

The modern theory of comparative advantage emphasizes the role of factor supplies and factor prices, while the classical theory emphasizes the differences in productivity levels on relative prices as the basis of international trade and related specialization between countries.

The evidence for Canada confirms Canada's advantage in the production of natural resource products, while levels of output per hour in manufacturing in Canada have been surpassed by productivity in Japan, France, Germany, and some other European countries.

An Appendix provides additional theory and evidence for Canada on the concepts of economies of scale. Modern cost theory provides a basis for the emphasis on the differences in cost and productivity levels between countries. These themes convey the continuing relevance of the Ricardian theory of comparative advantage to international trade.

## NOTES

1. *Bank of Canada Review*, December 1986, p. S. 118; and Statistics Canada, *National Income and Expenditure Accounts, Second Quarter 1986*, October 1986, p. 7. Both series are based on 1981 prices.

2. H. Grubel and P.J. Lloyd, *Intra-Industry Trade: The Theory and Measurement of International Trade in Differentiated Products* (New York: John Wiley & Sons, 1975); D.C. MacCharles, *Canadian Domestic and International Intra-Industry Trade* (Saint John, N.B.: University of New Brunswick, Mimeo, 1984); and D.J. Daly and D.C. MacCharles, *Canadian Manufactured Exports: Constraints and Opportunities* (Montreal: Institute for Research on Public Policy, 1986).

3. For additional information and some of the main sources on the literature see D.J. Daly, "Theory and Evidence on Canada's Comparative Advantage," in *International Business: a Canadian Perspective*, K.C. Dhawan, Hamid Etemad, and Richard W. Wright, eds. (Don Mills, Ont.: Addison-Wesley Publishing, 1981), pp. 32–47.

4. D.J. Daly and D.C. MacCharles, *Canadian Manufactured Exports: Constraints and Opportunities* (Montreal: Institute for Research on Public Policy, 1986) and references cited therein.

5. D.J. Daly, "Japanese Economic Developments, 1970–1976," in *Economic Growth and Resources, Vol. 5, Problems Related to Japan*, Shigeto Tsuru, ed. (London: Macmillan Press, 1980), pp. 315–36.

6. D.J. Daly, "Corporate Strategies and Productivity Performance in Japan's Manufacturing Industries," in *Canadian Perspectives on Economic Relations with Japan*, Keith A.J. Hay, ed. (Montreal: Institute for Research on Public Policy, 1980), pp. 125–65.

7. For discussions of Japanese management and its relevance to Canada, see Daly, "Corporate Strategies," pp. 125–65; Donald J. Lecraw, "Corporate Operations and Strategy in a Changing World Environment" in *Technological Change in Canadian Industry*, D.G. McFetridge (Toronto: University of Toronto Press, 1985), pp. 103–44; Charles J. McMillan, *The Japanese Industrial System* (Berlin: de Gruyter, 1984); William Ouchi, *Theory Z: How American Business Can Meet the Japanese Challenge* (Reading, Mass.: Addison-Wesley Publishing, 1981); Richard T. Pascale and Anthony G. Athos, *The Art of Japanese Management: Applications for American Executives* (New York: Simon & Schuster, 1981); Thomas J. Peters and Robert H. Waterman, *In Search of Excellence* (New York: Harper & Row, 1982); Richard J. Schonberger, *Japanese Manufacturing Techniques: Nine Hidden Lessons in Simplicity* (New York:

Free Press, 1982); Bruce Scott and George C. Lodge, *U.S. Competitiveness in the World Economy* (Boston: Harvard Business School, 1985); Joseph M. Weiler, "The Japanese Labour Relations System: Lessons for Canada" in *Labour-Management Co-operation in Canada*, Craig Riddell, ed. (Toronto: University of Toronto Press, 1985).

## APPENDIX: ECONOMIES OF SCALE

A key distinction between the Ricardian theory of comparative advantage and the modern theory introduced in Chapter 16 is that the Ricardian theory incorporates differences in production conditions in the same industry in different countries, whereas the modern theory assumes constant returns to scale and similar production conditions in different countries. Recent research on Canadian manufacturing and the effects of tariffs and the freer trade options has emphasized the empirical importance of economies of scale. In fact, research by Canadian economists contributed greatly to the theory and evidence on international trade and its relationships to industrial structure. In light of the importance of this topic, some of this theory and the related evidence will be summarized in this appendix.

The literature has distinguished between three sources of economies of scale, as follows:

Product-specific economies of scale.
Plant-specific economies of scale.
Nonproduction economies of scale.

These will be dealt with in separate sections. The plant-specific and product-specific economies of scale both relate to economies associated with production and purchasing, while the nonproduction economies of scale relate to such nonproduction overhead costs as finance, marketing, and managerial costs.

### Product-Specific Economies of Scale

The first clarification of product-specific economies of scale occurred in the analysis of the cost reductions associated with the production of air frames on the West Coast of the United States during World War II. If only one air frame of a particular model were built, the cost per unit was high, but the average cost per unit fell with a doubling of output to two air frames. A further cost reduction took place when output was increased to four and then to eight. An empirical generalization evolved that with each doubling of output, a given reduction in cost per unit occurred. The extent of decline in average cost per unit was frequently 15 or 20 percent — quite a significant reduction. Subsequent research has indicated that this concept applies to many products and processes, including manufacturing, transportation charges, publishing, and printing. Decline in average cost per unit is an important characteristic of product diversity with the type of production processes historically used in North America and other industrialized countries.

This phenomenon is sometimes termed the experience curve (the term used by the Boston Consulting Group) or the progress cost curve. A part of the reduction in average cost per unit is associated with the spreading of fixed costs over a longer run of a particular model variety. In addition, costs of some materials and components drop when purchased in large quantities. Lower average costs of labour inputs per unit of output are also typically obtained as employees develop faster processes when producing the same product. This reflects "learning by doing," something you have experienced yourself in doing essays or learning how to cope with a computer.

The experience curve is sometimes shown as in Figure 16A–1. The accumulated past production since the product first began to be manufactured is shown on the horizontal axis. The average cost or price per unit is shown on the vertical axis. Both the vertical and horizontal axes are shown in logarithmic form. A straight line on a double log chart would reflect a constant percentage reduction in cost with each dou-

---

**FIGURE 16A–1**  Average and Marginal Cost Curves, Experience Curve (logarithmic scale)

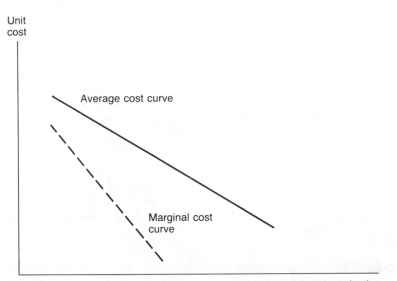

bling of output — say, 20 percent. In this situation, the marginal cost curve would also be a straight line but falling more steeply than the average cost curve.

The experience curve was developed by the staff of the Japanese subsidiary of the Boston Consulting Group. They were attempting to develop a rationale for the significant declines in cost per unit in Japanese manufacturing, and the comparable more rapid increase in output per hour than was taking place in North America.[1]

## Plant-Specific Economies of Scale

Plant-specific economies of scale have been much more widely recognized in the microeconomic literature of production and cost theory. The basic idea is that plants of different sizes (as measured by employment input or total capacity) can have different average costs per unit. If all inputs are doubled, the effects on average cost per unit lead to the same costs, higher average costs, or lower average costs per unit. Cost differences are associated with constant returns to scale, decreasing returns to scale, or increasing returns to scale, respectively. Costs are always measured at the low point on the average cost per unit schedule for a particular plant size. These differences are illustrated in Figure 16A–2. You may recall some of the distinctions that you have already encountered in your microeconomics course.

Although the economic literature has given a good deal of attention to plant-specific economies of scale, its importance has been diminished by two considerations. First, the idea was initially developed for a single-product plant. However, there are now almost no single-product plants, as almost all plants produce a tremendous range of different products and models. A further consideration is that most empirical studies conclude that different plant sizes tend to make only a relatively small difference in average cost per unit. For example, the major international comparison study by F. M. Scherer et al. found that the plants even one-third the minimum efficient scale for a wide range of products had costs per unit only slightly higher than the low-cost plants.[2] A similar conclusion was reached in a study by Zvi Griliches for a number of individual industries in the United States, using data on net value added per employee for different sized plants. He found that there were some economies of scale in moving from quite small plants up to the next larger size, but from there on, the individual industries tended to be approximated by a constant return-to-scale situation.[3]

## Nonproduction Economies of Scale

Product-specific and plant-specific economies of scale are associated with the production and purchasing costs of an individual plant. These

**FIGURE 16A–2**  Average and Marginal Cost Curves

Costs
per unit

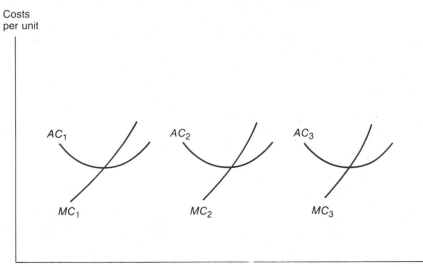

Production per unit of time

costs tend to be a very high proportion of total costs for the typical manufacturing firm. However, there are other nonproduction costs to consider—namely managerial costs, finance costs (such as debt and equity sources of funds), marketing and distribution costs, and research and development costs.

Marketing is an example of a nonproduction cost. The costs per minute of advertising are lower if the ad is run frequently than if it is only shown intermittently. This is why you sometimes see the same television ad repeated several times during one hour of programming.

Another nonproduction example is in finance, where the costs of borrowing in relation to a debt are lower for a well-known national company with a good financial performance than a smaller private company, whose financial position and prospects need special scrutiny by the potential lender. Some of these differences in cost reflect a different risk assessment by the lender.

## Evidence for Canada

Some evidence on the relative distribution of the various types of costs distinguished in the previous sections of this appendix can be seen in the accompanying table, based on data for a survey of 30 manufacturing firms (both subsidiaries and Canadian owned). Almost three-quarters of the total costs are production costs, and almost half are material costs.

**TABLE 16A–1**  Relative Structure of Existing Costs, Major Product Line (30 manufacturing firms)

| Cost Component | Percentage of Unit Cost Spent on Factor, Unweighted Average |
|---|---|
| Material | 48.9 |
| Labour | 9.7 |
| Factory costs | 15.7 |
| Total production costs | 74.3 |
| Research and development | 1.2 |
| Marketing, advertising, distribution | 10.7 |
| Administration | 5.5 |
| Financial and other | 2.5 |
| Total nonproduction costs | 19.9 |
| Residual (profit and tax) | 5.8 |
| Total cost | 100.0 |

SOURCE: D. J. Daly and D. C. MacCharles, *Canadian Manufactured Exports: Constraints and Opportunities* (Montreal: Institute for Research on Public Policy, 1986), p. 48.

The total nonproduction costs are about one-fifth of the total. If a particular company is interested in cost savings, it should concentrate on the larger items, rather than the small ones.

This survey also provided evidence on the average cost reduction with a tripling of output. Most of this cost reduction is in the product-specific, economies-of-scale category, although there may have been some instances where the companies also moved to a larger sized plant. The average cost reduction was 19 percent but with considerable variation between product groups. Chemicals and plastics, for example, experienced a cost reduction of less than 10 percent, while the reduction for electrical and electronics exceeded 30 percent (see Table 16A–2).

This evidence helps to clarify two things: first, it helps explain why Canada has a large net trade deficit in manufactured products, which is related to lower productivity and higher costs in Canada than in other countries, as pointed out in Chapter 16; and second, an important part of these cost problems can be offset by increased specialization by individual plants and firms and increased exports of a limited range of products.

A number of small Canadian-owned companies have been able to specialize and export in some niche in the world market overlooked by large firms in other industrialized countries with access to large markets. Successful companies tend to have aggressive, entrepreneurial managers, who have developed active training programmes for their employees. The gap in the world market must match the areas of interest and expertise of the firm, and managers must stay up to date on new technology in a highly competitive world market.

**TABLE 16A–2**  Unit Cost Reductions with a Tripling of Output (four manufacturing groups)

|  | Percentage Reduction in Unit Cost |
|---|---|
| Auto parts | 21 |
| Electrical and electronics | 32 |
| Chemicals and plastics | 9 |
| Machinery and equipment and miscellaneous | 14 |
| Average | 19 |

SOURCE: D. J. Daly and D. C. MacCharles, *Canadian Manufactured Exports: Constraints and Opportunities* (Montreal: Institute for Research on Public Policy, 1986), p. 54.

## Implementation of New Technological Developments

In recent years there has been increased interest in new technological developments involving the use of the computer in designing new products and in manufacturing—sometimes referred to as CAD/CAM. There has also been an increased interest in the use of robotics and flexible production systems that would permit faster changes from one type of product to another on the same machine. It has sometimes been suggested that these developments would be able to overcome Canada's traditional problems of high cost associated with short runs, and this is certainly a possibility.

However, these developments can only lead to an improvement in the Canadian position relative to other countries if Canada adopts them more rapidly than its competitors. The evidence, on the contrary, suggests that Canada has been slower in adopting new technology than other countries. The net effect is that the Canadian cost position becomes even more out of line. This is another illustration of the key importance of fast adoption of new technology. The managerial aspects of technological adoption are probably more important for Canada than the engineering and scientific aspects of the creation of new technology, since it is often feasible to buy new technology from abroad rather develop it all within Canada.[4]

## NOTES

1. J. C. Abegglen and W. V. Rapp, "Japanese Managerial Behavior and 'Excessive Competition'," *The Developing Economies*, December 1970 reprinted in *International Business—1973: A Selection of Readings*, Donald S. Henley (East Lansing, Mich.: MSU International Business and Economic Studies, 1973), pp. 65–82.

2. F. M. Scherer et al., *The Economies of Multi-Plant Operation* (Cambridge, Mass.: Harvard University Press, 1975); D. J. Daly and D. C. MacCharles, *Canadian Manufactured Exports: Constraints and Opportunities* (Montreal: Institute for Public Policy, 1986), especially Chapters 3 and 4.

3. Zvi Griliches, "Production Functions in Manufacturing: Some Preliminary Results," in *The Theory and Empirical Analysis of Production*, Murray Brown, ed. (New York: Columbia University Press, 1967), pp. 275–340.

4. D. J. Daly, "Technology Transfer and Canada's Competitive Performance," in *Current Issues in Trade and Investment in Service Industries: U.S.-Canadian Perspectives*, Robert M. Stern, ed. (Toronto: University of Toronto Press, 1985), pp. 304–33. Also Richard G. Harris, *Trade, Industrial Policy and International Competition* (Toronto: University of Toronto Press, 1985), pp. 93–109, and especially pp. 107–109. Richard Harris puts much more emphasis on the natural science and engineering aspects of market failure of the R & D side and plays down the managerial and social science aspects of technology transfer.

# 17

# Balance of Payments and International Capital Flows

The last chapter introduced the concept of comparative advantage and illustrated how it could clarify the structure of trade, particularly in Canada and Japan. This chapter will shift to more aggregate topics and concentrate on the position of a single country, with emphasis on Canada. These topics relate to what is referred to as international monetary economics.

After reading this chapter you should understand:

1. The main terms and concepts related to trade, balance of payments, and exchange rates.
2. What the trade and balance of payments statistics for Canada look like.
3. What the major determinants of the balance of payments are.
4. What purchasing power parity means, and how it can be applied to Canadian price and exchange rate developments since 1970.

## 17–1 CONCEPTS AND TERMS

The statistics on Canada's international trade and balance of payments are published by Statistics Canada, the same organization that produces the statistics on national accounts, prices, labour force, and capital stock that you encountered in previous chapters. The concepts and terms Statistics Canada uses are fairly standard and similar to those used by other countries and by international agencies that follow economic developments in the world economy.

Goods, services, and capital (purchases and sales of new and outstanding bonds and stocks) flow between nations. Such transactions are relatively large in relation to GDP for a country like Canada, with a

**TABLE 17–1** Canadian International Transactions, 1985 (dollars in billions)

| Line Number | Item | Credits (+) | Debits (−) | Net Credit (+) or Debit (−) |
|---|---|---|---|---|
| | Current Account | | | |
| 1. | Exports and imports of goods and services | | | |
| | a.   Goods | 120.3 | 102.8 | +17.5 |
| | b.   Current services | 15.7 | 20.0 | − 4.3 |
| | c.   Investment income | 7.4 | 22.0 | −14.6 |
| | d.   Transfers | 3.5 | 2.7 | + 0.8 |
| | e.   Net current account balance | | | − 0.6 |
| | Capital Account | | | |
| 2. | Net capital movements | | | + 7.7 |
| | Statistical discrepancy | | | − 7.1 |

SOURCE: *Bank of Canada Review,* December 1986, pp. S 133–S 135.

population of 25 million, that is relatively open to the rest of the world in terms of movements of both goods and capital.

These transactions between residents in Canada (both individuals and companies) and residents in other countries are recorded and assembled by Statistics Canada. Table 17–1 summarizes these international inflows and outflows for the calendar year 1985. Such transactions include goods and services *sold by* Canadians to foreigners, and also the *purchases* of goods and services *from* foreigners. Payments and receipts take place not only for goods (that you can see going back and forth across the border by truck, train, and ship), but also payments for past borrowing by governments and businesses (interest and dividend outpayments). The total balance of payments also includes capital movements (such as when Ontario Hydro sells bonds in New York or Paris, France).

## The Balance of Payments

Table 17–1 is divided into two sections. The top section summarizes the current account. The **current account of the balance of payments** shows the receipts and payments for goods and services currently produced and sold by Canadians to nonresidents. As you can see, the receipts and payments for goods (Item 1*a*) dominate the current account for Canada, as Item 1*a* is about three times as large as all the other receipts and payments combined. All receipts are shown as a credit (+) and all payments as a debit (−). Any transactions that provide foreigners with an additional supply of Canadian dollars are classed as debits, or minus items (−). **Current services**, Item (b), includes payments made for Canadians travelling on U.S. and other foreign airlines, and payments made for insurance (to Lloyd's of London, for example). **Investment income** (Item 1c) in the balance of payments includes the payments of interest and dividends on past issues of provincial and municipal bonds (bonds sold in New York, for example). It also includes payment of dividends by Canadian subsidiaries to their parent in New York or London, for example. **Transfers** (Item 1d) in the balance of payments include receipts from recent immigrants who bring their savings (from Italy or Hong Kong) when they relocate in Canada, and some tax payments.

The **net current account balance** (Item 1e) is the net difference on receipts and payments for all items 1a to 1d inclusive. As you can see, Items 1b and 1c show net payments abroad, a characteristic feature of the Canadian balance of payments historically. For 1985, the net current account balance was quite small ($−.6 billion) in relation to the large gross flows in both directions of almost $150 billion in 1985. In that year, the merchandise surplus (Item 1a) was sufficiently large that it covered the deficit on nonmerchandise trade.

The demand and supply for Canadian dollars can come from capital transactions in addition to the current account transactions shown in Items 1a to 1e. The **capital accounts** in the balance of payments relate to purchases and sales of assets and extensions of credit. For 1985, the data show larger receipts of Canadian dollars than payments on capital account. During earlier periods of rapid economic growth in Canada, both governments and corporations might sell bonds to finance domestic expansion, such as the sale of bonds by the Canadian Pacific Railway in London. In the 1950–73 period foreign companies made direct investment in Canadian subsidiaries (such as exploration for oil in Alberta or iron ore in Labrador). Such large capital inflows have slowed in recent years, and more foreign direct investment by Canadian companies has begun to take place.

Like all accounting statements, the total balance of payments should balance, but there was a statistical discrepancy of $7.1 billion in 1985. The discrepancy in the Canadian balance of payments has been negative every year since the middle of the 1960s, and the 1985 discrepancy was the second largest in the last two decades. The size of the discrepancy is bound to be worrisome to both the statisticians who assemble the numbers from a variety of sources and the users who may puzzle about its meaning and implications.

## Exchange Rates

Another new concept (and group of concepts) relates to the exchange rate. The **exchange rate** is the price of one currency in terms of another. For example, at the end of January 1987, the noon quotation for Canadian dollars was $1.3388 per U.S. dollar. In other words, you would have to pay $1.34 Canadian for each U.S. dollar you purchased. Newspapers quote the market rate, which is what the Canadian foreign exchange traders pay on large quantities. If you went into your local bank or trust company to buy some U.S. dollars for a weekend of skiing or shopping, you would pay more than this amount, and if you converted any U.S. funds that were left over back into Canadian dollars on your return, you would get less than this amount. This **spread** between a buying price and selling price is the commission that the financial institution charges for the service of providing the required foreign exchange close to your home.

Most quotations of the value of the Canadian dollar are made in terms of the U.S. dollar because today three-quarters of Canadian merchandise trade takes place with the United States. However, the financial pages (and the larger financial institutions) quote, buy, and sell foreign currencies for 50 countries. Since the early part of the 1970s, these various currencies have frequently fluctuated in relation to the U.S. and Canadian dollar — sometimes very sharply.

How can you make a comparison with a wider range of countries? Eventually you would want an index number based on the major countries in Canadian trade (much like the consumer price index that was introduced in Chapter 2, Section 2–4). Such an index is now published monthly based on what is called the G-10 countries. (The G-10 countries are the 10 largest trading countries, and the index is quoted on the basis of 1971 = 100.) It is thus a base-weighted price index, with the price quotations referring to exchange rates. Such a price index of exchange rates is referred to as an **effective exchange rate**, or a **trade-weighted exchange rate** (the latter being a more descriptive term).[1]

Figures 12–1 and 12–2 show the movements of the Canadian dollar both in relation to the U.S. dollar and on an index in relation to the G-10 currencies, with 1971 equal to 100. In October 1986, the Canadian dollar index was about 70, reflecting a drop in the value of the Canadian dollar of 30 percent since 1971 in relation to the exchange rates of the 10 major industrialized countries. Most of that change has taken place since 1976 by both measures of Canadian exchange rates. This is the largest change in the value of the Canadian dollar in relation to the U.S. dollar that has taken place in any decade during the present century.

One other topic related to balance of payments and exchange rates is the official foreign exchange reserves. The **foreign exchange reserves** are reserves of internationally accepted means of payment that a country holds to cover short-term deficits on its balance of payments. In Canada, these are held by the Bank of Canada. Very little of that reserve is held in gold bullion (although some is). Most of it is invested in Treasury bills issued by the U.S. government. The advantage in holding

**FIGURE 17–1**    Spot Exchange Rate — Average Noon Rate (Canada, 1982–1986)

Canadian dollar in U.S. cents - Monthly                    U.S. dollar in Canadian cents

SOURCE: *Bank of Canada Review*, December 1986, p. S 15.

**FIGURE 17–2**    Index of Canadian Dollars against G-10 Countries (Canada, 1982–1986)

Index of Canadian dollar against G-10 countries

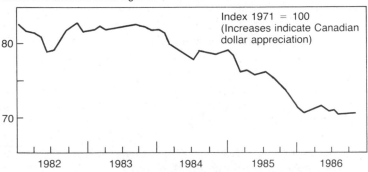

SOURCE: *Bank of Canada Review*, December 1986, p. S 15.

Treasury bills is that they earn an interest income and are easy to administer and safeguard. At the end of 1986, slightly more than $800 million was held in gold, while more than $2 billion was held in U.S. dollars (mostly invested). In total, the official reserves were $3.9 billion in late 1986, well below the level of $6 billion in 1972 (even though the value of foreign trade and other receipts and payments had increased more than fivefold over that period).

With these concepts and definitions introduced, we can now shift our attention to some of the main economic forces both within Canada and in the rest of the world that can influence the movements in receipts and payments in the Canadian balance of payments.

## 17–2 SOME KEY DETERMINANTS OF THE BALANCE OF PAYMENTS

To simplify the presentation, we will concentrate on providing an explanation for the movements in merchandise exports and imports. These amount to about three-fourths of the total receipts and payments on current account, and the changes in the nonmerchandise side of receipts and payments are normally less than on the merchandise side.

Changes in Canadian exports are bound to be heavily influenced by what happens in the rest of the world that we export to — especially the United States. When the United States is experiencing a period of rapid growth, this growth will stimulate Canadian exports (as well as exports from other countries, of course). When markets abroad are growing rapidly, Canadian exports of steel, lumber, and mineral products are encouraged. On the other hand, Canadian exports of a range of products are affected adversely during a recession in the United States. (It might be noted, however, that the timing of economic swings tends to differ in the United States from developments in Europe and Japan. Throughout the postwar period, declines in exports to the United States have often been partially offset by increases in exports to non-U.S. markets.)

Changes in Canadian imports are primarily influenced by what happens in Canada. When Canada is growing rapidly domestically, the high levels of domestic demand spill over into an increase in merchandise imports. Imports of automobiles, cameras, video casette recorders, and television sets increase rapidly.

In other words, all of the concepts introduced in earlier chapters are going to be relevant to your understanding of what has happened in the past and could happen in the future in relation to Canada's balance of payments (with special emphasis on merchandise trade, to simplify the presentation).

We will present some of these influences one at a time, following the points in the same order in which they have been developed in earlier chapters of this book.

## Economic Growth

Economic growth was introduced in Chapter 3, Section 3–1 and developed further in Chapters 5 and 6 in Part Two. High rates of growth in Canada are reflected in high rates of growth in merchandise imports (the largest component on the payments side of the balance of payments). Strong demands within Canada are reflected in increased market opportunities for both domestic producers and foreign suppliers — the latter being reflected in increased imports.

High economic growth in Canada does not occur in isolation, of course. Historically, rapid growth in Canada has always occurred when economic growth in the rest of the world (and especially in our major markets) was also high. Historically, this occurred in the United Kingdom before World War I, but the increase in the share of exports going to the United States since World War II has made developments there of major importance for the Canadian economy. Exports are affected directly, but there are also important indirect effects on business investment in Canada. The concern about the U.S. long-term supply of natural resources in the early 1950s and again in the 1970s was reflected in increased U.S. investment in Canadian mineral and forest products, and the price increases in petroleum in 1973 and 1978 (and the later declines in the 1984–86 period) drastically affected the Alberta economy.

## Cycles in Demand and Production

Superimposed on these longer-term periods of fast and slow growth are the shorter-term swings in demand (or business cycles), which were discussed in Part Three, especially in Chapter 10. These full cycles have averaged about four years historically in the United States (see Table 3–4).

You would expect to see such short-term business cycles in the United States and Canada reflected in both merchandise exports and merchandise imports. A recession in the United States would normally be reflected in a decline in exports from Canada to the United States. Such recessions normally produce a swing to inventory liquidation in North America, so sales of mineral and forest products are affected, as are sales of automobiles produced in Canadian plants.

Merchandise imports into Canada are also affected, of course. In a more severe depression, imports of machinery and equipment would decline if business investment dropped in Canada (as it did in the severe 1981–82 recession). A reduction in business inventories in Canada would also be reflected in lower imports of clothes and consumer durables (such as televisions and personal computers).

If the rates of growth and the extent of cycles (such as the severity of a recession) in Canada were similar to those that occurred in its major markets (such as the United States), receipts from exports and payments for imports would move in a broadly similar pattern and leave the net position on merchandise trade and the current account of the balance of payments essentially unchanged. This movement would be reflected in the declines in both merchandise exports and merchandise imports to the same degree, as both are influenced by developments in the foreign and Canadian markets, respectively. In fact, the evidence on cycles throughout the present century indicates that economic conditions do *not* behave identically in Canada and its major markets. These differences have an important impact on the current account of the balance of payments.

These differences can be illustrated by the developments during the periods of rapid long-term economic growth sometimes termed *long cycles* as opposed to short-term inventory cycles. During the present century three such periods of long cycles can be distinguished, each of which normally includes two or more business cycles. Important long cycles include the period from 1900 to 1914 (during which western expansion and prairie settlement followed the building of the railroads); the period from 1923 to 1929 (which witnessed hydro development and the early stages of the automobile industry); and the 1945 to 1957 period (the period of postwar reconstruction and the natural resource boom of the 1950s). The increases in growth in both the United States and Canada for the 1940s partly reflect the degree of underutilization in the 1930s, when actual output was well below potential output for an extended period.

During each of the three periods of high growth in the world economy, the Canadian economy experienced a higher rate of growth than the United States, as shown in Figure 17–3. Increases in the rate of growth in Canada increased demand for output and resulted in increased merchandise imports in the balance of payments. The higher rate of growth in Canada than in world markets showed up in faster increases in imports than exports. Markets within Canada were growing more rapidly than markets for Canada's products abroad.

During these periods of more rapid growth domestically than elsewhere, imports increased more rapidly than exports, so Canada experienced a larger deficit in the current account of its balance of payments. However, the discussion of Table 17–1 pointed out that the current account and capital account must balance. How could these accounts balance without a loss of foreign exchange reserves?

The periods of rapid growth within Canada have always occurred at the same time as a large net capital inflow into Canada. In some periods (such as the 1900–1914 period of railway building and western expansion), capital inflow primarily reflected sales of bonds (both public and private) to investors in other countries. In other periods, capital inflow took the form of direct investment in natural resource industries and manufacturing from a parent (or affiliated company), for instance, in the United States. This type of inflow of direct investment by multinationals tended to be relatively more important in the 1945–57 period than in the earlier and later periods of high growth. In some instances, the capital inflow was a major initiating factor in Canada's high-growth periods, such as the 1900–1914 period.

In other words, a high capital inflow and an enlarged current account deficit tended to go together historically — both partly responding to common favourable factors in domestic and world environments.

**FIGURE 17–3**    Long Cycles in Gross National Product (United States and Canada, 1870 to 1960)

Percent growth per annum

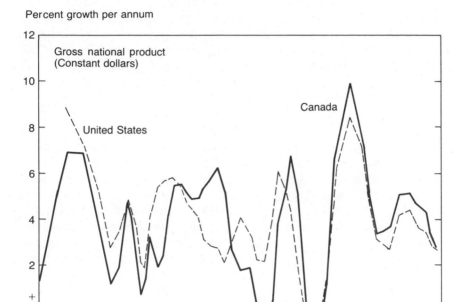

SOURCE: D. J. Daly, "Long Cycles and Recent Canadian Experience," in Royal Commission on Banking and Finance, *Appendix Volume* (Ottawa; Queen's Printer, 1964), p. 287.

During some of these periods of high growth, immigration added to the natural domestic increase in the labour force. Periods of immigration occurred primarily from 1900 to 1914 and from 1945 to 1957, although some net immigration occurred on a smaller scale in other periods as well. These periods thus tended to reflect a net inflow of men, money, and materials (the three m's).

The shorter-term business cycles (which were discussed in Chapter 10) also have an impact on the current account of the balance of payments. We have made the point on several previous occasions that, during business cycle recessions in Canada, part of the drop in domestic demand falls on domestic producers, but an important additional part has an impact on foreign suppliers (see Chapter 9, Section 9–8). For all the business cycle recessions in Canada from 1900 to 1980, the drop in the volume of imports was greater than the drop in the volume of the index of industrial production. This pattern appears both in the aggregate and also in the individual components of both domestic production and imports when the statistical classifications are comparable, which explains why the magnitude of business cycle recessions in Canada are normally less than in the United States. In terms of the impact on the balance of payments, recessions are usually reflected in a larger drop in merchandise imports than in merchandise exports.[2] Under these circumstances, if the current account was roughly in balance at a business cycle peak, a merchandise trade and current account surplus would normally appear in a recession. Thus the normal impact of a short-term recession is the development of a current account surplus. Even in economics, some clouds have silver linings.

Developments in the 1981–82 recession and the subsequent recovery correspond very closely to the historical experience of cyclical recessions and recoveries over the present century. From the business cycle peak in the second quarter of 1981, imports of goods and services dropped 18.5 percent to a low in the fourth quarter of 1982 (in 1981 prices), while the drop in GDP (in 1981 prices) was less than 5 percent. By the second quarter of 1986, GDP (in 1981 prices) had increased 17.8 percent over the trough in the fourth quarter of 1982 and 11.7 percent above the 1981 peak five years earlier. The increases in imports of goods and services were 44 percent over the trough and 12 percent over the previous peak. This greater volatility in imports than domestic production can be seen in Figure 17–4, covering the years 1981–86 by quarters.

Merchandise exports of goods and services were also affected by the U.S. recession and the greater strength of the subsequent recovery in the United States than in Canada. By the second quarter of 1986, merchandise exports (at 1981 prices) were 33 percent above the previous peak (a much larger increase than the 15-percent increase that had taken place in U.S. national product over the same period).

The greater strength in merchandise exports than in imports provided an important degree of support to demand in Canada. Of the change in GDP (in 1981 prices) between the second quarter of 1981 and the second quarter of 1986, above two-fifths of that increase was associated with the greater increase in exports of goods and services than in imports (all comparisons based on 1981 prices). By the second quarter of 1986, Canada had a surplus on current account (in both current dollars and in 1981 prices).

This current account situation in 1986 was quite different in the United States. The U.S. trade deficit was $170 billion in 1986, up from $148.5 billion in 1985, and the current account deficit was $125 billion at an annual rate over the first three quarters of 1986. The size of this deficit, the reasons for it, and possible solutions to it are still topics of active debate within the United States and in the rest of the world.[3]

**FIGURE 17–4** Changes in GDP, Output in Goods Producing Industries, Exports of Goods and Services, Canada, 1981 (II = 100.0, 1981 prices, 1981 to 1986)

Price (base quarter 1981 II = 100)

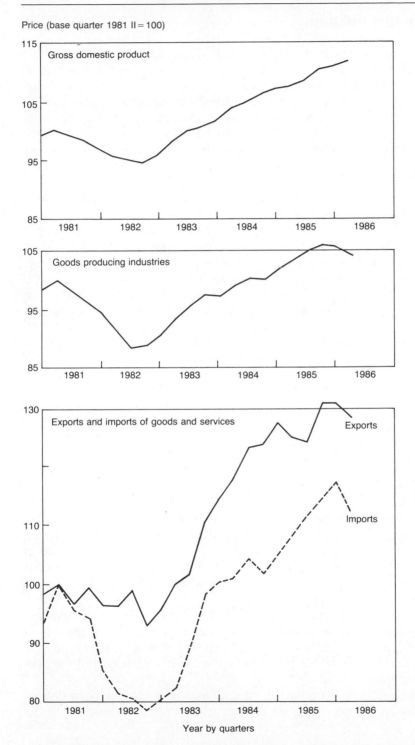

Year by quarters

SOURCE: Statistics Canada, *Gross Domestic Product by Industry, Second Quarter, 1986* (Ottawa: Supply and Services, 1986), p. 48. The data are seasonally adjusted at annual rates.

## Differential Inflation

Another development that can have implications for the balance of payments is a situation in which there are different rates of inflation in two countries. This situation can occur in a small open economy. Suppose that such a country is on a fixed exchange rate and begins to experience a more rapid rate of inflation. Also, suppose that the price level in world markets is roughly unchanged. The small country would be regarded as a **price-taker**, which implies that prices are determined in world markets on both the export and import side, and the supplies of goods and services in the small country are too small a part of the world market to affect prices internationally; i.e., the small country takes its prices from the world market. Typically, under these circumstances most contracts would be quoted in the currency of the larger country with which the small country was trading.

When a more rapid rate of inflation takes place in the small country, exporters find that their profit margins are eroded as their domestic costs go up, while the prices of their products in world markets are unchanged. If this situation continues for long, companies will find it more profitable to divert some production from the export market to the domestic market, especially for products that are just barely profitable on export sales. The net effect eventually will be a reduction in the volume of exports.

In our example, the prices of imports would be unchanged if there were no inflation in foreign countries. However, with the increase in costs and prices domestically, importers would find it cheaper to buy some products abroad, rather than domestically. The net effect would be an increase in import volume.

The net effects of these developments on the total merchandise trade and current account position would be a net reduction in foreign receipts and an increased current account deficit. Essentially, Canada, for instance, would be pricing itself out of the export market and also be raising prices in its own domestic market to the point where imports would become a larger share of the domestic market. This situation would lead to a loss of foreign exchange reserves, unless the deficit on current account were financed by a capital inflow.

The economic issues involved here would not be affected by relaxing the assumption of no inflation in the rest of the world economy. Any time the rate of inflation in Canada was more rapid than in the rest of the world, an increase in the current account deficit would occur, unless there were offsetting developments in some other part of the economic system.

Although this is a relatively simple example, it has a good deal of relevance to the economic developments in Canada in relation to the

**TABLE 17–2**  Measures of Domestic Inflation, United States and Canada (ratios, 1985/1970)

|  | Canada | United States | Canada-United States |
|---|---|---|---|
| Hourly compensation in manufacturing, domestic currency | 4.12 | 3.08 | 1.34 |
| Unit labour costs in manufacturing, domestic currency | 2.74 | 2.05 | 1.34 |

SOURCE: U.S. Department of Labor, *Output Per Hour, Hourly Compensation and United Labor Costs in Manufacturing, Twelve Countries, 1950–1985,* Bureau of Labor Statistics, December 1986. (See similar Table 11–2 in Chapter 11.)

United States since 1970 or so. In Table 17–2 it can be seen that the extent of the ratio of prices in Canada in 1985 compared to 1970 was about one-third higher than in the United States for the comprehensive measures of compensation per hour and unit labour costs for manufacturing, which are important measures of the changing international competitive position between the two countries. These measures are both in domestic currencies, so they do not take into account the exchange rate change between the two countries that has taken place since 1974. The reasons for this difference in behaviour of costs in the two countries were considered in Chapter 11, Section 11–8. Essentially what the table shows is that the degree of inflation in Canada was more marked than in the United States during the 1970–85 period.

The implications of these cost differences and the associated exchange rate changes shown in Table 17–2 will be discussed in the next two sections.

## 17–3 PURCHASING POWER PARITY

During World War I there were significant differences in the extent of inflation in various countries — a heritage of war finance. The Swedish economist Gustav Cassel (1866–1945) proposed an approach to deal with the question of the appropriate international exchange rates that should be adopted at the end of the war.[4] He proposed that the international purchasing power of a currency should be aligned to reflect its domestic purchasing power. Differences in domestic purchasing power could be measured by the differential rate of inflation in one country compared to the rate of inflation in the major countries with which it traded. One such measure could be the GDP deflator for the individual countries, or a measure of unit labour costs in the countries concerned. If a country had 30 percent greater inflation than the countries it traded with, it should adopt an exchange rate at the end of the war with a discount of 30 percent compared to the prewar exchange rate. This approach has been labelled purchasing power parity and has been discussed widely in the decades since it was first proposed, both by academic economists and economists in individual governments and international agencies. **Purchasing power parity** is the view that the international purchasing power (or the exchange rate) of a country should be brought into line with changes in its domestic purchasing power.

Purchasing power parity can be measured both in terms of levels of costs in various countries and by differential rates of change over time, as pointed out in an important article by Bela Balassa.[5]

One of the important assumptions in the purchasing power parity theory is that the exchange rate is primarily determined by the demand and supply of foreign exchange related to the current account (merchandise trade and trade in services). The theory does not give too much attention to international capital flows. One of the reasons that large and persisting differences in the degree of inflation could take place without much exchange rate change is that large international capital flows could persist, keeping the exchange rate up for the country with a high rate of inflation.

These ideas have some relevance to the Canadian situation in the early part of the 1970s. The rate of inflation in Canada had become more marked than in the United States for a series of years, and a current account deficit had begun to appear. However, a capital inflow occurred that moved the exchange rate even higher than parity for a few months in 1974 in spite of the size of the deficit on the current account. Eventually, however, the Canadian exchange rate began to decline. From 1974 to 1985 the extent of the decline was about 28 percent, and further declines occurred by the end of 1986. It is interesting that the extent of the exchange rate change by 1985 is very close to the differential extent of inflation in Canada compared to the United States as shown in Tables 11–2 and 17–2. Thus by 1985 the exchange rate had come roughly into line with the differential extent of inflation in Canada compared to the United States since 1970.

For Canada, purchasing power parity provided a rough indication of the extent of the exchange rate change to bring international purchasing power closer to the differentials in purchasing power of the two currencies domestically.

## 17–4 THE PRICE EFFECTS OF AN EXCHANGE RATE DEPRECIATION

We will now explore what the effects of an exchange rate depreciation will be (but keeping everything else unchanged), giving special attention to its effects on prices, costs, and profits. We will consider the effects initially on a natural resource company that is exporting a high proportion of its total output. We will assume that its market is primarily the United States, and we will continue to work with the small open economy model in which the prices of the major international commodities are determined in the U.S. market and contracts are quoted in U.S. currency. Let us assume that the Canadian exchange rate depreciates by 10 percent. This change would increase the prices of exports almost immediately by 10 percent, as the contracts are quoted in U.S. dollars. Measured in Canadian dollars, receipts would increase, contributing to a price increase in Canadian dollars for those products. The price increase associated with the decline in the value of the Canadian dollar will often be reflected in a comparable increase in the same products sold in the domestic market. However, most of the costs incurred by these natural resource exporters are incurred in Canadian dollars. Because profits are the residual between receipts and payments, a 10 percent change in the exchange rate can have a much larger percentage impact on corporate profits, especially if profit margins are narrow. Examples have been encountered in studies of individual companies and in statistics on the natural resource export industries where the elasticity of corporate profit changes can be as high as 5 or 6 percent for a 1 percent change in the exchange rate. There is a sufficiently wide awareness of this relationship both in the industries and in the stock market that a decline in the exchange rate can be reflected in greater strength for share prices in the natural resource companies.

The same type of analysis can be applied to the effects of an exchange rate on import prices. As these prices are all quoted in foreign currencies (primarily U.S. dollars), a drop in the Canadian exchange rate is quickly reflected in higher import prices. This change involves an increase in costs for importers, manufacturers, and other businesses in Canada who use imported parts, components, and raw materials. However, nothing has happened just from the exchange rate change that would increase the demand for these products sufficiently for the companies affected to be able to pass along the cost increases to the buyer. Companies may not adjust their selling prices at once, but would wait until their next price list was printed. A common occurrence, then, is for an important part of those cost increases to result in a squeeze in corporate profits for the companies affected.[6] There are some examples of stickiness in prices for manufactured products, when companies do not want to update catalogues and price lists too often. This is an example of transaction costs where prices are changed infrequently to reduce such costs.[7]

It should be noted that this phenomenon produces a short-term effect before companies have a chance to adjust prices domestically, which will occur with a lag. The higher prices for imports from an exchange rate depreciation will permit domestic firms to increase their share of the domestic market, so the longer-term effects will be more favourable for the domestic manufacturer than the short-term effect discussed in the previous paragraph.

One important implication of the analysis thus far is that an exchange rate depreciation will lead to upward pressure on the domestic price level. However, the direct effects would be limited to the commodity-producing industries, which account for over 30 percent of GDP. An exchange rate depreciation of, say, 33 percent (approximately the exchange rate depreciation that has occurred since 1974) would imply an increase in domestic prices of about 10 percentage points when the change to this sector is spread out over the whole economy (as reflected in the GDP deflator, for example). This is a relatively small part of a price increase of 120 percent in the GDP deflator from 1974 to 1985.[8] The exchange rate change would have a negligible influence on the prices in the large and growing service sector, where prices and costs are largely determined by domestic factors, rather than international developments.

Chapter 11, Section 11–8, summarized the factors contributing to inflation in Canada since 1970. We can now extend the discussion provided then in the context of the domestic economy to include the international influences from both United States monetary policy and the direct effects of an exchange rate depreciation.[9] Figure 17–5 shows the interrelations between inflation in Canada and the United States.

The top two boxes show the influence of U.S. monetary growth on U.S. inflation. The two boxes on the left show the potential influence of U.S. monetary growth on Canadian monetary growth. This connection could be close if Canada were on a fixed exchange rate or if the Bank of Canada and the government wanted to keep interest rates and the ex-

---

**FIGURE 17–5**   Direct and Indirect Influences of U.S. Monetary Growth on Canadian Inflation

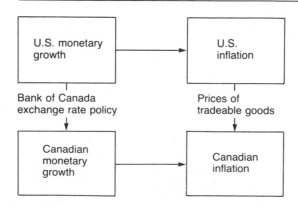

change rate of the Canadian dollar close to that of the United States. On the other hand, it could be rather limiting if Canadian authorities put high priority on domestic objectives and low priority on such international objectives as keeping the exchange rate close to the United States (or a wider group of countries such as the G-10 countries).

Canadian monetary growth can have an important influence on Canadian inflation because this is really the only influence on prices and costs in the large and growing service sector.

Inflation in the United States, and the rest of the world as well, can have an influence on Canadian inflation through the prices of tradeable goods. Canadian-dollar depreciation would further increase price levels in the tradeable-goods category, but this has not been a dominant part of the increases in the GDP deflator in Canada.[10]

In summary, an exchange rate change in isolation could have an influence on prices of traded goods, but the exchange rate depreciation of the Canadian dollar in relation to the U.S. dollar is primarily a response to the higher rate of inflation in Canada than in the United States and not really an independent causal influence. Inflation in the domestic service sector and in the traded-goods sector is primarily a response to domestic monetary policy rather than a reflection of exchange rate changes.

This discussion makes clear that exchange rate changes are going to be a lot more important to a manager in a commodity-producing firm than one in a firm whose revenues and costs are largely influenced by domestic developments.

A second important implication of this analysis is that an exchange rate depreciation is not neutral in its impact on corporate profits, but has a large positive effect on profits in the export industries and a negative effect in manufacturing and other importing industries in the short-term. Since there are significant contrasts in the industrial composition of the different regions in Canada, there is bound to be conflict between the regions on exchange rate policy. British Columbia and the prairies would favour exchange rate depreciation, while Ontario and Quebec would be concerned about the same development. These differences in view must be reconciled in Ottawa, but as long as more than 60 percent of the labour force resides in Ontario and Quebec, the political pressures against exchange rate depreciation are likely to be quite powerful. In this connection, it is significant that Gerald K. Bouey, when he was governor of the Bank of Canada, frequently expressed concern about exchange rate depreciation. In the most recent appraisal of monetary policy published by the C. D. Howe Institute, Peter Howitt criticised the priority given to avoiding further exchange rate declines.[11] An earlier and stronger move to monetary restraint in Canada would have reduced the pressures for exchange rate declines from extended larger increases in costs in Canada than in the United States.

This analysis also has implications for the **terms of trade**, which are measured by changes over time in the ratio of export prices to import prices. An exchange rate change will have comparable effects on both export prices and import prices, implying no change in the terms of trade in the small open economy model with which we have been working. This model has been used to test most of the major exchange rate changes that have occurred since the late 1940s, and very little change in the terms of trade has been observed. When such changes do take place, they occur for reasons other than changes in exchange rate.

## SUMMARY

The chapter initially introduced a number of new terms and concepts necessary to follow the data on international trade and balance of payments. The format of Canadian balance of payments statistics were set out.

Some of the key determinants of changes in the balance of payments were introduced, namely, long-run economic growth and the effects of business cycles on demand and production. These are particularly important if the timing and rates of change in Canada diverge from those of Canada's major trading partners.

Differential rates of inflation in Canada can also have an influence on the balance of payments, and the purchasing power parity theory of exchange rates shows how exchange rates can be affected. The interrelations between domestic monetary policy and exchange rate changes in influencing domestic prices were summarized. Exchange rate changes can be an important short-term influence on prices in the commodity-producing industries, but domestic monetary policies are key influences both for the large service sector *and* the goods-producing sector.

## NOTES

1.  For a discussion of the calculation and the weights for the 10 countries see *Bank of Canada Review*, September 1984, pp. 119–24.

2.  Derek A. White, *Business Cycles in Canada* (Ottawa: Queen's Printer for the Economic Council of Canada, 1967), p. 140 and related discussion. This discussion covered the 1903 to 1966 periods.

3.  *The Globe and Mail*, Jan. 31, 1987, p. B6 and U.S. Department of Commerce, *Business Conditions Digest*, December 1986, p. 93.

4.  Gustav Cassel, *Memorandum on the World's Monetary Problems*, (Brussels: International Financial Conference, 1920).

5.  Bela Balassa, "The Purchasing Power Parity Doctrine: A Reappraisal," *Journal of Political Economy*, December 1964, reprinted in *International Finance*, Richard N. Cooper, ed. (New York: Penguin Books, 1969).

6.  D. J. Daly and D. C. MacCharles, "Corporate Responses to Exchange Rate Depreciation," in *A.S.A.C. Proceedings, International Business,* Hamid Etemad, ed., 1983, pp. 52–62.

7.  Michael Bordo, "The Effect of Monetary Change and Relative Commodity Prices and the Role of Long-Term Contracts," *Journal of Political Economy,* December 1980, pp. 1088–1109. This article presents another example of lags which have been emphasized in other places in the text.

8.  *Bank of Canada Review,* December 1986, p. S 117. See Chapter 11, Section 11–8, for a discussion of inflation in Canada since 1970.

9.  Figure 17–5 and this discussion draw on Michael D. Bordo and Ehsan U. Choudri, "The Link Between Money and Prices in an Open Economy: The Canadian Evidence from 1971 to 1980," *Federal Reserve Board of St. Louis Review,* August/September 1982, pp. 13–23.

10. The small effect of exchange rate changes on domestic price increases was shown in *Responses of Various Econometric Models to Selected Policy Shocks,* Brian O'Reilly, Graydon Paulin, and Philip Smith, (Bank of Canada Technical Report No. 38, July 1982). See also Peter Howitt, *Monetary Policy in Transition: A Study of Bank of Canada Policy 1982–85* (Scarborough, Ont.: Prentice-Hall Canada, 1986), pp. 113–15.

11. Peter Howitt, *Monetary Policy in Transition: A Study of Bank of Canada Policy, 1982–85* (Scarborough, Ont.: Prentice-Hall Canada, 1986), pp. 113–19.

# 18

# Instability in the International Financial System

The last chapter introduced some of the concepts concerning the effects of changes in incomes and relative prices between countries as they relate to the Canadian balance of payments. We focused primarily on the current account of Canada's balance of payments in the face of these changes. At the end of the chapter, we analyzed a number of long-term developments which suggested that the international environment has changed to such a degree that it seems unlikely that a system of fixed exchange rates can be re-established for an extended period of time. Under these circumstances, it is important to examine some of the factors that have contributed to the major domestic and international exchange rate developments of industrialized countries.

This chapter will cover four topics:

1. It will discuss the key reasons for the abandonment of the system of fixed exchange rates that had worked so well for more than a century.
2. It will provide criteria to permit you to distinguish in a broad way what particular exchange rate system a country is working with.
3. It will analyze why inflation was so widespread and rapid in so many countries during the 1970s.
4. It will look at the recent impact of flows of private capital.

## 18–1 MAJOR CHANGES IN THE WORLD FINANCIAL SYSTEM

You can only assess whether exchange rate changes for a particular country will continue in the future by looking at the prospects for exchange rate stability for the world economy as a whole.

The question is whether the exchange rate instability that we have seen in the world economy since 1971 primarily reflects temporary circumstances, which will soon be reversed, or long-term and fundamental conditions, which are likely to persist.

## Decentralization of Economic Power

For most of the period from 1850 to 1972, the world economy as a whole operated on something fairly close to a fixed exchange rate. In the decades after 1850, the United Kingdom was a major power in the world economy, as it was the most important exporting country and the most important import market for such products as cotton, wool, tobacco, tea, and spices. The other industrialized countries and the natural resource supplying countries all maintained a fixed exchange rate in relation to the United Kingdom. William Adams Brown, Jr. called this occurrence a Sterling Exchange Standard to emphasize the unique role of the United Kingdom. The United Kingdom was also the major international centre providing both long-term and short-term funds, through the London money market, to companies and countries throughout the world.

Before World War I the United Kingdom's economic dominance began to erode due to the increased importance of such other industrial powers as the United States, France, and Germany. Since World War II, the role of the United Kingdom has continued to decline. Japan and some of the newly industrialized countries of the Pacific Rim have become more important. The net effect is a considerable decentralization of the world economy and the related concentration of economic power.

## Evolving Domestic and International Priorities

A second major development is the emergence of new goals and priorities in economic policy. Until the 1920s, most of the major countries and the smaller peripheral countries put a high priority on maintaining a fixed exchange rate. One of the important effects of Keynes's *General Theory* was an increased priority on maintaining employment stability domestically, even if doing so meant a departure from a fixed exchange rate. During the postwar period, a number of countries departed from fixed exchange rates during periods of worldwide inflation in order to achieve greater price stability through an exchange rate appreciation.

The circumstances of a decentralized world economy and differing policy goals among the major industrialized countries have made it increasingly difficult to maintain exchange rate stability in the world economy as a whole.

## Private Holdings of Foreign Exchange

A third major development has been a dramatic increase in the holdings of private balances of foreign exchange by corporations, financial institutions, and individuals. These holdings are often deposited in local commercial banks, creating a cycle of instability. Market participants, fearing changes in exchange rates, have tried to reduce their exchange risk exposure by diversifying their holdings of liquid assets into other currencies. A Canadian company that imports materials from the United States for resale might buy American funds when the Canadian dollar is strong to hedge against possible devaluations in Canadian currency. This practice can have its own impact on the exchange rate, because individuals and corporations can easily shift these funds from one currency to another if they feel that fundamental or temporary factors could lead to an exchange rate change affecting their asset or profit position. If large shifts occur, the expectations become self-fulfilling. These private-sector balances have become very large in relation to official foreign exchange reserves. Thus it has become difficult for individual countries or international agencies to maintain exchange rate stability if private capital movements become large.

All three of these factors are deep-seated and permanent, and they all combine to indicate that future planning should be premised on the basis of a continuance of exchange rate instability in the world economy as a whole. These factors also imply exchange rate instability for individual countries such as Canada, and even key currencies in the major industrialized countries have not been able to achieve any significant degree of exchange rate stability for any extended period since the early 1970s.

Individual companies in commodity-producing industries and in financial industries should give far more attention to exchange rate planning than was necessary in the 1960s and earlier. In some cases such planning may just involve diversification of exchange rate holdings, hedging, or other relatively low-cost options. In some cases more expensive and sophisticated analysis of the risks of lending to particular countries may be appropriate if large sums and higher risks are involved.

## 18–2 ALTERNATIVE EXCHANGE RATE SYSTEMS

A country has three options when co-ordinating exchange rates in relation to its major trading partners (recognizing that even wealthy countries do not have complete freedom in choosing a system). These three options are a fixed exchange rate system, a freely floating exchange rate system, and a managed floating exchange rate system.

An individual country might try to maintain a **fixed exchange rate** in relation to its major trading partners. (In practice there is always a small spread between the buying and selling prices for foreign exchange, reflecting the operating margin of the bank or foreign exchange dealer.) Under this system, any shorter-term or longer-term disequilibrium between the current account and capital account would be reflected in changes in the levels of official foreign exchange reserves. A basic balance of payments deficit (current and capital account combined) would be reflected in a loss of foreign exchange reserves, while a basic surplus would lead to a buildup of foreign exchange reserves. Such increases or decreases in official foreign exchange reserves would have some impact on the cash position of the central bank or foreign exchange authority for that country, which, in turn, could have an effect on the monetary base of the whole financial system. The result would be the same as if the central bank had bought government bonds from the public. (See Section 12–3 in Chapter 12 for a discussion of the money multiplier.)

Under a **freely fluctuating exchange rate** an individual country would keep its levels of official foreign exchange reserves unchanged, and thus any disequilibrium between the current and capital account in the balance of payments of that country would be fully reflected in the quoted exchange rates of that country's currency. In practice, some minor changes in the level of exchange reserves might take place to slightly moderate temporary situations, but no extended increases or decreases should occur if the system is to be truly freely floating. Under these circumstances, the government and foreign exchange reserve authorities would not have any view on an appropriate rate. They would usually emphasize that the exchange rate was determined entirely by the market.

A **managed floating exchange-rate system** (or a "dirty float") would be an intermediate position, where the government, central bank, and foreign exchange authority would not try to maintain a fixed exchange rate, but might have some idea of a rate they would prefer to maintain. If they were to announce their preferences publicly, private participants in the market would try to take advantage of future exchange rate movements. Although the rate is not announced publicly, those in the market are usually able to ascertain the general level of the preferred exchange rate.

It is possible to identify which exchange rate system a government favors, although only after the event. You can check the movements in the level of official foreign exchange reserves and movements in the exchange rate. If the exchange rate is steady, but there are fluctuations in the level of foreign exchange reserves, the country is on a fixed exchange rate. On the other hand, if the exchange rate changes frequently, and the level of foreign exchange reserves remains unchanged, the country is on a freely fluctuating exchange rate. If changes occur both in the exchange rate and the level of foreign exchange reserves, the country is operating a "managed" floating exchange rate system. In some circumstances these criteria cannot be clearly distinguished in the published data because some countries have reserves of foreign exchange, domestic cash balances, and holdings of government bonds. This diversity permits changes in the agencies' asset composition, without any necessary change in its total. This has been the situation in recent years with the Bank of Canada.

An important implication of the exchange rate system is that the systems have different effects on the country's monetary base. A large increase in foreign exchange reserves would have to be financed by making domestic currency available to those selling foreign exchange, and when domestic currency is deposited in a commercial bank, it can lead to an expansion in the total money supply, with all the accompanying effects that we explored in Part Four, Chapter 12. On the other hand, a system that leaves the level of foreign exchange reserves unchanged also gives the monetary authorities the scope to influence the money supply primarily on the basis of domestic considerations, giving a small country a greater degree of independence of monetary policy than would be possible under a fixed exchange rate system.

These criteria will be used in the next few sections to illustrate how domestic and international developments have affected some of the major currencies since the early 1970s.

## 18–3 INFLATION DURING THE 1970s

Inflation was more widespread early in the 1970s than it had ever been before in peacetime. For some countries, the rate of inflation approached 25 percent or more. Many of the previous periods of inflation occurred during periods of large government deficits financed by monetary expansion; however, the early 1970s were unusual as many countries were experiencing budget surpluses.

A key development in the early 1970s was the widespread increase in the monetary base and money supply in a number of the major industrialized countries at about the same time. If all countries had been on a gold standard system (which limits the reserves for the whole system), the increase in foreign exchange reserves in one country would have been matched by a reduction in the gold and foreign exchange reserves of another country. Some increases in the price level in the country gaining foreign exchange reserves would occur, but there would be price reductions in the country losing foreign exchange reserves, and no inflation on a widespread basis need occur for the system as a whole.

Here is what happened. The United States had been financing capital outflows in excess of the surpluses on current account during the 1970s. It was thus running a **basic balance of payments deficit** (that is, current and capital account combined). However, other countries, who were experiencing increases in their foreign exchange reserves, purchased U.S.-dollar securities, which permitted the monetary base in those countries to increase without a comparable reduction in U.S. official foreign exchange reserves or the U.S. monetary base. This was an unprecedented situation. It can be clarified by a monetarist interpretation of inflation that examines the interrelations between foreign exchange reserves and the money supply.[1]

There were some differences in the rate of inflation between individual countries. The United States had lower inflation rates during the 1970s and early 1980s than most of the countries in northwest Europe and the developing countries. Nonetheless, the price index for GDP roughly doubled between 1972 and 1982. From 1973 to 1983 the increase averaged 7.3 percent per year, ranging from a low of just over 5 percent to a bit over 9 percent per year.[2] The rate of increase for Canada exceeded these amounts for most of those individual years.[3] Over the same period, the rate of increase in Canada averaged 10.3 percent per year, and in 1974 the increase exceeded 14 percent. The rates of increase for many of the European countries were even higher than those in North America, with the increases in the United Kingdom, Italy, and Sweden in excess of 20 percent per year for a series of years.

More dramatic increases occurred in many other countries. In Israel, for example, the increases exceeded 300 percent per year during the 1980s. Inflation rates for some of the South American countries were even higher.

Differentials in the rate of price change of this extent for many years are probably without precedent in peacetime. If countries had stayed on a fixed exchange rate, countries with high rates of inflation would have experienced deterioration in their merchandise trade and current account position. The costs of their exports would have risen more rapidly than in the countries that they traded with, leading to a decline in corporate profits in the commodity-exporting industries and perhaps a fall in their share of the world market. Furthermore, costs of imports would have increased less than domestic costs, and imports would have begun to take an increasing share of their domestic markets. That shift in current account would eventually lead to pressure on the exchange rate and a loss of official foreign exchange reserves unless this was offset by capital flows. These differentials in domestic price changes were a contributing factor in the exchange rate changes of the 1970s and 80s. International capital flows also became increasingly important during this period. That development will be explored in the next section.

## 18–4 THE INCREASED IMPORTANCE OF INTERNATIONAL CAPITAL FLOWS

During the 1920s, a significant number of international flows of private capital took place. Some of these flows were financed by loans from commercial banks in the major industrialized countries. The severe depression of the 1930s, the declines in industrial production and employment in the industrialized countries, and the collapse of raw material prices prevented continued payments on those debts by many of the companies in the borrowing countries. Many companies went bankrupt. The large number of resulting bad debts to commercial banks in the industrialized countries contributed to a number of bankruptcies among commercial banks in the United States and some European countries. The memory of these losses led private banks to become extremely cautious in lending to companies in foreign countries. Only after prolonged prosperity for some decades in the postwar years did international flows of private capital begin once again (during the 1970s). Private lenders were reassured by the extended period of exchange rate stability through the 1960s and the low losses on bad debts through international lending.

During the 1970s the extent of private international lending began to increase once again. International capital flows took on a new importance in discussions of the international financial system. The move to complete currency convertibility by the members of the **International Monetary Fund (IMF)** provided a degree of reassurance to lenders that limitations on transfers of interest and repayments of capital would not be introduced, although temporary exceptions could be made for balance of payments purposes after consultation with the International Monetary Fund. The IMF is a specialized agency of the United Nations created in 1944 at a conference in Bretton Woods, New Hampshire. The "Bretton Woods System" was based on a policy of fixed exchange rates (with some scope for adjustment after consultation), the elimination of exchange restrictions, and complete convertibility between currencies.

In some cases, these capital flows operated to offset and to finance deficits on current account, permitting maintenance of an exchange rate even though it appeared to be overvalued on the basis of the trade and current account in isolation. This was clearly the situation in Sweden and some of the other countries in northwest Europe, where large inflows of private capital into the Eurocurrency market were important both in domestic and international accounts financing.

In other cases, international capital flows could intensify some of the problems on the current account. For example, if a country had a large current account deficit and participants in the market thought that an exchange rate depreciation was possible, speculative capital could flow out of the country and precipitate an exchange rate depreciation. In Canada during the 1970s, a minister of finance indicated publicly that he felt that a lower value of the Canadian dollar was appropriate. There were reports that the magnitude of the subsequent losses of official foreign exchange reserves ran as high as $300 million per day!

Private lending by commercial banks became important once again in the 1980s for the first time in four or five decades. Significant bank loans were made to such countries as Mexico, Poland, and some of the developing countries. Economic difficulties in some of these countries and the drop in petroleum prices raised questions about the likelihood of repayment, and the problems of developing countries' indebtedness took on new importance in the discussions of international economic and financial developments.

## SUMMARY

It is unlikely that a system of fixed exchange rates can be reintroduced due to the decentralization of economic power, the differences in policy priorities between key countries, and the massive holdings of private balances of foreign exchange. Rather, companies, individuals, and governments will have to learn how to live with continued exchange rate volatility and uncertainty.

Types of exchange rate systems a country might adopt (fixed, managed floating, and freely floating) were discussed.

The widespread and high inflation rates of the 1970s were made possible by large and simultaneous increases in official foreign exchange reserves in the major industrialized countries. When central banks provided domestic currencies to finance the increased exchange reserves, a multiple expansion occurred in the money supplies of a number of countries at the same time. This is an important illustration of the interconnection between domestic and international stability of prices and exchange rates.

Renewed international private capital flows began in the 1970s after limited private lending for four decades.

## NOTES

1. Robert Heller, "International Reserves, Money and Global Inflation," *Finance and Development*, March 1976, pp. 68–70. This article was written while the author was still with the International Monetary Fund.

2. *Economic Report of the President* (Washington, D.C.: U.S. Government Printing Office, January 1986), p. 258.

3. CANSIM Data Tapes, September 1986.

# 19

## International Trade in Manufactured Products

The increased relative importance of trade in manufactured products as a share of world trade has been pointed out several times in previous chapters. World trade in manufactured products has been heavily influenced by the worldwide increase in manufacturing capacity, significant reductions in tariff and nontariff barriers to trade, and changing inflation rates and exchange rates. The purpose of this chapter is to highlight some of the changes for manufacturing in an individual country or in a group of countries in relation to world trade and international competition. Some of these developments have been important sources of differences in view and policy between North American and other observers.

After reading this chapter you should understand:

1. Why world trade has continued to grow in spite of increased exchange rate uncertainty and slower economic growth since 1973.
2. How international trade has led to a narrowing in real income differences between the major industrialized countries, as suggested by Paul Samuelson some decades ago.
3. Why gains in real income for Canada from free trade can be large.
4. How Japan has been so successful in obtaining a larger share of the world market through marked productivity increases, small wage increases, and by passing a significant part of the productivity gains in manufacturing to buyers of those products within Japan and internationally.
5. The experience of the developing countries in world trade in manufactured products.

## 19–1 EXCHANGE RATE CHANGES AND WORLD TRADE

An important advantage of a fixed exchange rate is the increased certainty that it provides for business decision makers when planning contracts or arranging deliveries of internationally traded products. Observers who favour retaining fixed exchange rates argue that changing exchange rates for a large number of countries would adversely affect the level and growth of world trade. In fact, world trade has continued to grow both in volume and value since the early 1970s in spite of a great deal of variability in exchange rates, no matter how measured. The rate of growth in the volume of world trade has been slower since 1973 than before, reflecting the slowdown in economic growth for the world as a whole.

Uncertainty about future exchange rates has involved increased costs in a variety of forms for the individual firm. There has been an increase in the amount of exchange rate hedging, but some companies also have accepted the gains or costs from exchange rate changes as a part of current business operations. Companies engaged in international trade must now consider the currency in which contracts will be written and future exchange rates. Advanced courses in international finance have begun to give more attention to these topics. Commercial banks have had to develop improved information systems and recruit and train staff to deal with these volatile and frequently uncertain areas. Some specialized companies provide regular reviews and forecasts of exchange rate developments for their clients and subscribers.

A number of factors have contributed to the growth in volume of world trade in spite of the higher costs of handling international trade transactions in a world of flexible exchange rates. The most important of these factors are continued growth in real income for the world as a whole (although at a slower rate than before 1973) and a significant increase in the degree of specialization within an industry. These topics have been discussed in previous chapters.

## 19–2 INTERNATIONAL TRADE AND FACTOR PRICE EQUALIZATION

Several important articles on international trade were published by Paul Samuelson in the 1940s and 50s.[1] In these articles he suggested that international trade would tend to narrow the real income differences between countries, even without significant movements of the factors of production (such as labour and capital) between countries. During the 1930s and 40s, the presence of a wide range of tariff and nontariff barriers to trade and capital flows among the major industri-

**TABLE 19–1**   Real Gross Domestic Product per Person Employed
(OECD price weights, United States = 100)

|  | 1950 | 1970 | 1986 |
|---|---|---|---|
| United States | 100.0 | 100.0 | 100.0 |
| Canada | 75.2 | 82.3 | 92.7 |
| Japan | 15.0 | 45.1 | 68.7 |
| Belgium | 46.9 | 62.1 | 82.8 |
| Germany | 32.1 | 61.6 | 81.5 |
| Italy | 27.7 | 59.7 | 72.9 |
| United Kingdom | 60.1 | 64.3 | 66.3 |

SOURCE: Bureau of Labor Statistics, *Comparative Real Gross Domestic Product, Real GDP Per Capita and Real GPD Per Employed Person, 1950–1986* U.S. Department of Labor, April 1987.

alized countries limited the amount of international trade. With the reductions in tariff and nontariff barriers to trade that took place during the last four decades, the volume of international trade has increased appreciably. The question is whether the narrowing in real incomes that Paul Samuelson predicted has in fact taken place. We find that a significant narrowing in real incomes (as measured by GDP per person employed) has in fact occurred since 1950, as illustrated in Table 19–1. By 1986, Japan and the five European countries had real incomes within 35 percent of U.S. levels, while none of them were within 40 percent of U.S. levels in 1950. The United Kingdom dropped from the highest to the lowest of the European countries, reflecting the higher rates of increase in other European countries for more than three decades.

## 19–3 THE GAINS FOR CANADA FROM FREER TRADE

Many studies have examined the costs of tariffs and nontariff barriers to Canada and the potential gains in real income from reductions in such trade barriers. These studies have helped to clarify the conceptual and statistical issues of measuring such welfare costs, not just for Canada, but for other countries as well.

Canada is the only industrialized country in the northern hemisphere that does not have access on a free-trade basis to a market of 100 million or more people. Access to larger markets permits a degree of specialization and associated lower costs.

Early studies of the costs of Canadian tariff barriers only considered the costs to the consumer as reflected in higher prices. The major study by R. J. Wonnacott and Paul Wonnacott also included the costs to the producer in the form of lower levels of output of manufactured products in relation to labour and capital inputs. They also allowed for the costs of U.S. tariffs on prices received in Canada by Canadian exporters. The net effect of including these costs was a higher level of costs of existing tariffs between Canada and the United States and large potential gains in real income to Canada from freer trade. With the reductions in tariff and nontariff barriers to trade (both under a series of GATT negotiations and the Canada-U.S. Automotive Agreement) the potential gains at the start of the Tokyo Round of tariff negotiations was about 8 percent of Canadian GDP. The potential gains to the United States were large absolutely, but smaller as a percent of GDP, reflecting the much lower ratio of trade to GDP in that country.[2]

The approach taken by the Wonnacotts' study, which emphasized the costs to the producer of tariff and nontariff barriers to trade, implied a lower level of output per hour in manufacturing in Canada than in the United States. The theory we have developed predicts a reduction in the relative difference in output per hour with tariff reductions. This has happened. In 1950 real output per hour in Canadian manufacturing was only about 50 percent of the U.S. level. Since the early 1970s the gap has narrowed to between 25 and 35 percent.

Some estimates of the gains to Canada from freer trade have been much less. These lower estimates usually imply no difference in production conditions within an economy over time, with or without tariffs, and some of these estimates are based on unchanged production conditions.[3] We have seen that production conditions do change if tariffs are reduced, yet these studies did not take this important point into account.

Estimates of the gains for other countries from freer trade have frequently been lower than those summarized above for Canada. In some cases these lower estimates reflect lower ratios of trade to GDP for those countries, but in other cases the lower estimates did not allow for any costs of tariff and nontariff barriers to trade to the producers. They rarely allowed for increased productivity associated with specialization and tariff reductions.

The Wonnacotts' estimates of the Canadian gains from freer trade demonstrate the need for important adjustments within Canadian manufacturing in response to any reduction in trade barriers. In an atmosphere of freer trade, these adjustments can take place through longer production runs and an increased export of these lower cost products to the United States and other international markets. An important implication of the Wonnacotts' research has been that high costs of production of manufactured products in Canada are an important limiting factor on exports to the United States. In some cases, small Canadian-owned plants have responded to tariff reductions by developing a niche in the market previously overlooked by larger producers in larger countries. Knowledge of the markets in these countries and products must be cultivated. Specialized firms must conscientiously keep up to date with new engineering and managerial practices. If management and workers are willing to make the changes required to compete in larger markets, the necessary adjustments can take place fairly easily. There is no necessity for whole industries to disappear in Canada, although that fate could await some firms if they are unwilling or unable to adapt to the more open and competitive world environment.

The evidence from these studies suggests that Canadian gains from freer trade would be quite large and that the adjustment process to freer trade need not be difficult. It is important, however, to recognize that access to larger markets is a necessary but not sufficient condition for increased exports of manufactured products from Canada. It is also essential that productivity levels be raised closer to the levels of our major competitors and that our costs be brought down closer to international levels.[4]

## 19–4 JAPAN IN WORLD TRADE

There are three major developments affecting the performance of Japanese manufacturing in world trade. First, the productivity developments in Japanese manufacturing have been significant in comparison with the other major industrialized countries as pointed out in Chapter 16 and Table 16–6. Japan's level of output per hour was only about one-eighth of the U.S. level in 1950. But by the mid-1980s, Japan surpassed Canada and a number of countries in northwest Europe and was less than 15 percent below the United States. Thus, it was not just a matter of a higher rate of growth, but also significant achievements in terms of level.

A second major development was that Japan experienced a moderate rate of inflation after about 1974, partly due to significant slowing in the rate of increase in the money supply. The slowing of increase in money supply occurred because of the increased influence of monetarist ideas within the Bank of Japan. This more moderate rate of inflation was reflected in a significantly slower rate of increase in total compensation per hour in Japanese manufacturing. During the latter part of the 1980s the rate of increase in output per hour in Japanese manufacturing exceeded the increase in total compensation per hour, and unit labour costs in Japan actually fell in domestic currency. By the mid-1980s, unit labour costs were lower than in the late 1970s, as shown in Table 19–2. On the other hand, unit labour costs in Canada had almost doubled. They had risen more than 50 percent in the United States, more than doubled in the United Kingdom and France, and more

**TABLE 19–2**  Unit Labour Costs in Manufacturing, National Currency Basis (Japan and selected industrial countries, 1975 and 1985, 1977 = 100)

|  | 1975 | 1985 | Rate of Change |
|---|---|---|---|
| Japan | 96.0% | 92.7% | −0.3 |
| United States | 91.7 | 145.0 | +4.7 |
| Canada | 86.0 | 166.3 | +6.8 |
| France | 86.7 | 187.4 | +8.0 |
| Germany | 93.8 | 124.9 | +2.9 |
| Italy | 77.1 | 240.1 | +12.0 |
| United Kingdom | 79.2 | 198.1 | +9.6 |

SOURCE: U.S. Department of Labor *News*, "International Comparisons of Manufacturing Productivity and Labor Cost Trends, 1985," June 18, 1986.

than tripled in Italy. Such changes were bound to influence the competitive position of these countries, their exchange rates, or both.

A third major development occurred in the area of pricing and the distribution of productivity gains that were occurring in manufacturing. There are three ways significant productivity gains can be distributed. One is in the form of increased real wages to the workers in that industry. A second is in the form of lower prices to the buyers of the output of that industry. A third possibility is in the form of increased profits and higher rates of return to capital and equity in that industry.

The striking thing about the developments in Japanese manufacturing since the mid-1970s is the extent to which Japan has emphasized the second of these possibilities — namely, passing a significant part of the productivity gains to the buyers of manufactured products. During the annual spring period of wage rate settlements, the rates of increase in most individual industries and companies are fairly uniform. Industries that have above-average productivity gains end up with lower than average increases in prices. Manufacturing is a striking example of productivity increases above the national average, and the net effect is that an important part of the productivity gains in Japanese manufacturing are passed to those in other industries and consumers within Japan. Real wages in Japanese manufacturing have increased since 1973, but the extent of the increase is only about one-fifth of the rate of increase in output per hour.

Productivity gains in Japanese manufacturing have also benefitted the buyers of manufactured products in other countries. This benefit can be seen in the Japanese terms of trade (the ratio of export prices to import prices, usually compared over time to a base period). During the 1970s and 1980s, the Japanese terms of trade dropped significantly.

There was no similar drop in the terms of trade of any of the other industrialized countries that primarily exported manufactured products but imported raw materials, crude oil, and other petroleum products. From 1973 (before the major changes in oil prices occurred) to 1985, the drop in the terms of trade amounted to about 40 percent. Thus Japan had to export about 70 percent more by 1985 to pay for the same volume of imports as a decade or so earlier.[5]

This pattern of a drop in the Japanese terms of trade is not unique to the 1970s and 80s. Previous studies of Japanese international trade have shown similar drops in the terms of trade during every period of relatively slow economic growth in the world economy since World War I. During these periods of slow economic growth, the typical pattern is for raw material prices to drop more sharply than prices of manufactured products, so the terms of trade of most manufacturing countries tend to improve during periods of slow growth. This trend was very clear, for example, for the United Kingdom during the 1930s. (During this period prairie wheat farmers in Canada and the United States received very low prices for wheat. It has been suggested that the lower prices paid by British consumers helped to finance residential construction in the United Kingdom.) What was unusual in the Japanese pattern was that the prices of Japanese manufactured export products dropped even further than the prices of raw material imports. Thus Japan captured an enlarged share of the world market for manufactured products during periods of slow worldwide economic growth. Japanese manufacturers attempted to spread the heavy fixed costs of permanent employment over a larger volume of output. This tactic permitted a reduction in costs per unit, but the enlarged volume of output could only be sold if the prices of that output were also reduced.

In 1984, unit labour cost in Japan was about 40 percent below the U.S. level and half the Canadian level. A significant appreciation in the foreign exchange value of the Japanese yen since 1984 has reduced that cost advantage; however, Japan is still the lowest-cost producer of manufactured products among the major industrialized countries. A low-cost position permits exporters to get a larger share of the world market. It also makes it very difficult for other countries to export to Japan. Producers in both North America and Europe have sometimes expressed concern about the complexity of the Japanese distribution system. It is complex for Japanese suppliers as well. But they have the advantage of language and knowledge of the special features of Japanese business practice and Japanese legal philosophy. The need to understand differences in education, customs, and business practices to operate successfully in foreign countries is important for international business, and not just in Japan.

It has sometimes been alleged that the value of the Japanese yen internationally has been held artificially low. This supposition can be tested by examining the changes in foreign exchange reserves and the changes in exchange rates using the criteria introduced in Chapter 17. Although the Japanese foreign exchange reserves increased dramatically in the 1960s and early 1970s, this increase has not been apparent in the later 1970s and 1980s. During some of these years Japan had a large balance of payments surplus on current account, with a comparable outflow of capital. The capital outflow has been in the form of investment in bonds and some direct investment in Japanese subsidiaries and joint ventures. There has been no buildup in official foreign exchange reserves, although the levels of foreign trade have increased appreciably.

This interpretation of Japanese developments emphasizes the special features of productivity, total compensation (including bonuses and fringe benefits), and pricing as key parts of corporate strategy that have important implications for both domestic performance within Japan and the related position of Japanese trade and balance of payments. Japan's increased share of the world market for manufactured products has helped keep its unemployment rate low. The increase in real GDP per employee in the economy as a whole has been widely shared within Japan, through lower costs to consumers.

## 19-5 THE DEVELOPING COUNTRIES AND TRADE IN MANUFACTURED PRODUCTS

Population in the developing countries exceeded 2.7 billion in 1975 — about 80 percent of the world population. Developing countries' rate of population growth has been more rapid since 1950 than the rate of growth in developed countries. However, their exports totalled about $474 billion, or only about 25 percent of the world export total of almost $200 trillion in 1984. Their share of world national income is also much less than their share of world population.

The exports of manufactured products from the industrial areas to the developing areas is larger than the exports of manufactured products from the developing areas to the industrialized countries. This trend can be seen in Table 19-3. North Americans are often surprised that exports of manufactured products from industrial areas to developing countries exceeded trade the other way by a ratio of more than two to one during the 1980s. Exports of manufactured products from industrial areas to developing areas include a wide range of chemicals and engineering products. Exports from developing areas to industrial areas mostly consist of such primary products as food and fuels;

**TABLE 19–3**  Trade in Manufactured Products, Industrial Areas and Developing Areas (billions of dollars, 1981 and 1984)

| Exports of Total Manufactures | 1981 | 1984 |
|---|---|---|
| Industrial areas to developing areas | 248.4 | 205.3 |
| Developing areas to industrial areas | 63.5 | 92.2 |

SOURCE: *International Trade 1984/85* (Geneva: General Agreements on Tariffs and Trade, 1985), Appendix Table A39.

**TABLE 19–4**  Hourly Compensation Costs for Production Workers, All Manufacturing, Selected Countries, 1984 (United States = 100)

| | |
|---|---|
| United States | 100% |
| Canada | 89 |
| Japan | 50 |
| Brazil | 10 |
| Mexico | 14 |
| Hong Kong | 13 |
| Korea | 11 |
| Singapore | 19 |
| Taiwan | 12 |
| Portugal | 12 |

SOURCE: U.S. Department of Labor, Bureau of Labor Statistics, *Hourly Compensation Costs for Production Workers in Manufacturing, 34 Countries, 1975–1985.* May 1986.

exports of manufacturers are more heavily concentrated in textile and clothing categories.

Many observers would expect higher exports of manufactured products from the developing countries to the industrialized countries in light of the much lower level of hourly earnings and total compensation in manufacturing in Third World nations. You can see how wages in a number of developing countries compare to the levels in North America and Japan in Table 19–4.

There are essentially two reasons for the net trade deficit of the developing countries in industrial products. In spite of low total compensation per hour, output per hour in developing countries is still substantially lower than in industrialized countries. However, some newly industrialized countries have been quite successful in adopting new technology and exporting high-technology products to such countries as the United States. This is a major theme of a study by Bruce Scott and George C. Lodge.[6] This trend may provide some further narrowing of the export gap. Table 19–3 indicates that the developing areas are making some progress in that direction.

An additional reason for the limited exports of manufactured products from developing countries to the United States and other industrialized countries is the existence of higher effective tariff rates on labour-intensive products in the industrialized countries.[7] "Voluntary export agreements" and other nontariff barriers also limit exports of such labour-intensive products as clothing and textiles from developing countries. Such nontariff barriers have roots in the policies of 19th century imperial powers and form significant obstacles to Third-World development. Individuals and governments in developing countries prefer to solve their balance of payments and unemployment problems by increased trade rather than relying on foreign aid or greater international indebtedness.

## SUMMARY

International trade in manufactured products has continued to grow more rapidly than production and consumption of manufactured products, in spite of slower economic growth in the world economies, increased exchange rate volatility, increases in protectionist pressures in many countries, and new nontariff barriers. The major reason has been the widespread increase in specialization in individual plants and firms and the greater two-way flow of transactions both domestically and internationally that specialization involves.

These same forces have been reflected in a significant narrowing in the levels of real GDP per person employed and in output per hour in manufacturing since the 1950s, as predicted by Paul Samuelson three decades ago.

These influences are an essential part of the further large gains in GDP for the economy as a whole (and in manufacturing) that could occur in Canada with further movements in the direction of freer trade (either with the United States in a bilateral agreement or multilateral trade negotiations). Increased access to larger markets is a necessary part of that development, but further adjustments are necessary to take full advantage of larger markets through increased specialization, higher productivity, and lower unit costs.

Japan has been able to achieve an increased share of the world market in manufactured products by significant increases in productivity (to above Canadian levels by the mid-1980s), by low increases in wages and total compensation, and by passing a major part of the productivity gains to the buyers of manufactured products internationally. The lack of buildup in official foreign exchange reserves and the appreciation of the international value of the yen from early 1985 to the end of 1986 suggest that the yen has not been kept artificially low.

Developing countries still buy more manufactured products from industrialized countries than they sell to them, in spite of much lower rates of compensation per hour. This tendency is partly due to lower levels of output per hour and to industrialized countries' high effective tariff rates and nontariff barriers on labour-intensive products.

## NOTES

1. Joseph E. Stiglitz, ed., *The Collected Scientific Papers of Paul A. Samuelson* (Cambridge, Mass.: MIT Press, 1966), pp. 847–908.

2. Ronald J. Wonnacott and Paul Wonnacott, *Free Trade Between the United States and Canada, The Potential Economic Effects* (Cambridge, Mass.: Harvard University Press, 1967); Ronald J. Wonnacott, *Canada's Trade Options* (Ottawa: Information Canada for the Economic Council of Canada, 1975); Richard G. Harris, *Trade, Industrial Policy and Canadian Manufacturing* (Toronto: Ontario Economic Council, 1984); and John Whalley, *Canada-United States Free Trade* (Toronto: University of Toronto Press, 1985).

3. Robin W. Boadway and J. M. Treddenick, *The Impact of the Mining Industries on the Canadian Economy* (Kingston, Ont.: Centre for Resource Studies, 1977); Roma Dauphin, *The Impact of Free Trade in Canada* (Ottawa: Ministry of Supply and Services for the Economic Council of Canada, 1977); Harry H. Postner, *The Factor Content of Canadian International Trade: an Input-Output Analysis* (Ottawa: Information Canada for the Economic Council, 1975); and J. R. Williams, *Resources, Tariffs and Trade: Ontario's Stake* (Toronto: University of Toronto Press for the Ontario Economic Council, 1976). All these authors make these assumptions.

4. D. J. Daly and D. C. MacCharles, *Canadian Manufactured Exports: Constraints and Opportunities* (Montreal: Institute for Research on Public Policy, 1986).

5. D. J. Daly, "Japanese Economic Developments, 1970–1976," in *Economic Growth and Resources, Vol. 5, Problems Related to Japan*, Shigeto Tsuru, ed. (London: Macmillan Press, 1980), pp. 315–36.

6. Bruce R. Scott and George C. Lodge, *U.S. Competitiveness in the World Economy* (Boston: Harvard Business School, 1985), p. 62. Examples of high-technology products being exported by these countries include consumer electronics, electric components, watches, and telecommunications equipment and components.

7. Harry G. Johnson, *Economic Policies Toward Less Developed Countries* (Washington, D.C.: Brookings Institution, 1976), especially pp. 78–107, and D. J. Daly "Adaptation in Canadian Manufacturing," in *Conference on Industrial Adaptation* (Ottawa: Economic Council of Canada, 1978).

# PART SEVEN

# Public Policies for Growth and Stability

Earlier chapters developed the relevant theory and the related evidence on Canadian economic growth and cyclical experience. The evidence suggests that recessions will likely continue to be milder and shorter than those experienced before World War II, so concerns regarding recessions can now be given lower priority. The implications of monetary policy, fiscal policy, and international economic policies have also been developed in the appropriate sections. This part will now draw together the implications of the earlier discussions for discretionary short-term stabilization policies. This part will also deal with the greater practical problems of implementing such policies in light of the division of powers and revenues in a federal system, lack of flexibility in federal expenditures, and the serious lags in implementing monetary, fiscal, and international economic policies. Chapter 20 also considers whether we should place higher priority on policies related to longer-term economic growth and increased productivity to further improve the international competitive position of Canadian manufacturing. These problems of costs, productivity, and the low rates of return in manufacturing have contributed to high unemployment and hesitant business investment even during the expansion following the low point of the recession in late 1982.

# 20

# The Sources of Instability and Guiding Principles for Public Policy

In this chapter we will cull the various themes from theory and evidence in earlier parts of the text and focus on their implications for public policy. More specifically, we have seven main tasks in this chapter:

1. We will review the evidence on the changing severity of business cycle recessions.
2. We will summarize the discussion of moderate inflations, especially dealing with the question of whether the private sector could initiate more severe inflation on its own.
3. We will review the reasons for the continuing persistence of business cycles.
4. We will identify three alternative guiding principles for stabilization policy and other public policy options.
5. We will review the evidence and shifting opinions on the feasibility of improving short-term stabilization policy.
6. We will discuss the international aspects of policy, looking both at the macroeconomic issues of domestic and exchange rate stability and problems of productivity performance at a microeconomic level as well.
7. We will discuss the opportunity and need for higher priority on public policies to improve growth and increased real incomes, with special emphasis on the Canadian situation.

## 20–1 CHANGING SEVERITY OF BUSINESS CYCLES

It is clear from the evidence of the postwar period that the business cycle is not dead in industrialized market economies. In spite of many

decades of experience with the application of contemporary macroeconomic tools to follow and forecast current economic conditions, and
in spite of policies designed to moderate business cycle fluctuations,
cycles have persisted.

However, a significant amount of evidence and analysis indicates
that business cycle recessions in North America have been more moderate since World War II than in the longer-term historical experience.
A number of reasons for this change have been identified in previous
chapters, especially Chapter 10.

One important longer-term trend is the declining share of the GDP
derived from the cyclically sensitive industries of manufacturing, mining, and the industries most closely related to commodity production
and transportation. On the other hand, the service sectors have increased in importance, as measured by both employment and the industrial distribution of gross domestic product. Most observers expect this
shift to the service sector to continue and therefore expect milder recessions to persist.

A second, longer term institutional change has been the increased
importance of built-in stabilizers in the Canadian economy. The introduction of the Unemployment Insurance System during the 1940s
provided a degree of income support to individuals with previous employment experience if they became unemployed. A further important
change was the increase in federal tax collections as a percentage of
GDP. The marginal tax rate increased from about 13 percent of GDP in
1929 to about 42 percent in 1985 (as discussed in Chapter 14). This was
one of the most important institutional changes relating to economic
stability in Canada in the present century.

The relatively low values of the fiscal multipliers in Canada and
other small open economies are further evidence that the private sector
is highly stable in the current institutional environment. The evidence
points to a greater degree of stability during both recessions and periods
of potential inflation than we have experienced in earlier periods.

A further institutional change was the introduction of Federal Deposit Insurance for the Canadian banking system during the 1960s.
Canada had not experienced large-scale bankruptcies in the banking
system comparable to those in the United States, especially during the
1930s. However, the failure of two western banks during the 1980s was
a salutory warning that bank failures can occur here too.

An important development occurred in the world banking system
during the last decade. Commercial banks in most industrialized countries became involved in loans to businesses and governments in both
developing countries and some of the less fully industrialized countries
of Europe. Some of these loans may not be as secure as loans to established borrowers. This type of lending can make such banks increas-

ingly vulnerable if any of their major borrowers default or if interest and repayments fall into arrears. If problems occurred with a number of loans simultaneously, some of the financial institutions would have serious difficulties to deal with—difficulties that could affect the whole banking system.[1]

Recent recessions probably have not caused the same hardship to families and individuals as occurred during the 1930s. Families today usually have more income earners than they did five decades ago as more women have entered the labour force. And there are more young, part-time workers as well. In addition, the fairly widespread coverage of the unemployment insurance system provides a degree of income support that did not exist in the 1930s.[2] Some groups of workers, such as single-parent families (especially women) and older people (especially those receiving small pensions) will still experience economic hardship in periods of recession. However, these problems cannot really be remedied by any policy intended to stabilize demand.

## 20–2 INFLATION

On occasion, concern has been expressed that continuing mild inflation could cause individuals to shift their investments from financial instruments to real estate and physical assets. This view reflects a concern about instability in the demand function for money, either from the Cambridge cash balance view, or the velocity of circulation of money view (as discussed in Chapter 11). However, the possibility of individuals buying goods and services in advance of need is really quite limited. The decreased relative importance of commodity production (as measured by both employment and income by industry) means that buying in advance of need is only possible in a small and declining share of the total economy. Furthermore, the costs of holding goods in advance of need are quite high, frequently 20 percent or more per year. In these circumstances, the rates of inflation have to exceed 20 percent per year before there is much potential gain to individuals and businesses from buying in advance of need.

These considerations suggest that it is unlikely that changed attitudes and resulting actions in the private sector could intensify inflation. The main source of inflation in the future, as in the past, is most likely only to come from inappropriate public policies or serious problems in financial institutions.

Even mild inflation can have serious economic effects, such as the differing speed of response in various parts of the pricing system. Public policies have been modified to provide a partial offset to any inflation that does take place. For example, old-age pensions and family allowances in Canada have been "indexed" to changes in the price level to keep their real purchasing power fairly stable. There has been some discussion of partially de-indexing such payments, but public resistance to such a suggestion has been strong. In addition, private pensions and public old-age pensions are now much more widespread than four decades ago. Government pensions and annuities have been indexed for price inflation, but this is fairly rare in the private sector, and many pension specialists say that the costs of full indexing of pensions would be very high. There are still some individuals who have either no pension scheme or only a small one to provide real income if inflation re-emerges, but these problems seem to be more selective and less widespread than was true historically.

## 20–3 THE CAUSES OF PERSISTING BUSINESS CYCLES

If the private sector is basically very sluggish and slow to respond, you may wonder why business cycles persist. There are essentially two factors that contribute to the persistence of instability in the economy. One factor is the occurrence of random shocks from outside the private sector—for example, the oil price shocks of the 1970s. OPEC raised petroleum prices dramatically and shifted the terms of trade of the industrialized countries against the oil-importing countries. This move led to a marked increase in export earnings of the oil-exporting countries. Another example is the reduction in the money supply associated with the monetary policies of the Federal Reserve System of the 1930s and the widespread bankruptcies of the commercial banks that occurred. The impact of the Korean War of the 1950s and the Viet Nam War of the 1970s are more recent examples. Frequent wars and the associated problems of war finance have plagued the international economy for much of recorded history.

An important implication of the externally generated shock theory of cycles is the difficulty of forecasting the occurrence and severity of such shocks. Forecasters frequently recognize this risk and may make several forecasts of the main aggregates, depending on the eventual outcome of some of these variables, which are exogenous to their model. (Remember that *exogenous* is the term introduced in Chapter 9 for variables that are determined outside the economic model developed by the analyst, while *endogenous* is the term for variables that are explained within the model.)

Another important factor in the persistence of the cycles is the existence of lags in the system. You have encountered lags in a series of instances already, such as the lags in the process of planning, contracting, and construction of factories, shopping centres, and apartments. Another example is the delayed recognition of recent developments within a firm or an industry due to inappropriate use of year-to-year comparisons in economic processes that experience a high degree of seasonality. These examples were developed in Chapter 9 on business investment. Other examples of leads and lags were introduced in Chapter 13, illustrating the differing speed of adjustment in different parts of the pricing system.

These lags contribute to the persistence of cycles after any external shock impacts on the private sector. However, the evidence indicates that the economic system tends to be fairly highly damped, so that the economy would tend to return to a stable long-term growth path unless new shocks from outside impinge on the system.

The points emphasized in this section are consistent with the evidence referred to previously in Chapter 9 which shows that the values of the fiscal multipliers are quite low, reflecting the high degree of stability in the economic system.

## 20–4 ALTERNATIVE GUIDING PRINCIPLES FOR STABILIZATION POLICY

The late Harry G. Johnson wrote a paper for the Royal Commission on Banking and Finance entitled "Alternative Guiding Principles for the Use of Monetary Policy."[3] In that study he accepted the view that the performance of monetary policy had been definitely unsatisfactory in damping short-run cyclical fluctuations in the Canadian economy in the late 1950s and early 1960s. His main interest was advice for the future, rather than a systematic examination of the past or any attempt to find a scapegoat for past problems.

A central part of the study dealt with distinctions among three positions about the appropriate conduct of monetary policy in the future. He distinguished three options that can be broadened to apply to all instruments of stabilization policy. These options can be stated as follows:

1. Stabilization policy can be improved by better, more accurate, and farther-ranging economic forecasts, more and better current data, better public understanding, and more flexibility and better co-ordination in the decision-making process within the monetary and fiscal institutions, both domestically and internationally. The aim is improved performance on *short-term stabilization.*

2. Stabilization policy can be improved by placing greater priority on achieving *longer-term stability* to moderate the extreme instabilities associated with severe and prolonged periods of either inflation or deflation. This action would lower the objectives of

short-term stabilization and bring them more into line with historical achievements.

3. A third position would put a lower priority on stabilization policy can be improved by placing more emphasis on *other objectives* such as higher economic growth and more efficient use of resources. This position could be combined with the second approach above, with an emphasis on longer-term stabilization policy objectives.

The first option above has been the subject of a great deal of research and discussion in the two decades since Harry Johnson's paper was first published in 1963. Because it has received primary emphasis in macroeconomics for most of the last four decades, we will give it some additional attention now.

## 20–5 IMPROVING SHORT-TERM STABILIZATION POLICY

Accurate and current statistical data and careful forecasts of the economic future are essential to improve short-term stabilization policy. There has clearly been a considerable improvement in the timeliness and accuracy of economic statistics for the national economy since World War II. However, problems persist. The major monthly and quarterly statistics on employment, production, sales, corporate profits, and balance of payments become available weeks or months after the period to which they relate. First estimates frequently require extensive revision.[4] Studies of short-term economic forecasts indicate frequent errors, and the errors in quarterly forecasts are greater the further into the future the forecasts go.[5] Although progress in economic data and forecasting has occurred, the nature of the forecasting problem is persistant and difficult, and there seem to be no quick and easy solutions.

The topic of forecasting is closely related to the existence of lags in formulating and implementing public policy. Milton Friedman was one of the first economists who argued that lags are a serious problem for the effective implementation of discretionary stabilization policy to offset the business cycle. He distinguished three sources of lags, and since they tend to be independent of one another, their combined length is additive. The recognition lag occurs from the lag of published data behind the period to which they relate, and the uncertainties as to whether any changes in vigour and direction are based on temporary factors (which could be quickly reversed) and longer-term factors (which could persist). The decision lag occurs due to administrative and political inertia. Governments need time to review the problems and options before taking economic action. The outside lag is the length of time after a policy change is initiated and before it begins to have a significant impact on spending and production decisions in the private sector and the economy as a whole.[6]

Professional opinion in North America in the early 1960s generally suggested that lags were not a serious problem in operating a discretionary stabilization policy. Professional opinion also suggested that any problems could easily be overcome by improved forecasting methods and improvements in the decision-making process within the government. A few examples can illustrate the tenor of professional opinion. A major U.S. study of lags in fiscal and monetary policy by the Commission on Money and Credit in the United States was quite unsympathetic of an emphasis on lags but did not deal directly or systematically with the inside lags of recognition and decision-making.[7] A 1962 submission by the Bank of Canada to the Royal Commission on Banking and Finance emphasized the greater flexibility of monetary policy compared to fiscal policy. The submission emphasized "successive approximation" in adjusting monetary policy to the developing economic situation without any explicit discussion of how the approximation could be accomplished if the recognition and outside lags were long and variable. Robert M. Will had access to the forecasts made by the Economics Branch of the Department of Trade and Commerce and made studies of fiscal policy for both the Royal Commissions on Banking and Finance and Taxation. He recognized the length and variability of the inside lags for changes in tax rates and the even longer lags in changing government spending. His policy recommendations, however, emphasized methods to increase interbudget flexibility rather than lowering or abandoning the goal of discretionary changes in stabilization policy.[8] In the early 1960s, there was considerable discussion of **fine tuning** (a view that the difference between actual economic performance and some specified target variable could be kept relatively small). The length of the expansion of the 1960s and the success of the 1964 tax cut in the United States encouraged some observers to wonder whether the business cycle was obsolete.[9]

In a 1974 survey, R. M. Solow and Alan Blinder concluded that fine tuning is not feasible, although Solow still favours an activist fiscal policy. About three-fourths of the survey dealt with such topics as stable budget proposals, the interrelations between monetary and fiscal restraints, monetarism, and lags and uncertainties in fiscal policy.[10] The survey points out that

> Monetarists are not the only economists who are skeptical of fine tuning. Both Walter Heller and Arthur Okun, Chairmen of the Council of Economic Advisers under the activist Kennedy and Johnson administrations, have explicitly disavowed fine tuning.[11]

Similar recognition of the practical problems involved in implementing discretionary stabilization policy in Canada were stated by Simon Reisman in an address to the Canadian Economics Association in 1976. The adoption of a stated range of increase in the money supply by the Bank of Canada in 1976 is an illustration of the change in official thinking and practice. The Bank of Canada had been critical of monetarism during the 1960s, so its later adoption of some of the monetarist's themes reflected an important shift.[12]

The lags we are describing have existed for decades, but there has been a more widespread recognition and acceptance of their existence over the last decade than would have been true in the early 1960s. The evidence on and experience with the various lags in practice has led to the shift in views among professional economists that was described in the previous paragraph.

The lags in the internal decision-making process in fiscal policy have been recognized for a long time. In a period of deterioration in the economic situation, most politicians are unwilling to admit that such problems could have developed during their administration. At the beginning of the Kennedy administration, the Democrats argued that they had inherited serious economic problems from the previous Republican administration, and they wanted to get the economy moving again. When the late John G. Diefenbaker became Prime Minister in 1957, he was effective in arguing that the Liberals had been warned that the Canadian economy was moving into a recession. He based his attitude on the forecast made by the Economics Branch of the Department of Trade and Commerce. When the Progressive Conservative administration under Brian Mulroney took office in 1984, they argued that they had inherited serious problems and that "the cupboard was bare," meaning they had inherited a large and serious budget deficit when they took office.

If the problems emerge during the period of their own administration, politicians are usually unwilling to admit that action is necessary, but even after they recognize that it is necessary, changes cannot be quickly instituted. The budget making process in such a large organization as the federal government can be slow and cumbersome to change.[13] Changes on the revenue side can only be made in a budget, but such changes require approval before they can be implemented. During the 1980s there were long delays in approving some items included in the Budget Speech, due to pressure of other items of legislation. In total, these lags in the political and administrative process within the government are very long, frequently longer than the duration of the postwar recessions, which have averaged about 12 months as pointed out in Chapter 3. These lags can be even longer in the United States where the Senate and Congress have much more influence than is possible in the cabinet tradition in Canada.

It is widely accepted that the inside lags in monetary policy are shorter than for fiscal policy. However, it is also clear from the evidence that the outside lags in monetary policy are longer than those for fiscal policy. Evidence of very long lags within the major Canadian chartered banks was presented to the Royal Commission on Banking and Finance early in the 1960s. An extended period of time passed between a shift in monetary policy to restraint and directives going out from the head offices of the chartered banks to the branches. There was a further lag until the changed policies of the chartered banks affected the spending decisions on goods and services in the private sector, such as housing (the area of greatest sensitivity to the cost and availability of mortgage funds). These lags within the financial system shortened by the 1980s in light of the experience with policies of monetary restraint and high interest rates that had occurred in the intervening years. Long and variable lags were also identified in econometric models studying the timing and response of various expenditure decisions. The length of these lags varies, however, from one economic situation to another, partly reflecting the differing degree of initial liquidity in both the financial institutions and the nonfinancial spending sectors.[14]

It is likely that the lags in the financial system in the 1980s are now shorter than those of the 1950s and early 1960s. This shortening in lags reflects the increased degree of sophistication within the chartered banks, the increased use of seasonal adjustments in the analysis of banking operations, and the experience gained from the considerable amount of change in monetary policy over the last three decades.

The outside lags of fiscal policy are shorter than for monetary policy, the reverse of the inside lags. In summary, a reasonable working allowance for all three lags would seem to be about 24 months. However, there is bound to be considerable variation in lag depending on individual circumstances (reflecting the nature of the economic situation, the degree of public agreement on goals and priorities, and the political assessment of the situation). These lags are long relative to the duration of the business cycle.

The preceding information on lags is important evidence on the feasibility of a discretionary stabilization policy using the instruments of monetary and fiscal policy, if high standards of performance on short-term stability are desired. It is striking how widely this assessment would now be accepted by those who have had firsthand experience in the implementation of stabilization policies in the United States, the United Kingdom, and Canada. These conclusions are shared by economists with both monetarist and fiscalist leanings on analysis and policy.

The implications of this summary of the evidence and the changing assessment within the profession suggests that it is unlikely that we can do much better in operating short-run stabilization policies with a high degree of precision in the future, in spite of much more current data, analysis, and sophisticated econometric models.

We should shift our priorities more in the direction of Harry Johnson's last two principles. Rather than continuing to put priority on short-term stabilization policy, which has been a major priority for much of the profession in recent decades, we should shift our emphasis to long-run policies of stabilization.

Before turning to these areas, we will consider the international aspects of these issues, crucial for an economy of the size of Canada (in terms of population and national income), which is so closely and economically interdependent with the rest of the world.

## 20–6 INTERNATIONAL POLICY ASPECTS

We are all aware of the importance of international influences on the performance of the Canadian economy. It is not realistic to expect Canada to achieve high standards of domestic performance avoiding instability in domestic output, employment, and the general price, if instabilities persist in the countries that we trade with.

In Part Six, we saw that if the rates of growth (both long term and short term) in Canada diverged very far from what was occurring about the same time in the United States and the other countries we trade with, Canada would experience surpluses and deficits in the current account of the balance of payments. In the past, these current account surpluses and deficits were frequently financed by capital flows (both in and out). Current account deficits could also occur if the general price level in Canada moved up more rapidly than in the other countries where our trade in commodities is most heavily concentrated. This movement developed in the 1970s and early 1980s in Canada in relation to the United States to a greater extent than anything that had occurred previously in the present century.

It is important that Canada continue to give a good deal of attention to economic developments in the rest of the world. Canada participates in the exchange of information on current economic developments and short-term prospects that takes place in such international organizations as the International Monetary Fund, the Organization for Economic Co-operation and Development, and the United Nations. In addition, smaller and more informal meetings occur with the governors of the central banks in the major industrialized countries on a monthly basis at the Bank of International Settlements in Basel, Switzerland.[15] The smaller and more informal meetings permit a greater degree of frankness than can take place at such a meeting as the annual meeting of the International Monetary Fund, at which more than a thousand participants and observers are present. There is always a concern that proposed policy changes by a central bank could influence private speculators in the international financial system relating to future interest rates, stock prices, and exchange rates.

It seems important that Canada continue to follow a policy of some exchange rate flexibility, rather than attempt to operate on a fixed exchange rate. A fixed exchange rate ties Canada's policies, especially monetary policy, very closely to the United States. A fixed exchange rate would imply that Canada had become a 13th member of the U.S. Federal Reserve System, but without the option of participating in the important Open Market Committee of that system. A floating exchange rate permits Canada a greater degree of flexibility on domestic monetary policy, even though there are limits on the extent of independence permitted by such an exchange rate system.

Furthermore, the discussion in Part Six suggested that there were a number of important long-term and deep-seated changes in the world economy that would effectively prevent the return to a system of fixed exchange rates on a world basis. These changes included the decentralization of the world economy into a number of major economic regions, with those regions and individual countries within them having differing policy priorities and different emphases on domestic, as contrasted to international, objectives. Another important development is the dramatic increase in private-sector holdings of foreign exchange in most of the major industrialized countries. Many companies and individuals now hold foreign exchange balances in their own domestic banks, partly to diversify their assets away from a complete concentration on domestic cash balances only. This latter development has made it extremely easy for individuals and corporations to shift their holdings of currency from one country's currency to another. These three developments combined have led to marked changes in the exchange rates of the major industrialized countries since the beginning of the 1970s. This analysis emphasizes longer-term factors, on which such additional special circumstances as the OPEC oil price increases (and subsequent declines since 1983) and the Vietnam War, have only a temporary effect. We will continue to make the assumption that some exchange rate flexibility will persist for the world economy as a whole, as we do not expect to see a return to the type of world environment which made a system of fixed exchange rates feasible for much of the period from the middle of the 19th century to the beginning of the 1970s.

In light of this assessment of the world economy, we do not expect it to be feasible to operate a fixed exchange rate for Canada, certainly not for any extended period of time in the foreseeable future. We will have to learn to live with a world which has some flexibility in exchange rates, and we will return to the private-sector implications in the next chapter.

There are a number of micro aspects of international economic policy that are important for Canada. In Part Six we examined some of the evidence on the international comparisons of Canadian manufacturing with the other major industrialized countries with which we trade. Canada had the second highest level of output per hour in manufacturing of the major industrialized countries in the 1950s, and improvements have continued since then. However, the increases in Japan and most of the European countries have been so much more rapid than in North America that Canada has moved from the second highest to the third from the bottom of the major industrialized countries. Such countries as Japan, Belgium, France, West Germany, and Sweden had moved ahead of Canada by the middle of the 1980s.

The combination of lower level of productivity with high levels of money wages and real wages contributes to potential problems for Canadian international competitiveness, limiting opportunities to participate fully in the rapidly expanding area of world trade in manufactured products.[16] During the 1980s some of these problems were reflected in plant closures, corporate bankruptcies, take-overs, and reduced employment in domestic manufacturing. These problems of high costs at the micro level contributed to the high level of unemployment which Canada has experienced during the 1980s.

There have also been problems in some of the natural resource sectors during the 1980s, to a greater degree than anything experienced since World War II. The most dramatic, of course, is the large decline in the international prices of petroleum products, which has affected well-head prices in Alberta. Exploration and development has been sharply curtailed in the traditional areas of the prairies and on the frontier in the Beaufort Sea and the oil sands of the north. Layoffs have also occurred in other sectors of the petroleum industry, and the whole Alberta economy has been significantly affected, including such areas as construction and real estate prices.

Forestry and mining have also experienced problems, some of which have been intensified by the protectionist pressures in the U.S. Congress, and the decisions involving cedar shingles and shakes which have led to the levying of special duties by the United States on such imports. Some of these developments on the natural resource side reflect the longer-term decline in these products in world trade and in the domestic economies of the industrialized countries. The slower growth in demand in the major industrialized countries since 1973 (which was pointed out both in Chapter 3 and in Chapter 6) has contributed to a weakness in the prices of these items and a drop in the Canadian terms of trade (as measured by the ratio of export prices to import prices).

## 20–7 ENVIRONMENTAL POLICIES

A theme of this text is that the Canadian government should put higher priority on policies to increase real incomes of Canadians and reduce high unemployment. Greater attention must be paid to policies to achieve increased productivity, faster adoption of new technology, and measures that will improve performance on the supply side, issues which were first raised in Chapter 3 and Part Two. It is essential that individual firms and industries improve their economic performances in order to improve the economic picture for the economy as a whole.

Some observers in Canada have suggested that a much more active government program aimed at industries and firms is necessary to achieve improved performance. These observers sometimes rely on the "industrial policy" debate in the United States to support their views. **Industrial policies** are policies intended to influence the extent of research and development, to encourage particular sectors of manufacturing (such as the high-technology sector), to encourage growth industries and shift resources out of declining industries, or to influence the regional location of investment and production. Observers favouring such policies sometimes have serious doubts that the price system and the profit motive will achieve all of the intended social and economic goals. The Science Council of Canada and its staff have, over the years supported these views, and so have a number of the publications of the former Canadian Institute for Economic Policy.[17]

It seems unwise to give the government further authority in controlling and influencing the economy at a more detailed level. The evidence suggests that the government has not been too successful in operating the more aggregative policies of monetary and fiscal policy, which should be the easier of the two to implement.

Furthermore, it is very difficult in practice for any government agency to identify ahead of time what the most promising areas for future development might be. For example, some of the more dynamic and promising developments in manufactured exports are taking place in Canadian-owned firms of 100 to 300 employees. Such firms have specialized in producing a narrow range of products that have been overlooked by the large firms in the large countries. They have identified a "niche" in the world market that fits well with the skills and aptitudes of the existing management and key professional employees. The existing data sources available to the government at both the federal and provincial levels do not provide the information to identify such potential winners ahead of time.

Furthermore, pressure on politicians is more likely to force the adoption of policies that prop up losing firms by providing subsidies, financial bailouts, or nontariff barriers, rather than providing help and encouragement to potential winners. Selective industrial policies are more likely to prevent change and adjustment by maintaining the status quo and retaining the existing managerial elite rather than encouraging the change and specialization that might be more appropriate.

A number of concrete steps should be given increased emphasis in the longer term for consideration by the government. These include the following major suggestions. None of these proposals are new, but they might contribute to an improved performance for the Canadian economy in the future.

## Commercial Policy

Many of Canada's historic problems of high costs and low productivity levels in manufacturing are a heritage of the protectionist policies introduced in the latter part of the 19th century. An extended period of reduction in tariff barriers was initiated in the latter part of the 1930s and has continued throughout the postwar period in co-operation with the multilateral negotiations that have taken place under the General Agreement on Tariffs and Trade. The Canada-U.S. Automotive Agreement has been an important bilateral agreement. Negotiations were initiated between Canada and the United States on bilateral reductions in tariff and nontariff barriers in 1986. It is important for Canada that movements in this direction continue. Canada should resist the continuing pressure for nontariff barriers against imports, which have been directed against Japan and the less developed countries. The freeing up of trade and capital flows in the world economy over the last three decades has contributed to the major increase in world trade (especially in manufactured products) and has helped to increase living standards in both the industrialized and developing countries. The smaller countries have achieved the biggest increases in real income and international trade over the last four decades, and any reversals of this increased international interdependence could have serious adverse effects on smaller countries such as Canada.

The persistence of high cost of money, high real wages, and high unit labour costs in Canada is likely to lead to continued pressure for tariff and nontariff barriers to trade and the resistance to change that could result. It would be unfortunate if the federal and provincial governments were to respond to such an increase in protectionist pressures. Canada and other small industrialized countries have the most to lose if the complex system of an interdependent world economy that has evolved over three decades of favourable growth and international negotiations were to begin to disintegrate. Canadian movement toward more protectionist and interventionist policy during periods of difficulty would be bound to have adverse effects in other countries experiencing reduced employment in manufacturing to a greater extent and for a much longer period than has occurred in Canada. When Canada's level of real GDP per capita is so high by world standards, development of protectionist measures would be an unfortunate example to other countries. Canada itself would be seriously affected by any deterioration in free flows of trade and financial capital.

We should therefore press forward to conclude a free trade agreement with the United States. However, there are resistances to movements in this direction both within the United States and Canada, and if the current highly publicized negotiations were to fail, it is doubtful if Canada would get another opportunity for half a century or so.

## Adjustment Assistance

Some transitional assistance will be necessary to help both firms and workers adjust to lower tariff and nontariff barriers. Such policies of adjustment assistance continue to be more important for Canada in the 1980s than for other countries. For one thing, nominal tariff rates are higher in Canada than in the United States after the completion of the Tokyo Round reductions, and there are still significant variations in nominal and effective tariff rates from one sector to another. Furthermore, Canada has higher ratios of merchandise exports and imports to GDP than most other countries, especially the United States. As well, Canada has greater problems because of the differences between high real wages and real productivity levels in relation to comparable measures for other countries such as the United States and Japan.

It is not clear how severe any adjustments may be at the industry level in any future reduction in tariffs. Any further reductions in tariffs would be quite minor compared to the change in the exchange rate in relation to the U.S. dollar of more than 30 percent between 1974 and 1986. The extent of any interindustry adjustments would be much less if management in Canadian manufacturing firms aggressively specialized and moved into export markets by cutting costs down to competitive levels. A significant number of companies have already done this, and such changes will make it less likely and less necessary for significant employment reductions to take place. On the other hand, the continuation of the historic pattern of high costs, product diversity, and low productivity will increase the risks of employment cutbacks and corporate bankruptcies. Problems will also persist if the union leadership continue to oppose technological change and tariff reductions on the assumption that such changes will increase unemployment.

It would be useful to provide a variety of broad safety nets to facilitate any necessary and desirable shifts from declining industries to expanding industries and to provide a minimum degree of financial assistance when new jobs are not quickly found. A variety of measures along these lines have been proposed, and a number of them are already in place in Canada. The proposals include more information to management and workers on the nature of adjustments underway and more information on the success stories emerging in Canadian manufacturing; more training and re-training of workers; and some financial assistance to workers to cover the costs of moving to localities where jobs are available. Our basic philosophy should be to encourage, not prevent, the shift of resources out of declining industries to expanding ones.

## Inflation and the Corporate Profits Tax

The existing corporate profits tax regulations require corporations to report corporate profits on the basis of historic purchase costs for capital assets. However, in a period of rising prices, depreciation allowances and historic costs become an increasingly small proportion of the cost of replacing assets purchased in earlier periods at lower prices. Thus taxes on corporate profits are based on overstated levels of profits compared with the current and more realistic costs of replacing physical assets. Even if no further inflation takes place, this problem will continue until all the existing physical assets have been written off. Very few Canadian companies are using inflation accounting for either public or internal purposes. The lack of such adjustments, combined with a continued squeeze on corporate profit margins in manufacturing, could leave companies with an inadequate amount of internal funds for investment in the years ahead. Furthermore, rates of return on total assets appear to be so low in the mid-1980s that external financing of future expansion is not attractive to either companies or the capital market.

The federal government has thus far been reluctant to move in the direction of rationalizing corporate taxes, and the accounting associations seem to be more concerned about the problems of implementing inflation accounting than in the advantages of using it. Minister of Finance, Michael Wilson, stated on several occasions in late 1986 that he would like to reduce the share of the tax burden on individuals and increase it on corporations. This action could lead to a continuation of existing policies and high effective tax rates on corporate profits, which could contribute to a continued hesitancy in business investment.

## The Diffusion of Technology

Some recent research has indicated that the problem of science policy in Canada is related much more to the slow adoption of technology than to the lack of access of Canadian companies to natural science and engineering advances. When allowance is made for payments abroad for purchased research and development and the technology available to Canadian subsidiaries, science and technology is much more available in relation to other countries than you would gather from observing domestic expenditures on research and development. The primary problem is much more the *slow adoption* of new technology rather than the actual conduct of basic research and development in Canada.

The evidence indicates that Canada has been slower in adopting new technology in a variety of fields than other countries. Comparisons have been made with the United States, Japan, and some of the European countries. Canadian managers are usually familiar with practices elsewhere, but they are frequently much slower in incorporating current "best practice". Many senior Canadian managers learned their management skills while serving in World War II. Their managerial styles may be less effective in dealing with rapidly changing international influences than the better educated younger employees of the 1980s. This lack of openness to change and new ideas probably reflects the more conservative tendencies and resistance to change in Canadian society as a whole. Less competitive pressure is also an important factor in the slow adoption of new technology in the past.

## Labour-management Relations

During the 1970s and the early part of the 1980s, Canada had the dubious distinction of having one of the highest proportions of time lost due to strikes of the industrialized countries, second only to Italy. For the 1972–81 period this was still only 0.4 percent of total time worked. It is likely that the effects of adverse labour-management relations on productivity will have an even greater social cost in the form of decreased output than the actual time lost due to work stoppages. Lost time occurs when employees discuss labour-management issues during working hours, and low morale and absenteeism can have adverse effects on performance and output.

A new factor that can contribute to increased labour-management conflict during the 1980s is the degree to which real wages in Canada have largely caught up to the United States, while levels of real output per hour continue lower, especially in manufacturing. There is also an important contrast with Japan, where a major part of the productivity increases during the latter part of the 1970s and early 1980s have been passed on to the buyers of manufactured products both domestically and internationally, with much smaller increases in real wages per hour within Japanese manufacturing. These problems of high real wages in Canada seem likely to persist during a period of tariff reductions when lower-cost producers are actively looking for new markets.

Some of these issues are important topics for the agenda of the Canadian Labour Market and Productivity Centre, which was set up in 1984. The performance of the Centre will be dependent on the qualifications, expertise, and management abilities of the senior full-time staff. It is also important that there be broad agreement between the labour and management representatives who dominate the executive committee and the board of directors and who determine the key thrusts of the centre.[18]

In summary, the government should put a higher priority on improving the environment within which the more entrepreneurial, efficient, and lower-cost plants and firms can themselves identify the more promising market opportunities. Change must be fostered and encouraged rather than using subsidies, tariff, and nontariff barriers to slow and prevent change in firms that are not now, and are unlikely to become, cost competitive in the changing world economy.

The government should also provide a more stable policy environment. Inappropriate government policies have often been the source of the major severe instances of instability in the past, both deflationary (such as in the 1930s) or inflationary (such as in past wartime periods or during the widespread inflations of the 1970s and early 1980s). More stability in other policies is also desirable to facilitate longer-term decisions in the private sector. The petroleum industry has faced frequent changes in taxes, a major investigation under the Restrictive Trade Practices Commission, the policy changes under the National Energy Policy of 1980, and modifications in the mid-1980s.

In a small open economy, there are close interrelations between the domestic industrial structure and international trade, and any problems at the micro level are bound to affect macroeconomic performance. Thus, macroeconomic policy cannot afford to ignore problems at the micro level in a small country like Canada. Similarly, performance can also be affected by corporate policy and management. We will turn to these topics in the next and last chapter.

## SUMMARY

Recessions since World War II have been shorter and milder than earlier recessions, reflecting the declining share of the GDP derived from cyclically sensitive industries, the increased quantitative importance of the built-in stabilizers, and the introduction of insurance to depositors on liabilities of the major financial institutions in North America. However, cycles are expected to continue, although the private sector is inherently quite stable and resistant to shocks. There are now better measures to reduce the risks for personal and family hardship if and when unemployment occurs.

It is unlikely that moderate inflations will begin to accelerate from changes in the private sector on its own, due to the small and declining share of the commodity-producing industries where output can be bought and held in advance of need. In addition, only if the rate of inflation per year begins to exceed the costs of holding goods (20 percent or more per year) is there any opportunity for gain. This rate has rarely been reached in industrial countries in peacetime.

Many practical problems are encountered in trying to implement discretionary monetary and fiscal policies. These problems include internal lags in recognition and policy and long outside lags in monetary policy implementation. In light of the problems in implementing discretionary stabilization policy, short-term stabilization policies have begun to get lower priority, while more emphasis on longer-term stabilization objectives and such other goals as economic growth and more efficient use of resources have begun to receive greater attention.

International economic policy is important for a country like Canada. There is a need for co-operation and consultation with the other industrialized countries and the related international institutions. Freer trade and increased market access is also important and necessary to take fuller advantage of economics of scale in Canadian manufacturing. Further adjustments at firm level are also necessary to get productivity and costs more in line with Canada's closest competitors.

## NOTES

1. For a discussion of concern about the U.S. Federal Deposit Insurance system see Edward J. Kane, *The Gathering Crisis in Federal Deposit Insurance* (Cambridge, Mass.: MIT Press, 1985), reviewed by David H. Pyle in *Journal of Economic Literature*, September 1986, pp. 1249–1950.

2. A recent study by the Fraser Institute shows that the ratio of payments under the Canadian Unemployment Insurance System is quite high relative to income while employed. This ratio is higher for Canada in the 1980s than it was in earlier decades. It is also higher than current ratios in the United States. See Herbert G. Grubel and Josef Bonnici, *Why Is Canada's Unemployment Rate So High?* (Vancouver: Fraser Institute, 1986), pp. 45–47.

3. Harry G. Johnson, "Alternative Guiding Principles for the Use of Monetary Policy" in *Essays in International Finance*, No. 44, October 1963, reprinted in H. G. Johnson, *The Canadian Quandary* (Toronto: McGraw-Hill, 1963), pp. 188–224.

4. Rosanne Cole, *Errors in Provisional Estimates of Gross National Product* (New York: Columbia University Press for the National Bureau of Economic Research) and studies of the revisions in the monthly business-cycle indicators by the late Julius Shiskin. A recent Canadian example is the extent of revisions in the annual and quarterly national accounts with the most recent benchmark revision. See Department of Finance, *Quarterly Economic Review September 1986* (Ottawa: Ministry of Supply and Services, 1986), pp. 39–45.

5. Victor Zarnowitz, *An Appraisal of Short-Term Economic Forecasting* (New York: Columbia University Press for the National Bureau of Economic Research, 1967) and Mervin A. C. Daub, "On the Accuracy of Canadian Short-Term Forecasts," *Canadian Journal of Economics*, February 1973, pp. 90–107 and subsequent work by the same author. Regular summaries of economic forecasts for Canada are provided in the *Canadian Business Review*, occasional issues.

6. Milton Friedman, "A Monetary and Fiscal Framework for Economic Stability," *American Economic Review* 38 (June 1948), pp. 245–64 and "The Effects of Full-

Employment Policy on Economic Stability: A Formal Analysis," in *Essays in Positive Economics*, Milton Friedman ed. (Chicago: University of Chicago Press, 1953).

7.   Albert Ando, E. Cary Brown, Robert M. Solow, and John Kareken, "Lags in Fiscal and Monetary Policy" in *Stabilization Policies*, Brown, et al. (Englewood Cliffs, N.J.: Prentice Hall for the Commission on Money and Credit, 1963), pp. 1–162, especially pp. 3, 4, and 8.

8.   Robert M. Will, "The Time Lags of Fiscal Policy" in *Conference on Stabilization Policies* (Ottawa: Queen's Printer for the Economic Council of Canada, 1966), pp. 133–154.

9.   Martin Bronfenbrenner, ed., *Is the Business Cycle Obsolete?* (New York: John Wiley & Sons, 1969). Most of the papers from all the countries represented argued that the business cycle was *not* obsolete.

10.  Alan S. Blinder and Robert M. Solow, "Analytical Foundations of Fiscal Policy" in *The Economics of Public Finance* (Washington, D.C.: Brookings Institution, 1974) pp. 3–115.

11.  Ibid., p. 63. The authors refer to similar conclusions by Otto Eckstein (based on his experience on the staff of the Joint Economic Committee and as a member of the Council of Economic Advisers) and to Christopher Dow's conclusions on his experience with the British fiscal policy. Ibid., p. 44. Similar conclusions were made by two senior U.S. officials in the Republican Administration. See Chapter Two, "The Myth of Budget Tuning" in *Economic Policy Beyond the Headlines*, George P. Shulty and Kenneth W. Dam (New York: W. W. Norton, 1977), pp. 23–41.

12.  The changes in bank policy and summaries of the statements made by Bank of Canada Annual Reports and speeches by senior bank officials have been well set out in a series of studies by Tom Courchene. See his "Recent Canadian Monetary Policy: An Appraisal," *Journal of Money, Credit and Banking* 3 (February 1971); T. C. Courchene, *Money, Inflation and the Bank of Canada* (Montreal: C. D. Howe Research Institute, 1976); T. C. Courchene, *Monetarism and Controls: The Inflation Fighters* (Montreal: C. D. Howe Research Institute, 1976). These studies contain quotations and references to speeches, annual reports, and studies by Bank of Canada staff. For the latest assessment see Peter Howitt, *Monetary Policy in Transition: A Study of Bank of Canada Policy, 1982–85* (Toronto: Prentice Hall for C. D. Howe Institute, 1986). See also the comprehensive study by W. R. White, *The Demand for Money in Canada: Evidence from the Monthly Data*, Bank of Canada Staff Research Study 12, 1976.

13.  Statistics Canada, "Financial Administration" in *1972 Canada Year Book* (Ottawa: Information Canada, 1972), pp. 134–38 and Will, "Time Lags" in *Stabilization Policies*, and his larger study on fiscal policy for the Royal Commission on Taxation.

14.  *Royal Commission on Banking and Finance, Report* (Ottawa: Queen's Printer, 1974), pp. 129–36; Harry G. Johnson and John W. L. Winder, *Lags in the Effects of Monetary Policy in Canada* (mimeo), November 1962, pp. 36–40; D. J. Daly, "The Scope for Monetary Policy — A Synthesis" in *Conference in Stabilization Policies* (Ottawa: Queen's Printer, 1966), pp. 27–37. It should be borne in mind that many of the attempts to estimate the lags in monetary policy (by both the monetarists and the Keynesians) figure on the basis of the differences in timing between rates of change in the money supply to the resulting subsequent change in physical activity. Thus only the outside lag is measured resulting in an underestimate of the total length of the lag as no allowance for the inside lags of recognition and policy response, which have been distinguished previously, is made.

15.  The Bank of International Settlements was established early in the 1920s to facilitate the settlement of reparations and war debts that were a heritage of World War I. It is interesting that the organization did not disappear with the eventual resolution of the problems it had been designed to deal with, but has continued to thrive and have an important but little-publicized influence on economic developments in a quite different world environment 60 years later.

16. For much fuller documentation of the previous paragraphs see two research mono-
    graphs published during 1986. They are: D. J. Daly and D. C. MacCharles, *Canadian
    Manufactured Exports: Constraints and Opportunities* (Montreal: Institute for Re-
    search on Public Policy, 1986), and D. J. Daly and D. C. MacCharles, *Focus on Real
    Wage Unemployment* (Vancouver: Fraser Institute, 1986).

17. The fullest statement of the Science Council views is in John N. H. Britton, James G.
    Gilmour, assisted by Mark G. Murphy, *The Weakest Link — A Technological Per-
    spective on Canadian Industrial Development* (Ottawa: Science Council of Canada,
    1978). For a critical assessment of this study see D. J. Daly, "Weak Links in 'The
    Weakest Link,'" *Canadian Public Policy*, 1979, pp. 307–317 and Kristian S. Palda,
    *The Science Council's Weakest Link: A Critique of the Science Council's Tech-
    nocratic Industrial Strategy for Canada* (Vancouver: Fraser Institute, 1979). For an
    earlier discussion of these issues see A. Rotstein, ed., *An Industrial Strategy for
    Canada* (Toronto: New Press, 1972). See also Fred Lazar, *The New Protectionism:
    Non-Tariff Barriers and Their Effects on Canada* (Toronto: James Lorimer, 1981). See
    also Richard G. Harris, *Trade, Industrial Policy and International Competition* (Tor-
    onto: University of Toronto Press, 1985), which deals with international trade and
    competition aspects for Canada. However, Chapter 3 does not deal with the evidence
    on productivity differences by industry and Chapter 6 does not deal with the mana-
    gerial aspects of change.

18. Section 20–7 draws on the study by D. J. Daly and D. C. MacCharles, *Focus on Real
    Wage Unemployment* (Vancouver: Fraser Institute, 1986), pp. 51–57.

# PART EIGHT

# Implications for Business Decisions

Previous chapters have developed the main theoretical underpinnings of macroeconomic theory for the determination of the main aggregates for the economy as a whole, on both the demand and the supply side. The purpose of this section is to summarize the various applications to business decisions that have been introduced previously. Macroeconomic policies that have been designed to influence the main aggregates will only have an impact on output, employment, prices, and exchange rates if they have some influence on the decision-making process in the (financial and nonfinancial) business sector (corporate and unincorporated business) or the personal sector. This summary will explain some of the main effects that changes emerging from international economic developments and policies and from domestic economic policy will have on private decision making, with special emphasis on the business sector.

# 21

## Macroeconomic Developments and Business Decision Making

After reading this chapter you should understand the effects of macro-economic developments on six main areas of business decision making. We will:

1. Review the problem of business cycles and economic fore-casting.
2. Review the impacts of fiscal and monetary policy on the main areas of business decision making.
3. Summarize the influence of changes in the price level on interest rates and reported profits of the firm.
4. Review the effects of major developments in the international side on business operations, with special emphasis on the main aggregates.
5. Summarize the main elements relating to the international competitive position of Canadian manufacturing in an increasingly interdependent and competitive world market.
6. Identify some ways of detecting main growth areas and declining areas for industries and firms in Canada.

## 21–1 BUSINESS CYCLES AND FORECASTING

Business cycles have been an important characteristic of the major industrialized economies since the 19th century, and they have persisted into the 1980s. Earlier chapters pointed out some of the reasons for the decreased severity of business cycle recessions since World War II. However, they continue to be important for the commodity-producing industries, construction, and real estate, and thereby can continue to have a secondary effect on other industries, including retail sales and the service industries.

In the past, business firms have typically recognized a change in the business cycle (especially the turning points at business cycle peaks and troughs) only after the change had already taken place. This lag in recognition continues in spite of the increased availability of more economic data, quicker release of economic statistics, and much more discussion of recent economic developments in the media.

Part of the difficulty of making accurate forecasts of the short-term economic outlook is the effect of external shocks and disturbances from international developments or unanticipated changes in economic policy. Such shocks can have an impact on the economy not just at the time they occur (and in the months immediately following), but for a year or two afterwards, because of the existence of lags in many of the major economic processes in the economy. Examples of such lags were introduced previously, in Chapter 9 on investment, Chapter 13 on the differing sensitivity of various parts of the pricing system (such as the tendency for corporate profit margins to lead and wage rates and unit labour costs to lag behind business-cycle turning points), and in the discussion of the lags in decision making in fiscal and monetary policy, summarized in Chapter 20.

The problem of identifying a business-cycle peak is particularly difficult. An important characteristic of a business cycle peak is that the number of expanding industries is usually about the same as the number of contracting industries. It is only after the peak has passed that the number of industries declining begins to exceed the number expanding. (In practice the differing relative weights of different industries in the aggregate can also influence the total, but the proportion of expanding industries is closely related in theory and in practice to the rate of change in the aggregate.) A further factor contributing to the uncertainty at the peak is that random factors and disturbances in particular industries and regions can contribute to short-term declines which can quickly be reversed. A strike, for example, can depress production, or a period of inclement weather can depress retail sales for a week or two. Such temporary disturbances can sometimes be enough to affect the national totals, if the underlying change in the aggregate has become hesitant due to more deep-seated factors in the business cycle. Discussions of economic developments at such a period will often reflect these conflicting cross-currents.

Another characteristic of a business-cycle peak is that corporate profit margins frequently have begun to narrow with the diminishing vigour of the underlying demand forces and the delayed responses in wages, interest rates, and other costs. The business community will frequently have begun to talk about profitless prosperity in these circumstances. The emergence of some of these symptoms should be a caution that the economy could have moved into the later stages of a business-cycle expansion.

One relatively low-cost way of trying to identify such changes at about the time they occur is to use the system of statistical indicators that has emerged from theoretical and historical studies of the U.S. National Bureau of Economic Research. Current releases of such data are made by Statistics Canada in *Current Economic Analysis* in Canada, *Business Conditions Digest* released by the U.S. Department of Commerce, and by Statistical Indicator Associates, a weekly U.S. publication. In assessing the use of this system to identify business-cycle turning points, Geoffrey Moore has said that at best a turning point can be identified at about the time it occurs. This is, however, an improvement over past experience, which has often only identified a business-cycle turn after it has occurred.

The individual leading indicators rarely conform perfectly to business cycles. They also experience a fair amount of month-to-month irregularity in their movement. It is for this reason that leaders are usually combined in a composite index. A **composite index** is a summary of a number of individual series, measuring the percentages of that group of series which are expanding from one month to the next. Such composite indexes of the leading indicators typically lead the business-cycle peak, but the leads are sometimes short.

There has been a good deal of discussion over the years about the tendency for such a composite index to give "false signals". A major problem in identifying a business cycle peak is that the economy typically experiences a pause in the rate of growth at about the mid-stage of a full expansion from a business-cycle trough to a business-cycle peak. In its early stages the expansion is typically vigorous, due to a good deal of initial slack, considerable strength from housing, and a swing from inventory liquidation during the recession phase to an inventory buildup in the early stages of expansion. These sources of strength begin to moderate in the mid-stages of the expansion, before the strengthening in business investment in plant and equipment has become strong, carrying the economy along in the later stages of the expansion. The leading indicators show weakness at the mid-cycle pause as well as at the peak itself, and even experienced users of business-cycle indicators can sometimes have difficulty in identifying a pause in growth from a true business-cycle peak.

These business-cycle indicators can be used to indicate orders of magnitude of potential change as well as changes in direction. For example, Geoffrey Moore has been working for some years on measuring the severity of a recession in its early stages based on the extent of the decline in the leading indicators in the first five or six months. He has also used the system of statistical indicators available in the last month of a calendar year to forecast the extent of change in GNP for the coming year.[1]

It is somewhat easier to do short-term forecasts during periods of economic expansion. The average duration of expansions in North America during the post-war period is 45 months, although some expansions have been much shorter. (However, one expansion began in 1961 and lasted almost nine full years.) Most of the successes in economic forecasting come from such extended periods of growth.

A number of forecasts of the economic situation are now available on a regular basis for Canada. Some of these are summarized regularly in the *Canadian Business Review,* published by the Conference Board in Canada, and others are made by private organizations such as Informetrica in Ottawa and Data Resources International in Toronto.

A small proportion of the larger companies in Canada do their own short-term forecasts, but the number of these is rather small. Also, the cost cutting introduced by the severity of the 1981–82 recession and the sluggish subsequent recovery may have reduced the number further. Some companies, such as Ontario Hydro and some of the chartered banks, have used more sophisticated econometric models. Some also subscribe to the forecasting services provided by a number of private organizations, such as the Conference Board in Canada.

One of the more promising routes for individual firms is to develop more seasonally adjusted data from their own internal statistics. About six years of monthly data is the minimum required to do a seasonal adjustment. It can be done quickly and inexpensively using a mainframe computer. As forecasts deal with finer levels of disaggregation, there is frequently a higher degree of irregular movement. Thus seasonal adjustment is most useful for large companies or the whole industry.

In light of this somewhat skeptical appraisal of the reliability of forecasting for individual businesses, it is important for companies to follow developments with care and to be prepared to make adjustments in production scheduling and inventory control once a change seems to have begun.

## 21–2 THE EFFECTS OF FISCAL AND MONETARY POLICY

A major emphasis of macroeconomic discussions during recent decades has dealt with the impacts of fiscal and monetary policy on the short-term performance of the economy. The empirical evidence in previous chapters provides a basis for assessing the importance of these policy aspects for the individual firm.

A major theme of the empirical work for Canada (and other industrialized countries as well) is that the quantitative size of the fiscal multipliers is quite low. This low size reflects the significant quantitative importance of the marginal tax rate at the federal level in Canada. An important part of any potential increase in the economy associated with changed government expenditure is partly offset by the increase in tax collections. Furthermore, another part of the increase in domestic demand is reflected in higher imports, based on the high marginal propensity to import. The resulting low multipliers reflect the inherent high degree of stability in the private sector in the current institutional environment within Canada.

Under these circumstances the impact of a change in government expenditure or revenue is likely to be small. Much public discussion has probably exaggerated the importance of this topic. Governments frequently find themselves experiencing so many restraints on their policy flexibility that they can normally only introduce small changes in any particular year, and the secondary effects are also small. The size of the federal deficit during the early part of the 1980s was an important constraint, even though the government and the public were well aware that unemployment levels were at new postwar highs and were expected to remain high over a number of years.

At some time in the future, if people in your organization come running in to ask your advice on what the company should do to respond to the latest speculation or announcement on government policy, your best advice would be to encourage them to concentrate on the major internal issues that are facing the organization rather than being too concerned about broad fiscal policy.

There has been extensive discussion over the years about the effects of monetary policy and interest rates on business investment. The evidence summarized for Canada in Chapter 9 indicates that such direct responsiveness is quite limited. Factors other than interest rates are far more important in the decision-making process relating to business investment.

Changes in interest rates are much more important in residential construction, both for individual homes and multiple units. In the housing or mortgage financing industry, interest rate changes can be crucial for business. However, these changes operate with a lag, so there is usually adequate time to respond to any changes in interest rates, reflecting changes in either the demand or supply for money balances.

Changes in housing investment can have some secondary effects on such related industries as construction materials (asphalt shingles, plumbing supplies, plaster, and paint). Sales of existing houses can also be affected by changes in interest rates, as lower mortgage rates encourage more purchases of older homes, as well.

## 21–3 INFLATION, INTEREST RATES, AND REPORTED PROFITS

An important theme in Part Four was that a high and persisting rate of increase in the money supply can eventually lead to inflation. It was also pointed out that high rates of price increase for goods and services eventually lead to increases in nominal interest rates. This theory, developed by Irving Fisher, is crucial to understanding why high rates of interest occurred in North America and in most other countries in the world in the early 1980s. The subsequent moderation in the rate of inflation has been crucial to understanding why interest rates then declined, even though the federal deficits have continued at high levels in both the United States and Canada.

Such significant changes in long-term interest rates tend to have a much greater impact on financial markets, financial institutions, and the distribution of the holdings of financial assets by individuals in the institutions than in the market for goods and services. The significant inflations of the 1970s and 1980s have appreciably reduced the real purchasing power of many pensions. Very few pensions are indexed to changes in the general price level, although the federal government has had indexed superannuation payments for retired members of Parliament and civil servants for some time. Many individuals have had to reassess their financial planning to allow for the probable effects of inflation on their retirement incomes. These inflationary developments have benefitted companies and individuals who had undertaken large mortgage or bond indebtedness at lower interest rates but had adverse effects on individuals and companies who had large holdings of monetary and financial assets. Important changes in the distribution of wealth have occurred in response to these developments in the general price level.

Inflation has also had an important impact on the reported corporate profits of firms. The accounting information used by managers is usually based on historical costs of buying physical assets (such as plant, machinery, and inventory) rather than replacement costs. This practice has a long tradition in accounting and is based on objective records from market transactions. The use of historical costs is an appropriate practice when there has been little change in the general level of prices over extended periods of time. When the general price level has increased significantly, historical cost data do not provide reliable information for managerial decision making and can even affect the ability of a firm to survive in the longer term. The cumulative cash provisions for depreciation based on historical costs would not be adequate to replace those assets at the new and higher price level. Firms using historically determined costs in an inflationary era would be overstating profits available for distribution as dividends (perhaps even paying out capital rather than earned income only), overstating rates of return on investment, and setting prices too low to cover all costs in the long term. They would have paid taxes on reported corporation profits, rather than on the replacement cost of physical assets and inventories.

Incomplete evidence would suggest that only a small minority of even large Canadian companies are making inflation accounting adjustments for internal purposes. Even rough allowances to put corporate profits and the major items from the balance sheet on a replacement cost basis would be better for management decision making than making no allowance at all. This will continue to be an important issue for economists and accountants for some decades to come, even if prices remain unchanged in the future, since it takes many years to fully write off physical assets that were purchased some time ago.

## 21–4 INTERNATIONAL ASPECTS

One of the major developments during recent decades is an increased degree of economic interdependence between Canada and the rest of the world. This interdependence is reflected in a wide range of economic processes. There has been an increase in the two-way flow of international trade, both in absolute terms and as a share of GDP. This increase for Canada has concentrated heavily in the commodity-producing industries, where commodity exports amount to about 85 percent of GDP in the goods-producing industries. Receipts from sales of services internationally to Canada amount to only about 5 percent of GDP in the rapidly growing service industries. This increased international interdependence of trade in commodities is associated with an increased degree of similarity in price levels and movements (after any necessary adjustment for changes in exchange rates).

There has also been an increase in international connections on interest rates and stock prices. There has always been a significant amount of foreign ownership of Canadian bonds (provincial, municipal, and corporate), and the improved flow of information by telephone, teletype, and computers has further speeded up communication at low cost. A number of the larger corporations in Canada have their stocks listed and traded in the New York market as well as in either Toronto or Montreal. Interest rates are also closely connected, and some of the larger corporations and financial institutions in Canada can invest any temporarily idle cash balances in either the New York or Canadian market, depending on the latest interest rate levels and any possible changes in the value of the Canadian dollar.

One of the important themes developed in Part Six was the discussion of the reasons for the increased volatility in international exchange rates that have taken place since the early 1970s. A number of changes have taken place in the world environment that have contributed to this volatility. These changes are deep seated and fundamental and are unlikely to be reversed. This volatility is reflected in the Canadian exchange rate, both in relation to the United States (our most important partner for trade and capital flows) and the other major currencies as well. Thus company planning should be based on the idea of continued movements in foreign exchange rates, affecting many areas of trade, capital flows, long-term investment decisions, and aspects of the composition of assets and liabilities on corporate balance sheets.

The importance of changes in the exchange rate can be illustrated by the effects of exchange rate changes on corporate profits in the commodity-producing industries. This area was explored in Part Six using a relatively simple model of a small open economy, which assumed that prices were set in world markets and many contracts for both exports and imports were quoted in U.S. dollars. Under these circumstances, a decline in the value of the Canadian dollar (an increase in the amount of Canadian currency that would have to be paid to buy one U.S. dollar) would be reflected in an increase in the Canadian dollar receipts for exports of natural resource products. Most of the costs of labour, materials, and taxes are paid in Canadian dollars. Corporate profits are the net difference between these receipts and costs, and when they are a relatively small residual, small percentage changes in the exchange rate can be reflected in much larger percentage changes in corporate profits. This high elasticity of corporate profits in the natural resource export industries is well recognized in those industries within Canada and in the stock market.

Corporate profits in manufacturing and the importing industries can also be affected by an exchange rate change. For example, a depreciation in the value of the Canadian dollar will be reflected in an increased price in Canadian dollars, even when no change in the world price has taken place. In the short term (say, until the company revises its next catalogue or price list) the higher prices of the imported items may be a negative influence on corporate profits in the affected industries.

This difference in response in the natural resource export industries, on the one hand, and manufacturing, on the other, is reflected in the different regional responses to exchange rate changes within Canada. British Columbia and the Prairie provinces tend to favour exchange rate depreciation, while the central provinces of Ontario and Quebec tend to oppose exchange rate depreciation. In light of the much larger population concentrations (and related number of seats in the

House of Commons) in the manufacturing centre of the country, exchange rate policy during the last decade has tended to limit or delay declines in the exchange rate.

Corporations in the commodity-producing industries have had to take notice of the effects of exchange rate changes on their operating statements and on the distribution of their assets and liabilities between domestic and foreign currencies. Some companies have resorted to hedging or other methods to insulate and reduce the risk of losses from adverse movements in the exchange rates. In other instances, they have accepted exchange rate risks as just one other type of uncertainty and have continued to operate essentially as before.

One other development is the much more widespread practice, for both companies and individuals, of holding a large part of their cash and other liquid assets in U.S. dollars or other foreign currencies. There has been a dramatic increase in the foreign currency deposit liabilities of the Canadian chartered banks to Canadian residents that have been booked in Canada. These liabilities amounted to roughly $35 billion in mid-1986, while such foreign currency deposit liabilities would have been negligible in the early 1970s. Companies and individuals have been trying to reduce the risk of loss from declines in the value of the Canadian dollar internationally by diversifying their holdings of cash into other currencies. They have been able to do this at their own local financial institutions within Canada.

This pattern of an increase in local holdings of foreign currencies has become quite widespread in other countries as well. It is unlikely that these types of changes would have occurred if an environment that permitted stability in exchange rates had continued.

## 21–5 INTERNATIONAL COMPETITIVENESS

Part Six included some discussion of the position of Canadian manufacturing in relation to international competition. Manufacturing has begun to be a falling share of domestic income and employment for some of the industrialized countries. At the same time, it has become an increasing share of international trade since World War II. This recent trend is important, especially in light of the discussion in North America and elsewhere about freer international trade. Protectionist pressures have increased in a number of the industrialized countries, and advocates of freer trade are being pressed to explain their reasoning and evidence.

During the 1950s, Canada had the second highest level of output per hour of the major industrialized countries, second only to the United States. However, output per hour in Canada was appreciably lower than in the United States, as it had been for some decades. As a heritage of the previous period of higher tariff rates, Canada developed a pattern of secondary industry which involved a high degree of product diversity in the individual plants and firms within the manufacturing sector. The associated high costs limited the scope to export manufactured products to any significant degree once postwar shortages began to dwindle. The tariff reductions during the postwar years, part of the successive tariff negotiations under the General Agreement on Tariffs and Trade and under the Canada-United States Automotive Agreement, encouraged a greater degree of specialization. Thus the productivity gap between Canada and the United States had narrowed somewhat by the early 1970s, although Canada's level of output per hour remained 25 to 30 percent below that of the United States throughout the last decade. Increases in output per hour in manufacturing in both the United States and Canada have taken place during the 1970s and 1980s, but at a slower rate since 1973 than in the two or three decades before that.

The increases in Japan and the European countries have been much more rapid than in North America throughout most of the postwar period, due partly to the lower levels of productivity in those countries initially. However, by the middle of the 1980s such countries as Japan, France, Germany, Belgium, and Sweden had all achieved levels of output per hour higher than Canada's. The declines in the exchange rates of some of those countries in relation to North America brought their costs down to approximately North American levels. Thus they were more price competitive than they had been in 1980, for example.

There has also been an increase in international trade in manufactured products coming from some of the developing countries in Asia and South America. However, their exports tend to be concentrated in a relatively narrow range of products such as clothing, textiles, and footwear. But some of these industries have been experiencing relative declines in industrialized countries. In some cases nontariff barriers have been introduced to protect these domestic industries.

The problems of low productivity in Canadian manufacturing are not present in every industry, of course, and a number of industries have higher productivity levels than in the United States and are fully competitive internationally. The lower levels of output per hour tend to be more apparent in the smaller Canadian-owned plants and firms, where levels of value added per employee tend to be below the comparable-sized plants and firms that are foreign owned.

At this writing, discussions are under way for a possible Canada-U.S. agreement for freer trade. The completion of any such agreement will encourage the continued movement toward the increased specialization that has been developing in recent decades. Such an agreement would be an important step in permitting Canadian manufacturers to achieve the increased access to foreign markets that lower tariffs are designed to achieve. Specialization and increased exportation to the United States and elsewhere will require further changes in corporate strategy for companies planning to serve the domestic market behind the tariff and nontariff barriers that protected them in the past.

Small Canadian-owned companies have been moving fairly rapidly toward specialization and greater export capability during the 1970s. Their greater flexibility is made possible by their smaller size. They are reacting to greater necessity because of lower profit margins, lower rates of return, and sometimes lower cash resources than are customary for the larger firms, some of which are foreign owned. Some of the foreign-owned firms have been changing as well, but they are sometimes slower to develop the required changes in corporate strategy and implementation since they must first seek approval from their parent companies.

In our current business environment, adaptation is not just a matter of achieving a "once and for all" increase in productivity. Other countries have not been standing still. It will be a continuing challenge to achieve the increases in productivity and the fast adoption of new technology that will be needed to match Canada's closest competitors.

Achieving higher levels of productivity and lower costs per unit will often require organizations to use many of the skills and tools that are a normal part of the business school curriculum. Production management, for example, will provide guidance on plant lay-out, inventory control, and planning, the use of robotics, and computer-assisted design and manufacturing. These techniques provide the basis for lower costs, higher productivity, and more flexible changes in production scheduling.

Managerial accounting can provide data on costs for past levels of production. It can also provide guides on what cost levels may emerge under different levels of rate and volume. Financial accounting can provide information on profits and rates of return based on historical costs of fixed assets and also on the effects on the operating statements and balance sheet of valuing these assets on the basis of replacement costs. Management must use such information in order to make informed decisions in a world of uncertainty.

The achievement of high performance on many of these dimensions will require the active involvement of the people in the organization. Chapter 5 pointed out the high share of labour income in net national income, which was also reflected in the value-added costs within the organization. Recruitment, training, promotion, morale, and motivation are all essential parts of a successful company.

Successful adaptation of new technology is also important, both from the natural sciences and engineering areas and from the managerial and social science areas of applied psychology and sociology. Such new approaches may be even more important to the company and the country that can adopt them quickly than to the company and country who first developed them.

It was pointed out in Part Six that Canada's unit labour costs and real wages are high, particularly in relation to the United States and Japan, our two closest competitors. In addition to achieving significant increases in productivity, it is also important that a major part of any productivity increase be passed along to the buyers of manufactured products both domestically and internationally.

Such developments will be important if Canadian firms are to participate more fully in the rapidly growing areas of international trade in manufactured products. Canadian firms will also need to adapt just to maintain a share of the domestic market from competitive suppliers in other countries. It will be important to achieve some agreement on the distribution of these productivity gains between labour and management. Organizations, especially in manufacturing, are bound to find this an area of active debate for some years to come.

It has also been suggested in early parts of this book that some of these problems of high costs and low productivity performance on the supply side in some sectors of Canadian manufacturing have an important indirect influence on the levels of demand at the more aggregative level. Levels of business investment in real terms in late 1986 were still well below the previous peak in 1981. Low levels of business investment have clearly been a factor in the higher levels of unemployment that prevailed in Canada during the 1980s. Symptoms of these problems are also apparent in the number of plant closures and corporate bankruptcies.

A theme of this book has been that you cannot make a sharp line of demarcation between macroeconomics and microeconomics in a small open economy like Canada. The previous paragraphs are good illustrations of this theme.

## 21–6 IDENTIFICATION OF GROWTH AREAS

In order to assess the more promising areas of future growth as contrasted to the declining commodities and industries, it is necessary to look at world trends, and especially at the countries with which Canada continues to be closely interrelated such as the United States and Japan. It is always better for the products produced by a company to be in high growth areas, rather than in areas of declining demand or areas facing severe competition from alternative sources of supply.

Companies must assess the areas of relative strength and relative weakness in relation to world markets. This assessment is essential in a small country like Canada, which has a relatively small part of the world market in many production areas. This need was recognized in the emphasis given in Part Six to the theories and evidence related to Canada's comparative advantage in relation to world markets. It is not clear that Canada can completely abandon some areas of traditional comparative advantage, even if these are declining products in world trade. On the other hand, it may not be appropriate for Canada to try to develop "knowledge intensive" industries, even if they are an area of high growth for the world as a whole, if Canada does not have the engineering and management personnel to produce these products on a competitive basis. There is no simple answer to these potentially conflicting criteria of long-term growth, on the one hand, and areas of strength and weakness for Canada, on the other.

Another emerging growth area in Canada and in a number of the other industrialized countries is the increased importance of small plants and firms. This important development seems likely to continue, even though all the reasons for the successes of such small companies are not clear, and many new small companies fail quickly. This area is likely to be quite an important one for banks and other sources of investment funds, as there is some uncertainty and some risk in lending to such small organizations.

One new development in countries such as Sweden, as well as in Canada, is the emergence of companies who have identified a niche in the world market overlooked by large companies in the major industrialized countries. This trend was already clearly under way in the 1970s and is likely to continue in the decade ahead. What companies should be looking for are gaps for individual commodities in the world market which match the skills and interests of the management and staff.

## SUMMARY

Some large business organizations have their own internal forecasting units or staff who provide economic analysis for sales and production planning. An increasing number of forecasts are publicly available, also. More companies could benefit from seasonally adjusting some of their own operating data, especially the larger companies.

Most companies are not likely to be affected to any great extent by broad domestic fiscal and monetary policy changes, although firms in residential construction, construction materials, and real estate can be significantly affected by changes in mortgage interest rates.

There would be gains in understanding the economic climate if more companies made adjustments to their financial statements putting depreciation, inventories, and some items of their balance sheet on a replacement cost basis. This change could also affect their plans on pricing, wages, dividend, and investment policy.

International economic changes can be important for Canadian companies in the commodity-producing industries. Changes in the international value of the Canadian dollar can also be quite important to profits, especially in the natural resource export sector.

An important recent development in Canada (as well as in the United States and Japan) is the emergence of new small firms. Some of the small successful companies in manufacturing have developed a niche in the world market overlooked by the large companies in the major industrialized countries.

## NOTES

1.  Geoffrey H. Moore, *Business Cycles, Inflation and Forecasting* (Cambridge, Mass.: Ballinger Publications, 1980), pp. 389–435.

# Key Sources and Selected References

This section contains an annotated list of sources and selected references that may be of help for term papers in this and related courses, or for additional viewpoints. Some important references have become available since the text was finished. They are grouped for each main part of the text. The endnotes identify references used in each chapter, and only major ones are also included here.

## SELECTED REFERENCES FOR PART ONE

*Bank of Canada Review*. A monthly publication with text, charts, and tables on general economic trends, with special emphasis on monetary and financial developments.

Department of Finance. *Quarterly Economic Review*. A quarterly review of economic developments and special reports on particular topics.

Statistics Canada. *Canada Yearbook*. A major annual publication that gives a comprehensive summary of the major economic and political developments in the past year in Canada.

———. *Current Economic Analysis*. A monthly publication with text, charts, and tables with an emphasis on business cycles. More technical than other monthly Canadian publications.

———. *Historical Statistics of Canada. Second Edition*. Ottawa: Ministry of Supply and Services, 1983. A comprehensive and detailed presentation of historical statistics under 22 major headings, with descriptions of series and sources. Produced with advice from a number of advisory committees. Current data released on a monthly basis in *Canadian Statistical Review*.

————. *National Income and Expenditure Accounts, Volume 3.* Ottawa: Information Canada, 1975. The major explanation of concepts for the national accounts and the sector, industrial and provincial breakdowns cover both the annual and quarterly estimates. Some later changes introduced in 1986 revision.

U.S. Department of Commerce. *Long-Term Economic Growth, 1860–1970.* Washington, D.C.: U.S. Government Printing Office, 1973. Major economic series for the United States and the major industrialized countries. Later data for some series for the United States in the monthly publication *Survey of Current Business.*

————. *Handbook of Cyclical Indicators.* Washington, D.C.: U.S. Government Printing Office, 1984. Contains historical data by months and quarters from 1974 to 1982. Later data with all regular revisions in individual series in the monthly *Business Conditions Digest* from the same agency. Some series included for other major industrialized countries.

## SELECTED REFERENCES FOR PART TWO

BEIGIE, CARL E., and ALFRED O. HERO, JR. *Natural Resources in U.S.-Canadian Relations, Volume 1. The Evolution of Policies and Issues.* Boulder, Colorado: Westview Press, 1980.

BROOKS, DAVID B., ed. *Resource Economics: Selected Works of Orris C. Herfindahl.* Washington, D.C.: Resources for the Future, 1974. Some important topics in the economics of natural resources.

BROWN, MURRAY, ed. *The Theory and Empirical Analysis of Production.* New York: Columbia University Press for the NBER, 1967. Proceedings of a conference with surveys of many of the major issues in production analysis.

DENISON, EDWARD F. *Accounting for United States Economic Growth, 1929–1969.* Washington, D.C.: Brookings Institution, 1974. A comprehensive review of the approach and sources for economic growth accounting in the United States.

———— and WILLIAM K. CHUNG. *How Japan's Economy Grew So Fast.* Washington, D.C.: Brookings Institution, 1976. An application of the methodology of economic growth accounting to Japan, covering both level comparisons and changes over time.

———— and JEAN-PIERRE POULLIER. *Why Growth Rates Differ.* Washington, D.C.: Brookings Institution, 1967. The first major intercountry comparison (with both level comparisons and changes over time) for nine western countries. The application of current approaches in accounting for economic growth to the interests of the classical economists in comparisons of levels and growth rates of different countries.

KENDRICK, JOHN W., and BEATRICE N. VACCARA, eds. *New Developments in Productivity Measurement and Analysis*. Chicago: University of Chicago Press for the NBER, 1980. Research studies on productivity by industry, the effects of research and development, and international comparisons of productivity.

KUMAR, PRADEEP, and associates. *The Current Industrial Relations Scene in Canada*. Kingston, Ont.: Industrial Relations Centre, 1986. An annual publication in industrial relations, trade unions, and labour legislation with a supplement which includes sources, technical notes, and glossary.

KUZNETS, SIMON. *Modern Economic Growth: Rate, Structure and Spread*. New Haven, Conn.: Yale University Press, 1966. A comprehensive study of population, industrial structure, and international comparisons, covering both developed and underdeveloped countries.

PURVIS, DOUGLAS D., ed. *Declining Productivity and Growth*. Kingston, Ont.: John Deutsch Roundtable on Economic Policy, 1984. Developments in manufacturing and total productivity performance and prospects and the role of research and development.

SARGENT, JOHN, ed. *Economic Growth: Prospects and Determinants*. Toronto: University of Toronto Press, Volume 22 for the Royal Commission on the Economic Union and Development Prospects for Canada, 1985. Surveys of economic growth in Canada and the role of population, productivity, and savings in past growth and growth prospects.

SARGENT, JOHN. *Long-Term Economic Prospects for Canada: A Symposium*. Toronto: University of Toronto Press, Volume 23 for the Royal Commission on the Economic Union and Development Prospects for Canada, 1985. An assessment of economic growth prospects for Canada, both macro and by sector, and an evaluation of past projections for Canada.

SCOTT, ANTHONY. *Natural Resources: The Economics of Conservation*. Ottawa: Carleton Library No. 68, 1973. An important economic study of natural resources and natural resource conservation.

## SELECTED REFERENCES FOR PART THREE

BRONFENBRENNER, MARTIN, ed. *Is the Business Cycle Obsolete?* New York: Wiley-Interscience, 1969. A number of studies of the industrialized economies that conclude that the business cycle is not obsolete. The international transmission of cycles is also discussed.

Federal Reserve of Boston. *Consumer Spending and Monetary Policy.* Boston: 1971. Some of the papers reflect the importance of monetary influences on consumer durables and housing investment.

FRIEDMAN, MILTON, *A Theory of the Consumption Function.* Princeton, N.J.: Princeton University Press, 1957. An important contribution that distinguishes between the long-term and short behaviour of consumption and the role of permanent income in consumption.

GORDON, ROBERT J., ed. *The American Business Cycle: Continuity and Change.* Chicago: University of Chicago Press, 1986. A major study of business cycles, covering the sources of cycles, changes in cyclical behaviour, and the role of fiscal and monetary policy.

KLEIN, LAWRENCE R., and A. S. GOLBERGER, *An Econometric Model of the United States, 1929–1952.* New York: Wiley-Interscience, 1955. An important medium-sized macroeconometric model for the United States which influenced later studies in the United States and other countries. An important illustration of econometric business-cycle research.

MOORE, GEOFFREY H. *Business Cycles, Inflation and Forecasting.* Cambridge, Mass.: Ballinger for the NBER, 1980. A number of studies applying the National Bureau approach to business-cycle research to recessions, inflations, and short-term forecasting.

WHITE, DEREK. *Business Cycles in Canada.* Ottawa: Queen's Printer, 1967. A comprehensive study of Canadian business cycles, including the role of investment on business fixed capital and inventories and international trade. Comparisons of timing and amplitude of cycles with the United States.

## SELECTED REFERENCES FOR PART FOUR

DALY, D. J. "Inflation Accounting and Its Effect, Canadian Manufacturing, 1966–1982," *Review of Income and Wealth,* December 1985, pp. 355–74. An application of inflation accounting to corporate profits and rates of return in Canadian manufacturing.

COURCHENE, THOMAS J. *Money, Inflation and the Bank of Canada, Volume II: An Analysis of Monetary Gradualism, 1975–80.* Montreal: C.D. Howe Institute, 1981. One of a series by the same author on monetary policy. This one concentrates on the period of the use of monetary targets to moderate inflation but emphasizes a gradual slowing in the rate of monetary expansion.

FRIEDMAN, MILTON, and ANNA J. SCHWARTZ. *A Monetary History of the United States, 1867–1960*. Princeton, N.J.: Princeton University Press, 1963. An important study of monetary developments over an important century of experience, including formation of the Federal Reserve System, the depression of the 1930s, and three wartime periods. Chapter 7 is an important interpretation of the 1930s, including Federal Reserve policy and the period of bank failures.

FRIEDMAN, MILTON, and ROSE FRIEDMAN. *Free to Choose*. New York: Harcourt Brace Jovanovich, 1980. Chapter 9 deals with inflation and the role of monetary expansions in recent inflations in a number of countries.

HOWITT, PETER. *Monetary Policy in Transition: A Study of Bank of Canada Policy, 1982–85*. Scarborough, Ont.: Prentice-Hall Canada for the C. D. Howe Institute, 1986. A critical assessment of monetary policy in the early 1980s and the shift away from monetary targets towards moderating exchange rate fluctuations by the Bank of Canada.

LAIDLER, DAVID E. W. *The Demand for Money: Theories, Evidence and Problems*. 3rd ed. New York; Harper & Row, 1985. A careful assessment of the demand for money and a discussion of the reasons for present problems in finding stable relationships.

SARGENT, JOHN, ed. *Postwar Macroeconomic Developments*. Toronto: University of Toronto Press, Volume 20 for the Royal Commission on the Economic Union and Development Prospects for Canada, 1985. Surveys of Canadian postwar performance, including prices, price flexibility, and international monetary aspects.

## SELECTED REFERENCES FOR PART FIVE

BARROW, ROBERT J. *Macroeconomics*. New York: John Wiley & Sons, 1984. Contains considerable evidence on nominal and real interest rates, inflation, and financing deficits.

Canadian Tax Foundation: *The National Finances, 1985–86*. Toronto: 1986. An annual publication surveying revenues, expenditures, debt, payments to other governments, and the role of crown corporations. Includes both description and basic historical tables.

CONKLIN, DAVID, and THOMAS J. COURCHENE, eds. *Deficits: How Big and How Bad?* Toronto: University of Toronto Press for Ontario Economic Council, 1983. Important assessment of the reasons for the large federal deficits and their effects, reflecting a variety of viewpoints.

Federal Reserve Bank of St. Louis. *Review,* October 1986. Special issue reviewing the evidence on the relative importance of monetary and fiscal actions and reprints of two early important articles explaining the monetarist type models they have developed and tested for many years.

SARGENT, JOHN, ed. *Fiscal and Monetary Policy.* Toronto: University of Toronto Press, Volume 21 for the Royal Commission on the Economic Union and Development Prospects for Canada, 1985. Surveys of the implementation of fiscal and monetary policies in Canada up to the early 1980s.

TOBIN, JAMES. *The New Economics One Decade Older.* Princeton, N.J.: Princeton University Press, 1974. Reflects important extensions of Keynesian macroeconomics, including the author's experience with the President's Council of Economic Advisers in Washington.

## SELECTED REFERENCES FOR PART SIX

BHANDARI, JAGDEEP S., and BLUFORD H. PUTNAM, eds. *Economic Interdependence and Flexible Exchange Rates.* Cambridge, Mass.: MIT Press, 1983. A series of studies on the determinants of exchange rates and the interdependence of domestic and international economic policies.

COOPER, RICHARD N. *The International Monetary System: Essays in World Economics.* Cambridge, Mass.: MIT Press, 1987. A group of essays by a clear writer with a good grasp of both theory and practical experience in government about the international monetary system and the reconciliation of domestic policies and exchange rate stability.

DALY, DONALD J., and DONALD C. MACCHARLES. *Canadian Manufactured Exports: Constraints and Opportunities.* Montreal: Institute for Research on Public Policy, 1986. A major conclusion is that high unit costs and low output per hour have been the major constraint on exports, but an important number of small Canadian-owned companies have become successful exporters by specializing. Discusses the implications for corporate strategy.

KRUGMAN, PAUL R. *Strategic Trade Policy and the New International Economics.* Cambridge, Mass.: MIT Press, 1986. A number of chapters propose a more active policy for governments to identify areas to create a comparative advantage.

LIPSEY, RICHARD G., and WENDY DOBSON. *Shaping Comparative Advantage.* Scarborough, Ont.: Prentice-Hall Canada, 1987. Some new research and discussion on the interrelations between trade and industrial policy.

LIPSEY, RICHARD G., and MURRAY SMITH. *Taking the Initiative: Canada's Trade Options in a Turbulent World.* Toronto: C.D. Howe Institute, 1985. A comprehensive and well-written study on the advantages to Canada of a Canada-U.S. free trade arrangement, including an assessment of the contrary arguments.

Royal Commission on the Economic Union and Development Prospects for Canada. *Report Volume One.* Toronto: University of Toronto Press, 1985. Part II contains the important recommendation on the gains to Canada from improved market access to the United States. Additional detailed studies are included in Volumes 9 to 14 of the research studies.

WONNACOTT, R. J. *Canada's Trade Options.* Ottawa: Information Canada, 1975. An assessment of the various options for Canada to follow (e.g., multilateral, Canada-U.S., etc.) and an updated quantitative assessment of the gains to Canada from freer trade.

## SELECTED REFERENCES FOR PART SEVEN

DALY, D. J. "Micro Economic Performance: Interrelations between Trade and Industrial Policies." In *Canadian Trade at a Crossroads: Options for New International Trade Agreements,* eds. DAVID V. CONKLIN and THOMAS J. COURCHENE. Toronto: Ontario Economic Council, 1985, pp. 156–87. The importance of combining policies for adjustment assistance, technological diffusion, and management to achieve the full benefits of improved market access.

———. "Technology Transfer and Canada's Competitive Performance." In *Current Issues in Trade and Investment in Service Industries: U.S.-Canadian Perspectives,* ed. ROBERT M. STERN. Toronto: University of Toronto Press, 1986, pp. 304–33. Emphasizes the managerial aspects of technology adoption and the availability of scientific and engineering technology to Canadian firms, including comparisons with Japan.

——— and D. C. MACCHARLES. *Focus on Real Wage Unemployment.* Vancouver: Fraser Institute, 1986. Emphasizes the importance of high money and real wages and the related low rates of return and low business investment as a factor in the persistence of high unemployment in Canada and discussion of the public policy options.

FRIEDMAN, MILTON, ed. *Essays in Positive Economics.* Chicago: University of Chicago Press, 1953, pp. 245–64. A classic statement of the rationale for emphasizing longer-term objectives for monetary and fiscal policy, rather than short-term discretionary changes.

GRUBEL, HERBERT G., and JOSEF BONNICI. *Focus on Why is Canada's Unemployment Rate So High?* Vancouver: Fraser Institute, 1986.

Emphasizes the importance of unions and Canada's unemployment insurance system as factors in the persistence of high unemployment rates.

HARRIS, RICHARD G. *Trade, Industrial Policy and International Competition.* Toronto: University of Toronto Press for Ministry of Supply and Services, 1985. An integration of international trade and industrial developments in a small open economy with an emphasis on the scientific aspects of technological change.

JOHNSON, HARRY G. *The Canadian Quandary.* Toronto: McGraw-Hill, 1963, pp. 188–224. Discusses three alternative guiding principles for the conduct of monetary policy in an open economy.

Royal Commission on the Economic Union and Development Prospects for Canada. *Final Report, Volume Two.* Ottawa: Ministry of Supply and Services, 1985. This volume deals with growth and employment, natural resources and human resources, drawing on the related research studies and public hearings.

# Glossary of Major Terms and Concepts

**Acceleration principle.** The theory that net investment is influenced by the expected change in output in the economy, with higher expected output leading to higher planned investment.

**Action lag.** The length of time taken by the government to decide on policy changes, introduce them, and implement them.

**Ad valorem tariff.** A flat-rate tax on the value of specific merchandise imports.

**Aggregate(s).** A total of the components that constitute the broad economic categories of national income, total employment, or the general price level. It encompasses the entire national economy. It is the sum of the major microeconomic variables, wages, and profits paid in a particular firm or industry, employment in an individual firm or industry, and the price for a particular product produced by that economic unit.

**Auditor general.** An official responsible to parliament on the auditing function for all federal departments and agencies. His report also deals with his views on the appropriateness of certain functions of government.

**Average consumption ratio.** The ratio of consumption to personal disposable income.

**Average savings ratio.** The ratio of personal savings to personal disposable income.

**Balance of payments.** Summarizes all receipts and payments for goods and services and movements of capital between Canadians and nonresidents over a specified time period.

**Bank of Canada.** The central bank in Canada, established in 1935. It is responsible for issuing paper currency, acts as fiscal agency for the federal government, and formulates and implements monetary policy. Its essential purpose is to help achieve price, employment, and economic growth conditions that are "in the best interests of the economic life of the nation."

**Basic balance of payments.** Refers to the current and long-term capital accounts combined, a specific total in the full balance of payments statistics.

**Bretton Woods Conference.** Conference held in New Hampshire in 1944 that led to the formation of the International Monetary Fund to assist in the coordination of international economic policies of member countries.

**Budget deficit.** See Deficit.

**Built-in (automatic) stabilizers.** Institutional factors that reduce the extent of cyclical fluctuations without any direct, discretionary action by governments. One of the most important built-in stabilizers is the progressive personal income tax which leads to a prompt reduction in personal income tax collections when personal incomes decline during a recession.

**Business cycles.** Fluctuations in aggregate economic activity; they recur, but with irregular timing.

**Cambridge cash balance theory.** (See also Quantity theory of money). This theory emphasized that the demand for money balances was a stable ratio of national income.

**Canada-U.S. Automotive Products Trade Agreement** (auto pact). This agreement permitted duty-free trade in automobiles, trucks, and parts for existing North American producers with certain production and capital-investment conditions.

**CANSIM.** The abbreviation for Canadian Socioeconomic Information Management, which is a fully computerized and regularly updated data bank.

**Capital.** Goods produced by firms for the purpose of producing further goods and services. It normally includes nonresidential construction (such as factories and shopping centres), which have a very long life, and machinery and equipment, which wear out or become obsolete quickly.

**Capital accounts.** A component of the balance of payments that relates to purchases and sales of assets and extensions of credit.

**Capital intensive.** A process of production that involves a high ratio of capital to other factors of production. Measured by the stock of capital per person employed.

**Capital market.** The raising of funds by the sale of stocks and bonds through the specialized financial institutions that provide such services.

**Cash reserve ratio.** The percentage of total deposits that the chartered banks are legally required to keep in their vaults and tills or on deposit with the Bank of Canada. No interest is paid to the banks on such deposits.

**C. D. Howe Research Institute.** A nonprofit organization established in 1973 to conduct nonpartisan research and analysis of economic policy issues in Canada.

**Circular flow of income.** The flow of payments and receipts between firms and households. It illustrates the income and expenditure sides of the national accounts.

**Club of Rome.** A private international organization of about 75 individuals with interests in long-term economic growth and environmental issues.

**Cobb-Douglas production function.** A widely used specification of a production function named after Charles W. Cobb (a mathematician) and Paul H. Douglas (an economist and U.S. Senator). It was built on the marginal productivity theory of income distribution.

**Comparative advantage.** An explanation of specialization in international trade between countries, based on differences in relative costs. Each country concentrates on what it can produce more economically than other countries.

**Composite index.**    A summary of a number of individual series, measuring the percentage of that group of series which are expanding from one month to the next. Composite indices are designed to help in the current analysis of business cycles. Composite indices of the leading indicators typically lead the business-cycle peak, but the leads are sometimes short.

**Conference Board in Canada.**    A nonprofit institution that produces national and provincial economic forecasts and surveys on business attitudes and data on labour compensation.

**Constant prices.**    A measure of the physical volume of output (such as GDP) by valuing all output at the prices of a base period.

**Constant returns to scale.**    A situation where an increase of 1 percent in *all* of the factor inputs will be reflected in an increase of 1 percent in total output.

**Consumer expenditures on goods and services.**    Covers current expenditures on all goods (both durables and nondurables) and services.

**Consumer price index (CPI).**    Measures the total change in the prices of a comprehensive specified set of consumer goods and services that would be bought on a regular basis by the average urban family.

**Consumption expenditure.**    The spending by households on goods and services, usually presented for a calendar year or by quarters, seasonally adjusted at an annual rate.

**Consumption function.**    The relationship between the consumption expenditures that households desire to spend and their disposable income. (Normally both consumption expenditures and personal disposable income would be measured in constant prices.) $C = a + bY$ is a common form of the relationship.

**Consumption ratio.**    See Average consumption ratio.

**Cost-push inflation.**    Inflation that is said to come from excessive wage and cost increases reflecting market power rather than excess demand.

**Crowding out.**    The effect that a larger government deficit (and its financing) has in reducing private investment or consumption. Such crowding out occurs through higher interest rates and could occur even if the economy was operating at less than full employment.

**Currency outside banks.**    Notes (produced on behalf of the Bank of Canada by two specialized printing plants) and coin (minted primarily by the Royal Canadian Mint in Ottawa).

**Current account of the balance of payments.**    Shows the receipts and payments for goods and services currently produced and sold by Canadians to nonresidents.

**Current prices.**    The actual prices at which transactions occur in the national accounts. Most prices in the late 1980s will be much higher than the prices for the same items would have been in the early 1970s, for example.

**Current services.**    A category in the balance of payments for payments made abroad; these include the payments made for Canadians travelling on U.S. and other foreign airlines, and payments made for insurance to Lloyd's of London, for example.

**Damped cycle.** A cyclical fluctuation which decreases in amplitude (the extent of change from the peak to the trough of the cycle) over time.

**Deficit.** Occurs when spending exceeds government revenues; a government deficit means that current and capital expenditures are in excess of current tax collections.

**Demand for money.** Depends on the level of national income (a positive relation) and the rate of interest (a negative relation).

**Demand-pull inflation.** Inflation caused by too much demand relative to potential output at full employment.

**Demand side.** The demand side of macroeconomics refers to the expenditures on goods and services in the economy. The volume of these expenditures determines the volume of output and employment.

**Deposit liabilities.** These are the deposits of both individuals and businesses with the chartered banks. They are liabilities from the point of view of the banks, but these same accounts are assets from the point of view of the depositors.

**Depression.** A term for a very severe recession such as occurred during the 1930s in North America.

**Diminishing returns.** A condition that is said to occur when increasing quantities of a variable factor of production combined with a fixed factor of production lead to a decline in the marginal return to the variable factor.

**Discretionary monetary policy.** Monetary policy that is adjusted to offset undesirable developments in the private sector, such as inflation or unemployment.

**Disequilibrium.** A state of the economy when economic forces are pressing the participants in the economic process to change their current actions.

**Dissavings.** The amount by which the expenditures of the personal sector as a whole on consumption in a given year exceeds personal disposable income after direct taxes and transfers. This situation could come about in a recession when people with existing assets sell some of them to maintain a level of consumption closer to the style to which they have been accustomed.

**Dual economy.** An economy that contains a mixture of large, modern, and highly mechanized plants and some small, old, and more labour-intensive plants.

**Durables.** Goods, such as new cars and appliances, that are purchased by the personal sector.

**Econometric model.** This is a statistical summary of the behaviour of the economy, based on the historical experience of the country as captured in its statistical records.

**Economic Council of Canada.** A federally funded crown corporation established in 1963 as an independent body to provide projections of the medium-term growth prospects for Canada and advice to governments, business, and labour on how Canada's broad economic goals can be achieved. It is composed of three full-time members (a chairman and two directors) and up to 25 other members from business, labour, agriculture, and the general public (although labour representatives have not participated in this and other federal advisory bodies for some years). It produces annual reports on the economy and publishes research studies compiled by its staff and associated economists.

**Economic processes.**  A term covering such economic developments as production, sales, labour income, profits, business bankruptcies, and exports.

**Economies of scale.**  The increase in output per unit of input that is made possible by increases in the size of the markets that a business serves.

**Effective exchange rate.**  A summary exchange rate comparison based on a number of currencies, with their trade being used as weights to combine them into an index number.

**Elasticity.**  The percentage change in a dependent variable for a 1-percent change in an independent variable.

**Endogenous theory.**  A theory that emphasizes that business cycles are caused entirely by inherent problems within the private sector in the market-oriented industrialized economies.

**Endogenous variables.**  These are variables that are determined or explained by the model or system, such as consumption in the consumption function, which is dependent on income.

**Equilibrium.**  The position that, if attained, would be maintained; it is assumed that the participants in the economic process are all satisfied with their current level or position.

**Equilibrium level of national income.**  A level of national income that, if attained, would be maintained without any unintended building up or running down of business inventory.

**Establishment surveys.**  Surveys of individual plants (or establishments) that provide data on employment and compensation per hour and total labour income.

**European Economic Community (EEC).**  A regional free-trade association which now covers countries with a combined population of more than 300 million people. It was formally established in 1957.

**Exchange rate.**  The price of one currency in terms of another currency.

**Exchange rate depreciation.**  A reduction in the exchange rate of a given country against other currencies.

**Exogenous theory.**  A theory of business cycles that emphasizes the role of shocks or disturbances from *outside* the system as a central part of the persistence of cycles.

**Exogenous variables.**  Variables that are determined outside the model or economic system, such as government expenditures.

**Expansionary fiscal policy.**  A policy involving an increase in expenditures (or a tax cut) that leads to a larger federal deficit and a higher level of national income.

**Expansionary monetary policy.**  See Monetary expansion.

**Expansions.**  The period between a business-cycle trough and the next business-cycle peak.

**Expenditure flows.**   Current production measured by the payments made by consumers and other final purchasers of goods and services. (See Expenditure side).

**Expenditure side.**   The expenditure side of the national accounts refers to the major areas of final expenditures (consumption, business investment, and government expenditure on goods and services) in the GDP.

**Experience curve.**   The term for a reduction in average cost of production per unit of output with additional volume. The curve can partly reflect learning by doing, the spreading of fixed costs over a larger production volume, and also economies of scale.

**Factor prices.**   The prices paid by firms for the factors of production (labour, capital, and land).

**Factor services.**   The services provided by households to business units; these include working for a company on an hourly, monthly, or commission basis, loaning of funds to a company by the purchase and holding of a corporate bond.

**Factors of production.**   The resources of society that are used in production — labour, capital, and land.

**Federal Reserve System (FED).**   This system was established in 1913 to provide the functions of a central bank and a strengthened system of regulatory control over the commercial banking system of the United States. It has a federal structure composed of 12 Federal Reserve District banks. The Federal Open Market Committee has a key role in forming U.S. monetary policy.

**Federal system of government.**   A system where the central government has some areas of responsibility (on both functions of government and sources of revenue), while the provinces and municipalities have different areas of responsibility and sources of revenue.

**Fine tuning.**   Policy position based on the view that the difference between actual economic performance and some specified target variable can be kept relatively small.

**Fiscal drag.**   A situation in which the growth in tax revenues could cause a dampening effect on the rate of growth of economic activity.

**Fiscal policy.**   Government expenditures and taxes (and their difference — budget surpluses and deficits) and their effects on the private sector.

**Fixed exchange rate.**   A system in which a country is committed to maintain a fixed international value of its currency in relation to the currencies of other countries.

**Flexibility in government expenditures.**   The possibility of adjusting some types of expenditures in response to changes in the economic situation. This is done to try to offset any instability in the economy coming from international forces or from changes in the domestic private sector.

**Floating exchange rates.**   A system in which the relative international value of two currencies is allowed to fluctuate in response to international market forces. Central banks might sometimes intervene to smooth out short-term fluctuations but not to oppose longer-term and deep-seated forces.

**Flow.**   The quantity of an economic variable measured over a period of time. (See also Stock).

**Foreign exchange reserves.** Reserves of internationally accepted means of payment which a country holds to cover short-term deficits on its balance of payments.

**Foreign sector.** Economic transactions involving receipts and payments between Canadians and foreigners for goods and services sold and purchased.

**Four pillars of the financial system.** These are the commercial banks, the trust and loan companies, the insurance companies, and the securities dealers. Traditionally, they have had separate, specialized functions, but there has been a move to reduce the regulatory barriers that separate their spheres of activity and to increase competition among these institutions.

**Freely fluctuating exchange rate.** A system by which a country keeps its level of official foreign exchange reserves unchanged. Any disequilibrium between the current and capital account in the balance of payments of that country would be fully reflected in the quoted exchange rates of that country's currency. In practice, some minor changes in the level of exchange reserves might take place to slightly moderate temporary situations, but no extended increases or decreases should occur if the system is to be truly freely floating.

**General Agreement on Tariffs and Trade (GATT).** This agreement, which came into effect in 1948, provides a forum for negotiations between countries on the gradual reduction or elimination of tariffs and other barriers to trade, and also sets out rules of conduct for international trade relations.

**GDP.** See Gross domestic product.

**GDP deflator (or implicit price index of GDP).** An aggregate price index for the economy as a whole. It is defined and measured as the ratio of nominal GDP to real GDP.

**Government sector.** The incomes and expenditures of government departments and agencies. Only their expenditures on goods and services are included on the expenditure side of GDP.

**Gross domestic product (GDP).** A summary measure of current goods and services produced within Canada's borders by Canadians and non-residents. GDP is measured in prices of the current period.

**Gross national product (GNP).** Measures current production of all goods and services produced by Canadian nationals (both within and outside Canada). This was the concept emphasized until 1986 when gross domestic product became the standard measure.

**Hedging.** In international trade, this is an action taken by a buyer or seller to protect income or assets against possible adverse future exchange rate changes.

**Household sector.** See Personal sector.

**Hyperinflation.** Extreme inflation when the rates of price increase exceed 45 percent, not per year, but per month.

**Implicit price index.** See GDP deflator.

**Imports of goods and services.** The payments in Canadian currency for the purchase of such items as tea, coffee, crude petroleum, and manufactured products from foreign producers and payments of interest and dividends abroad.

**Income elasticity.** The percentage change in purchases for a change of 1 percent in income. It is normally positive.

**Income flows.** Payments made for current productive services by business and government; payments for civil servants and members of the armed forces (See Income side).

**Income side.** The major sources of income (labour income, corporation profits, depreciation allowances, and indirect taxes) in the GDP.

**Index number of prices.** A figure derived by combining the prices of a large number of individual products to obtain a total price level, which is then compared to the price level of a base period (1981 for Canada, for example).

**Indexation of personal income taxes.** The process of adjusting personal income tax allowances and tax brackets upward in proportion with increases in the general price level.

**Industrial policies.** Policies which are intended to influence the extent of research and development, to encourage particular sectors of manufacturing (such as the high-technology sector), to encourage growth industries and shift resources out of declining industries, or to influence the regional location of investment and production.

**Industrial sector.** Refers primarily to the manufacturing industries.

**Inflation.** A widespread increase in prices for many products that continues for a sustained period of time. It is measured best by a comprehensive price index (such as the GDP deflator) or by a measure of costs (such as unit labour costs or compensation per hour).

**Inside lags.** Delays in forecasting and recognizing economic changes as well as political and administrative delays in adjusting policies to major economic changes. These affect both fiscal and monetary policy.

**Interest on the public debt.** Comprises the annual payments to holders of government bonds and treasury bills.

**International Monetary Fund (IMF).** An agency of the United Nations established in 1945 and consisting of many individual countries. It relies upon members' contributions and borrowing arrangements to finance its operations. The major international body to co-ordinate exchange rates and capital flows between individual countries. Located in Washington, D.C.

**Investment income (paid or received).** In the balance of payments, this category includes the payments of interest and dividends on past issues of provincial and municipal bonds sold in other countries. It also includes the payment of dividends by Canadian subsidiaries to their parent companies in other countries.

*IS* **curve.** This curve shows all the combinations of income and interest rates in the economy where desired investment and saving are equal. It is a schedule that is downward sloping, reflecting the relationship that a higher level of investment will take place at a low rate of interest than at a high rate of interest (especially in housing).

**Kennedy Round.** Named after the late President J. F. Kennedy, these agreements reduced the average level of world industrial tariffs by approximately one-third when fully implemented in 1973.

**Labour force.**   The adult population 15 years of age and over who are either employed or unemployed.

**Labour force survey.**   This survey is produced and published each month by Statistics Canada. Approximately 56,000 households, about 1 percent of the households in Canada, are included in each survey.

**Lags.**   Lags occur when decisions or developments in one time period have an influence on other economic variables in some later time period.

**Liquidity trap.**   A situation in which individuals hold large money balances without using them to buy bonds, stocks, or goods. This situation would make increases in the money supply ineffective in stimulating the economy. This was a concern of J. M. Keynes and his early followers, especially during the 1930s and 1940s.

**LM curve.**   Shows all the combinations of income and interest rates in the economy where the demand for money equals the supply of money. The term *LM* reflects the importance of *liquidity* and *money* in such a market, and any given *LM* curve is based on a given and fixed supply of money. It is an upward-sloping curve, as contrasted to the *IS* curve which is downward sloping.

**$M_1$.**   A narrow definition of the money supply covering only notes and coin outside the chartered banks and chequing account balances. It is only about 20 percent of the more comprehensive measure of the money supply and has moved quite differently than the other monetary aggregates during the 1980s.

**$M_2$.**   The wide definition of the money supply, including notes and coin outside the chartered banks and all deposits in Canadian currency.

**Macroeconomics.**   The study of the behaviour of the national economy as a whole, rather than of the relative prices and output for an individual firm or industry.

**Managed floating exchange rate (or a "dirty float").**   A system in which the government, central bank, and foreign exchange authority do not try to maintain a fixed exchange rate but intervene to maintain some target rate that is not announced publicly. (See also Freely fluctuating exchange rate).

**Marginal productivity theory of income distribution.**   A theory of the demand for a factor of production developed from the relevant microeconomic theory of production and costs at the level of the firm. An employer who seeks to maximize profits will hire additional units of labour as long as the value of the additional output is greater than the increase in costs from the additional labour.

**Marginal propensity to consume.**   The change in consumption compared to a change in disposable income.

**Marginal propensity to save.**   The proportion of an increase in personal disposable income that is saved.

**Marginal tax rate.**   The proportion of an increase in GDP that would accrue to the federal government with an unchanged tax structure.

**Merchandise exports.**   The receipts in Canadian currency from the sale of goods to foreign countries.

**Microeconomics.**   The study of the behaviour of individual units such as households, firms, and sectors of the economy.

**Model.**   A framework of analysis that simplifies those characteristics that are crucial to an understanding of the relationships underlying an economic system.

**Monetarism.**   A body of economic thought that emphasizes the importance of the supply of money in the determination of interest rates, price level, and national income. It argues that disturbances within the banking and financial sector are the principal cause of instability in the economy.

**Monetarization hypothesis.**   Emphasizes the risk that the existence of public debt (or its potential increase) can lead to increases in the money supply.

**Monetary expansion.**   The rate of increase in the supply of money.

**Monetary policy.**   Changes by the central bank (Bank of Canada) that influence the supply of money and interest rates and the related aspects of the private sector.

**Money.**   A unit of account which is broadly acceptable by other participants in the economic process as payment for something that they are buying or selling, or as payment of a debt.

**Money multiplier.**   The change in the equilibrium level of the money supply for a given change in the cash reserves of the banking system.

**Money supply.**   Includes the notes, coin, and deposit liabilities of the chartered banks. The narrow definition of the money supply ($M_1$) includes notes, coin, and chequing deposits, while the broad definition of the money supply ($M_2$) also includes savings deposits.

**Monopolistic competition.**   A situation of nonprice competition based on differentiated products (such as a variety of models or brand names) and a small number of producers.

**Multiplier.**   The change in the equilibrium level of national income for a given change in investment or government expenditures.

**National accounts.**   A term relating to all the major aggregates (such as GDP) and the corresponding sector accounts (such as the personal and government sectors).

**National accounts presentation of government transactions.**   The payments and receipts that relate to the general public. This set of tables consolidates the extra-budgetary funds (such as the Unemployment Insurance Fund and the Canada and Quebec Pension Plan) and excludes bookkeeping transactions (such as writing off bad debts).

**Natural resource sector.**   Includes agriculture, forestry, fishing and trapping, and mining (including petroleum).

**Net current account balance.**   The net difference between receipts and payments for all merchandise and nonmerchandise items in the balance of payments.

**Net national income (or product).**   A measure on the income side of the accounts; it excludes depreciation and indirect taxes.

**Net wealth hypothesis.**   A theory that an increase in the supply of government debt would lead to an increase in real interest rates (assuming the money supply to be constant), because private borrowers would be competing with government for investment dollars. Nominal interest rates would increase faster than the price level.

**Net worth.**   The difference between all the assets and all the liabilities of a family.

**Nominal GDP.**   Measures the output of goods and services at current prices.

**Nominal interest rates.**   The market rates charged by banks or received by bondholders, measured in current prices.

**Nonaccelerating inflation rate of unemployment.**   At this unemployment rate, there would not be any tendency to experience accelerating inflation.

**Nondurable consumer expenditures.**   Spending for such items as perishable foods and clothing.

**Nonfactor services.**   The receipts and payments of interest, dividends, and royalties in the current account of the balance of payments.

**Nonproduction economies of scale.**   Reductions in costs per unit with improvements in efficiency in overhead costs such as managerial salaries, research and development, finance costs, and marketing costs, resulting from increases in the size of an organization.

**Nontariff barriers.**   Limitations on imports. Quotas are the most prevalent nontariff barrier, but there are other varieties of nontariff barriers, such as "voluntary" export controls.

**Nontraded goods and services.**   Goods and (especially) services that are produced and consumed in a locality with limited trade to nonresidents.

**Okun's Law.**   The quantitative extent of the loss in aggregate output associated with a short-run increase in the unemployment rate in a recession. Named after the late Arthur M. Okun.

**Organization of Petroleum Exporting Countries (OPEC).**   Established in 1960 to co-ordinate petroleum production and prices in the member petroleum exporting countries.

**Open economy.**   An economy that is heavily interdependent with the rest of the world's economies in terms of international trade and capital movements.

**Open market operations.**   Sales or purchases of government securities by the Bank of Canada. These purchases and sales would be made through one of the larger investment dealers.

**Open market purchase.**   Purchase of government bonds by the central bank in the open market (i.e., from the private sector rather than directly from the government). Such a purchase will lead to an increase in the supply of money that can be much greater than the size of the initial open market purchases. (See also money multiplier).

**Outside lags.**   The delay between the time a change in either monetary or fiscal policy takes place and the time it has its full impact on the economy.

**Outstanding debt.**   The accumulated overall deficit since Confederation. It is thus a *stock*, and it will continue to increase each year as long as budget deficits continue.

**Peak.**   The high point in a business-cycle expansion. Peaks are followed by recessions.

**Perfect competition.**  A situation where a large number of buyers and sellers buy and sell a standardized product.

**Personal disposable income.**  The total of personal income remaining after the deduction of personal direct taxes.

**Personal savings.**  The part of personal income remaining after the payment of personal direct taxes and the purchase of consumer goods and services. It is estimated as a residual.

**Personal sector (or household sector).**  The incomes and expenditures of households (including associations of individuals, such as churches).

**Plant-specific economies of scale.**  A condition that occurs when larger plants have lower minimum average costs than smaller plants.

**Porter Commission.**  The Royal Commission on Banking and Finance which reported in 1964 is sometimes named after the chairman, the late Dana H. Porter. It reviewed the operation of the financial system and the conduct of monetary policy and made recommendations.

**Potential employment.**  The total number of persons who would be employed if the economy were operating at a low unemployment rate.

**Potential output.**  A measure of what the economy would produce if the country's labour resources were fully employed (with the level of capital stock then current and the technology then in use); estimates of what the level of output in a given period would be assuming full employment.

**Precautionary motive for handling money.**  Recognizes that all individuals and organizations are always faced with some degree of uncertainty in the timing of their receipts and expenditures or in the risk of illness or accident, in the case of individuals, and they are inclined to hold money balances as protection against such risks.

**Price elasticity.**  The percentage change in purchases for a small percentage change in price.

**Price taker.**  A firm or country that accepts the price established in the market as a given, usually because it is so small a part of the world market for that product that it cannot influence world prices.

**Primary products (or natural resource products).**  Refers to agricultural, forestry, and mineral products.

**Private sector.**  The nongovernment part of the economy.

**Production function.**  When applied to a particular good it relates the amount of output of that good to the various combinations of factors of production that are used in its creation. The calculation is used to find the maximum output that can be produced by a given combination of inputs. The same term and concept is used for the total economy.

**Product-specific economies of scale.**  Reductions in marginal and average costs that result from a larger accumulated volume of production of narrowly specified products or models.

**Progressive personal income tax.**  A tax that takes a higher proportion of income in tax at higher incomes.

**Protectionist policies.**   Policies that employ tariff or nontariff barriers to trade to protect domestic producers against imports.

**Public debt.**   The amount of outstanding debt of the federal government accumulated since Confederation.

**Purchasing power parity.**   The view that the international purchasing power (or the exchange rate) of a country should be brought into line with changes in its domestic purchasing power. The concept was initially developed by Gustav Cassel after World War I.

**Quality of labour.**   A measure to allow for differences in age, sex, education, and experience that affect the contribution of labour input to output.

**Quantity theory of money.**   The theory that the demand and supply of money are important influences on changes in output in the short-term and the price level in the long-term.

**Real GDP.**   A measure of the output of goods and services at prices of a base year (1981 for the revised set of national accounts published in 1986).

**Real Gross Domestic Product (or real national income).**   A measure of the total output of the economy at constant prices. It is also measured by the *volume* of output in each individual industry, at constant prices.

**Real interest rate.**   The interest rate people pay or receive after allowing for increases in the general price level. It is calculated by nominal interest rate minus the rate of inflation.

**Recession.**   The period of decline from a business-cycle peak to a business-cycle trough.

**Reduced form of a model.**   A model in which all the endogenous variables to be explained in the system are on the left-hand side of the equation, while the exogenous variables (determined outside the model) are shown on the right-hand side.

**Research and development.**   The activity devoted to increasing scientific and technical knowledge and the improvement of existing products and production processes.

**Residual savings.**   A measure of the amount remaining after deducting personal expenditure and taxes from personal income.

**Ricardian hypothesis.**   A theory that government debt has no influence on the economy, either through the money supply or through other channels. People who support this theory would view a tax of a certain amount as equivalent to a current budget deficit of the same amount.

**Ricardian theory of comparative advantage.**   A theory that emphasizes differences in labour productivities between industries as the major source of differences in comparative costs and comparative advantage between countries.

**Royal Commission on the Economic Union and Development Prospects for Canada.**   This commission was chaired by Donald Macdonald. It held numerous meetings across Canada and submitted a three-volume report, together with 72 volumes of studies prepared by a large research staff.

**Say's Law.**   A view that supply creates its own demand. Named after J. B. Say (1767–1832), an influential French economist.

**Seasonal adjustment.**   A statistical procedure to remove the average seasonal movement from the original data. This adjustment permits the underlying changes to be seen more easily and earlier.

**Secular stagnation.**   The hypothesis that the North American economy would return to a period of persisting inadequate private investment and high personal savings at the end of World War II.

**Securities dealers.**   Dealers who assist companies and governments to issue new securities (either bonds or shares) to the public and who assist in the purchase and sales of outstanding shares and bonds. They provide advice to corporate and individual clients.

**Services.**   Personal expenditures on intangible items, such as laundry and dry-cleaning services or residential rent.

**Shocks.**   Unexpected influences on the private sector, such as wars or the OPEC petroleum price increases of the 1970s.

**Specialization.**   Concentration on a limited range of products or processes. The term can be applied to an individual, a firm, or a country.

**Speculative motive.**   The readiness of individuals and corporations to hold cash balances in expectation of being able to buy stocks or bonds at a lower price in the future. In the meantime, they will be willing to hold idle balances which would not be used for transaction purposes. This motive is particularly relevant to attitudes and expectations about future developments in financial markets related to expected changes in stock prices and interest rates.

**Stability.**   Economic processes (or series) that undergo only small changes from quarter to quarter and over the business cycle.

**Stabilization policies.**   The use of monetary or fiscal policies in a conscious, discretionary manner to offset instability in the economy.

**Staple theory.**   A theory that emphasized the role of natural resource exports as a factor in Canadian economic and political growth and development. The theory was developed by Harold A. Innis and W. A. Mackintosh.

**Statistics Canada.**   The central statistical agency of the federal government. Statistics Canada collects and publishes statistics on the national accounts, labour force, prices, trade, and balance of payments.

**Stock (as opposed to flow).**   An economic magnitude at a particular point in time. The stock of capital and money supply are examples in macroeconomics.

**Stock of capital.**   Produced goods with a long life that are used as factor inputs for further production along with other factor inputs (such as labour and natural resources).

**Stock of money.**   The quantity of currency and bank deposits at a *point in time* (such as December 31, 1986).

**Subsidies.**   Payments by governments, usually to producers, to increase incomes or lower the selling price of selected products. Agricultural subsidies are an example.

**Supply side.**   The determination of output (see potential output), based on the inputs of labour and capital and the contribution of output per factor input.

**Surplus.**   Occurs when government revenues exceed expenditures.

**Tariff.**   A tax imposed on goods imported into a country, frequently as a percentage of the value of the import (see Ad valorem tariff).

**Technological change.**   An innovation that allows more output to be produced from an unchanged quantity of labour and capital.

**Terms of trade.**   A measure of changes over time in the ratio of export prices to import prices.

**Time-series data.**   Data on national income, consumption, or employment for a series of years or time periods.

**Theory of aggregate demand.**   An explanation that emphasizes the stability of the consumer and the key impact of an unstable and volatile level of business investment in leading to fluctuations in national income.

**Tokyo Round.**   Tariff negotiations to reduce tariffs that were completed in 1979. Further resulting industrial tariff reductions of 25 to 30 percent will have been implemented by 1987.

**Total factor inputs.**   The change in an index number of all the factors of production (labour, capital, and natural resources). They are combined in an index in which their shares in national income are used as weights.

**Traded goods and services.**   Products and services that can easily be transferred between countries.

**Trade-weighted exchange rate (see Exchange rate).**   A trade-weighted exchange rate is desirable if a country conducts trade with a number of other countries. It is a price index of exchange rates with the weights being determined by the extent of trade with each country.

**Transfer payments.**   Payments which are made with no service or good being produced in return. Examples are family allowances and old-age pensions. These are included as income in the personal sector, but are *not* included in GDP which measures only payments for services rendered in current production.

**Transfers.**   Transfers in the balance of payments would include receipts from recent immigrants who bring their savings when they relocate in Canada, and some tax payments.

**Trough.**   The low point in a business-cycle recession; it is followed by a recovery phase.

**Trust companies.**   Institutions that provide regular banking services and can clear cheques through the Canadian Payments System, but they are not classed as chartered banks. They are the only corporations that act as executors, trustees, and administrators of wills and are active in the total mortgage market.

**Undistributed corporate profits.**   The net profits of the company after the payment of taxes and dividends to shareholders.

**Unemployed.**   Adults who are without work and are also actively seeking work.

**Unemployment rate.**   The number of jobless adults who are actively seeking work, as a percentage of the total labour force.

**Value-added costs.**   The costs of production at the firm or industry level, excluding purchased materials. Value-added costs include wages, profits, and internal overhead costs.

**Velocity of circulation of money.**   The level of national income divided by the value of the stock of money. This concept was developed by Irving Fisher as part of the quantity theory of money.

**Volatility.**   Economic processes (or series) that undergo large changes from quarter to quarter and over the business cycle, such as corporate profits, inventory investment, and merchandise imports.

# Index

Abegglen, J. C., 265 n
Accelerator principle, 135–36
Accounting
  economic growth, 59–61
  for inflation, 205–8, 322, 336–37
  management use of, 341
Action lag; see Lags
Adaptive expectations, 120
Adelman, Frank L., 141, 144 n
Adelman, Irma, 141, 144 n
Ad valorum tariffs, 249
Aggregates, 3–4, 8–9, 11
Agriculture
  comparative advantage in, 255
  employment in, 56–57, 84–86, 90–92,
    103–4, 157
 in world trade, 250–51
Allen, Robert C., 111 n
Ando, Albert, 326 n
Athos, Anthony G., 259 n
Auditor general, 225
Australia, 220, 253
Automatic stabilizers; see Built-in
  stabilizers
Automotive Products Trade Agreement,
  Canada—U.S., 256, 320, 340


Balance of payments
  and alternative exchange rate systems,
    289–90
  for Canada, 267–69, 272–79, 316
  and capital flows in 1970s, 292–93
  deficit in, 291
  of developing countries, 302–3
  and inflation in 1970s, 290–91
  for United States, 276, 291
Balassa, Bela, 280, 284 n
Bank Act, 184
Bank of Canada
  econometric models of, 146–47
  foreign exchange reserves of, 270–71,
    290
  labour productivity study by, 81–82

  and money supply, 181–85, 194–95,
    202, 211–12, 233, 282–83
  and stabilization policy, 313–14
  as statistics source, 8, 140
Bank of Canada Review, 171, 184
Bank of International Settlements, 212,
  316
Bank of Japan, 298
Banks; see Commercial banks
Barter, 167
Base-weighted indexes, 17–18, 270
Beattie, J. R., 125 n
Belgium
  economic growth and productivity in,
    40, 254, 257, 296, 318, 340
  employment growth in, 72
  exports by, 247–48
Bertram, G. W., 58 n
Blinder, Alan S., 123–24, 125 n, 313,
  326 n
Boadway, Robin W., 304 n
Bordo, Michael, 285 n
Borrowers, final, and money supply,
  183–85
Boston Consulting Group, 261–62
Bouey, Gerald K., 183, 283
Bretton Woods System, 292
Britton, John N. H., 327 n
Bronfenbrenner, Martin, 328 n
Brown, E. Cary, 326 n
Brown, William Adams, Jr., 287
Built-in stabilizers, 159, 308
Burns, Arthur F., 45 n
Business Conditions Digest, 146, 333
Business cycles, 32–36; see also
  Depressions and Recessions
  and aggregate demand fluctuations,
    32–36
  approaches to research on, 145–47
  and balance of payments, 273–77
  in Canada; see Canada
  causes of persisting, 310–11
  damped, 141–42, 311
  and discretionary fiscal policy, 242

duration and severity of, 104, 153–60,
213, 307–9
and exogenous shocks, 147–49
federal revenue variability during,
228–29
forecasting, 145–47, 331–34
and lags, 149–53
and price change rate, 37
pricing system and speed of
adjustment over, 208–9
and unemployment, 100, 218
in United States; *see* United States
Business investment
in aggregate demand theory, 105–9
and corporate profits, 208, 322
factors determining level of, 127–30
and federal deficit, 237–38
income and accelerator effects on,
135–36
and interest rates, 127–32, 134–35, 335
Japanese, 91
and lags, 149–50, 242
and multiplier, 136–39
and unemployment, 342
Business sector, 11–13
Business units, 105

CAD/CAM, 265
Cagan, Philip, 45 n, 174, 178 n, 179 n
Cambridge theory of interest rates,
167–69
Canada
balance of payments for, 268–69,
272–79, 316
business cycles in, 33–36, 154–56
and balance of payments, 273–77
and exogenous shocks, 147–49
forecasting of, 334
length and severity of, 154–60, 308
output and employment during, 161
research on, 146
and U.S. business cycles compared,
154–56
consumption function in, 117–18, 124
economic growth and productivity in,
29–32
and balance of payments, 272–73,
316
and comparative advantage, 254–57
ECC objectives for, 218–19
and economic policy, 317–18
and economies of scale, 263–65
and factor input changes, 62–63,
68–69, 71–73
and federal revenue growth, 226–28
fluctuations in, and employment,
80–82

and international competitiveness,
337–42
and Japanese economic growth
compared, 92, 257–58, 298–300
and natural resources, 56–57
and real wages growth, 323–24
slowdown since 1973 in, 89–90
and U.S. growth and productivity
compared, 86–88, 92, 257–58, 340
environmental policies in, 318–24
and exchange rates, 42, 172, 177,
269–71, 279–84, 288, 293, 317,
337–39
exports to GDP ratio for, 248–50
federal budget deficits for; *see* Federal
budget deficits
federal system in, 219–21, 224
fiscal multiplier in, 136, 138, 142
and free trade, 296–98, 320–21,
340–41
government expenditures and revenues
for; *see* Government expenditures
*and* Government revenues, sources
of
inflation in, 37–38, 176–78, 309–10
accounting for, 205–8, 336–37
and international trade, 278–80,
282–84, 291
measures of, 172–73
since 1970, 176–78, 291
interest elasticity of business
investment in, 131
labour force in, 63–66, 68–69, 71–73
money multiplier in, 187
money supply in, 165–66, 171–72,
177–78, 183–85, 187–88
natural resources of, 41, 49, 56–57, 255
personnel planning in, 74
savings rate in, 121, 124
stabilization policy in, 311–16
statistics sources for, 8
stock of capital in, 67–69
unemployment in, 3, 72, 218–19, 236,
318–19, 335, 342
unionization in, 74–76
and world trade, 41, 248–50, 337–39
Canada Deposit Insurance Corporation,
188
*Canadian Business Review*, 334
Canadian Institute for Economic Policy,
319
Canadian Labour Market and
Productivity Centre, 323–24
Canadian Payments System, 187–88
Canadian Socioeconomic Information
Management (CANSIM), 8
Capacity, and economic growth, 31
Capital; *see also* Investment
and growth in output, 68–71

per person employed, changes in level of, 61–63

as production factor, 54, 59, 61, 68, 80, 254

stock of, 60, 62–63, 66–67, 128

as substitute for labour, 76

Capital accounts, of the balance of payments, 269; *see also* Balance of payments

Capital flows, and exchange rate changes, 291–93

Capital intensive countries, 89

Capital market, 106

Cash reserve ratio, 185–87

Cassel, Gustav, 279, 284 n

Census X-11 program, 152

Central Mortgage and Housing Corporation, 8

Chartered banks; *see* Commercial banks

Cheques, and money supply, 166–67

Chequing deposits, cash reserve ratio for, 186

Choudri, Ehsan U., 285 n

Circular flow of income, 11–14

Civil service, expenditures on, 223, 225

Civil War (U.S.), 37, 176, 190

Clark, Colin, 58 n

Clark, Peter K., 143 n

Clinton, Kevin, 191 n

Closed shops, 75

Club of Rome, 55

Cobb, Charles W., 60

Coinage
and internal cash drain, 185–86
in money supply, 165–66

Cole, Rosanne, 325 n

Commercial banks
deposit liabilities of, 165–66, 186
and exchange rate changes, 295
failures of, 148–49, 159, 188–89, 292, 308
foreign exchange holdings of, 288
international loans of, 292–93, 308–9
and money supply, 165–66, 171, 183–86, 188

Commission on Money and Credit in the United States, 313

Commodity-producing industries; *see also* Manufacturing
employment in, during recessions, 156–58
and exchange-rate changes, 282–83, 338–39
importance of, 308–9, 337
inflation and profits in, 209

Common Market; *see* European Economic Community (EEC)

Comparative advantage, 252–57, 343

Compensation, hourly; *see* Wages

Competition, perfect and monopolistic, 71

Composite indexes, 333

Computers, 50, 140, 147, 152, 187, 265, 334

Conference Board in Canada, 8, 146–47, 334

Constant returns to scale, 71, 254, 260, 262

Constitution Act of 1981, 220

Consumer expenditures on goods and services, 20–21, 99, 105

Consumer price index (CPI), 16–17, 69–70
and business cycles, 37–38
income tax indexation to, 228
as inflation measure, 172–73

Consumption
average ratio of, 107, 114–16
and income redistribution, 122–24
and interest rates, 122
in life-cycle hypothesis, 120–21
in permanent income hypothesis, 119–20
stability of, 33
and wealth, 121–22

Consumption function
Keynesian, 107–10, 113–16, 121–22
for postwar years, 116–19

Corporate bond rate, 131–32, 206

Corporate profits; *see* Profits

Corporate profits tax, 132–33, 220, 225–26, 322

Cost-push inflation, 209–10

Cost reductions with volume, 263–65

Courchene, Tom, 326 n

Crow, John W., 183

Crowding out, 197–98, 237

Currency
domestic, 177
foreign, 171
in money supply, 165–66, 185–86
outside banks, 166
ratio of, to deposit liabilities, 186–87

Current account of the balance of payments, 268–69; *see also* Balance of payments

*Current Economic Analysis*, 333

Current services, 269

Current-weighted price indexes, 17–18

Customs collections, 226

Daly, Donald J., 45 n, 58 n, 78 n, 96 n, 143 n, 162 n, 214 n, 230 n, 244 n, 259 n, 265 n, 266 n, 285 n, 304 n, 327 n

Dam, Kenneth W., 236 n

Damped cycles, 141–42, 311

Data Resources International, 334
Data Resources of Canada, 146–47
Daub, Melvin A. C., 325 n
Dauphin, Roma, 304 n
David, Paul A., 125 n
Death rate, 53
Decision lag; see Lag, inside
Deficits, federal; see Federal budget
    deficits
Della Valle, P. A., 125 n
Demand, aggregate
    curve for, 4, 49–50
    economic growth and changes in, 79,
        88–89
    fluctuations in, and business cycles,
        32–36
    Malthus on, 50–54
    overview of, 104–10
Demand deposits, 187
Demand-pull inflation, 209–10
Denison, Edward F., 78 n, 79–80, 82, 84,
    86, 88–91, 96 n, 118, 254
Denison's Law, 118
Denmark, 254
Department of Commerce (U.S.), 78–80,
    146, 154, 333
Department of Employment and
    Immigration, 8
Department of Finance, 8, 81, 146–47,
    236, 238–39
Department of Insurance, 188
Department of National Revenue, 8
Department of Trade and Commerce,
    313–14
Deposit liabilities, 165–66
    Bank of Canada, 183
    cash reserve ratios on, 185–87
    and chartered banks, 184
    ratio of cash reserves to, 186–87
    ratio of currency to, 186–87
Depreciation, 14, 67, 206, 322, 336
Depression, Great
    bank failures during, 149
    capital flows during, 292
    consumption and savings during,
        117–18
    and economic growth, 29
    and exchange rate changes, 42
    and macroeconomics, shift in theory
        of, 104
    money demand curve during, 170
    and price change, 37
    and unemployment, 36
    U.S. monetary policy during, 188–90
Depressions; see also Recessions
    and balance of payments, 272–76
    consumption and savings during, 114,
        119–21
    and money supply, 190

Developing countries, 301–3, 340
Diefenbaker, John G., 314
Diminishing returns, 51, 53
Dirty float; see Managed floating
    exchange rate system
Discretionary policy; see Fiscal policy
    and Monetary policy
Dissavings, 114, 116, 121
Dollar, Canadian, exchange value of, 42,
    172, 177, 269–71, 279–84, 288,
    293, 317, 337–39
Dollar, U.S., exchange value of, 42, 281,
    288, 339
Domestic currency, 177
Douglas, Paul H., 60, 77 n
Dow, Christopher, 326 n
Dual economy, 257
Durables, 99, 134
Dye, Kenneth, 225

Easterbrook, W. T., 58 n
Eckstein, Otto, 326 n
Econometric models, 139–41
    in business cycle forecasts, 146–47
    reduced form of, 137
Economic Council of Canada, 8, 72, 81,
    131, 135, 146–47, 218–19
Economic growth, 28–32, 47; see also
    Business cycles and Productivity
    accounting for, 59–61
    as balance of payments determinant,
        272–77
    and business cycles, 32–36, 160–61
    in Canada; see Canada
    employment and fluctuations in, 80–83
    and federal revenue growth, 226–28
    identification of areas of, 342–43
    in Japan; see Japan
    long cycles of, 274
    in Malthusian model, 50–54
    and natural resource scarcity, 54–56
    and output per unit of input, changes
        in, 79–80, 83–85
    and production factors, 68–71
    slowdown in North American since
        1973, 88–91
    in United States; see United States
    and world trade growth, 295
Economic processes, 33–34
Economics, methodology of, 49–50
Economies of scale, 256, 260–65
    in Canada, 87, 263–65
    and economic growth, 79, 83–84
    in Japan, 92
    nonproduction, 260, 262–63
    plant-specific, 260, 262
    product-specific, 260–62
    for small countries, 248

in United States; 85, 87
Education, of labour force, 72–73
Effective exchange rate, 270
Eisenhower, Dwight D., 148
Elasticity
  income, 103–4
  interest rate, of investment, 130–31,
    134–35
  of money demand, 170
  tax revenue, 227–29
*Elements of Political Economy*, (Mill),
  100
Employed category, 64–65
Employment; *see also* Labour *and*
    Unemployment
  and aggregates, 11
  and business cycles, 35–36
  full, 81
  measurement of, 63–66
  and monetary policy, 213–14
  permanent, 92–94, 300
  and potential national income, 80–83
  productivity changes versus changes
    in, during recessions, 160–61
  total, 9
  trends in, and recession severity,
    156–58
Employment Service (Canada), 66
Endogenous theory of business cycles,
  145, 147
Energy prices; *see* Petroleum prices
Equilibrium
  in *IS-LM* framework, 192
  labour supply function, 53
  partial, 105
Equilibrium level of national income,
  109–10, 136–38, 191–204, 210
Equipment investments, 67, 105–6
Establishment surveys, 65–66
European Economic Community (EEC),
  248–49
Evans, John C., 78 n
Evans, Paul, 237, 244 n
Exchange rates, 41, 141, 269–71
  and Canada; *see* Canada
  capital outflows and pressure on,
    292–93
  effective or trade-weighted, 270
  fixed, 278, 287–89, 291–92, 295, 317
  floating, 288–90, 317
  and inflation, 91, 172–73, 176–77
  and Japanese yen, 300–301
  and price effects of depreciation,
    280–84
  purchasing power parity as basis for,
    279–80
  stability/volatility of, 41–44, 210–11,
    286–88, 338–39
  tariff reductions versus changes in, 321

and United States, 42, 281, 288, 339
world trade and changes in, 295
Exogenous shocks
  and business cycles, 36, 145, 147–49,
    153, 310, 332
  and economic stability, 139, 141–42
Exogenous theory of business cycles, 145,
  147
Expansions, 33; *see also* Business cycles
Experience curve, 261
Exports, 23–24; *see also* International
    trade
  and balance of payments, 272–78, 291
  of Canadian natural resources, 41, 49,
    56–57, 255
  developing country, 301–3
  and exchange-rates, 281, 283, 338
  to GDP, ratio of, 35, 247–50, 321
  and inflation measures, 172–73
  Japanese, 257–58
  postwar increases in, 41
Ex post results, 7

Factor inputs
  in Canada, 62–63, 68–69, 71–73
  index of, 68–71
Factor services, 12
Factors of production, 51, 68–71, 80, 87,
  91, 252–54
Farber, Henry S., 78 n
Federal budget deficits, 233
  effects of, 236–38
  factors in emergence of, 234–36
  growth of, 39, 232–33
  in *IS-LM* analysis, 231–32
  and monetary policy, 335
  options for reduction of, 238–39
Federal Deposit Insurance, 159, 190, 308
Federal expenditures; *see also* Federal
    budget deficits *and* Fiscal policy
  distribution of, 223–24
  and federal deficit, 234
  flexibility in, 224–25
  growth of, 39, 220–23, 234–36
Federal Open Market Committee, 188–89,
  317
Federal Reserve Bank of Philadelphia,
  237
Federal Reserve Board, 189
Federal Reserve System, 149, 188–90,
  310, 317
Federal revenues
  and federal deficit, 235–36
  growth of, 38–39, 235
  structure of, 225–29
Federal system of government, in
    Canada, 219–21, 224
Final buyers, 14

Finance costs, 263
Fine tuning, 313
Fiscal drag, 227, 229
Fiscal policy, 131, 215
  and cost-push inflation, 209–10
  discretionary changes in, 236, 239–40
  effects of, 334–35
  expansionary, 194
  income redistribution using, 122
  and *IS-LM* framework, 193–94, 196–99
  lags and timing of, 240–43
  scope of, 130–31, 135, 219
  in short-term stabilization, 312–16
Fisher, Irving, 168, 204–5, 238, 336
Fixed-basket-type price indexes, 17
Flexibility, in government expenditures, 222
Floating exchange rates, 42, 288–90, 317
Food
  Malthus on supply of, 51–54
  prices of, 173
Foreign banks, in Canada, 184
Foreign currency deposits, 171
Foreign exchange, private holdings of, 288, 317
Foreign exchange reserves, 270–71
  balance of payments and loss of, 274, 278, 289–90
  capital flows and financing of, 291–93
  and inflation in 1970s, 290–91
  Japanese, 301
Foreign sector, 138–39
Forestry, 318
Four pillars of financial system, 188
France
  economic growth and productivity in, 30, 40, 254, 257, 296, 340
  employment growth in, 72
  exports by, 248
  savings rate in, 121
Freely floating exchange rate system, 288–90
Freeman, Christopher, 58 n
Freeman, Richard B., 78 n
Friedman, Milton, 119–20, 125 n, 147, 153, 162 n, 174–75, 178 n, 179 n, 189, 190, 191 n, 312, 325 n
Friedman, Rose, 178 n


G-10 countries, 270
GATT; *see* General Agreement on Tariffs and Trade
GDP; *see* Gross domestic product (GDP)
General Agreement on Tariffs and Trade (GATT), 249, 256, 297, 320–21, 340

*General Theory of Employment, Interest and Money, The* (Keynes), 5, 112–16; *see also* Keynesian theory
General wholesale price index, 37
Germany, 30, 174, 176; *see also* West Germany
Gilmour, James G., 327 n
Gold, 165, 270–71, 290
Goldberger, Arthur, 141
Gordon, Robert J., 96 n
Government; *see also* Federal budget deficits; Federal expenditures; *and* Federal revenues
  and circular flow of income, 13
  as final buyer, 14
  and multiplier in econometric model, 138–39
  role of, in economic performance, 38–39
Government expenditures; *see also* Federal expenditures
  growth of, 220–23
  sources of, 22–23
Government revenues, sources of, 22–23; *see also* Federal revenues
Government sector, 7–8, 20, 22–23
Great Britain; *see also* United Kingdom
  Malthus on population and economic growth in, 50–51, 53–54
  textile industry of, 102–3
Griliches, Zvi, 262, 266 n
Gross domestic product (GDP), 6–7, 10
  commodity production as percentage of, 308, 337
  and consumer expenditures on goods and services, 99, 105
  coverage of, 14–16
  exports to, ratio of, 35, 247–50, 321
  federal deficit as percentage of, 231–32, 234, 236
  federal revenue and changes in, 226–29
  government expenditures as percentage of, 221–22
  implicit price index (deflator) for, 18, 172
    ECC goal for increases in, 219
    in Great Depression, 37
    during inflation, 37–38, 206, 291
    and purchasing power parity, 279
  international transactions in, 23–24, 337
  nominal, 18
  price and quantity changes in, 16–20
  real, 11, 16, 18
    employment, stock of capital, and, 62, 67–68

per capita, increases in, 54, 101, 103, 320
per employee, 29–31, 39–40, 62, 91, 296
and production function, 60
total, 29–31
unemployment and increases in, 82, 161
in recession of 1981–82, 276
tax collections as percentage of, 308
Gross national product (GNP), 6
foreign trade as percentage of, 172
implicit price index (deflator) for, 172–73
Grubel, H., 259 n
Grubel, Herbert G., 325 n

Hansen, Alvin H., 118, 125 n
Harberger, A. C., 78 n
Harris, Richard G., 266 n, 304 n, 327 n
Heckscher, Eli, 253
Hedging, exchange-rate, 295
Heller, Robert, 293 n
Heller, Walter, 313
Helliwell, J. F., 143 n
Hickman, Bert G., 142, 144 n
Hicks, Sir John, 191–92, 200 n
High-powered money, 186
Historical costs, 205–6, 322, 336
Household sector, 11–13, 105; see also Personal sector
Housing investment, 126–27
and expansionary fiscal policy, 199 .
and federal deficit, 237–38
and interest rates, 132–35, 335
and lags, 150–51
and money supply changes, 202–4
Howe, C. D., Research Institute, 8
Howitt, Peter, 191 n, 244 n, 283, 285 n
Hultgren, Thor, 81, 96 n
Hyperinflation, 36, 38, 167, 173–74, 176, 211

Immigration, 72, 87, 275
Imports, 24; see also International trade
and balance of payments, 272–78, 291
and exchange-rates, 281, 338
fluctuations of, during business cycles, 228
and inflation measures, 172–73
postwar increase in, 41
Income; see also National income
and consumption function, 113
elasticity of, 103–4
flows of, 182

investment, 269
and labour quality, 66, 70, 73
in life-cycle hypothesis, 120–21
and marginal propensity to consume, 107
personal disposable, 21
real, 219, 295–96
redistribution of, 122–24
and saving function, 107–8
Income taxes; see Personal income taxes
Indexation
of pensions, 239, 309–10, 336
of personal income taxes, 228, 235–36, 241
Industrial policies, 319–20
Inflation; see also Prices
accounting for, 205–8, 322, 336–37
and balance of payments, 278–80
in Canada; see Canada
cost-push, 209–10
and currency depreciation, 280–84
demand-pull, 209–10
and exchange rate instability, 287
and federal deficit, 237–38
federal tax revenue buoyancy during, 227–28
financial market effects of, 336
and GDP measurement, 16–20
hyper-, 36, 38, 167, 173–74, 176, 211
intensification of, as possibility, 309–10
and interest rates, 91, 204–5
in IS-LM framework, 191–92, 100–200
in Japan, 298
measures of, 172–74
and money supply, 174–76, 189, 203–4, 210, 213–14
in 1970s, 36–38, 290–91
and Poor Laws, 50
and productivity, 90–91
in United States; see United States
Informetrica, 146–47, 334
Innis, H. A., 58 n
Inside lags; see Lags
Inspector General of Banks, Office of the, 188
Insurance companies, 187–88
Interest on the public debt, 224–25, 233–35
Interest rates
and business investment, 127–32, 134–35, 335
and demand for goods and services, 174
determination of, and money supply/demand, 167–69, 180–83, 190

in econometric models, 140
and federal deficits, 232, 235, 237–38
and foreign investment, 337
and housing investment, 132–35, 335
and inflation, 91, 204–5
in *IS-LM* framework, 191–200
in Keynesian theory, 107, 122, 169–70
and money supply changes, 167–69,
   180–83, 190, 202–4
in 1980s, 38–39
nominal, 38
timing of movements in, over business
   cycle, 208, 210
Intermediate transactions, 13–14
Internal cash drain, 185–86
International Monetary Fund (IMF), 42,
   113, 212, 292, 316
International trade; see also Balance of
   payments; Exports; and Imports
composition of, 41
exchange rate changes and growth of,
   295
as GDP component, 23–24
growth of, 41
importance of, 247–50, 337
and Japanese manufacturing
   performance, 257–58
statistics on, 267
trends in, 250–52, 257
Inventories, 158, 205–6
Investment, 126–27; see also Business
   investment and Housing
   investment
and balance of payments, 274–75
and business cycles, 33, 36
and consumption, in Keynes's *General
   Theory*, 113–16
and economic growth since 1973, 89
gross, and stock of capital, 67
income from, in GDP, 6
Investment dealers, 183, 187–88
Investment income, 269
*IS* curve, 192; see also *IS-LM* framework
*IS-LM* framework, 190–200
and budget deficits, 231–32
money supply shift in, 202–3
Israel, 291
Italy
economic growth and productivity in,
   30, 40, 121, 254, 257, 296, 298–99
exports by, 248
inflation in, 37, 291
strikes in, 323

Japan
business cycle research in, 146
capital growth in, 61–62

economic growth and productivity in,
   29–30, 32, 87, 89, 296, 318, 323
and comparative advantage, 254–55,
   257–58
and economic power
   decentralization, 287
and experience curve, 262
and inflation, 211
in postwar period, 91–95
and savings rate, 121
and unemployment, 101
U.S. growth and productivity
   compared with, 39–40, 80, 92,
   257–58, 298–300, 340
employment growth rate for, 72
exports to GDP ratio for, 247–48
inflation in, 37, 211
labour contracts in, 175
trade barriers against, 249, 320
in world trade, 298–301
Johnson, Harry G., 253, 304 n, 311–12,
   316, 325 n, 326 n
Johnson, Lyndon, 81


Kane, Edward J., 325 n
Kareken, John, 326 n
Kaysen, Carl, 58 n
Kennedy Round; see General Agreement
   on Tariffs and Trade (GATT)
Keynes, John Maynard, 5, 112–13, 125 n,
   126, 130, 141, 191; see also
   Keynesian theory
Keynesian theory
aggregate demand in, 107
consumption function in, 107, 113–16,
   121–22
and economic instability, 141
and exchange rates, 287
and income redistribution, 122
interest rates in, 122, 130
investment in, 126
*IS-LM* curves in, 196–97
money demand in, 169–71
on secular stagnation, 118
Klein, L. R., 125 n, 141, 146
Knowledge advances, and economic
   growth, 79, 83–86, 91–92
Korean War, 310
Kumar, Pradeep, 78 n
Kuznets, Simon, 58 n, 118, 125 n


Labour; *See also* Employment; Labour
   costs, Labour force; and
   Unemployment
and growth in output, 62–63, 68–71
and immigration, 275

Malthus's supply function for, 53–54
and management, relation between,
    323–24
as production factor, 51, 68, 80
in production function for economy, 60
productivity of, and comparative
    advantage, 253–54
Labour costs
adjustment of, over business cycle,
    208, 210
in Canada, 323, 342
and economies of scale, 261
Japanese, 298–301, 323, 342
and planning/implementation, 73–74
Labour force, 64
categories of, 64–65
growth of Canadian, 71–73
*Labour Force Survey* of, 63–66
quality of, 70
unionization of, 74–77, 175, 208, 321
Lags
and business cycles, 149–53, 310–11
and fiscal policy timing, 240–43
and monetary expansion, 175
monetary policy, 211–13
in pricing system adjustments, 208–9
Land, as production factor, 51, 54, 80
Laspeyres indexes, 17–18
Lazar, Fred, 327 n
Lecraw, Donald J., 259 n
Lenders, final, and money supply,
    183–85
Lewis, H. G., 76, 78 n
Life-cycle hypothesis, 120–21
Liquidity trap, 170
Lloyd, P. J., 259 n
*LM* curve, 192; *see also* IS-LM framework
Lodge, George C., 260 n, 302, 304 n
Long cycles, 274
Lower, A. R. M., 58 n
Lubell, Harold, 123–24, 125 n
Ludd, Ned, 100
Luddites, 100
Lynch, Kevin, 191 n


$M_1$ money supply, 171–72, 178
$M_2$ money supply, 171–72, 177–78, 187,
    232
MacCharles, D. C., 78 n, 214 n, 259 n,
    265 n, 285 n, 304 n, 327 n
Macdonald, Donald, 221
MacDonald, Glenn M., 78 n
Machinery, 65, 105–6
Mackintosh, W. A., 58 n
McMillan, Charles J., 259 n
Macroeconomics
defined, 3–6

microeconomic implications of, 8–9
Malthus, T. R., 5, 50–55, 58 n, 59
Managed floating exchange rate system,
    288–90
Manufacturing; *see also* Productivity
and business cycles, 32–33, 308
comparative advantage in, 253, 255–57
compensation per hour in, 173, 176–77
economies of scale in, 260–65
employment in, during recessions,
    156–57
and exchange-rate changes, 283,
    338–39
foreign investment in, and balance of
    trade, 274
international trade in, 41
    and developing countries, 301–3
    and factor price equalization, 295–96
    reduction of trade barriers to, 296–98
Japanese; *see* Japan
profit margins in, and inflation type,
    209
unit labour costs in, 173, 176–77
valuation of return rates in, 206–8
in world trade, 250–52
Marginal productivity theory of income
    distribution, 71
Marginal propensity to consume, 107–8,
    113–18, 122–23, 137–39
Marginal propensity to import, 139, 142
Marginal propensity to save, 114–16
Marginal tax rate, 139, 159, 205, 227, 229,
    308, 335
Marketing costs, 263
Marshall, Alfred, 5
May, S. J., 142, 144 n
Medoff, James L., 78 n
Merchandise exports; *see* Exports
Mexico, 293
Microeconomics, 4, 8–9
Mill, James, 100
Mining, 56–57, 252–53, 255–57, 308, 318
Mitchell, Wesley Clair, 45 n, 81, 146–47,
    153
Models, 49–50; *see also* Econometric
    models
Modigliani, Franco, 120–21, 125 nn
Monetarism
and fine tuning, 313
on inflation cause, 174–75
IS-LM curves in, 197–99
in Japan, 298
Monetary expansion, 174–76; *see also*
    Money supply
Monetary policy, 36, 131
alternative strategies in, 213–14
Bank of Canada, 183–85
and cost-push inflation, 209–10

effects of, 334–35
expansionary, 195
indicators of, 211
in *IS-LM* framework, 194–97
lags in, 211–13, 242–43
scope of, 130–31, 135
in short-term stabilization, 311–16
of United States, 188–90, 282–83
Monetization hypothesis, 237
Money
definition of, 166–67
in price system, 167
quantity theory of, 168–69, 174
Money, demand for
and interest rate determination,
167–69, 180–83, 190
in *IS-LM* framework, 191–92
Keynesian theory of, 169–71
Money multiplier, 185–87
Money supply
in Canada, 165–66, 171–72, 177–78,
183–85, 187–88
components of, 165–66
economic activity and changes in,
202–4
and federal deficits, 232–33
and foreign exchange reserves, 290–91
and inflation, 174–76, 189, 199–200,
203–4, 210, 213–14
and interest rates, 167–69, 180–83, 190,
202–4
in *IS-LM* framework, 191–200
Japanese, 298
monetary strategies and growth of,
213–14
and money multiplier, 185–87
participants in process of, 183–85
in United States during Great
Depression, 188–90
Money Workshop, at the University of
Chicago, 174
Monopolistic competition, 71
Monroe, Jack, 75–76
Moore, Geoffrey H., 45 n, 82, 96 n, 146,
154, 162 n, 333–34, 344 n
Mortgage loan rates, 132–35, 335–36
Mulroney, Brian, 225, 314
Multinational corporations, 252, 274
Multiplier; *see also* Money multiplier
and discretionary fiscal policy, 239–40
and economic stability, 142, 308, 311
government/foreign sector and size of,
138–39, 159
and marginal tax rate, 335
money multiplier compared with, 187
simple model of, 136–38
Murphy, Mark G., 327 n
Musgrove, P., 125 n
Mutual insurance companies, 188

National accounts presentation of
government transactions, 223; *see
also* National income
National Bureau of Economic Research,
81, 146, 154, 242, 333
National Economic Conference in
Ottawa, 239
National Energy Policy, 324
National income, 6–8; *see also* Economic
growth *and* Gross domestic
product (GDP)
advantages in use of, 10–11
and business investment, 127–30,
135–38
circular flow of, 11–14
and demand for money, 169, 180–82
equilibrium level of, 109–10, 136–38,
191–204, 210
and federal deficits, 232, 234
government sector of, 22–23
money value of, and interest rates,
167–68
personal sector of, 20–22
potential, 80–83, 174–75
summary of, 24–26
Natural resources, 318
Canadian exports of, 41, 49, 56–57,
255, 318
foreign investment in, and balance of
trade, 274
of Japan, 257
scarcity of, 54–56
sector of, 56
in world trade, 41
Near banks, 188
Net current account balance, 269
Netherlands, 40, 254
Net public debt, 233
Net wealth hypothesis, 237
Net worth, 21
Nominal interest rates, 38
Nonaccelerating inflation rate of
unemployment, 218
Nondurables, 99
Nonproduction economies of scale, 260,
262–63
Nonresidential construction, investment
in, 105–6
Nontariff barriers, 249
and agricultural trade, 251–52
and commercial policy, 320, 324
costs of, to Canada, 296–98
and developing countries, 303, 340
and world trade growth, 295–96
Nontraded goods and services, 249
Nordhaus, William S., 27 n
Notes
and internal cash drain, 185–86
in money supply, 165–67

"Not in labour force" category, 64–65

Oguchi, N., 125 n
Ohlin, Bertil, 253
Oil prices; see Petroleum prices
Okun, Arthur, 81, 96 n, 161, 313
Okun's Law, 81, 161
OPEC, 36, 55, 89, 148, 310, 317
Open-market operations, 183, 194–95
O'Reilly, Brian, 285 n
Organization for Economic Co-operation
    and Development, 316
Ouchi, William, 259 n
Output per unit of input; see
    Productivity
Outside lag; see Lags
Outstanding debt, 233
Owner's equity, for housing investments,
    132

Paasche indexes, 17–18
Palda, Kristian S., 327 n
Parkin, Michael, 238, 244 n
Parsley, C. J., 78 n
Partial equilibrium, 105
Pascale, Richard T., 259 n
Paulin, Graydon, 285 n
Pavitt, K. L. R., 58 n
Peaks, 32; see also Business cycles
Pearson, Lester B., 75
Pensions, indexation of, 239, 309–10, 336
Perfect competition, 71
Permanent employment, 92–94, 300
Permanent-income hypothesis, 119–21
Perpetual inventory method, 67
Personal disposable income, 21
Personal income taxes, 38–39
    as built-in stabilizer, 159
    and federal system, 220
    and income growth, 226–28
    indexation of, 228, 235–36, 241
    on interest income, 205
    as share of federal revenues, 225–26
Personal savings, 20–21
Personal sector, 7, 20–22, 24; see also
    Household sector
Personnel, planning for, 74
Peters, Thomas J., 259 n
Petroleum prices, 55–56, 89, 148–49, 173,
    273, 310, 317, 318
Pigou, A. C., 5
Plant-specific economies of scale, 260,
    262
Poland, 293
Policy lag, 211–13

Poor Laws, 50–51
Population growth
    in developing countries, 301
    in Malthusian model, 51–53
Porter Commission; see Royal
    Commission on Banking and
    Finance
Portugal, 37, 175–76
Postner, Harry H., 304 n
Potential output, 80–83, 174–75
Precautionary motive for holding money,
    169
Price indexes, 16–20
Prices; see also Inflation
    and aggregates, 11
    and comparative advantage, 253
    constant, 18
    current, 18
    and demand curve, 49–50
    elasticity of, 103–4
    and GDP, 6–7
    and Japanese manufacturing, 299, 301
    market, in GDP, 14
    natural resource, 55–56
    producer, speed of adjustment of, 208
    and productivity, 102–4
    and quantity changes in GDP, 16–20
    and quantity theory of money, 168
    and unionization, 76–77
Price-takers, 278
Pricing system, speed of adjustment of,
    208–11
Primary products; see Natural resources
Principle of Population, As It Affects the
    Future Improvement of Society,
    The (Malthus), 50
Production, factors of; see Factors of
    production
Production function
    Cobb-Douglas, 60–61
    Malthusian, 51
Productivity; see also Economic growth
    and Gross domestic product (GDP)
    and business cycles, 160–61
    in Canada; see Canada
    and comparative advantage, 255–57
    of developing countries, 302–3
    and economic growth, 29–31, 80
    and economies of scale, 260–65
    and employment, 80–83, 100–104
    and inflation, 211
    Japanese; see Japan
    in life-cycle hypothesis, 121
    sources of change in, 83–85
    and trade barrier reductions, 296–98
    and unionization, 75–77
    United States; see United States
Product-specific economies of scale,
    260–62

Profits
   and aggregates, 11
   and business cycles, 33, 36, 228,
      332–33
   and exchange rates, 280–81, 338
   and price change, 37–38, 205–8, 322,
      336–37
   timing of peaks in, over business cycle,
      208–9
   undistributed, 106
Progress cost curve, 261
Protectionism; *see* Nontariff barriers *and*
   Tariffs
Protopapadakis, Aris A., 244 n
Public debt, interest on, 224–25, 233–35
Public sector unionization, 75
Purchasing power, 204
Purchasing power parity, 279–80
Pyle, David H., 325 n


Quality of labour, 70
Quantity of production; *see* Volume of
   production
Quantity theory of money, 168–69, 174


Random samples, 64
Rapp, W. V., 265 n
Reagan, Ronald, 238
Real GDP per employed person, 40, 62
Real parts of the economy, 105
Recession of 1981–82
   corporate profits during, 206–7
   and economic forecasting, 334
   and federal deficit, 39, 235–36
   and international trade, 276
   investment during, 127, 136
   unemployment during, 36, 82, 218–19
Recessions, 32–36; *see also* Business
      cycles *and* Depressions
   and balance of payments, 272–76
   duration and severity of, 153–60, 239,
      307–9
   and exogenous shocks, 148–49
   federal revenue during, 229–30
   and lags, 151, 153
   and money supply, 190
   and productivity, 81–82, 100, 160–61
   transfer payments during, 222
   and unemployment, 100
Recognition lag; *see* Lags, outside
Reduced form of models, 137
Reisman, Simon, 313
Rental unit construction, and mortgage
      rates, 133
Replacement costs, 206–8, 336

Research and development, 89–90,
      322–23; *see also* Technology
Reserve requirements; *see* Cash reserve
      ratio
Residential construction, 106; *see also*
      Housing investment
Resource allocation, and economic
      growth, 79, 83–84
Resource industries, 57
Response lag; *see* Lags, outside
Restrictive Trade Practices Commission,
      324
Ricardian hypothesis, on government
      debt, 237
Ricardo, David, 5, 237, 252–54, 260
Riddell, W. Craig, 178 n
Right-to-work laws, 75
Rotstein, A., 327 n
Royal Bank, 146
Royal Commission on Banking and
      Finance, 130, 186, 212, 313, 315
Royal Commission on Taxation, 313
Royal Commission on the Economic
      Union and Development Prospects
      for Canada, 221


Salaries, as labour costs, 74
Salter, W. E. G., 102, 111 n
Samuelson, Paul, 253, 295–96
Saving function
   Keynesian, 107–10, 114–16
   in *IS-LM* framework, 191–92
   for postwar years, 116–19
Savings
   in aggregate demand model, 106–9
   and income redistribution, 122–24
   and interest rates, 122
   Japanese, 91
   in life-cycle hypothesis, 120
   in permanent income hypothesis,
      119–20
   personal, 20–21
   and wealth, 121–22
Savings deposits, 186
Say, Jean-Baptiste, 100, 111 n
Say's Law, 100
Scadding, John L., 125 n
Scherer, F. M., 262, 265 n
Schmookler, J., 77 n
Schonberger, Richard J., 259 n
Schwartz, Anna Jacobson, 45 n, 178 n,
      179 n, 189, 190, 191 n
Science Council of Canada, 319
Scott, Bruce R., 260 n, 302, 304 n
Seasonal adjustment, 151–53, 334
Seasonal variations, 151–53, 311, 334

Secular stagnation, 118
Securities dealers, 188
Self-employment, 84–85, 91
Service sector industries
    and balance of payments, 268–69
    and business cycles, 308
    and exchange-rate depreciation,
        282–83
    growth of, 90, 249–50, 337
    and international trade, 249–50
Shaffner, Richard, 58 n
Sharpe, Andrew, 96 n
Shocks; see Exogenous shocks
Shulty, George P., 326 n
Siegel, Jeremy J., 244 n
Silver, 165
Smith, Adam, 5, 100
Smith, Philip, 285 n
Solow, Robert M., 313, 326 n
Sowell, Thomas, 111 n
Spain, 37, 175–76
Specialization, 252, 256, 264, 297, 319,
    321, 340–41
Speculative motive for holding money,
    169
Spread, 270
Stability
    economic, 33, 139, 141–42, 145, 147,
        229
    price, 37
Stabilization policy; see Fiscal policy
    and Monetary policy
Stabilizers; see Built-in stabilizers
Stagnationist school, 118
Standard of living, 40, 53
Staple theory, 56
Statistical Indicator Associates, 333
Statistical indicators of business cycles,
    146–47, 333–34
Statistics, economic, major sources of, 8
Statistics Canada, 6, 7, 8, 16–17, 19,
    63–65, 140, 146, 240, 267–68, 333
Sterling Exchange Standard, 287
Stiglitz, Joseph E., 304 n
Stock insurance companies, 188
Stock market crash of 1929, 189
Stock prices, 337
Stocks of capital, 60, 62–63, 66–67, 128
Stocks of money, 182
Strikes, 323, 332
Stuber, Gerald, 81–82, 96 n
Subsidies, agricultural, 251–52
Supply, aggregate, 4–6, 50–54; see also
    Money supply
Sweden
    and capital flows, 292
    economic growth and productivity in,
        211, 257, 318, 340

exports by, 247–48
inflation in, 291
and specialization, 393


Tariffs, 249
    and agricultural trade, 251–52
    and commercial policy, 320, 324
    costs of, to Canada, 296–98
    and developing countries, 303
    and GATT, 249, 256, 297, 320–21, 340
    and world trade growth, 295–96
Taxation; See also Corporate profits tax
        and Personal income taxes
    and GDP, 20–21
    of interest expense, 132–33
    and multiplier size, 139
Technology
    developing country exports of, 302–3
    diffusion of, 322–23
    and economic growth, 89–90, 118, 342
    and economies of scale, 265
    Japanese purchases of, 94–95
    in Keynes's General Theory, 113
    and knowledge advances, 84
    Malthus and change in, 54
    in production function for economy,
        59–61
Term deposits, 187
Terms of trade, 284, 299–300
Textile industry, 102–4
Third World; see Developing countries
Tinbergen, Jan, 141–42, 144 n
Tobin, James, 27 n
Tokyo Round; see General Agreement on
        Tariffs and Trade (GATT)
Traded goods and services, 249
Trade-weighted exchange rate, 270
Traité d'économie politique (Say), 100
Transactions motive, 168–69
Transfer payments
    expenditures for, 223, 225
    growth of, 38, 222
    in national accounts, 20, 22, 24
Transfers, in balance of payments, 269
Treasury bills, 270–71
Treddenick, J. M., 304 n
Trendicator, 146
Trust companies, 187–88


Undistributed corporate profits, 106
Unemployed category, 64–65
Unemployment; see also Employment
    and business cycles, 35–36, 160–61
    in Canada, 3, 72, 218–19, 236, 318–19,
        335, 342
    and deficit, 39

in developing countries, 303
and economic growth, 29
government programs for, 160
during Great Depression, 189
in Japan, 301
measurement of, 64–66
nonaccelerating inflation rate of, 218
and output changes, 81–82
and technological change, 100–104
in United States, 236
Unemployment compensation, 160
Unemployment Insurance Commission, 8
Unemployment Insurance System, 239,
    308–9
Unions, 74–77, 175, 208, 321
United Auto Workers, 75–76
United Kingdom; see also Great Britain
  cash reserve ratio in, 186
  cost accounting in, 206
  demand for money in, 170
  economic growth and productivity in,
      30, 40, 72, 121, 211, 254, 257, 273,
      298–99
  exports by, 248
  federal system in, 219–20
  and fixed exchange rate system, 287
  inflation in, 37, 211, 291
  interest elasticity of business
      investment in, 130
  stabilization policy in, 315
  terms of trade in, 300
United Nations, 316
United States
  balance of payments for, 272–80, 291
  bank failures in, 159, 189, 292, 308
  business cycle dates, 34
  business cycles in, 33–36, 153–54
    and Canadian business cycles
        compared, 154–56
    and exogenous shocks, 148–49
    reduced severity of, 104, 158–60
    research on, 146
    speed of adjustment over, 208
    Tinbergen model of, 141–42
  economic growth and productivity in,
      29–31, 39–40, 85–86
    and Canadian growth and
        productivity compared, 86–88, 92,
        257–58, 340
    and comparative advantage, 254–57
    and employment, 102
    and Japanese growth and
        productivity compared, 39–40, 80,
        92, 257–58, 340
    slowdown in, since 1973, 88–90
  exchange value of dollar for, 42, 281,
      288, 317, 339
  exports to GDP ratio for, 247–48

federal deficit for, 236
federal system in, 219–20
inflation in, 37–38
  accounting for, 206
  and Canadian inflation, 172–73,
      176–77, 279, 280, 282–84, 291
interest elasticity of investment in, 130
Japanese technology purchases from,
    94–95
labour force growth in, 72
measures of cyclical variability, 35
monetary policy in, during Great
    Depression, 188–90
money supply in, 166
natural resources of, 55–56
personnel planning in, 74
savings rate in, 118, 121
stabilization policy in, 313–15
tariffs of, 297, 318, 321
unionization in, 74–76
and world economy, 39–40
Unit labour costs in manufacturing, 173,
    176–77; see also Productivity
University of Toronto, 146–47
Usher, Dan, 27 n

Value-added costs, 74, 94
Value of production, 6–7, 16
Velocity of circulation of money, 168, 204
Viet Nam War, 310, 317
Volatility of economic processes, 33
Volume of production, 6–7, 11, 16–20
Voluntary export agreements, 303

Wages
  and aggregates, 11
  developing country, 302
  and inflation, 37–38, 173, 176–77, 209
  Japanese, 298–301
  as labour costs, 74
  natural resource prices compared with,
      55
  in personal sector, 20
  and productivity, 318
  real, 323, 342
  stability of, 33
  timing of changes in, and business
      cycle, 208
  unions and relative, 75–76
Walker, Michael, 78 n
Walters, Dorothy, 78 n
Wars
  and economic instability, 147–48, 310
  as exogenous shocks, 147–48
  and inflation, 176
Wartime Tax Agreements, 220

Waterman, Robert H., 259 n
Watkins, M. H., 58 n
Wealth
  and consumption-savings relationship, 120–22
  in Keynesian theory, 107
*Wealth of Nations, The* (Smith), 5, 100
Weiler, Joseph M., 260 n
Welfare, and national income, 25–26
West Germany; *see also* Germany
  economic growth and productivity in, 40, 72, 92, 121, 211, 254, 257, 296, 299, 318, 340
  exports by, 248
  federal system in, 220
Wharton Econometric Forecasting Model, 146
White, Bob, 75–76
White, Derek A., 45 n, 162 n, 284 n
White, W. R., 326 n
Will, Robert M., 313, 326 n
Williams, J. R., 304 n
Wilson, Michael, 239, 322

Winder, John W. L., 326 n
Women, in labour force, 66, 70, 73, 87
Wonnacott, Paul, 296–97, 304 n
Wonnacott, Ronald J., 296–97, 304 n
Woodworkers of America, 75–76
World War I, 37, 41–42, 176, 189, 279
World War II
  business cycle duration since, 158–60, 213
  consumption function during, 116–18
  economic growth since, 29, 39, 60, 62
  economies of scale during, 260
  as exogenous shock, 147–48
  federal deficit growth during, 234, 236
  and inflation, 37, 176

Yen, Japanese, 300–301
Young, J. H., 143 n
Young persons, in labour force, 66, 70, 73

Zarnowitz, Victor, 325 n